DATE DUE			

ABOUT ISLAND PRESS

Island Press, a nonprofit organization, publishes, markets, and distributes the most advanced thinking on the conservation of our natural resources– books about soil, land, water, forests, wildlife, and hazardous and toxic wastes. These books are practical tools used by public officials, business and industry leaders, natural resource managers, and concerned citizens working to solve both local and global resource problems.

Founded in 1978, Island Press reorganized in 1984 to meet the increasing demand for substantive books on all resource-related issues. Island Press publishes and distributes under its own imprint and offers these services to other organizations.

Support for Island Press is provided by Apple Computers, Inc., The Mary Reynolds Babcock Foundation, The Educational Foundation of America, The Charles Engelhard Foundation, The Ford Foundation, The George Gund Foundation, The William and Flora Hewlett Foundation, The Joyce Foundation, The J. M. Kaplan Fund, The John D. and Catherine T. MacArthur Foundation, The Andrew W. Mellon Foundation, The Joyce Mertz-Gilmore Foundation, The New-Land Foundation, Northwest Area Foundation, The Jessie Smith Noyes Foundation, The J. N. Pew, Jr. Charitable Trust, The Rockefeller Brothers Fund, The Florence and John Schumann Foundation, The Tides Foundation, and individual donors.

Natural Resources for the 21st Century

Natural Resources
for the 21st Century

Edited by R. Neil Sampson
and Dwight Hair

AMERICAN FORESTRY ASSOCIATION

ISLAND PRESS

Washington, D.C. □ *Covelo, California*

Cover design by Ben Santora

Library of Congress Cataloging-in-Publication Data

Natural resources for the 21st century.

    1. Renewable natural resources— United States— Management. 2. Environmental policy— United States. I. Sampson, R. Neil. II. Hair, Dwight, 1921-
III. Title: Natural resources for the twenty-first century.
HC103.7.N296 1989   333.7'0973   89-19946
ISBN 1-55963-003-5
ISBN 1-55963-002-7 (pbk.)

Printed on recycled, acid-free paper

Manufactured in the United States of America

10 9 8 7 6 5 4 3 2

Contents

viii

Part II: Perspectives and Analyses

Acknowledgments

This book is composed of papers presented at a conference on "Natural Resources for the 21st Century" held in Washington, D.C., on November 14-17, 1988. It is a product of a collaborative effort among the organizers of the conference; the authors of papers, reviewers, and the moderators and panelists who participated; and the conference sponsors and co-sponsors.

An organizing committee determined the objectives of the conference, provided guidance on appropriate papers and authors, and served as a communicating link with the organizations and interests the members represented. The committee included: R. Neil Sampson— Chairman (American Forestry Association), Frederick J. Deneke— Co-chairman (Extension Service), Keith A. Argow (American Resources Group), William H. Banzhaf (Society of American Foresters), Norman A. Berg (Soil and Water Conservation Society), Jack H. Berryman (Internationl Association of Fish and Wildlife Agencies), Melinda A. Cohen (National Association of State Foresters), Derrick A. Crandall (American Recreation Coalition), John Fedkiw (Department of Agriculture), Roy M. Gray (Soil Conservation Service), Harry E. Hodgden (The Wildlife Society), Ray M. Housley (Society of Range Management), Douglas W. MacCleery (Department of Agriculture), James E. Miller (Extension Service), Roger A. Sedjo (Resources for the Future), William E. Shands (Conservation Foundation), Ernie C. Shea (National Association of Conservation Districts), Jeff M. Sirmon (Forest Service), Carl R. Sullivan (American Fisheries Society) and John A. Vance (Extension Service).

The principal author(s) of each paper are listed under the chapter titles. Many others contributed by preparing supporting papers and material, providing technical review, and presenting material (as panelists and moderators) during the conference. These included: Vaughn C. Anthony (National Marine Fisheries Service), William Aron (National Marine Fisheries Service), William H. Banzhaf (Society of American Foresters), Mollie H. Beattie (Vermont Department of Forests, Parks and Recreation), Michael Bender (Fish and Wildlife Service), John R. Block (National Wholesale Grocers Association), Frank E.

ix

Busby (Winrock International Institute for Agricultural Development), Peter Caulkins (Environmental Protection Agency), Rodney L. Clouser (University of Florida), Rupert M. Cutler (Defenders of Wildlife), Derrick A. Crandall (American Recreation Coalition), David G. Davis (Environmental Protection Agency), Gary L. Edwards (Fish and Wildlife Service), Carlos M. Fetterolf (Great Lakes Fish Commission), Joseph Fletcher (National Oceanic and Atmospheric Administration), Alberto Goetzel (National Forest Products Association), John C. Gordon (Yale University), Roy M. Gray (Soil Conservation Service), Ralph E. Grossi (American Farmland Trust), Richard W. Guldin (Forest Service), Dwight Hair (American Forestry Association), James Hildreth (Farm Foundation), Laurence R. Jahn (Wildlife Management Institute), David W. Moody (Geological Survey), Harvey K. Nelson (Fish and Wildlife Service), Laird Noh (Idaho State Senate), Jerry J. Presley (Missouri Department of Conservation), Michael L. Parrick (National Marine Fisheries Service), Thomas M. Quigley (Forest Service), F. Dale Robertson (Forest Service), Robert Rodale (Rodale Press), Roger A. Sedjo (Resources for the Future), Thomas N. Schiflet (retired— Soil Conservation Service), Milo J. Shult (Texas Agricultural Extension Service), Robert A. Siegel (National Oceanic and Atmospheric Administration), George H. Siehl (Congressional Research Service), Zane G. Smith, Jr. (American Forestry Association), Lee W. Stokes (Boise State University), Norton Strommen (World Agricultural Outlook Board), Gerald W. Thomas (retired-New Mexico State University), Virginia K. Tippie (National Oceanic and Atmospheric Administration), Dale E. Toweil (Idaho Fish and Game Department), Stewart Udall (author and lecturer), Jared Verner (Forest Service), R. Scott Wallinger (Westvaco Corporation), Robert Wetherbee (National Association of Conservation Districts), Ross S. Whaley (SUNY College of Environmenal Science and Forestry), Douglas P. Wheeler (Conservation Foundation), Bill O. Wilen (Fish and Wildlife Service), Robert M. Williamson (Forest Service), Gerald W. Winegrad (Maryland State Senate), and Robert E. Wolf (retired— Congressional Research Service).

The general planning, direction, and management of the conference and this book were by R. Neil Sampson (American Forestry Association) and Frederick J. Deneke (Extension Service). All papers were edited by Melany C. Neilson (Soil Conservation Service). Technical coordination for the papers and technical editorial assistance was provided by Dwight Hair (American Forestry Asociation). The primary support for the preparation of text, graphics, and other materials for printing was provided by Eric S. Sampson (American Forestry Association).

A number of sponsors and co-sponsors provided support and assistance for the conference and this book. The sponsors were the American Forestry Association, Extension Service, Fish and Wildlife Service, Forest Service, Soil Conservation Service, and Waste Management, Inc. The co-sponsors were the

Agricultural Research Service, American Farmland Trust, American Fisheries Society, American Recreation Coalition, Bureau of Land Management, Cooperative States Research Service, Conservation Foundation, Council on Environmental Quality, Defenders of Wildlife, Environmental Protection Agency, Geological Survey, International Association of Fish and Wildlife Agencies, National Association of Conservation Districts, National Association of Professional Schools and Colleges, National Association of State Conservation Administrators, National Association of State Foresters, National Park Service, National Woodland Owners Association, Renewable Natural Resources Foundation, Resources For the Future, Rodale Press, Society of American Foresters, Society for Range Management, Soil and Water Conservation Society, The Wildlife Society, and the Wildlife Management Institute.

Foreword

Peter C. Myers

We live in an information age. Nowhere is that more true than in the natural resources and environmental arena. Acid rain, global warming, ocean dumping, oil spills, and other environmental topics are all regularly in the media headlines.

Anyone who is interested in the wise use and management of our natural resources is faced with even more voluminous, and often conflicting, information about the condition of our natural resources and environment. Information is generated by a wide variety of sources, both public and private, about the opportunities, problems, and alleged crises related to our wildlife, recreation, water, forests, croplands, grazing lands, and air.

Moreover, it is normal in our democracy that special interest groups and even public agencies will compete for attention to their particular concerns. It is also natural for such groups to place their own value and their particular spin on an issue in seeking public attention.

As a result of all these factors, there is a continuing challenge involved in putting the large amount of information we receive on resource issues into an integrated perspective of scientific facts and long-term resource trends. In the Old Testament, Zechariah (8:16) admonishes: "These then are the things you should do: Speak the truth to one another; let there be honesty and peace in the judgment at your gates." Putting all of the information we receive from many sources into a proper truthful perspective is essential for reaching enlightened decisions. Thus, the purpose of this book, to encourage the development of a balanced perspective and to sort fact from fiction, is truly important.

Much of this book focuses on assessing the current condition of our natural resource base and on identifying those factors that were most influential in leading to its current condition. This is a sound approach. Before deciding where we want to go, we first need to agree on where we are and understand how we got there.

As the use of our renewable resources has increased, the relationships and connections among them have become better known and understood. We are increasingly interested in the multiple resource context and the holistic view that the whole of natural resources is greater than the simple sum of its individual parts. We are also interested in how resources are performing in the aggregate over time and space. Public officials are constantly receiving snapshots of conditions and problems which are difficult to evaluate without the overall understanding that reflects the background of resource trends over time and their geographic distribution.

Other factors influencing the performance of our resources also need better understanding. While public resource policies have been well scrutinized, economics and new technology are factors whose roles are often *not* clearly seen, defined, or analyzed. The environmental sensitivity of our natural resources is often cited, but we need to know and understand much more about the resilience of resources and their ability to respond to management.

We need to better understand that resource management is concerned with both the use and management of our heritage of natural capital. Resource management assures effective short-term use and production. More important, it provides for long-term capital investment and maintenance that generate a long stream of benefits into the future. Each year's investment tends not only to sustain the stream of benefits into the future but to increase that stream. New technology performs like a capital investment. It has an important sustaining and enhancing role.

Wise use of our resources is necessary for maintaining and increasing the productive capacity of our planet to meet the needs of a growing population. Our resources also have an important environmental and aesthetic role in sustaining and enhancing the enjoyment of life on this earth. Quality of life has always been an important dimension of our national interest in natural resources. As the affluence of our population has grown, quality-of-life concerns have risen. Assuring that those quality issues are properly addressed has become an important part of resource management objectives.

In many ways, resource policy officials can be viewed as caretakers. Among the most valuable tools for assisting them in exercising good stewardship over our natural resources is good information about their use, management, and condition. The information in this book can provide better understanding about what is happening to our resources. Just as important, it can help open a new dialogue between resource officials and the public about the future of those resources.

PART I
An Inventory of
Renewable Natural Resources

Introduction

R. Neil Sampson
and Fred Deneke

This book began with a vision. Simply stated, we think that the most important ingredient in framing the future of America is people and the decisions they make as part of their daily lives. As natural resource professionals, we are dedicated to the idea that people who use the natural bounty of the world wisely will prosper in many ways, in matters of the soul as well as in matters of practical survival and economic prosperity. We further believe that people who have a realistic view of the facts surrounding their situation, and the most likely results of their actions, will make better decisions than those working without good information.

The present moment offers some exceptional opportunities to the American people. New political leadership is taking charge of the federal agencies, and the "environment," as a political issue, has come back into public consciousness after a few years on the back burner. At the local level, many recent elections in the past year have turned on the public's perception of the quality of their lives, with the main issues often surrounding growth, development, land use, transportation, pollution, and related topics.

On the private scene, farmers in 1988 came through a significant drought that added to a decade of economic stress, and forest products industries are now going through intensive pressures from corporate realignments. Fishermen are running into depleted or pollution-poisoned populations, and cattlemen fear that lowered per-capita red meat consumption will cause their industry problems for years to come. Clearly, people need to make strategic decisions in natural resource management, and the idea that better decisions will be based on better information is easy to reach.

On the other side of the decision ledger, the recent months have seen an exceptional flurry of natural resource information studies. In the Department of Agriculture, the Resources Planning Act (RPA) assessment carried out by the Forest Service was recently released for public review, as was the Resources Conservation Act (RCA) assessment done by the Soil Conservation Service. In the Department of the Interior, a major assessment of waterfowl population dynamics is underway in connection with the North American Waterfowl Plan, and there is widespread concern over growing evidence of population problems in several major fisheries. At the Environmental Protection Agency, concerns for air and water quality, the impact of the greenhouse effect, and other topics are resulting in a series of assessment reports.

Thus, we seem to be at a critical juncture — a time when a significant need for reliable information occurs in conjunction with the release of dozens of major natural resource studies that could, if properly interpreted, be put to very good use. The challenge is to get the information to those who need it, in a form that they can use. Massive scientific or government documents produced by teams of credible scientists may, by their very bulk, hide information from the "end users" rather than make it readily available.

This book is one attempt to break down that communications gap. It is based on the premise that there is a cadre of "natural resource educators" in both public and private service whose education or job role places them in the position of being part-scientist, part-educator. They are asked to plow through the heavy scientific or data-laden reports, then translate that information into usefully abbreviated versions that retain their scientific honesty, but cut away as much of the "overhead" information as possible. One such cadre is contained in the Cooperative Extension Service. In adopting "Conservation and Management of Natural Resources" as one of its primary issue initiatives, the Service has signaled that it expects its employees and cooperative partners at the state universities to increase their knowledge of and attention to natural resource issues.

This book presents these educators with a resource, from which we hope many new and improved natural resource information and education programs will emerge.

Another major audience is composed of those who actually manage land and water: farmers, ranchers, foresters, fishermen, and others. There are significant needs in the corporate boardrooms of America, where major decisions affecting natural resources are made. And, in the minds of many, the most important audience of all is that vast majority of the American people who do not work directly with natural resources, but who frame the public opinion that drives actions in both the private and public sectors.

We make no pretense to having covered all of the relevant information on natural resources in this book. Some critical topics weren't even explored, simply to keep the scope of the project within manageable limits. Energy is probably the most notable omission, accompanied by minerals and related non-renewable resource facts. Even on the topics covered, the information is carefully chosen and limited, and not everyone will agree that what has been selected is the most important. But with those caveats, we believe much is to be learned from the following assessments.

In working with over 100 people to put together the conference which led to this book, we learned a great deal, both about natural resources and about how the natural world has reacted to the actions of people. We learned that, when viewed as objectively as possible, things aren't all that bad. Neither are they all good. Unfortunately, too many times we are given one or the other of these messages by people who want us to join them in one or another type of policy action. But when scientists look at the natural resource situation, what they find is a very complex situation. Easy, simple answers aren't common. Most renewable resources respond to good management, and there are many examples where the actions of people have resulted in improved conditions. In many respects, the natural world is remarkably resilient. Even after significant insult, it can bounce back if given the proper investment, care and treatment.

The forests of the United States have responded well to a century of increasing knowledge and attention to management, for example. But there are some problems, many opportunities for improvement that would be both economically and environmentally beneficial. The same can be said of rangelands. In other resource areas things aren't going very well at all — some fisheries are seriously depleted and the waterfowl situation in North America indicates a significant need to make some changes in both land use and human activities. The potential threat to ecosystems posed by global warming is a long-term concern that concerns natural resource experts.

We have more information about natural resources than ever before in history, but data and the wisdom to make the best management decisions are not automatically linked. People still strive to do their best in the midst of a complex stream of events — political, economic, natural, social. They don't always think about the long-term impacts of their actions on the natural resource base, and might not be able to accurately assess the true impacts in every case, even if they tried. So, in large measure, natural resource management is a people problem. More people, making more significant impacts on their environment, need more and better information if they are to live without ruining the natural resource base upon which all life depends.

There are many ways to go about managing resources, and it is not always clear that some management techniques are right and others are wrong. Often, scientists and educators will find it both easy and honest to be fairly neutral on the means of achieving society's goals. But few can afford the luxury of being neutral on the goals themselves. There are right and wrong ways to use land and water, and their renewable resources. Identifying the boundary between prudent use and waste is not always easy. But it can be done, and it must be done. So natural resource education programs must teach people how to make those judgments, and how to identify those boundaries. In the process, the education program must show people what the boundary is, why it is where it is, and how to tell when you are approaching it. There's little room for neutrality here.

Nobody has magic answers. Political leaders and scientists alike work most of the time on sketchy information that too often gives few clues about future outcomes. They make recommendations or decisions because they are forced to do so by circumstances, not because all of the evidence is at hand, or the best course of action plainly shown. The least productive strategy may be the "we-they" construct, where people attempt to show that the reason problems exist is because "they" (whoever "they" are) refuse to be reasonable or do the right thing. Just like there are few true prophets, there are few clearly identifiable ogres.

Truly integrating resource understandings into a "holistic" point of view is hard work, and it takes a lot of people — well-trained and talented people. But it is critical if we are to try to really understand the world and what is happening to it as a result of human activities. We must, therefore, try to train ourselves in two skills at once: a technical skill where we truly understand one aspect of the natural world; and an integrative skill where we gain the ability to relate that aspect to the rest of the world around it. It may not be a matter of being either a "specialist" or a "generalist," so much as the challenge to be some of each.

At the same time, we must build many more bridges between professional disciplines, agencies and institutions. The boundaries built to protect "turf" impose heavy penalties on society, because they deprive the ultimate users — private land users and public decisionmakers — of the full range of integrated and holistic resource information that they need. That is a cost burden that was never helpful, but is rapidly becoming unacceptable.

At the conference which led to this book, we asked four panels of experienced leaders to share with us their insight into the meaning of resource trends and needed directions for future management. As well, we asked four experienced natural resource writers and several analysts to add their insights to those panels and present the results here in reflective articles. These are gathered at the back of the volume as an opening to dialogue on the implications of the data.

In reading the material that follows, both in Part I, which contains chapters assessing resource trends and situations, and in the second section, which interprets the interactions and importance of those trends, keep in mind that the authors have tried to minimize value judgments, predictions, and alarm bells. Those are, for the most part, left to the reader. It is our hope that what you find here will be the basis for you to make reasoned judgments about natural resources. Whether the facts presented herein alarm or comfort you, we hope they bring you new information and insight into ways that people can work to make natural resources more productive and plentiful.

In the final analysis, we believe that the difference between a society that will survive and one whose future is in doubt will be the difference between a people whose actions (intended or otherwise) destroy the natural resources on which they depend, and one whose people and institutions take *intentional, constructive* actions to use natural resources for human benefit, and to protect and improve their sustainable productivity through wise stewardship. It is hoped that the information presented in this book will help Americans attain that goal.

CHAPTER 1

Population and Global Economic Patterns

Lawrence W. Libby
Rodney L. Clouser

Natural resources are the physical context for all human activity. They facilitate, constrain, embody what we as human beings do with or to each other. With population changes over time come inevitable changes in the natural resource context, exerting new constraints or providing new opportunities for people. The purpose of this chapter is to help clarify future natural resource consequences of two major forces— population and global economics. Beginning with an identification of key concepts, it reviews evidence of demographic and economic patterns and identifies policy needs of highest priority for the 21st century.

Futurist Daniel Bell has observed that the only real "time bombs" associated with people and natural resources of the future are polity and demography. The former concerns how people in meaningful public entities such as counties, states, provinces, or nations organize themselves to solve natural resource problems. The latter concerns both the number of people and their distribution relative to natural resource systems. More people within any natural resource setting implies a greater frequency of interaction with resources, greater likelihood of scarcity or conflict, and greater challenge for political and economic institutions.

IMPORTANCE OF RESOURCES

The inevitable controversies over natural resource policy will center on the various ways in which those resources generate utility for people. Resource conflict means a difference of opinion about the rate, form and spatial character of resource-based utility. The apparent tautology needs restating— natural resources are relevant to policy only because of what they do for, or to people. No one truly speaks for resources. They argue to protect resource use patterns that they prefer. Resource utility comes in many forms.

Resources as Production Inputs

Farmers and foresters have learned how to facilitate the conversion of soil, water, sunlight, and various added nutrients into a product that has value to people. Effective economic demand for the natural resource, then, is derived from demand for the product resulting from organized resource conversion. Food, building materials, and the ornamentals that grace the home or landscape are broad categories of valued products that convert or consume available resources.

Resources as Consumer Goods

Some resources or systems of natural resources are consumed directly with little physical conversion— fish, firewood, coal, or natural gas— though there are costly and essential services added to the resource to make it usable. These services generate jobs and political support; they consume additional resources. Other resources create on-site utility. They are valued *because* they are not consumed, converted, or altered by human action, as with wilderness, wetlands, groundwater recharge areas, shorelands. People are willing to bear considerable cost or inconvenience to keep these resources as they are and petition governments to enact programs to protect them. Accessibility of these systems will affect the quality of utility generated. Some are subject to the cost of excessive enjoyment of people— congestion or deterioration. For others, private ownership may restrict access.

Resources as Store of Wealth

Because they are limited in supply, many resources are valued for the likelihood that greater contact with people will increase their monetary value. People buy land or minerals in anticipation of physical and economic scarcity. They anticipate conversion or consumption at some future time.

Natural resource issues and policies of the 21st century will involve conflicts among these sources of human utility as world populations increase and redistribute, technologies develop, and preferences change. Conflict will not be uniformly distributed throughout the landscape or across political boundaries.

Economics of Scarcity

In their seminal work at Resources for the Future, Barnett and Morse (1963) established the essential distinctions between physical and economic scarcity. As the physical supply of a particular resource becomes harder to find or develop, its price is bid up. Users have an incentive to find substitutes, and they do. New production technologies alter the required resource mix for a given output. Agricultural development programs, for example, focus on getting more product from a land unit and substituting other inputs for land. Economic scarcity is a central ingredient of resource conflict as competing users bid for resource services or petition governments to protect certain natural systems.

Institutional Context
Conflicts in the use of natural resources are resolved (some more success-fully than others) through specific institutions. Resource markets, for example, can handle much of the allocation problem, with direct government action when needed to allocate resource services that are not handled well by markets. We know from experience that markets are inadequate to allocate access to an ocean fishery, a fragile eco-system, or the waste-processing capacity of land. People request that governments exercise the powers to tax, to regulate, or to spend funds in the public interest on behalf of forms of natural resource utility not handled well by a market. The choice among available and acceptable policy instruments becomes the substance of natural resource policy. An individual or political group will lobby for or against a particular natural resource policy proposal, based on the resource utility being acquired *and* distribution or the potential distribution of the burden. Even when there is agreement on the resource service desired (e.g., protect a fragile wetland), there may be sharp differences over whether that resource should be acquired with tax money or protected through regulation.

We contend at the outset that people and resource imbalances in the United States are at their root institutional or policy problems rather than matters of physical scarcity. Differences of opinion over the form or rate of resource conversion, the importance of protecting fragile eco-systems, the need for controlling frequency of interaction between people and resources, even the rate of population increase, will define the natural resource issues of coming decades.

POPULATION TRENDS AND RESOURCE CONFLICT

The Population Reference Bureau, a private nonprofit Washington, D.C., think tank on population matters, monitors the vital statistics of national population patterns of virtually all nations of the world. Their estimates help clarify the natural resource consequences of population change on a macro scale. The other major component of change is migration of people from one nation or locality to another. Age, sex, and other characteristics of the population change suggest the kinds of resource pressures involved. Emphasis here is on the United States, though brief discussion of world totals is included.

World Population
The overall pattern of projected change in population between 1988 and 2020 is shown in Table 1.1. The most dramatic differences here are between the

developed and less developed nations of the world. The developed world *is* developed partly because of natural resource endowment. Thus, those nations least able to sustain population increase are those with the most pronounced rates of change. A few key facts emerge:

1) The rate of natural increase, comparing births to deaths, in the less developed world is nearly *quadruple* that of the developed world (.6 percent in developed, 2.4 percent in undeveloped excluding China; 2.1 percent, including China).

2) Fertility in the developed nations is below replacement and is continuing to increase in less developed (Bouvier 1984).

3) Infant mortality rates are startlingly different between more and less developed nations, with 15 deaths per 1,000 infants under age one in the former and 86 to 96 in the latter.

While not shown in Table 1.1, the age and sex distribution of the population also differs dramatically between the more and less developed countries (Crews and Cancellier 1988). The less developed countries show a much younger profile than more developed nations where the numbers of men and women in each age category are roughly the same up to age 68 or so, when the inevitable reductions begin to show up, with slightly more women than men. Further, the proportion of the population that is classified as urban in more developed nations is more than twice that in the less developed areas.

The obvious inference is that generalizations about the population/resource interaction around the world are virtually impossible. Population densities suggest a source of resource pressure.

United States Population

Total population in the United States is estimated at 246.1 million in 1988, expanding at an average of about 1.6 million per year through 2020 (Haub and Kent 1988). The United States birth rate remains fairly low among developed nations, at 16 births per 1,000 population (compared to 11 in Sweden, 11 in Japan, 13 in the United Kingdom, 12 in western Europe, 20 in the Soviet Union), down from 55 in the early 19th century when families averaged eight to 10 children (van der Tak 1982). The rate has fluctuated with various baby booms, boom "echoes," wars, and other major events, but has declined consistently. Birth rates differ by ethnic category— 1980 rates were 68.5 births per 1,000 women of child-bearing age for whites, 84.0 for blacks, 106 for Hispanics. Birth rates also vary by region, with higher rates in West and South, and among rural women. Family size is influenced by various religious and cultural factors. The rates of teenage births have increased dramatically from 1950 with an equally dramatic increase in the proportion of out-of-wedlock births over that period. The number of households doubled from 1950 to 1986, partly a result of the

Table 1.1 World Population: 1988-2020

	1988 (mil)	Birth Rate (per 1,000)	Death Rate (per 1,000)	2000 (mil)	2020 (mil)	Infant Mortality (per 1,000 births)	Percent < 15 and > 65
World	5,128	28	10	6,178	8,053	77	33/6
More Developed	1,198	15	9	1,266	1,337	15	22/11
Less Developed	3,931	31	10	4,911	6,716	86	37/4
Less Developed (excluding China)	2,844	35	12	3,699	5,312	96	40/4

Source: Information abstracted from "1988 World Population Data Sheet," Population Reference Bureau, Washington, D.C. "More developed" are all nations of North America, Europe, Australia, Japan, New Zealand, and the Soviet Union. All others are considered "less developed."

number of single person and nontraditional family households (van der Tak 1982).

Mortality, the other determinant of natural increase, has declined steadily in the United States from 17.2 deaths per 1,000 in 1900, to nine in 1988. However, mortality rates for black infants are nearly double those for whites, with some regional variation. Life expectancy is 75 years in 1988, compared to 78 in Japan, 75 in the United Kingdom, 47 in Western Africa, 61 in Southeast Asia, 65 in the Soviet Union, 77 in Sweden, with slightly higher life expectancy among females than males. In 1980, nearly half of all deaths in the United States were from heart disease, another 21 percent from cancer. Those two causes have grown far more prominent over time despite improvements in treatment technology.

Immigration is a factor of growing importance in the overall population level in the United States as natural growth rates stabilize. Net migration accounted for 40 percent of population growth in the late 1800s when the United States opened its doors to the world. Some 85,000 more people left the United States than came in during the 1930s, the years of the Great Depression. In the 1980s, the rate again approaches 30 percent as the quality of opportunity in the United States attracts immigrants from around the world. The United States is now the destination of more than half of all immigrants (Holden 1988). Illegal immigration has made the accounting difficult, but demographers predict between 900,000 and one million immigrants annually for the 1980s, nearly matching the first decade of this century. New arrivals are primarily Asian and Hispanic rather than European, as they were in the earlier period (Arocha 1988). Also included are more than 2.5 million illegal immigrants likely to be granted amnesty under the 1986 Immigration Reform and Control Act.

Regional Differences

As noted with world population patterns, the most consistent feature of United States population change is its regional diversity. The natural resource character of a place affects its drawing power, imposes constraints on location, and is often irretrievably altered by population change. While there are some regional differences in natural increase— large families in Utah, other south-western states, and the South— most of the regional diversity is explained by differences in the rate of immigration and internal migration. Wage rates, tax levels, and other economic factors are significant determinants of inter-regional migration. The general patterns have been well documented (van der Tak 1982; Crews and Cancellier 1988).

The South and West have consistently shown highest rates of population increase, with internal migration being the greatest factor. Several of these states— Florida, California, and Texas, for example— are the intended destinations of many immigrants, as well. The Northeast (except for New Hampshire), Midwest (particularly the industrial Great Lakes states), and Northwest (except Washington) have either lost population or barely held even in the 1980s. Greatest mobility occurs in the 20-to-35 age group when children of the family are younger. Migrants tend to be better educated than non-migrants, with higher job skills. Self-employed people move less than those on salary.

Within states or regions, migration between urban and rural areas adds to the population flow. Until 1970, urban areas were the population magnets, drawing people from rural areas to better jobs and opportunity in the city. Improvements in farm production technology released people from farming, pushing them toward non-farm possibilities elsewhere. Human capital needs remain high in agriculture but with more emphasis on management than physical labor. The demographic turnaround of the 1970s pulled people back to the countryside, some to work but more just to live and retain urban employment. Some returned to retire or just enjoy their higher income (Dillman 1979; Beale 1976). Financial pain in rural America, which in the mid-1980s added to the attraction of revitalized downtowns, has again caused an urban migration.

Implications

What are the implications of all of this for people and resources of the 21st century? A few conclusions emerge:

1) Population pressures on natural resources will be highly localized. While there may not be overall scarcity of renewable resources in the next century, there will continue to be intense resource pressure where population increase is most dramatic. The degree of pain associated with population pressure depends on how "polity deals with demography," in Bell's terms (1987).

Florida provides the most convenient current laboratory for observing the resource consequence of localized population pressure. In July 1980, the *Wall Street Journal* predicted that Florida would surge past Pennsylvania to be the fourth largest state by 1990 (Morgenthaler 1986). It happened by 1987. The population increased 24 percent in seven years, with an net average of 900 new residents per day in 1987-88. The Naples metropolitan area in southwest Florida led the nation with a 35 percent increase in five years. Collier County, containing Naples, is expected to grow another 45 percent by 1998. Contrary to the popular image, 40 percent of the new arrivals are in the 30-to-64 age category, coming for new jobs rather than retirement in the sun, though the climate is likely a factor in any relocation decision. Needs for housing, schools, roads and public services will create serious growing pains in the 20 or so of Florida's 67 counties expected to increase 35 percent or more by 1998 (Kiplinger 1988). Fresh water, building space, and materials will be scarce in areas with the most rapid growth. Florida has one of the nation's most progressive sets of institutions for growth management, water allocation and water quality protection but may lack the collective will to employ these institutions effectively. Physical development makes some people and some municipalities wealthy in a hurry. The pressure is not easily capped or controlled. Yet Florida's primary exporting sector is still resource dependent — agriculture. Citrus, beef, vegetables and ornamentals are the leaders. *In situ* resources in the form of coastal beaches, ocean access, and friendly climate are the heart of Florida. Yet these attributes are for sale and threatened by poor management in areas of greatest population pressure. Developers and citrus growers compete directly in Collier County, while many other Florida counties experience little resource pressure.

Florida's natural resource picture is uneven for the 21st century. There will be localized pain, even real economic scarcity, where collective will and institutional innovation fall behind the monetary attraction of physical growth. Tax effort remains low in Florida, 47th in the nation relative to income, limiting the capacity to cope with population pressure. The consequence of population increase is a function of institutional response, which in turn is a function of the general social commitment for managed change. We fear for Florida on that count. Other areas of rapid change may handle it better. In *all* cases, though, deliberate thoughtful action is necessary.

2) Age and occupational mix of increased population is an important determinant of impact. Again, that mix varies from place to place.

Age mix in a state or locality is obviously affected by those who move in and those who move out. The United States population is an aging population, with median age increasing. Utah has the highest ratio of young to old while Florida has the lowest. Older people require less housing space per capita while demanding more living space. Retired people require fewer schools but more hospitals (perhaps the resource impacts of that are off-setting). They require nearby accessible shops and other services. A declining proportion of working Americans are in the natural resource sectors such as agriculture and mining while a growing segment are service employees. Perhaps the lack of direct association with natural resource industries breeds insensitivity to resource problems. Alternatively, a better educated service-oriented society with more leisure time may demand protection of resource amenities. The character of the people/resource interaction will vary with population differences.

3) Population declines in some areas will *increase* the reliance on natural resources. Those states and localities losing population will depend more on the natural resource base for livelihood, often with less opportunity to employ advanced farm or forest production technologies. Development programs for those left behind by migration to other areas must begin with resource-oriented opportunities. Major federal and state development efforts for people in resource-limited regions like Appalachia or isolated counties in Maine, Oregon, and Texas have begun with resource-based employment possibilities. Much of the public domain is tax-reverted land or other lands too rough or infertile to generate income. With public investment, some of these lands may yield salable

timber or minerals or provide valuable wildlife habitat. Programs may be instituted to direct more of the revenue back to the local units for development needs.

The consequences of population pressure on resources are subject to policy action. Deliberate thoughtful steps may be taken to avert or mitigate the resource impacts of population change. We need not be unwitting victims of change. The sense of urgency for action on any particular population/resource problem is a function of prevailing expectations. To some extent, changing expectations represent a mitigating force. Higher population densities are unavoidable facts, evidence for some that civilization has finally arrived. No one expects the vast wilderness areas of a century ago. Artificial facsimiles of natural wonders have been created and provide utility for people. With each new generation comes a new set of values about the human condition and the appropriate role of natural resources in that condition. Concerns for the protection of endangered species habitat, and control of certain global environmental problems have emerged. Public actions designed to realign rights and obligations of competing resource users are up for consideration at all levels. Attention here is focused on three areas— population policy, managing the pace and pattern of physical change, and waste control.

GLOBAL ECONOMIC PATTERNS AND IMPLICATIONS FOR RESOURCE USE

What impact do global economic conditions have on resource use? A review of existing economic literature would suggest that the question is often explored though never adequately answered. Although considerable research has covered issues such as the impact of debt, inflation, and exchange rates on the United States and global economy, attempts to associate global economic trends with resource use are precarious at best. The sole exception to this assessment is the energy crisis in the late 1970s, which many economists and other social scientists agree led to a worldwide recession and reduction in oil consumption.

The problematic relationship between economic conditions and future resource use has not dampened individual aspiration for prediction. It has been more than 200 years since economist Robert Malthus concluded that economic growth would be stifled by a fixed and finite supply of land. Of course, that prediction was wrong, as many predictions are. (Another leading economist of his time predicted that the population of New York City would stabilize at 100,000 because of the shortage of space for stabling horses.) Where did Malthus go wrong in his analysis? It was impossible for him to foresee future technological advances in fertilizers, seed, pesticides, herbicides, machinery and other factor inputs. Malthus' analysis was limited by availability of data and although data collection has improved immensely over the last two centuries it still remains a limiting factor in analysis. It is most troublesome in developing countries. However, the precision with which future trends are defined is probably less important than direction of those trends.

Theorizing and speculating on future resource use and how it will be affected by global economic conditions is similar to trying to make one's way through a large, complex labyrinth. The labyrinth is complicated because it is dynamic. Every decision results in a new twist in the maze. Again, this is most easily seen during the 1978 energy crisis. Who could have speculated that a group of countries, several of which were unlikely to agree on anything, would form a cartel that would drastically reduce oil supply and cause economic havoc around the world (especially for fuel importing countries)? Keeping all these caveats in mind, we proceed with our analysis of how global economic conditions will affect resource use in the future.

Economic Variables and Resource Use

It is important before beginning discussion of various economic variables to acknowledge that global measurements of economic variables do not exist. The "world" is unfortunately not a meaningful political entity. Rather, specific continents, global regions, and countries have individual measurements of economic variables. Worldwide aggregate inflation rates, unemployment rates, and interest rates do not exist.

Consumer Price Increases

During the past decade consumer price increases have varied significantly across the world. Data indicate that inflation in developing countries and regions during this period exceeded rates in many industrialized countries by a factor of two to eight times. Rates in developing countries are even more divergent when oil exporting and oil importing countries are separated (International Monetary Fund 1985).

The oil situation of the late 1970s affected many countries. Interest rates were high for most countries between 1979 and 1981. However, some individuals believe that the energy situation in the late 1970s was not as severe as the earlier crisis around 1973 (International Bank for Reconstruction and Development 1983). Anticipated inflation and restrictive monetary policies by several countries that wanted to bring the expected inflation under control led to higher interest rates.

This latter point is extremely meaningful because it brings into view the issue of causality. Do world economic conditions affect resource use or does resource availability affect economic conditions? The correct answer is probably both. The energy predicament of the 1970s is a classic example of how resource scarcity created economic uncertainty about supply and prices. The resulting price increase has been six-fold since 1972 (Repetto 1986) and eventually led to a worldwide reduction in energy use (specifically oil). Reduction in resource use was primarily brought about by substitution of other energy resources, regulation, conservation and the price increase.

It is just as easy to cite examples where inflationary conditions have altered resource use. Higher energy prices resulted in decreasing demand for energy inputs. Decreased use also contributed to increases in unemployment rates throughout the world. However, during this time period many countries of the world were experiencing higher inflation, unemployment, interest rates and debt, and it is difficult to determine how much of the unemployment increase can be attributed to the decreased resource demand. Opposite resource effects due to inflation can also be identified. Consider the case of farmland in the U.S. during the early 1980 inflationary period. The price of farmland skyrocketed, yet the demand for farmland remained strong because output prices were also relatively high. Farmland was considered a good investment because of its rising value, and the value of the resource was buffeted from down-side market impacts through government support programs.

Most economists would agree that inflation results in the depreciation of currency. This makes imports more expensive and could have dampening effects on raw material demand directed to exporting countries. However, this impact appears to be relative to inflation, interest, and growth rates in the importing and exporting countries. During the inflationary period of the early 80s, for example, United States imports and exports both declined while short-term real interest rates remained relatively high. Funds and capital from outside investors and nations continued to flow into the United States during this period. This may be partially explained by the stability of the United States government.

As we approach the 21st century, historical patterns will likely continue. There will be various economic inflationary shocks that will affect resource use. Likewise, there will be "resource shocks" that affect economic conditions, initiated by external political forces. Energy resources seem the most likely to cause these economic shocks, impacting both energy consumers and producers who use the resource as an input in a production process. As available supplies continue to decrease, upward pressure on prices can be expected in the absence of government regulation or subsidy. Inflationary impacts associated with rising prices will not be distributed evenly among countries. Greatest impacts will be felt in countries and regions that are heavily dependent upon energy imports.

Debt and Capital Flows

Most economists associate worldwide debt problems with the oil/energy crisis of the 1970s (Shane and Stallings, 1988; International Monetary Fund, 1983). In general, increased debt acts as a constraint on trade. This has important connotations for resource-based trade sectors, specifically agriculture. Shane and Stallings summarized the debt predicament in the following manner.

During the 1960s and 1970s developing countries were borrowing funds to invest internally. The borrowing stimulated growth in their economies. Export markets were expanding and prices for the exports were increasing. Due to substantial increases in oil prices during 1973-74, abundant revenues were generated by oil exporting countries. These excess funds were available to developing countries throughout the world and economic growth remained high despite those increasing energy prices. Funds borrowed by developing countries were used to enhance the domestic economy, and exports of the countries doubled between 1970 and 1980. Shortages of various raw commodities resulted in even higher export incomes. A second round of energy price hikes in the 1979-80 time period raised concerns with inflation. Restrictive monetary policies were adopted. Interest rates were increasing. World credit availability was reduced. Export markets were declining. Many developing countries devalued currencies to induce increased exports. Raw food commodity prices dropped by 25 percent in developing countries between 1980 and 1985. Since these countries were not generating export income to purchase imports, export markets for industrialized countries such as the United States dried up.

Debt problems are still prevalent as the end of the decade approaches. Many countries are seeking debt forgiveness and a restructuring of payment schedules. Shane and Stallings note that between 1956 and 1975, 11 countries revised payment schedules on $8 billion in debt; but between January and September of 1987, 18 countries rescheduled payment schedules on $144 billion.

The debt crisis is further complicated by deficit financing in both industrialized and developing countries. Not only are government deficits increasing internal interest payments but relatively high rates of interest are also attracting funds to finance the deficit rather than making these funds available for capital investment.

The debt problem has had major impacts on both industrialized and developing countries. The industrialized countries have experienced reduced trade. Developing countries therefore are not importing as many goods and their export markets have also been reduced as they try to meet their debt obligations. The bottom line is that developing countries are experiencing stagnant or deteriorating per capita incomes.

Resource use has been affected by the debt situation. In the early 1970s, for example, U.S. agricultural producers, because of favorable world economic conditions, were planting from "fence row to fence row." Agricultural commodity exports were increasing in both value and volume. Marginal lands were brought into production. The emphasis shifted from managing excess supply to generating adequate production to meet demand. Suddenly, world economic conditions changed. Exports from U.S. agriculture declined in both value and volume, partially as a result of the world debt problem. Programs switched back to an excess supply management mode. Policies were adopted encouraging marginal lands to be removed from production. Impacts from this latest set of policy actions varied throughout the United States. Areas in the country most affected were states in the Midwest or corn belt that produce our major export commodities. However, policy actions such as the conservation reserve program have resulted in marginal lands across the country being removed from production.

Expenditures on land, chemicals, labor and machinery have been reduced sharply. Future impacts on crop production also extend beyond the row crops mentioned previously. Low per capita income growth rates in developing countries will most likely translate into less demand for fruits and vegetables. Ramifications of the debt problem and policy actions taken by countries to alleviate this problem will no doubt have consequences well into the 21st century. The debt situation underscores the need for U.S. agriculture to remain competitive in world markets in order to retain current markets and expand export markets in the future.

Other Important Global Conditions

Economic factors are not the only variables that will affect resource use in the 21st century. At least three non-economic variables have the potential for global impacts on resource use.

Peter Drucker (Marston, 1988), the well-known management guru, has recently noted that the "raw material economy has become uncoupled from the industrial economy." Shortly after World War II almost 40 percent of major consumption costs were associated with the costs of such raw materials as copper, steel and rubber. However, Drucker estimates that about 3 percent of costs of current consumption items can be directly attributed to raw materials used in their production. The remainder of production costs include research, interest on the investment, development of software, etc. The world has changed from a raw material economy to an information, research and technology economy.

Implications of Drucker's convictions are far reaching, especially for developing countries and rural regions of industrialized countries. Most resource based raw materials are derived from rural areas and many developing countries' economies are resource based. If indeed the raw materials component of production remains relatively low, areas in the world dependent upon these materials to provide economic growth will suffer, not only in terms of the rate of extraction of the resource but also in depressed income levels. This in turn will require long-term structural adjustments in raw material based economics.

A second non-economic concern is raised by Smith and Krutilla (1982). Natural resource availability and use are dependent on both economic and physical science considerations. Their conclusion is that many economic analyses oversimplify physical science constraints. In discussion of extractive industry they conclude "that most economists, if polled, would subscribe to a view that as firms are forced to mine lower grade deposits, there will be larger volumes of mineral ore available in them." The economic assumption is that additional ore is available for mining or that technology will be available to extract ore deposits not currently available. They note that geologists, on the other hand, might conclude that as chemical characteristics affect physical occurrence, geochemical properties will influence costs of extraction, and that chemical properties are likely to be important in determining the end use of the resource.

Smith and Krutilla note that Zimmerman's quote, "resources are not, they become," might best summarize the importance of the two-dimensional concern of economic and physical considerations. Their argument seems valid. It takes thousands or millions of years for some resources to form. There may not be perfect substitutability among different qualities of resources. Scarcity of resources becomes a more important issue when physical constraints are contemplated.

The final non-economic issue we want to discuss is domestic political policy of countries throughout the world. The specific application is related to an agricultural commodity. In the past decade Brazil has emerged as a major competitor to the U.S. citrus industry, primarily in frozen concentrated orange juice (FCOJ). During the 1979-80 season Florida produced 251.1 million gallons of concentrate and Brazil 146.2 million gallons. During the 1985-86 season Florida production was 132.4 million gallons and Brazil produced 292.4 million gallons (Florida Department of Citrus 1986). Likewise, orange production in Brazil has increased in excess of 2.7 million metric tons between the 1982-83 season and the 1986-87 season. At the same time U.S. orange production decreased by almost 1.7 million metric tons over the same time period (Florida Agricultural Statistical Service 1988). Experts who have visited Brazil note that much money has been invested in state of the art processing facilities. Additionally, thousands of acres of new bearing groves have been planted.

Citrus in Brazil, especially for FCOJ production, will remain a force in world markets no matter what world economic conditions are. With monetary and physical investments in acres planted, investments in state of the art processing facilities, and with an internal domestic policy built around increased export opportunities, the choices for the future have already been determined. Even if the economics of citrus production deteriorated during the next several years, it is unlikely that investments made in the industry would be abandoned. Politics and policies of countries may be more significant determinants of resource use, especially in the short-term, than economics.

U.S. Agricultural Trends
Before concluding the discussion of global economics and resource use,

some comments must be made about U.S. resource use, especially in agriculture. About three-fourths of the U.S. land base can be accounted for in terms of use as cropland, grassland pasture or forests (USDA 1984). In addition, agriculture is a major consumer of water. What trends on resource use are evident in U.S. agriculture?

Data used to evaluate changes are U.S. production and output indices collected and maintained by the U.S. Department of Agriculture. We acknowledge potential shortcomings of certain indices as identified by Crosson and Brubaker (1982), but conclude that these indices exhibit selected resource use patterns that are reliable for our discussion. What has happened to U.S. farm output since 1950? Total output increased in the vicinity of 80 percent (the precise increase is not as important as the direction of the change). Use of farm labor decreased by about two-thirds during the same time period. Use of agricultural chemicals has increased almost six-fold between 1950 and 1986. During many of the years between 1950 and 1986, agricultural policy can be characterized as a group of policies designed to alleviate excess supply. Acreage reductions and land set-aside programs were major components of U.S. agricultural policy. Statistics indicate we can produce more commodities with less land and fewer people but with more intensive production practices, including increased chemical use.

These substitutions will likely continue into the 21st century but at a lower rate than experienced during the 1950 and 1986 period. There will be increased pressure, mainly from consumers, to reduce the use of chemicals. Fewer people will be required to produce the necessary food supply. This will have important implications for farm and rural income policy. If increased usage of chemicals were to slow dramatically, the land base needed for production would decrease only moderately. If biotechnology can be easily adopted at the farm level, expect more substantial reductions in the land base. Agriculture is a major barometer of resource use in the United States. Changes in trends can and will have implications worldwide.

POLICY IMPLICATIONS

We now turn to possible institutional response to global economic and population forces affecting renewable resources of the 21st century. People can and do act collectively, given sufficient incentive and opportunity. Considered here are policy directions for rural income, population, and waste management.

Rural Income Policy

One of the most difficult tasks decision makers will encounter in the remainder of the 20th century and the 21st century is improving incomes and standards of living. This issue will be most significant in developing countries and rural regions of industrialized countries where government seeks to mitigate the consequence of global population and economic trends for rural people.

It is well documented in an industrialized country such as the United States that disposable per capita income of the farm population is significantly less than the non-farm population (USDA 1984). During the 1980s, farm per capita disposable income ranged between 68 to 80 percent of non-farm per capita disposable income. These depressed levels are prevalent despite the fact that between 1969 and 1983 the number of farms decreased by 7.5 percent. Farm population has also decreased dramatically. Until about 1940 the U.S. farm population exceeded 30 million people, and it is currently less than 6 million (USDA 1971). Also disturbing is the incidence of rural poverty. As of 1986 the farm population poverty rate was almost 20 percent, and non-metro poverty was approximately 15 percent, compared to a metro poverty rate of approximately 10 percent (USDA 1988). What can be done to improve economic conditions?

The above statistics would seem to indicate that in an industrialized and relatively affluent country such as the United States migration of people and resources out of rural areas has not significantly improved rural income levels. If conditions can't be improved in an industrialized country, what hope is there for improving incomes within developing countries? We conclude that the primary policy options available to alleviate income problems in rural areas and developing countries are to encourage further migration of resources out of the agricultural sector and enhance employment opportunities. Effective policies in these areas will require additional actions with respect to monetary and trade policy, agricultural and resource policy, and educational policy.

Improvement in rural incomes will clearly depend on continued conversion of people and land out of farming. Data on farm population change in the United States suggest that migration policy is already in place, or at least that no effort has been made to stem the transitions underway. Other policy actions must be consistent with continued out-migration. Farm population decreased 7.5 percent in the United States between 1969 to 1983, but land in farms only decreased 3.8 percent (USDA 1984). While policy has been effective in reallocating people from the agricultural sector to other sectors of the economy, it has been less effective in the reallocation of the primary physical resource (land). Given that farm size and production per acre are increasing, it is not surprising that U.S. agricultural policy has focused on supply management problems.

Farm policy has been adopted to improve incomes through acreage reduction, land set-aside, price support and loan programs for selected commodities. Because commodity price support and loan levels are above world market prices, these policies have directly contributed to the oversupply problem and caused more land to remain in production than is necessary to supply world food needs.

Solutions to U.S. rural income problems through resource and agriculture policy may not be applicable in other industrialized and developing countries. It seems obvious in developing countries that population, health, trade, education and resource policies will need to be more closely coordinated. Quotas and tariffs often limit import goods from reaching markets in developing countries. This can have a direct impact on incomes and standards of living. Population and health policy in developing countries could dramatically improve income levels if the size of families could be reduced and life expectancy increased. Education policies that expand skills and training improve the possibility of enhanced job opportunities and mobility. Resource policies that promote pricing of farm production inputs closer to world price levels would alter input factor substitutability, which in turn would affect production levels. There are numerous solutions to income problems but politically those decisions are difficult to make.

There are two possible ways that countries could enact some of the resource, agricultural, and trade policies needed to improve income standards. One alternative would be to let the market allocate use. While this alternative might be attractive to some, it could have catastrophic impacts in rural areas and countries with resource based economies. The necessary adjustments would create further hardships in terms of unemployment and poverty for those individuals least able to withstand those hardships. Pragmatically, complete elimination of existing policies is unlikely. The second alternative would result in a number of government actions to phase out existing policies and move more towards the market as a means of allocating resources. Current GATT (General Agreement on Tariffs and Trade) negotiations are structured around this concept. Quotas, tariffs, price support structures, etc. would be phased out over a set time frame, allowing for a more orderly adjustment. It is doubtful that any single policy can be effective, but a combination including market-based resource pricing, increased emphasis on long-term trade agreements, and market development programs may be more successful in accomplishing desired goals and objectives.

Increased employment opportunities for rural people can most likely be accomplished through a combination of population, health, and education policies. Educational policy may prove most promising but represents a very long-term investment. Again, consider the United States as an example. As of 1986 it is estimated that approximately 30.4 percent of the adult population in the Northeast, 25.8 percent in the Midwest, 22.6 percent in the South and 37.5 percent in the West are not high school graduates (USDA 1988). In several southern states, only 50 to 60 percent of the adult population are high school graduates (Clouser and Libby 1987). Conditions are even worse in developing countries. Only about 70 percent of the population in the Dominican Republic and El Salvador is considered literate (roughly estimated as an 8th grade education equivalent), and 47 percent of the population in Guatemala (Isaacson et al., 1985). These countries are representative of many developing countries. There can be little hope for enhanced employment opportunities with education and skill levels that are so substandard.

Education policy in developing countries cannot be separated from population and health policy. Many of these countries are in a vicious cycle where large families are required to work at subsistence farm activities to provide for the family. Health conditions are substandard and life expectancy is shortened. This in turn encourages more births. Repetto summarizes the condition in the following manner, "[W]hen half a country's deaths are those of infants and children younger than five, many closely spaced births result in high infant mortality, which in turn weakens parents' motivation to plan their families. Poverty and population growth reinforce each other," (Repetto 1985). This cycle must be broken if conditions are to improve. Programs will be required that make family planning and other health care services accessible to all people. Programs such as this have the possibility to make education services more attainable for children as well as adults. Money will also have to be targeted for educational facilities and curriculum development.

These policy actions will not guarantee improved employment opportunities but they can improve individuals' probability of better incomes. Firms are showing interest in establishing international operations, but only in stable environments that include educated workers, a secure and consistent government, availability of labor, adequate transportation systems, accessibility to markets and a variety of other factors. If these conditions do not exist, the possibility of attracting industry may decrease. In addition, these factors identify many other potential areas where policy actions may be required to provide the conditions desired by industry.

A final policy option that may improve income levels is technology transfer. Industrialized countries such as the United States are heavily dependent on mechanical equipment, fertilizers and other chemicals, and other forms of technology that augment production levels. On the other extreme, agriculture in developing countries still is dependent on human labor, limited chemicals and fertilizer use, and limited technology. A desperate need in developing countries is for additional agricultural research. While research support for improved hybrids, fertilizers, and chemicals will not necessarily improve incomes, it may influence the movement of people and resources out of the agricultural sector. Johnson notes that research has dispelled the old rumor that poor and illiterate farmers will not adopt new profitable technologies. Rather, he concludes these individuals adopt new, profitable and complicated production systems with which they have had little practice.

It is difficult to consider technology transfer without addressing the issues of sustainable or low-input agriculture. Repetto argues that if factor inputs, such as energy inputs, were priced at market levels and not subsidized, that mechanical equipment might be displaced by human labor. This shift would then eliminate some potential unemployment problems. We believe that long-term improvements in economic standards can be achicvcd only if people and resources leave agriculture. This will require adoption of new technologies and new inputs. It may require land reform policies (FAO 1981). Technology policy can encompass low-input agriculture, but should not exclude the use of new and more intensive farm production inputs.

Kuznets in his 1971 Nobel address noted that ". . . the spread of modern economic growth . . . is limited in that the economic performance in countries accounting for three-quarters of world population still falls far short of the minimum levels feasible with the potential of modern technology." His conclusion on developing countries was ". . . substantial economic advance . . . may require modifications in the available stock of material technology and probably even greater innovations in political and social structure." Technology, by itself will not be a solution to rural income problems. There is no prescription on transferability of technology policy from country to country although there may be some useful models from industrialized countries. We conclude it will be essential to improve incomes in developing countries.

Population Policy

Population size and distribution *will* be matters for policy attention as citizens consider how to avoid resource/population conflicts in the 21st century. The latter is reasonably well established on the local, state and national policy agenda. The former is more delicate. As discussed, population pressures are uneven, creating life-threatening imbalance with supply of food and materials in some parts of the world. Technology of producing food and services from land and materials mitigates meaningful scarcity, yet the sheer numbers of people overwhelm technology in Bangladesh and parts of Sahel where climate imposes additional limits. In his important critique of scarcity predictions, economist Julian Simon pointed to the human capital generated with population increase as an asset for improving worldwide well-being (1980). Educated people develop new substitutes for scarce raw materials if the relative price of those materials is a sufficient signal of need. While there is debate about the urgency of population/resource conflict (Council on Environmental Quality 1978), population policy will move more prominently to national and international policy agendas. Surprisingly little has been written on population policy— more intellectual investment is needed.

The central theme of population policy in less developed countries will be education with targeted incentives designed to encourage reduced family size. The immediate family costs of additional children need to be identified, measured, and communicated. High fertility rates increase health risks for mothers, affect family nutritional status and create other problems. Family planning assistance, including information on the full spectrum of birth control technologies from abstinence to sterilization, must be made available. These programs do make a difference— 30 percent decrease in fertility in countries employing such programs compared to 4 percent reduction in other countries (Meyer 1987). Changes in more developed countries show the value of family planning, providing models for other nations. Population policy may be seen as prerequisite to sustained economic development. Ironically, the incentives for large families are particularly evident where state of technology and education are lowest— as a source of family farm labor where labor saving technologies do not exist and as old age insurance for parents lacking such service from other sources. Mexico has undertaken a "social marketing" program to alter human values on family size and the age at which young people begin families (Meyer 1987).

Direct economic incentives such as tax credits or public bonus for smaller families and limited access to day care or other services beyond a certain family size are difficult, but worthy of attention. Unless individuals feel that their contribution to global population should be limited in their *own* interest, population policy is hopeless in a free society. Lack of methods or techniques for birth control is far less important than lack of motivation (Repetto 1985). Improved status of women in a society may exert constraining influence on population growth as women gain greater control of fertility choices as well as other aspects of rural life. Improved services for the elderly may remove an incentive for large families.

It appears that continued economic development assistance by the United States and other developed nations can help create the economic conditions favoring smaller families in developing nations. Direct United States involvement in family planning efforts has been curbed in recent years because of the sensitivity of the abortion issue and the sanctity of individual freedom. Yet the Population Reference Bureau has asserted ". . . it is almost certain that withdrawal of U.S. funds has resulted in more unwanted pregnancies and more abortions . . . in countless cities and villages around the globe" (Meyer 1987, p. 24). The Bureau calls for restored U.S. investment, including development of new contraceptive techniques.

Within the United States and other developed nations, immigration policy will be the main element of population policy in the 21st century. Rules that determine who may immigrate and conditions for staying will affect mix, distribution, and total numbers of people. The United States is destination for half of the total immigrants around the world, accounting for one-third of U.S. population growth (Holden 1988). That proportion is likely to increase. Immigrants are organizing to assure that their needs are heard — family reunification accounts for 90 percent of new immigrant admissions. Immigrants are significant components of the political economy in many parts of the country. They dominate certain business or service sectors in some cities and dramatically affect the political and social climate. Ability to speak Spanish is a distinct advantage for travelers through the Miami airport. Southeast Asian domination of the Gulf fishing industry in some ports is obvious. These and other changes are not necessarily cause for alarm, but they do shape the character of population/resource interface in the next century. Significant immigration reform began with the 1986 Simpson-Mazzoli-Rodino bill and will continue.

Future U.S. policy will likely place greater restrictions on legal immigration as a deliberate effort to affect future quality of life. A proposal by Senators Simpson and Kennedy would emphasize occupational skills rather than the traditional family unification rationale. There will be emphasis on firm ceilings rather than the porous current system that exempts family members from the ceiling. While there is little consistent scientific rationale for immigration policy, more research is needed to understand the social, economic and resource consequences of alternative immigration streams. Traditional liberal and conservative labels do not fit for immigration policy (Holden 1988). Farmers and other business owners who tend to be politically, socially and economically conservative support liberal immigration policies for their effects on labor supply. Environmentalists are generally progressive on social issues yet worry publicly about becoming over-run with uneducated "third world" masses.

Control Policy

The most compelling policy need for the 21st century bearing on the increased intensity of population/resource interaction concerns management of the residual of physical change. Included are the familiar environmental hazards of point and non-point water pollution, ozone depletion, ground water contamination, air pollution and related acid precipitation, hazardous and solid waste management and the less familiar human costs of noise and congestion in the space for living and moving. No attempt is made here to review the problems and policy experience in these diverse areas. The general roots of these issues and major policy directions are suggested, however.

Perhaps the most difficult challenge of dealing with waste management needs is the prevailing though implicit assumption of unlimited resources. Waste problems are problems of abundance, not scarcity. When quality resources do become scarce the importance of action becomes more apparent. Until there is at least the perception of impending cost from failing to act, the body politic tends to remain at rest. The facts are that the private financial gains from physical growth are substantial for a few people and groups. Population increase and mobility make some people rich. The costs of growth, on the other hand, are often ephemeral, widely distributed, and dispersed in small increments. The tragedy of the commons is apparent in waste control, where the waste processing capacity of the land, air, and water is available for the taking. The consequence of each waste-generating action is so small compared to the vastness of the resource system that individuals see little reason to change. Yet the sum of individual actions so compromises the quality of the air, water, and land as to remove them from usable supply. Some collective sense of responsibility is needed, based on projected consequence, to adjust the incentives for private action in appropriate ways. Resistance to such change can be formidable from those who gain the most from continuation of the present situation as well as from those who resist change in general.

Some local, state, and federal policy actions have been taken to manage residual wastes, but far more is needed. In some places, institutional change is far ahead of the political will to employ those rules. Florida, for example, has an impressive structure of groundwater and growth management rules, but implementation is far less impressive. The cross-jurisdictional aspect of waste problems makes them even more difficult. Cities generate most of the waste yet have no place to dispose of or process it. Surrounding counties understandably resent being the waste dump. Vast holdings of federal lands in the West become attractive and inexpensive disposal sites for hazardous and nuclear waste. Any such attempts are deeply resented. The oceans are dumping grounds for untold tons of waste— some of which floats home to roost.

We are an interdependent national and global economy, no state or county or nation can go it alone. Solutions will have to be broad enough to transcend the boundary problems. For the United States, imaginative *federal* waste control initiatives are essential to overcome the distributional character of the gains and burdens involved. Reimbursement schemes can be a part of those programs. Federal investment is also necessary to find new ways to manage waste or, more important, to use it differently.

CONCLUSIONS

Reasonable people will continue to disagree on the urgency of future natural resource problems associated with population and economic trends; yet policy analysis and innovations are essential insurance against the possibility of crisis. While per capita incomes and technological changes in production are far more important influences on future welfare than population, population policy is still an essential component of a sound future.

The most compelling message to emerge from our analysis of the consequences of global economic and population trends is the degree to which the U.S. future is tied to futures of less developed nations. We in the United States have a real stake in the welfare of people around the world. It is not altruism, though concern for others is laudable; it is enlightened self-interest, built on the realization that informed people with adequate incomes, food, and shelter must design institutions to avoid the trauma of future scarcity, poisoning of global resources, or economic collapse. The global economy binds us together. Unchecked population expansion in lesser developed countries is no less critical to worldwide security than gluttonous abuse of the natural resource endowment in the United States and other developed nations. Both phenomena can be avoided if leaders with real vision and strength will establish the setting for meaningful cooperation and institutional change.

REFERENCES

Arocha, Z. 1988. A Wave of Immigration to Match the Turn of the Century's. pp. 31-32 in The Washington Post National Weekly Edition. Washington, D.C.: The Washington Post, August 1-7, 1988.

Barnett, H. and C. Morse. 1963. Scarcity and Growth: The Economics of Natural Resource Availability. Baltimore, Maryland: Johns Hopkins Press.

Beale, C. 1976. A Further Look at Non-Metropolitan Population Growth Since 1970. pp. 953-958 in American Journal of Agricultural Economics, Volume 58, No. 5, December 1976.

Bell, D. 1987. The World and the United States in 2013. pp. 1-31 in Daedalus, Volume 116, No. 3.

Bouvier, L. 1984. Planet Earth 1984-2034: A Demographic Vision. Washington, D.C.: Population Reference Bureau, Inc. Volume 39, No. 1.

Caldwell, L. 1985. Population and Environment: Inseparable Policy Issues. Washington, D.C.: The Environmental Fund.

Clouser, Rodney L. and Lawrence Libby. 1987. Rural Development in the South: In Search of Priorities. Agriculture and Development Issues in the South. Proceedings of a Regional Workshop, May 1987. Mississippi: Mississippi State University.

Council on Environmental Quality. 1978. The Global 2000 Report to the President: Entering the 21st Century. Washington, D.C.

Crews, K. and P. Cancellier. 1988. U.S. Population: Charting the Change. Washington, D.C.: Population Reference Bureau, Inc.

Crosson, Pierre R. and Sterling Brubaker. 1982. Resource and Environmental Effects of U.S. Agriculture. Washington, D.C. Resources for the Future.

Dillman, D. 1979. Residential Preferences, Quality of Life, and the Population Turn Around. pp. 960-966 in American Journal of Agricultural Economics, Volume 61, No. 5.

Florida Agricultural Statistics Service. 1988. Citrus Summary 1986-87. Florida Agricultural Statistics.

Florida Department of Citrus. 1986. Economic Research Department. Florida Citrus Outlook 1986-87 Season. Gainesville: University of Florida. Orlando, FL.

Food and Agricultural Organization. 1981. Agriculture: Toward 2000. Rome.

Haub, C. 1988. The World Population Crisis Was Forgotten, But Not Gone. p. 23 in The Washington Post National Weekly Edition. Washington, D.C.: The Washington Post, September 5-11, 1988.

Haub, C. and M. Kent. 1988. 1988 World Population Data Sheet. Washington, D.C.: Population Reference Bureau, Inc.

Haub, C. and M. Yanagishita. 1988. The United States Population Data Sheet. Washington, D.C.: Population Reference Bureau, Inc.

Holden, C. 1988. Debate Warming Up on Legal Migration Policy. pp. 286-290 in Science, Volume 241.

International Bank for Reconstruction and Development/The World Bank. 1983. World Development Report, 1983. New York: Oxford University Press.

International Monetary Fund. 1985. World Economic Outlook, April 1985. Washington: Oxford University Press.

Isaacson, Bruce, Rodney Clouser and Gary Fairchild. 1985. Data on Selected Caribbean Basin Initiative Countries. Economic Information Report No. 217. Gainesville: Institute of Food and Agricultural Sciences.

Jacobsen, J. 1983. Population Change, Resources, and the Environment. Washington, D.C.: The Population Reference Bureau, Inc.

Johnson, D. Gale. 1975. World Food Problems and Prospects. Foreign Affairs Study 20, June 1975. Washington: American Enterprise Institute for Public Policy Research.

Kiplinger Washington Editors. 1988. "Florida's Population: A Forecast of Florida's Growth by County During the Next Ten Years." Washington, D.C.

Kuznets, Simon. 1973. "Modern Economic Growth: Findings and Reflections." 1971 Nobel Address. Reprinted in The American Economic Review. Vol. 63, No. 3.

Marston, Ed. 1988. Global Economy Turns 'Lite.' High Country News. Colorado: High Country News Foundation.

Meyer, D. 1987. A Blueprint for World Population Stabilization. Washington, D.C.: The Population Institute.

Morgenthaler, E. July 15, 1986. "Florida Grows Apace, Aided by Retiree Cash, Disney, Demographics." The Wall Street Journal, Volume 208, No. 10.

Organization for Economic Cooperation and Development. 1985. Historical Statistics 1960-1983. OECD Economic Outlook. Paris: OECD.

Organization for Economic Cooperation and Development. 1986. Historical Statistics 1960-1984. OECD Economic Outlook. Paris: OECD.

Repetto, R. 1985. Population, Resource Pressures, and Poverty. pp. 131-170 in R. Repetto, The Global Possible: Resources, Development, and the New Century. New Haven, Connecticut: Yale University Press.

Repetto, Robert. 1986. World Enough and Time. Successful Strategies for Resource Management. New Haven: Yale University Press.

Ridker, R. 1979. Resource and Environmental Consequences of Population and Economic Growth. pp. 99-123 in P. M. Houser, World Population and Development: Challenges and Prospects. Syracuse, New York: Syracuse University Press.

Rowen, H. 1988. Facing Facts. p. 5 in The Washington Post National Weekly Edition. Washington, D.C.: The Washington Post, September 19-25, 1988.

Shane, Mathew and David Stallings. 1988. Debt Crisis in Developing Countries Hurts U.S. Agriculture. Agricultural Information Bulletin No. 546. U.S.D.A. Washington: U.S. Printing Office.

Simon, J. 1980. Resources, Population, Environment: An Over Supply of False Bad News. pp. 1431-1437, in Science, Volume 208.

Smith, V. Kerry and John V. Krutilla. 1982. Explorations in Natural Resource Economics. Baltimore: Johns Hopkins University Press.

United States Department of Agriculture. 1988. 1988 Agricultural Chartbook. Agricultural Handbook No. 673. Washington: U.S. Government Printing Office.

United States Department of Agriculture. 1984. Agricultural Statistics, 1984. Washington: U.S. Government Printing Office.

United States Department of Agriculture. 1988. Economic Indicators of the Farm Sector. Production and Efficiency Statistics, 1986. Washington: U.S. Government Printing Office.

United States Department of Agriculture. 1971. 1971 Handbook of Agricultural Charts. Agricultural Handbook No. 423. Washington: U.S. Government Printing Office.

van der Tak, J. 1982. U.S. Population: Where We Are; Where We Are Going. Washington, D.C.: Population Reference Bureau, Inc. Volume 32, No. 2.

CHAPTER 2

Climate Trends and Prospects

William E. Easterling

The climate of the earth is hospitable to life. On average it is neither too hot nor too cold and the gases which compose the atmosphere rarely combine naturally in ways that are toxic to life. Yet seemingly small variations in climate, just a few degrees of temperature or a few millimeters of rainfall, can trigger massive glaciation or cause the appearance of lakes where there were once deserts. The purpose of this chapter is to discuss how climate has varied in the recent past and to speculate on what climate might look like in the 21st century. To begin, it is helpful to consider how climate can be defined.

What Is Climate?

Climate is the characteristic weather of an area. It is a composite of all states of the atmosphere including, for example, mean temperatures and precipitation and also meteorological events such as heat waves, cold waves, and severe storms (Landsberg 1984). In this sense, climate is an extension of its past performance. Implicitly, climate is determined by factors that occur with such regularity that the random states of the atmosphere have probability distributions with finite means and variances (Hare 1985).

Climate is viewed both as a natural hazard and a natural resource (Riebsame 1985). The view of climate as hazard discounts the importance of climate as a mean condition and focuses on the disruptive role of climatic extremes such as droughts, cold waves, heat waves and other climatic variations— in short, on the harmful and threatening aspects of climate.

Many natural resource economists have begun to focus on climate as a natural resource, a manageable environmental asset (d'Arge 1980). Climate here is conceived as "matter and energy organized in a certain way" (Ausubel 1980). Traditional economic concepts such as scarcity, exhaustibility, and renewability can be argued to exist in the atmosphere. As a somewhat simplified example, some municipal water systems depend on annual precipitation to replenish reservoir levels. Occasional droughts cause precipitation to diminish to levels that are insufficient to keep reservoirs adequately filled. In such events precipitation becomes a scarce resource. If, for some reason, longer-term changes in precipitation cause a shift to a new annual mean that is not enough to fill the reservoir, then the climate resource has been exhausted. However, if adequate precipitation returns or if steps are taken to adjust the reservoir to the new precipitation regime, then it can be argued that the resource has been renewed.

Climate is a common property resource. It is owned by no one and is there to be utilized by anyone. Also, when utilized by some the resource may be diminished in quantity or quality for others.

Climate serves as a factor input to many vital production processes including, for example, photosynthesis, water-intensive manufacturing, construction and transport distribution services and, on longer time scales, the formation of fossil fuels. It also enters directly into final consumption where it has utility as, say, solar energy or as simply a warm sunny day. As a common property resource, climate falls outside the realm of the market, making it difficult to value and thus difficult to manage.

Climate is dynamic. It varies rhythmically with the seasons but it also varies quite apart from natural seasonal cycles. That is, climatic conditions can depart from previous seasonal patterns. These departures may last for weeks, years, decades, centuries, and beyond. Normal seasonal cycles of climate are not particularly troublesome to most human activities. As long as climate performs reliably, it can be ignored (Hare 1985). However, failure of expected seasonal changes often leads to human hardship, a point to which I will return below.

FACTORS WHICH GOVERN CLIMATE VARIATION

What causes climate to vary? Why have vast areas of the earth at times been covered by kilometers-thick glaciers while at other times these same areas have been bathed by warm inland seas? Causes of climatic variation may be separated into two categories: 1) *external forcing factors* and 2) *internal forcing factors* (Gates and McCracken 1985).

External Forcing Factors
A number of factors operate outside of or external to the climate system to cause major swings in climate. These factors, for the most part, operate by causing sweeping long-term changes in the earth's radiation budget. The earth's radiation budget is the balance between incoming energy from the sun and outgoing earth radiation. At present, about 50 percent of the total incoming solar radiation that enters the top of the earth's atmosphere is

absorbed at the earth's surface and about 20 percent is absorbed by the atmosphere. The remainder is scattered or reflected to space by clouds, by the gases of the atmosphere and by the earth itself.

Once absorbed, solar radiation is re-radiated as long wave or infrared radiation. Radiatively active trace gases in the atmosphere such as, for example, water vapor, carbon dioxide, and ozone absorb a certain proportion of outgoing long wave radiation as it passes through the atmosphere (and on out to space). This absorption serves to warm the atmosphere. Without this absorption and heating, the earth would be too cold for life. In an equilibrium state, incoming radiation is essentially balanced by outgoing radiation. The earth's climate system is driven by this energy balance. Changes in the earth's radiation balance will result in changes in climate.

How do changes in the radiation balance occur? Long-term changes in earth-sun relationships can affect the amount and timing of incoming solar radiation. One such change involves the tilt of the earth on its axis with respect to the imaginary plane that intersects the center of the earth and the center of the sun. This is known as the "plane of the ecliptic." At present the axis of the earth is tilted 23.5Z with respect to the plane of the ecliptic. This tilt is responsible for the changing seasons as the earth revolves around the sun. Changes in the angle of tilt caused by earth axis wobbles or by axis changes can affect the timing of radiation received at the earth's surface and greatly influence the earth's seasonality.

Another set of earth-sun relationships relates to changes in the shape of the earth's orbit and to changes in the time of year at which the earth is closest to or farthest from the sun. In its present orbital configuration, the earth is closest to the sun during the Southern Hemisphere summer and farthest from the sun during Northern Hemisphere summer. A change in this configuration would affect the average amount and timing of radiation received by the earth.

The presence of aerosols suspended in the atmosphere such as those that result from certain types of volcanic eruptions may externally force climate. Such aerosols, especially if injected into the upper atmosphere, can form a shiny blanket around the earth. There they increase the albedo (reflectance) of the planet and reduce the amount of radiation received at the earth's surface. The result may be surface cooling. In the case of the eruption of Krakatoa in 1883, aerosols remained suspended in the upper atmosphere for several years after the eruption. Anomalous global cooling was observed during these years. The anomaly has been generally attributed to the higher global albedo following the Krakatoa eruption.

Yet another external forcing factor is the changing distribution of surface biomass. Changes in the surface biomass, perhaps initially brought on by climate variation, may, in turn, serve as a feedback to alter the surface albedo and evapotranspiration rates, thus changing the climate. Though not well understood, this may be a particularly important factor in some sub-tropical climates (Gates and McCracken 1985), particularly in areas undergoing rapid land transformations such as desertification.

An external forcing factor that I will have more to say about later is the role of radiatively active trace gases in the atmosphere. These gases include water vapor, carbon dioxide, methane, nitrous oxide, ozone, and others. Changes in these trace gas concentrations will alter the atmospheric absorption of long wave radiation.

Internal Forcing Factors

Climatic variations can occur in the absence of external forcing. Such climatic variations are the result of physical processes that are internal to the climate system. These processes represent the many interactions and feedbacks of the climate system. They include, for example, effects such as the horizontal advection and vertical convection transport of temperature, moisture and momentum; the interaction of clouds, radiation and temperature; and the interactions of temperature with surface snow, ice, and ground moisture (Gates and McCracken 1985). These internal forcing factors keep the atmosphere in a state of continual transition. Put another way, the atmosphere at any time seeks a particular equilibrium state, but before that state can be reached internal forcing may cause it to begin seeking a new equilibrium state. Sometimes an equilibrium state is sought which causes the occurrence of anomalous climate conditions. In practical terms, the result is the occurrence of climatic fluctuations such as drought that may persist for days, months, seasons, or even years, but eventually nondrought conditions will return.

Can we pinpoint exact causes of observed climate variations in the earth's climatic record? Not very well. There are many things that we cannot explain. For example, why were summer temperatures warmest in central North America about 6,000 years ago while the summer radiation maximum occurred some 3,000 to 6,000 years before then (COHMAP Members 1988)?

Indeed, we are only now beginning to recognize and characterize the many forms or modes of past and present climatic variation. In some cases, we can only approximate the past climate conditions for which we seek causes. How do we reconstruct past climates? What have climate reconstructions told us about the recent climatological history of the earth? I address these questions in the next section.

CHARACTERIZING HISTORICAL CLIMATES

Variations in climate can be characterized by, for example, their intensity, spatial extent, and duration. Atmospheric scientists have attempted to identify different modes of climate variation in order to sort out their causes and to characterize the effects of such variation on broad ecosystems and, more lately, on society. Hare (1985) has identified four major modes of climatic variability: noise, variability, change, and fluctuations.

Climatic noise is the result of weather events, especially extreme weather events (e.g., heat waves, droughts), on mean climate conditions within very short averaging periods. *Climatic variability* refers to internal oscillations within a given averaging period. A period of high climatic variability would be characterized by large swings in weather conditions. *Climatic change* represents a long-term shift in mean climate conditions. It is a shift to a new quasi-steady state of the atmosphere. The change should be persistent and distinct enough to be easily detected regardless of the averaging period used to portray the climate. *Climate fluctuations* mimic climatic change. They are often referred to as "mini-climate changes." They may persist for decades and may be the result of either external or internal forcing factors. They are, in essence, extended departures from longer-term mean climatic conditions.

In the following section I provide examples of these different modes of climate variation. Though I focus primarily on the contiguous United States, examples are drawn worldwide.

Historical Climates

Instrumental records of climate are only slightly over a century old. Reconstruction of climates prior to instrumentation is not easy. Such reconstruction is done with "proxy" information. Proxy information is not derived from direct measurement of the atmosphere but rather from sources that allow inferences to be drawn about what past climate was like. Examples include information about vegetation and animal life, sedimentary structure of lake beds, and air composition in glacial ice. Such information has allowed limited reconstruction of climates on geologic time scales. A great deal of progress is being made by joining proxy information with global climate circulation models (discussed below) to "backcast" climate conditions (COHMAP Members 1988). Such backcasts make it possible to establish relatively detailed circulation features such as locations of jet streams and storm tracks which, in turn, allows a much more detailed climate reconstruction than is possible with proxy methods alone.

For periods within recorded human history, it is possible to reconstruct climate on the basis of historical accounts of weather as reported in a variety of documents and books. Archives of the great trading companies, government documents, monastic and ministerial papers, and other sources contain remarkably precise descriptions of climate (Flohn and Fantechi 1984).

What do proxy techniques tell us about past climates of the earth? Frakes (1979) has compiled his interpretation of generalized surface temperatures throughout the earth's history based on a compilation of proxy data (see Figure 2.1). Schneider and Londer (1984) have pointed out that there is much uncertainty in Frakes' figure and that errors could exist on the order of /10ZC. However, the algebraic signs of the reconstruction are instructive. Throughout the long sweep of geologic time, climates have oscillated between warmth and cold. These oscillations represent periods of climate change. For example, glaciers covered vast portions of the tropics during the late Paleozoic Era (some 230 million years ago). By the Mesozoic era (230 to 65 million years ago), conditions were very nearly as they are today (Budyko 1982).

Ten thousand years ago the Pleistocene epoch ended, signaling the beginning of the current epoch. The Pleistocene was a time of widespread glaciation. At times during the Pleistocene, glaciers penetrated as far south in North America as what is now the confluence of the Ohio and Mississippi rivers. It was the last major ice age and it gave way to the current Holocene epoch. The Holocene is considered an interglacial period and has been generally warmer than the Pleistocene.

Within the last 1,100 years, the earth has experienced swings in climate that have been severe enough and that have persisted long enough to be classified as climatic changes. In the Middle Ages a warm and benevolent climate, lasting from about A.D. 900 to A.D. 1200, known as the Medieval Optimum, permitted human habitation to extend to normally harsh regions such as Greenland. During the Medieval Optimum, oats and barley were regularly grown in Iceland; Canadian forests were tens of kilometers north of their present limits and Scottish agricultural settlements flourished in the Highlands (Schneider and Londer 1984). This period is clearly seen in the temperatures shown in Figure 2.2.

The end of the Medieval Optimum in the 13th century marked the beginning of a 600-year period of pronounced cooling. As the cooling intensified this became known as the "Little Ice Age." During this period snow and ice cover were more extensive than at any time since the Pleistocene. Viking colonies which had thrived in Greenland under the Medieval Optimum gradually died out. North American boreal forests retreated southward and Dutch canals were often frozen in winter, bringing water transportation to a halt (Schneider and Londer 1984).

By the time the Little Ice Age lessened its grip on global climate (about the mid-1800's) instrumental measurements of various climatic elements were beginning to be routinely recorded. Scientists at the University of East Anglia in England, in collaboration with fellow scientists at the United States National Oceanic and Atmospheric Administration, have compiled and analyzed these measurements for as much of the globe as data were available (Jones et al. 1988). These data show that by the close of the 19th century a warming trend began to occur globally. (Figure 2.3) [1] The warming reached an initial peak in

---

[1] There is some debate in the research literature about whether this is broad secular warming or an artifact of the heating effect of cities growing up around the recording stations.

Figure 2.1.   Generalized Surface Temperature Changes over the Geological History of the Earth

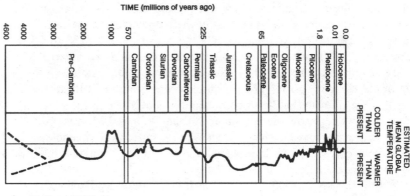

Source: Frakes 1979.

Figure 2.2.   Climate of the Last 1000 Years Estimated from Evidence Relating to East European Winters

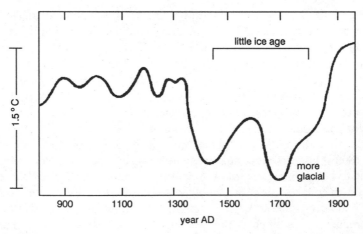

Source: After Lamb 1966.

the 1930s. In the years immediately following the 1930s maximum, global temperatures cooled slightly before resuming their more general upward trend. The record for the last two decades shows global surface air temperatures increasing above even the 1930s maximum. Indeed, Jones et al (1988) point out that 1987 is the warmest year recorded in this century. This warming trend extends to both the Southern and Northern Hemispheres, but the Southern Hemisphere, where seven of the past eight warmest years in this century have occurred in the 1980s, has been slightly warmer than the Northern Hemisphere. However, the two warmest years in the Northern Hemisphere's 20th century record were also in the 1980s (1981 and 1987). Jones et al. (1988) suggest that the record warmth in 1987 may have been partly the result of an unusually strong El Nino/Southern Oscillation (ENSO).[2]

RECENT TRENDS IN UNITED STATES CLIMATE

We can look with confidence on the climate trends compiled from instrumental data in the United States. These data are of the highest quality. Such records permit us to consider fine temporal and spatial resolution features of climate such as, for example, decadal fluctuations, the frequency of occurrence of extreme events, and changes in interannual variability.

Temperature and Precipitation

Can clear trends be identified in the 20th century temperature and precipitation data in the United States? Karl (1988) has compiled areally averaged[3] mean annual temperature (adjusted for urbanization effects) and precipitation data for the contiguous United States over the period 1895-1985. Though the average annual temperature of the contiguous United States today is not much different from what it was in 1895, there have been some pronounced trends between 1895 and the present. Temperatures rose gradually from 1895 to an initial maximum in the mid-1930s. After a brief period of cooling following the 1930s maximum, a secondary maximum was struck in the mid-1950s. Following the mid-1950s maximum, mean annual temperatures sharply fell until around 1970. Since 1970, temperatures have been generally cooler than the long-term mean (1895-1985) but there has not been any pronounced trend toward warming or further cooling.

---

[2] El Nino/Southern Oscillation (ENSO) is a term used to describe an anomalous warming of southern Pacific Ocean sea surface temperatures. ENSO has been attributed with a number of worldwide weather anomalies including generally higher temperatures, droughts in Northeast Brazil and Australia, heavier than normal rainfall in the North American west, and failure of the Indian monsoon.

[3] Areal temperature and precipitation averages were calculated for each of the 344 state climate divisions by taking the mean over a set of stations within each climate division.

Figure 2.3.   Global Mean Annual Surface Air Temperature, 1901-1987

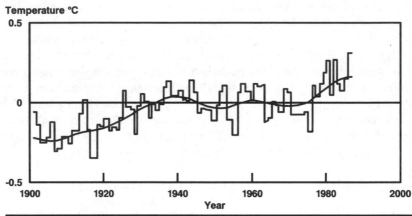

Source: Jones et al. 1988.

The disaggregation of mean annual temperatures of the United States into seasonal means reveals few interseasonal differences. Winter, spring, and fall mean temperatures over the last two decades tend to reflect the general cooling observed in the annual means. Summer temperatures, however, have exhibited a slight warming trend during this period. Thus, except for summer, mean seasonal temperatures of the United States are currently out-of-kilter with the rising global temperatures described above.

Turning to precipitation, the United States is on average about 100 mm per year wetter today than it was in 1895. This trend toward wetter conditions began in the mid-1950s. Moreover, the last half of this decade has been wetter than at any time so far in this century. Virtually all parts of the contiguous United States reflect this moistening in the annual statistics. However, not all regions in the United States show moistening in all seasons. For example, over the past two decades, the agriculturally critical summer months in the southeast, west north central, and central regions were mostly drier than the 90-year mean.

Despite the general trend toward moistening, serious episodic droughts have not disappeared, 1988 being a case in point. The occurrence of widespread droughts is even evident in the national means. Note the national drying during the extended droughts of the 1930s, 1950s and, more recently, the mid-1970s.

How severe have droughts been in recent years? The Palmer Drought

Severity Index (PDSI) is a well-known tool for monitoring the intensity of drought (Palmer 1965). As Karl and Quayle (1980) note, there has been a general trend toward less severe widespread droughts since about 1965. However, episodic extreme droughts occurring in localized pockets of the country have recurred throughout the last 25 years (e.g., Great Plains, Northeast, and Southeast). More recently, the 1988 drought in the Midwest has been, as of this writing in fall 1988, as severe as the droughts of the 1930s from a moisture deficiency standpoint.

Climate Fluctuations

Recent works by Karl and Riebsame (1985), Karl (1988), and Richman and Easterling (1988) have documented the occurrence of fluctuations in temperature and/or precipitation which may persist for relatively long periods (say, one to two decades). They occur at many spatial scales. Karl and Riebsame (1984), for example, found such fluctuations in regions as small as collections of counties and as large as the entire eastern one-third of the United States. These fluctuations are not intense enough nor do they persist long enough to qualify as climate changes. Yet, the above studies suggest that such fluctuations are common.

The causes of these decadal fluctuations are difficult to identify (Karl 1988). Practically speaking, such fluctuations may represent mini-climate changes for natural resource systems such as water (Riebsame 1988) and agriculture (Richman and Easterling 1988). Riebsame found that reservoir managers in the western United States actually altered their operating rules in response to precipitation fluctuations. Richman and Easterling identified a 15-year period of wet springs combined with dry summers in northwest Illinois. They found that this fluctuation was reflected in corn yields in the area, taking into account the positive effect of technology on yields. We are only beginning to identify and catalogue such fluctuations (Karl 1988). It is important to continue to develop our knowledge of these fluctuations since they may serve as partial analogs to future climate change.

In summary, there is evidence that the average surface air temperature of the earth is slightly warmer now than it was nearly 100 years ago. This has been the result of a gradual warming trend. The United States has become slightly cooler over this same time period, primarily because of a cooling trend that began in the 1950s. The United States has also experienced a general trend toward increased wetness in the last two decades. Droughts have persisted through this period of moistening.

However, with the exception of localized events and this past summer's drought, they have been less severe in recent years than those of the 1930s and 1950s. Climatic fluctuations, some persisting for decades, have been detected in the recent climate record of the United States and their effects on certain natural resource systems may have limited value in anticipating some of the effects of long-term climate change.

CLIMATE IN THE 21ST CENTURY

What will climate be like in the 21st century? Are there any surprises in store? It is now accepted that the climate a few decades hence may be quite different from today. In fact, it is widely believed by researchers that present climate trends may be a poor guide to depicting the climate of the 21st century (Schneider and Rosenberg 1989, in press). Climate changes greater in magnitude than any in recorded human experience could be just a few decades away. What is happening in the climate system that makes us think such changes are in store? The answer, in large part, comes down to two words: human activity.

The global economy has grown dramatically in the wake of the Industrial Revolution. A necessary component of this economic expansion has been the energy derived from the burning of fossil fuels. Among the by-products of fossil fuel burning are carbon dioxide and a host of other radiatively active trace gases (e.g., methane, oxides of sulfur and nitrogen, and others). These radiatively active trace gases (henceforth referred to collectively as "greenhouse gases") are polluting the atmosphere and may already be changing the earth's climate through the so-called "greenhouse effect." Figure 2.4 is a well-known graphic which shows the amount and rate of increase in atmospheric carbon dioxide since the mid-1950s. This increase has been taking place at least as far back as the early 19th century although its earlier rate of rise was not as rapid as it has been for the last 30 years or so.

What do increasing concentrations of greenhouse gases have to do with climate? Schneider and Rosenberg (1989, in press) argue that greenhouse gases are relatively transparent to visible sunlight (shortwave solar radiation). However, these gases are more efficient at absorbing longwave radiation emitted by the earth. The result is that the lower atmosphere, where greenhouse gases are becoming more concentrated, heats up. This process is known as the greenhouse effect and its existence and basic function are not questioned by atmospheric scientists (Schneider and Rosenberg 1989, in press).

The uncertainty lies in how the greenhouse effect will change the earth's climate. How much will climate change? How fast will changes occur? What will the regional pattern of change look like? Will there be accompanying changes in climatic variability? Is climate now responding to the greenhouse effect? What will be the impacts? Though we are beginning to be able to make some educated guesses at the answers, these are open scientific questions.

Most of our understanding of the potential climate effects of greenhouse warming comes from experiments involving large and complex global circulation models (GCMs). These models are numerical representations of the

Figure 2.4.   Concentration of Atmospheric CO$_2$ at Mauna Loa Observatory

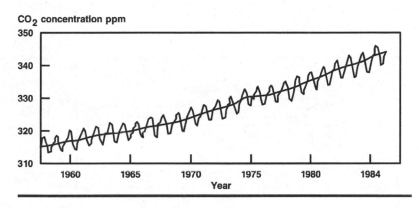

large-scale motions of the atmosphere. They are based on Newtonian equations of motion and laws of conservation of thermal energy. GCMs attempt to simulate climate by simulating day-to-day weather (Dickinson 1986). At present, GCMs do not fully represent all of the determinants of climate and they are computationally demanding. However, their development and refinement is the key to increasing our understanding of the greenhouse effect.

How Much Might Climate Change?
If we arbitrarily choose a reference mark to gauge climate change, we can ask how much climate might change. The "equivalent doubling"[4] of atmospheric carbon dioxide over preindustrial levels is often used as such a reference mark. Bolin et al. (1986) examined results from the main GCMs and concluded that equivalent doubling of carbon dioxide is likely to raise mean global surface temperatures by between 1.5Z-5.5ZC. This temperature increase would be approximately of the same magnitude as the change in global temperature from the last glacial period to the present. It is useful to point out that the low end of the range of projected temperature changes (+1.5ZC) is two and a half times greater than the observed amount of global warming experienced in this century (Figure 2.3). The time of doubling of atmospheric carbon dioxide only is conservatively projected to occur some time around

[4] "Equivalent doubling" is a term used to describe the level of atmospheric concentration of all greenhouse gases (including carbon dioxide) necessary to equal the radiative effect of a doubling of only atmospheric carbon dioxide over preindustrial levels.

Figure 2.5. Cumulative Equilibrium Surface Temperature Warming Due to Increase in CO₂ and Other Trace Gases from A.D. 1980 to 2030

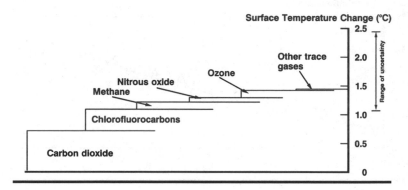

Source: Ramanathan et al. 1986.

2100 (Bolin et al. 1985); equivalent doubling can be expected before then.

What might the individual temperature contribution of each of the greenhouse gases be to the total global temperature rise? Ramanathan et al. (1986) used a simple climate model to project the range of temperature change associated with each of the major greenhouse gases, assuming that these gases increase in the atmosphere over the next 40 years as expected. Figure 2.5 shows that the combined temperature contribution of all of the greenhouse gases, exclusive of carbon dioxide, is about equal to the contribution of carbon dioxide only. Thus, greenhouse warming is not simply a problem of increasing concentrations of atmospheric carbon dioxide. The other greenhouse gases are at least as important, maybe even more so.

How Fast Might Climate Change?

The rate at which climate might change from greenhouse warming is highly dependent upon the sensitivity of climate to the greenhouse effect and the future rate of emissions of greenhouse gases. The report of the 1987 Villach and Bellagio workshops (Jager 1988) gives a range of projected decadal temperature increases based on different scenarios of climate response sensitivity and greenhouse gas emissions. The upper bound scenario, which assumes a large increase in emissions and a high sensitivity of climate response, calls for a global surface temperature increase of 0.8ZC/decade. The middle scenario, based on an assumed extension of current emissions trends, except for a small reduction in radiatively active chlorofluorocarbons (to reflect compliance with the Montreal Protocol Treaty) and a moderate climate sensitivity, calls for an increase in temperature of 0.3ZC/decade. The lower bound scenario, in which emissions are greatly reduced and climate sensitivity is low, calls for an increase of 0.06ZC/decade. Keep in mind that the global temperature decrease that ushered in the Little Ice Age was slightly more than 1.0ZC over a century. Not only might the amount of temperature change from greenhouse forcing be unprecedented in human history but the rate of warming could also be unprecedented.

What Might the Spatial Pattern of Climate Change Look Like?

There is good general agreement among the GCMs developed by different research groups as to the very broad latitudinal response of climate to the greenhouse effect. Bolin et al. (1986) conclude that there are indications that warming will be much greater at the high latitudes and much less at the low latitudes. The most extreme temperature increases are likely to occur in winter in the high latitudes of the Northern Hemisphere where changes could be as much as two and a half times greater and faster than the globally averaged values. The least amount of change is predicted to occur in the tropics.

The picture becomes less clear when we look at GCM projections of regional patterns of climate change. There is wide divergence among models concerning regional patterns of change (Rosenberg 1987). This is particularly true for projected regional precipitation patterns. However, Kellogg (1988) has synthesized the results of equilibrium runs of five different GCMs in which carbon dioxide was doubled. He found that these models generally agree that increased evaporation could lead to increased summer dryness in mid-latitude continental interiors. This consistency does not necessarily prove that summer dryness will occur, but it does suggest that such dryness in these regions, many of which are agriculturally important, is certainly plausible.

How Might Climate Variability Change?

Schneider and Rosenberg (1989, in press) argue that even more uncertain than changes in regional climatic means are expected changes in climate variability. They argue that changes in variability are likely to be marked by the altered frequency and magnitude of extreme events. On the one hand, negative events such as severe storms and heat waves could become more frequent. On the other hand, damaging frosts and cold snaps may become less frequent. From a natural resources management standpoint, these kinds of changes can be more important than changes in mean conditions. For example, the effects of late and early freezes, droughts, and heat waves on agricultural yields are usually much greater than simple changes in mean temperature.

Mearns, Katz, and Schneider (1984) considered how the probability of heat waves in three United States locations might change if only mean temperature were to change by +1.7ZC and there were no changes to the standard deviation of maximum daily temperature or the autocorrelation of daily temperature variations. The probability of July heat waves would increase by 30 percent in Washington, D.C., by 16 percent in Des Moines, and by 30 percent in Dallas.

Does the Greenhouse Effect Explain Recent Climate Variations?

The 1988 summer drought in North America has prompted speculation from some scientists and laymen on whether or not climate is now responding to the greenhouse effect. I contend that it is simply too early to tell. Karl (1988) argues that the features of the 1988 summer drought are not inconsistent with features of droughts that have occurred earlier in this century. This would seem to suggest that there was nothing new or particularly surprising about this drought from the standpoint of historical climatology. In fact, over the last decade precipitation has been noted to be above normal in the Midwest, particularly during the summer. This moistening trend is contrary to what some of the GCMs suggest for a greenhouse response in that region. I believe it is difficult to argue convincingly that the greenhouse effect was the dominant factor in that drought.

Can we attribute observed trends in global temperature to the greenhouse effect? Most of the global warming depicted in Figure 2.3 is accounted for by the Southern Hemisphere (Jones et al. 1986). Climate data in the Southern Hemisphere, especially from the earlier part of this century, are sparse and generally less reliable than those in the Northern Hemisphere. Because of the large percentage of oceans in the Southern Hemisphere, much of the data are from shipboard measurements. Such are less reliable than land-based observations. In short, the Southern Hemisphere warming needs to be viewed with some skepticism. Northern Hemisphere temperature trends are not as consistent with the global temperature warming trend. For example, I have already discussed the recent cooling in the United States; Great Britain as well shows cooling in recent years (Kenneth Bergman, personal communication).

I do not mean to imply that the greenhouse effect is not affecting climate today in some way. In fact, as our understanding of greenhouse warming increases we may look back on many of the recent global climate anomalies and find that the greenhouse effect was indeed a major protagonist. But for now we should be cautious in announcing the connection of observed climate anomalies with greenhouse warming. The detection of the so-called carbon dioxide "fingerprint," the unique response of climate to the greenhouse effect, is a facet of climate research that has only just begun in earnest and results are still sketchy (*Science* 1988).

Impacts of Climatic Change

The impacts of climate change could be far reaching. The direct effect of climate change could be felt in several natural resource sectors including, for example, agriculture, forestry, and water resources. If climate change causes sea level to rise, then surely a variety of wetlands and other low-lying ecosystems will be affected. Indirectly, climate change may affect a variety of related resource sectors such as agribusiness, transportation, recreation and so on. At present, we can only speculate on how future climate change might impact these resources. As a case in point I focus on agriculture and the plight of the midwestern United States farmer in particular.[5]

How might the midwestern United States farmer be affected by climate change? To answer this question we must first attempt to understand what agriculture will be like 50 to 75 years hence. By then, the signal of climate change will have become apparent. Three types of change are relevant to this question: a) the growth of world agricultural demand; b) the growth of world agricultural capacity; and c) changes in regional comparative advantage.

Consider the situation if there is no future climate change. Over the long term, population and income growth are the two major determinants of the growth in demand for food and fiber. World population is expected to rise from its present level of 5 billion to about 8 billion by the middle of the 21st century (World Bank 1984). Most of this growth is expected to occur in the Third World. In this scenario world per capita income rises 2 percent annually (Crosson 1986). The combination of population and per capita income growth results in a 1.0 to 1.4 percent annual increase in world demand for food over the next 50 to 75 years (Easterling, Parry, and Crosson 1989, in press).

Since 1950, world output of food and fiber increased about 2.5 percent annually and prices fell, indicating that the expansion of capacity outpaced the growth in demand. Climate change apart, this trend seems likely to continue. The projected growth in world demand will be less than it was in the past 35 years. The potential for continued advances in agricultural technology and management is high and should continue to raise crop productivity. In the without-climate-change scenario, therefore, future economic costs of production decline. Environmental costs associated with production may increase, but not enough to offset the decline in economic costs.

World agricultural trade has been increasing and will continue to increase in the years ahead. However, production will be more diffused geographically, reflecting shifts in regional comparative advantages. No country will have as

---

[5] Portions of this section were taken from Easterling, Parry, and Crosson (1989, in press).

large a share of world trade as the United States does today (Crosson, forthcoming).

Climate change is not likely to affect growth in world income or population in the coming 50 years or so (Schelling 1983). Thus, the effect of climate change on world food demand is likely to be negligible. Nor is climate change likely to limit the expansion of world food and fiber capacity in step with world demand. Even if yield reductions due to climate change are on the high end of current estimates, the projected yield increases from technology advances alone should offset these yield reductions and still accommodate increased world demand. Moreover, given that climate changes in some regions may favorably impact agriculture and that farmers are likely to make short-term adjustments within existing technological and managerial regimes and to adapt in the long-term with new technologies, there is even more room for optimism. I share Crosson's (1989, forthcoming) conclusion that even with climate change, the increasing productivity of world agriculture together with slowing growth in world agricultural demand will result in falling prices for crops.

This scenario does not mean that climate change will not create problems in some regions. What about the midwestern United States? How will the midwestern farmer fare with climate change and falling prices? The answer depends on how climate in the Midwest changes, how unpriced environmental costs of production are handled on the farm, and how quickly farmers can adjust and adapt to climate and associated environmental changes.

Assuming that climate in the Midwest changes for the worse, meaning warmer and drier, what is likely to be the effect on crop productivity? Research on this question is sketchy and is based on today's agriculture, not the future. But its results are instructive. Waggoner (1983) assumed a 1ZC increase in temperature and, with the use of a simple statistical crop-climate model, found yield decreases of 2 to 12 percent in all major grain and oilseed crops in the Midwest (Table 2.1). But these yield responses fail to take account of the direct influence of increasing atmospheric carbon dioxide on plant photosynthesis and water use efficiency (see Rosenberg 1987 or Kimball 1983 on plant response to atmospheric carbon dioxide). Decker and Achutuni (1988) have done a first approximation analysis of the combined effect of doubled carbon dioxide direct effects and climate change effects on Missouri corn production. Based on a review of the literature, they assumed that a doubling of atmospheric carbon dioxide, all else equal, would increase corn yields by 29 percent. They found that with lesser amounts of climate change (+1.0ZC and a 10 percent decrease in annual precipitation) and doubled carbon dioxide, yields would increase by 15 percent over the yields achieved with present climate and carbon dioxide levels. However, with greater amounts of climate change (+2ZC and a 10 percent decrease in annual precipitation) and doubled carbon dioxide, yield would decrease by 1 percent under present yields. These findings suggest that for some crops a negative

Table 2.1. Effect of Climate Change on Crop Yields in the Midwest

Crop	Region/ State	Estimated Change in Yield (qu/ha)	Percentage Change in Yield from 1978-1980 Avg.
Spring wheat	Red River Valley	-1.32	- 7%
Spring wheat	North Dakota	-1.77	-12%
Spring wheat	South Dakota	-1.36	-11%
Winter wheat	Nebraska	-1.04	- 5%
Winter wheat	Kansas	-1.04	- 5%
Winter wheat	Oklahoma	-0.37	- 2%
Corn	Iowa	-2.36	- 3%
Corn	Illinois	-1.72	- 3%
Corn	Indiana	-2.80	- 4%
Soybeans	Iowa	-1.55	- 7%
Soybeans	Illinois	-0.82	- 4%
Soybeans	Indiana	-1.25	- 6%

Source: Waggoner 1983.

climate change could override the positive carbon dioxide effect on yields. Might larger amounts of climate change— say of the magnitude projected for midlatitude regions by some GCM's— decrease yield that much more? Based on simple extrapolation of the Decker and Achutuni (1988) methodology, the answer would be yes.

The above results need to be viewed with some caution. They fail to take account of the adjustments and adaptations that farmers are almost certain to make in attempts to lessen the costs of climate change. I have argued in recent work for the U.S. Environmental Protection Agency that farmers may be able to make some adjustments within the existing technological and managerial regime in order to partly offset the impacts of the climate change (Easterling 1989, in press). Examples include altering the choice of crop varieties, planting dates, and fertilization and tillage practices. Indeed, a negative climate change without adjustments by farmers could be made into a positive growth situation if farmers do make such adjustments.

It is reasonable to expect the development of new technologies through research for dealing with climate warming. Although I cannot predict with certainty that this will happen, neither can I offer a compelling argument that research will not develop new technologies, maybe at a rate that keeps pace with the climate changes. Historical performance of agriculture in this connection is revealing. Rosenberg (1982) found that the area of the Great Plains planted in hard red winter wheat expanded across steep spatial climatic gradients between 1920 and 1980 (Figure 2.6). These spatial climatic gradients far exceed the expected climate changes from greenhouse warming. A follow-on study at Resources for the Future suggests that the expansion continues today

Figure 2.6. Hard Red Winter Wheat Zone in 1920 and 1980

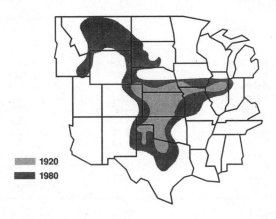

1920
1980

Source: Rosenberg 1982.

into southern Canada. What allowed this expansion to occur? It was mostly attributable to the development of cold hardy varieties and the adoption of soil and moisture conserving practices such as stubble mulching and fallowing. There is no reason to believe that if faced with a future climate challenge, agricultural research will not respond as it has in the past.

This brings us to the issue of unpriced environmental costs associated with farm operations. There is little question that a large share of the gains in U.S. agricultural productivity over the past few decades was won at the expense of environmental damage such as decreasing water quality and loss of wildlife habitat. The costs of this damage have, until now, remained unpriced and have not been charged to farmers (Crosson, forthcoming). Climate change, if it causes increased pressure to irrigate crops, will almost certainly cause these environmental costs to rise faster than if climate were not to change. How these environmental costs will affect midwestern farmers as a group will depend largely on how such costs will be handled in the future. If environmental costs remain unpriced and farmers are not held accountable for them in some way, then their impacts on costs of production on any given farm will be minimal, with or without climate change. If pressures from beyond the farm gate (e.g. conservation and environmental protection policies) succeed in forcing farmers to value and incorporate some of these environmental damages into their real costs of production, and I think they will, then surely costs of production will rise. And if farmers are not given some assistance in meeting these costs, such as the provision of less environmentally destructive technologies, then some loss in comparative advantage is certain.

Given the above, how might a farmer in the Midwest be affected by

Figure 2.7. Geographic Shift of the Corn Belt Estimated for a 3ZC Temperature Increase and a Slight Decrease in Summer Precipitation

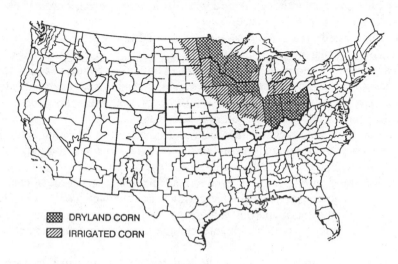

DRYLAND CORN
IRRIGATED CORN

Source: Blasing and Solomon 1982.

climate change? If crop prices fall, if the midwestern climate changes for the worse as far as crop productivity is concerned, if adjustments and adaptations cannot keep pace with such changes and if farmers are forced to pay by themselves for the environmental costs of their operations, then there almost certainly will be a loss of comparative advantage in crops currently grown in the Midwest. I believe this to be a "worst-case scenario" which could result in the geographic shift of certain crops. As Blasing and Solomon (1982) have shown, climate change could result in a shift of several hundred kilometers of the North American Corn Belt on an axis from the Southwest to the Northeast (Figure 2.7). Other crops could behave similarly. How will this affect farm incomes and larger regional economies? We do not know. Research at Resources for the Future and other institutions is just beginning to address this question.

CONCLUSION

Climate is dynamic. It varies on time scales ranging from weeks and months to geologic eras. We are currently in an interglacial period known as the Holocene. The last 1,000 years or so in the Holocene have been punctuated by interludes of climate change (which have lasted for centuries) such as the Medieval Optimum and the Little Ice Age. More recently we have experienced a trend toward gradual global warming. This warming trend, which extends back into the latter 19th century, is largely a Southern Hemisphere phenomenon, although record warmth has been experienced lately in the Northern Hemisphere as well.

In the United States, national average annual temperatures the last few decades have been generally cooler than the 100-year mean and there has been no clear national trend in the last few years. The United States has also been getting wetter over the last few years. However, droughts, though possibly less severe from a national standpoint than those of the 1930s, have occurred frequently during this recent period of moistening.

A facet of climate variation that has received attention lately has been the high frequency of interannual fluctuations in climate which last too long to be climatic noise but too short to be considered as climatic changes. These fluctuations tend to be persistent excursions from longer-term mean climate conditions. The causes of such fluctuations are not well understood, but nonetheless they serve as partial analogs to climate change and have been useful for the study of possible climate change impacts on environment and society.

In the future, greenhouse warming is almost certain to cause climate to change more rapidly than at any time in human experience. There are not many virtual certainties in what is known about future global climate change. Much is based on educated guesses. It is virtually certain that global temperatures will rise in response to the greenhouse effect. It is less certain what the amount of surface warming will be from an equivalent doubling of atmospheric carbon dioxide over preindustrial levels but the consensus is that it will probably range from 1.5 to 5.5ZC on a global average. It is also highly probable that more warming will take place at high latitudes than at low latitudes. The probable mid-range estimate of the rate of mean global warming is about 0.3ZC/decade but with wide margins of error. The regional pattern of climate change is even less certain, though drying out of midlatitude continental interiors is a plausible outcome. It is least certain how climatic variability will change as warming occurs.

Climate change will almost certainly affect a number of natural resource systems. A case in point is midwestern United States agriculture. Whether climate changes or not, it seems likely that prices for crops will either hold steady or fall in the coming decades. If climate change results in a warmer and drier midwestern climate then crops could be stressed, even taking account of the positive influence of increasing ambient levels of carbon dioxide on yields. If farmers are unable to adjust and adapt to these climate changes and if they are forced to make restitution on the environmental costs of their operations, then losses in comparative advantage could occur. Such losses of comparative advantage could force geographic shifts in crops currently grown in the Midwest.

REFERENCES

Ausubel, J. H. 1980. "Economics in the Air," in J. H. Ausubel and A. K. Biswas, eds., Climatic Constraints and Human Activities, IIASA Proceedings Series (London, Pergamon Press), pp. 13-60.

Ayres, R. V. and A. Kneese. Unpublished. Externalities: Economics and Thermodynamics (unpublished manuscript).

Blasing, T. J. and A. M. Solomon. 1982. Response of the North American Corn Belt to Climatic Warming. Oak Ridge National Laboratory Environmental Science Division (Oak Ridge, Tenn.) Publication No. 2134, pp. 1-16.

Bolin, B., B. R. Doos, J. Jaeger, and R. A. Warrick, eds. 1986. The Greenhouse Effect, Climatic Change, and Ecosystems. SCOPE 29 (Chichester, U.K., Wiley), 541 pp.

Budyko, M. I. 1982. The Earth's Climate: Past and Future, International Geophysics Series, vol. 29 (London, Academic Press), 307 pp.

COHMAP Members. 1988. "Climatic Changes of the Last 18,000 Years: Observations and Model Simulations," Science, vol. 241, pp. 1043-1052.

Crosson, Pierre. 1986. "Agricultural Development— Looking to the Future," in W. C. Clark and R. E. Munn, eds., Sustainable Development of the Biosphere (Cambridge, Cambridge University Press).

Crosson, Pierre. Forthcoming. "Climate Change and Mid-Latitudes Agriculture: Perspectives on Consequences and Policy Responses," Climatic Change.

d'Arge, Ralph. 1980. "Climate and Economic Activity," in World Meteorological Organization Proceedings of the World Climate Conference (Geneva), pp. 652-681.

Decker, W. L. and R. Achutuni. 1988. "The Use of Statistical Climate-Crop Models for Simulating Yield to Project the Impacts of CO_2-Induced Climate Change. DOE/ER. 60444-H1 (Washington, D.C., U.S. Department of Energy, Carbon Dioxide Research Division).

Dickinson, R. E. 1986. "Impact of Human Activities on Climate— A Framework," in W. W. Clark, and R. Munn, eds., Sustainable Development of the Biosphere (Cambridge, Cambridge University Press).

Easterling, W. E. Forthcoming. Farm-Level Adjustments to Climatic Change by Illinois Corn Producers, Report to the United States Environmental Protection Agency, Office of Policy, Planning, and Evaluation.

Easterling, W. E., M. L. Parry, and P. Crosson. 1989 (in press). "Adapting Agriculture to Climate Change," in N. J. Rosenberg, W. E. Easterling, P. Crosson, and J. Darmstadter, eds., Greenhouse Warming: Abatement and Adaptation (Washington, D.C., Resources for the Future Press).

Flohn, Herman and R. Fantechi. 1984. The Climate of Europe: Past, Present and Future (Dordrecht, Reidel), 356 pp.

Frakes, L. A. 1979. Climates Throughout Geologic Time (Amsterdam, Elsevier), p. 261.

Gates, W. L. and M. C. McCracken. 1985. "The Challenge of Detecting Climate Change Induced by Increasing Carbon Dioxide" in M. McCracken and F. M. Luther, eds., Detecting the Climatic Effects of Increasing Carbon Dioxide, U.S. Department of Energy (Washington, D.C., NTIS), pp. 1-12.

Hare, F. K. 1985. "Climatic Variability and Change," in J. H. Ausubel and M. Berberian, eds., Climate Impact Assessment, SCOPE 27 (New York, Wiley), pp. 37-68.

Jager, J. 1988. Developing Policies for Responding to Climatic Change, World Meteorological Organization and United Nations Environment Programme (Geneva).

Jones, P. D., T. M. L. Wigley, C. Folland, D. Parker, J. Angell, S. Lebedeff, and J. E. Hansen. 1988. "Evidence for Global Warming in the Past Decade," Nature vol. 332, no. 28, p.790

Jones, P. D., S. C. Raper, and T. M. L. Wigley. 1986. "Southern Hemisphere Surface Air Temperature Variations: 1851-1985." **Journal of Climate and Applied Meteorology** vol. 25, no. 9, pp. 1213-30.

Karl, T. R. 1988. "Multi-Year Fluctuations of Temperature and Precipitation: The Gray Area of Climate Change." **Climatic Change** vol. 12, no. 2, pp. 179-198.

Karl, T.R. and Quayle, R.G. 1981. "The 1980 Summer Heatwave and Drought in Historical Perspective." **Monthly Weather** Review, Vol. 109, No. 10, pp. 55-73

Karl, T. R. and W. E. Riebsame. 1984. "The Identification of 10- to 20-Year Temperature and Precipitation Fluctuations in the Contiguous United States," **Journal of** Climate **and Applied Meteorology** vol. 23, no. 6, pp. 950-966.

Kellogg, W. W. and Zhao Zong-Ci. 1988. "Sensitivity of Soil Moisture to Doubling of Carbon Dioxide in Climate Model Experiments. Part I: North America," Journal of Climate vol. 1, pp. 348-366.

Kerr, R. A. 1988. "Research News: Is the Greenhouse Here?" **Science** vol. 239, pp. 559-561.

Kimball, B. A. 1983. "Carbon Dioxide and Agricultural Yield: An Assemblage and Analysis of 430 Prior Observations," **Agronomy** Journal vol. 75, pp. 779-88.

Lamb, H.H. 1966. **The Changing Climate**. London.

Landsberg, Helmut. 1984. "Global Climate Trends," in J. Simon and H. Kahn, eds., **The Resourceful Earth** (Oxford, Blackwell Publishers Ltd), pp. 272-315.

Mearns, L., R. W. Katz, and S. H. Schneider. 1984. "Changes in the Probabilities of Extreme High Temperature Events with Changes in Global Mean Temperature," **Journal of** Climate and Applied Meteorology vol. 23, pp. 1601-1613.

National Climate Data Center. 1988. **Time Series of Regional Season Averages of Maximum, Minimum, and Average Temperature, and Diurnal Temperature Range Across the United States: 1901-1984**, National Oceanic and Atmospheric Administration, NESDIS/NCDC.

Palmer, W. C. 1965. **Meteorological Drought**. Research paper No. 45, U.S. Department of Commerce, Weather Bureau, Washington, D.C., USGPO.

Parry, M. L. and T. R. Carter. 1988. "The Assessment of Effects of Climatic Variations on Agriculture," in M. L. Parry et al. (eds.), Ibid.

Parry, M. L., T. Carter, and N. Konigen, eds. 1988. Assessment of Climatic Variations on Agriculture, Vol. 1 Assessment in **Cool Temperature and Cold Regions** (The Netherlands, Reidel).

Ramanathan, V., R. J. Cicerone, H. B. Singh, and J. T. Kiehl. 1985. "Trace Gas Trends and Their Potential Role in Climate Change," **Journal of Geophysical Research** vol. 90, pp. 5547-66.

Richman, M. B. and W. E. Easterling. 1988. "Procrustes Target Analysis: A Multivariate Tool for the Identification of Climate Fluctuations," **Journal of Geophysical Research** vol. 93, no. D9, pp. 10,989-11,003.

Riebsame, W. 1985. "Research in Climate-Society Interaction," in Kates et al., Ibid, pp. 69-84.

Rosenberg, N. J. 1982. "The Increasing CO_2 Concentration in the Atmosphere and Its Implication on Agricultural Productivity. II. Effects Through CO_2-Induced Climatic Change," **Climatic** Change vol. 4, pp. 239-254.

Rosenberg, N. J. 1987. "Drought and Climate Change: For Better or Worse," pp. 317-347 in D. A. Wilhite and W. E. Easterling, eds., **Planning for Drought: Toward a Reduction of Societal** Vulnerability (Boulder, Colo., Westview Press).

Schelling, T. 1983. "Climate Change: Implications for Welfare and Policy," in National Academy of Sciences **Changing Climate: Report of the Carbon Dioxide Assessment Committee** (Washington, D.C., National Academy of Sciences).

Schneider, S. and R. Londer. 1984. The Coevolution of Climate and Life (San Francisco, Sierra Club Books), 563 pp.

Schneider, S. H. and N. J. Rosenberg. 1989 (in press). "The Greenhouse Effect: Its Causes, Possible Impacts and Associated Uncertainties," in N. J. Rosenberg, W. E. Easterling, P. Crosson, and J. Darmstadter, eds., **Greenhouse Warming: Abatement and Adaptation** (Resources for the Future Press).

Waggoner, P. E. 1983. "Agriculture and a Climate Changed by More Carbon Dioxide," in **Changing Climate: Report of the Carbon Dioxide Assessment Committee** (Washington, D.C., National Academy Press), pp. 383-418.

World Bank. 1984. **World Development Report 1984** (New York and London, Oxford University Press for the World Bank).

CHAPTER 3

Cropland and Soil Sustainability

Sandra S. Batie
Daniel B. Taylor

"Forming images of the future is one of the most important activities of the human mind. It is important because human behavior . . . is guided constantly by the making of decisions, and a decision always involves a choice among images of the future that we believe at the time are realistic" (Boulding 1984).

The forming of images is the purpose of this book— and image-formation is important to our future decisions about natural resource use. Thus, determination of the status and trends with respect to agricultural land quantity and quality is important because it is only by examining our past that we are able to form alternative images of tomorrow with which we guide today's decision making. Furthermore, if we understand the forces that produced the trends, we have guidance on how those trends can be influenced in the future. Still, such image-formation is not the same as designing a road map of the future; it is not forecasting. Yet it is an effort to position ourselves to be prepared for the highly uncertain world of tomorrow.

There are two main components of image-formation with respect to agricultural land use. The first involves concern over the adequacy of future food and fiber production; the second has to do with satisfaction or dissatisfaction over the current agricultural production system. These are necessarily interrelated.

Factors Influencing the Adequacy of Future Food and Fiber Production
Virtually all countries either have a farm policy or a food policy. As the General Agreement on Tariffs and Trade negotiations illustrate, these policies are not easily altered. Once policies are implemented, they create wealth for some people, who then fight to maintain the policy's original design. More fundamentally, national leaders have a commitment to feeding their people; too high a price for bread can overthrow the current country's leadership. In

addition, the Malthusian specter of a growing population's food needs swamping agricultural harvests (and distributional networks) is all too real for many nations. Even in this country, where surplus disposal has been the more frequent concern in this century, "excess" cropland and "excess" farmers are seen— at least implicitly— as good insurance options.

A latent anxiety about food supply occurs periodically throughout the United States' history. In the 1920s and 1930s, for example, studies were conducted concerning the adequacy of cropland for future food and fiber production and projections were made to the 1950s (Gray et al. 1924; Ickes et al. 1934). Because the potential of scientific agricultural practices— fertilizers, chemicals, hybrid seed, antibiotics, improved machinery — were not foreseen, there was substantial concern about the adequacy of the future supply of cropland to feed the nation:

> The . . . [estimate] emphasizes the fact that without important changes in methods of production, standards of consumption, or both, we could not provide for a population of 150,000,000 people [in 1950] . . . It is exceedingly unlikely that we shall increase the productivity of our cropland by 47 percent [from 1923 to 1950] . . . (Gray et al. 1924).

Technological and scientific advances made these concerns seem ill-placed; yields from the 1920s to the 1950s were more in the range of 98 percent (measured as crop production per acre; U.S. Department of Agriculture 1978) than 47 percent. It should be noted that these projections were made by individuals who were engaged in an activity similar to what we are doing in this book. They projected the future given the information available to them; and, as we now know, the projections proved to be inaccurate.

In the 1970s, a set of factors converged that led to "fence row to fence row" food production, and concern was once again raised among scientists that the United States was facing resource limits. Numerous books and articles addressed various dimensions of the problem (Batie and Healy 1980; Crosson and Brubaker 1982; The Conservation Foundation 1982; Sampson 1981; NALS 1981; OTA 1981; Runge 1986; English et al. 1984; CAST 1988).

Of these recent studies, the non-alarmist, more objective analyses focused on factors underlying adequacy concerns. These factors encompassed both domestic and foreign conditions and trends. As Table 3.1 indicates, the factors perceived as crucial to forecasting the adequacy of agricultural resources were those affecting demand and supply of food and fiber, as well as the efficiency of the processing and transportation sectors. Lags and relative prices were incorporated into the analyses, which were then subjected to optimistic, pessimistic,

Table 3.1. Factors Influencing the Adequacy of Food and Fiber

Demand for Services of Land
    Foreign and Domestic Consumption
    Competition for Land and Agricultural Inputs
        Urbanization
        Non-agricultural uses of water
        Energy, mineral, and forestry production
        Recreation
        Speculative investment
        Grazing and cropland

Supply of the Products of the Land
    Substitution for Land
        Agricultural chemicals
        Fertilizers
        Water
        Hybrid plants
        Other technologies (e.g. biotechnology advances)
    Complements to Land (e.g. agricultural inputs)
        Relative prices of inputs (e.g. energy, fertilizer, pesticides)
    Environmental Limits
        Pollution
        Productivity constraints (e.g. fertility, salinity, erosion)
        Climate influences--seasonal and long-term trends
        Crop and animal diseases
    Infrastructure Availability, Efficiency and Price Processing
        Processing
        Storage
        Transportation

Social and Economic Factors
    Public Policies--Domestic and Foreign
        Export and import policies
        Farm and food policies
        Environmental and health policies
        Finance and credit policies
    Social Forces
        Farmer adoption behavior
        Community infrastructure viability
    Macroeconomic Forces
        Exchange rates
        Interest rates

Table 3.2. Cropland Conversion in Millions of Acres per Year

Use	1958-1967	1967-1975
Urban, Built-up, and Transportation	1.14	2.08
Waterbodies	.73	.84
Total	1.87	2.92

Source: Brewer and Boxley 1982.

or realistic projections of their actual values and interactions. These analyses are continuing today, but with less intensity as surpluses rise and with greater intensity as surpluses diminish.

Resource Use Trends

Table 3.1 provides an organization by which to consider some of the factors influencing the adequacy of food and fiber production as reflected in resource use trends. We discuss these factors not to predict the future, but to understand the current use and condition of agricultural resources in order to develop policy implications for better positioning the agricultural sector to respond to future conditions.

Demand for Services of Land

The trends in foreign and domestic consumption of the products of land are illustrated by Figure 3.1. While there have been increases and decreases in the harvested acreage of cropland from 1970 through 1987, the total harvested cropland has remained relatively constant, with 286 million acres harvested in 1970, and 284 million acres harvested in 1987. This variation in the quantity of harvested cropland, strongly influenced by exports, is expected to continue in the future. In 1970, harvested acres for export were 72 million, while in 1987, the products of 107 million acres were exported.

Table 3.2 presents information on cropland conversion, one measure of competition for land. In the period of 1958-1967, cropland was removed from agriculture and converted into urban areas, transportation routes, other built-up

Figure 3.1. Harvested Cropland: Exported vs. Domestic Use

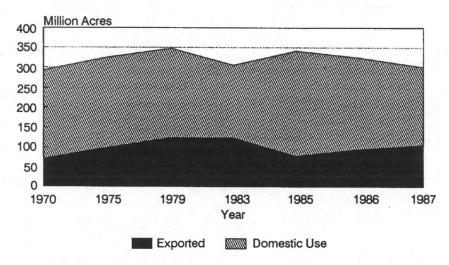

Source: USDA 1988.

areas, and water bodies at a rate of 1.87 million acres per year. In the period 1967 to 1975, this rate increased to 2.92 million acres per year. While land continues to be converted to essentially permanent non-agricultural use, both transportation construction and water body development have slowed since the 1970s.

The major use of agricultural land has been for feed and food grain production (Figure 3.2). In 1945, 215 million acres of feed and food grains were harvested— with feed grains comprising 146 million acres of this total. Total harvest acreage of feed and food grains declined over time, and by 1985 only 180 million acres were harvested. This decline in harvested acreage can be attributed to a decline in feed grain acreage, which was only 112 million acres in 1985. Food grain acreage has been relatively stable over time with 69 million acres harvested in 1945 and 68 million acres harvested in 1985.

The general downward trend in harvested grain acreage can also be observed in total planted cropland acreage (Figure 3.3). In 1945, 356 million acres of cropland were planted, while in 1985, only 324 million acres were planted. A downward trend in planted acreage is expected to continue mainly due to declines in grain acreage. As will be discussed shortly, this decline in grain acreage is largely due to the Conservation Reserve Program. Another interesting phenomenon illustrated in Figure 3.3 is the rise in planted acreage, from 303 to 356 million acres during the 1970 to 1980 period. In 1980, the planted acreage

Figure 3.2. Feed and Food Grains: Harvested Land

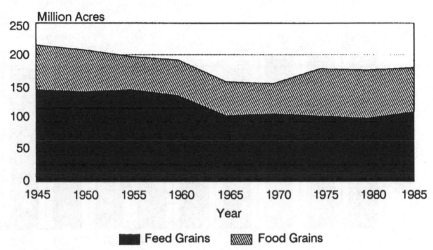

Source: USDA 1988.

equaled that of 1945. This increase in planted acreage represents the return to "fence row to fence row" production.

However, a look at the total cropland base (Figure 3.4) reveals that the nation's cropland base has remained relatively stable at around 400 million acres. As will be presented later, a large proportion of the "other" category of land in the late 1980s is comprised of CRP land.

Supply of the Products of Land

In addition to the demand for the services of land are factors that have influenced the supply of the products of land. Pesticides have acted as substitutes for land in that they have made it possible to employ less complex and therefore less "land-using" rotations. Fertilizers have been employed as substitutes for the inherent productivity of the land. The relatively low prices of pesticides and fertilizers have acted as complements to the land base— encouraging the use of these substitutes.

The dramatic rise in pesticide use is illustrated in Figure 3.5. In 1964, just under 200 million pounds of pesticides were applied to the nation's agricultural land, while by 1976 the amount of pesticides applied had grown to over 500 million pounds. This is a trend that is not likely to continue into the future, due to environmental concerns, reduction in planted cropland acreage, and im-

Figure 3.3. Cropland Acreage: Planted Acreage

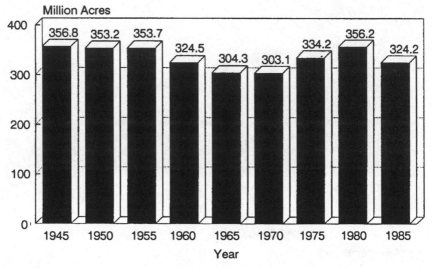

Source: USDA 1985a.

Figure 3.4. Total Cropland: Harvested vs. Other

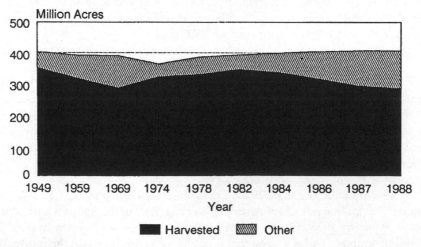

Source: USDA 1985a.

provcments in the techniques of pesticide use, such as integrated pest management. Management techniques have increased the efficacy of pesticides and made it possible to reduce both quantity applied and the frequency of application. In 1982, the influence of these factors was evident with pesticide application falling to 479 million pounds.

As suggested in the above discussion on the quantity of pesticides, the upward trend in total acreage treated (primarily influenced by herbicides) is not likely to continue (Figure 3.6). The changes in acreage treated with herbicides illustrate the difficulty of predicting the future from observations of the past. In 1964, just over 80 million acres were treated with herbicides, while by 1982 over 200 million acres were treated. A naive projection into the future would be to suggest that this upward trend will continue. However, environmental concerns relating primarily to water quality, particularly drinking water, as well as concerns about pesticide residues on food, are likely to limit the use of these substitutes in the future.

The relationship of past fertilizer application to future trends is also uncertain (Figure 3.7). For example, if this book were being published in 1980, only an increasing trend in fertilizer use would have been observed with about 25 million tons being applied in 1960 to over 50 million tons being applied in 1980. By 1987, fertilizer use had declined to about 45 million tons. Land retirement, as well as improved application techniques, such as split applica-

Figure 3.5. Pesticide Use on Major Field Crops

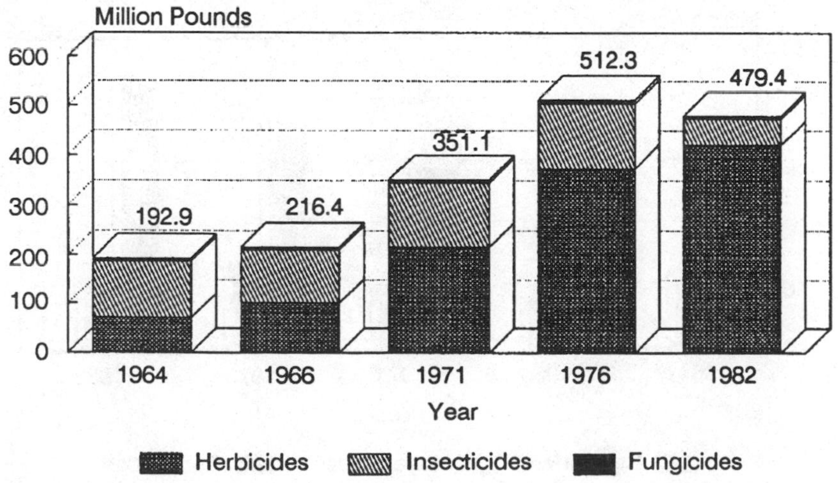

Source: USDA 1983.

tions, has reduced the amount of fertilizer employed in the United States.

Irrigation water represents another complement to land. Where available in the West, it permits crops to be grown where they could not otherwise be produced, and it removes the requirement of summer fallow. On all land, it can increase yields and reduce the yield risk faced by farmers. To an extent, irrigation can be viewed as substituting for the moisture holding capacity of the soil. Information on irrigated acreage (Figures 3.8 and 3.9) once again suggest the difficulty of trend analysis. An examination of Figure 3.8, based on irrigated acreage from 1969 through 1988, suggests that irrigated acreage has stabilized at just under 50 million acres. However, considering irrigated acreage over a longer time span, beginning in 1900 (Figure 3.9), will present a different scenario with irrigated acreage increasing from 7.7 million acres in 1900 to 47.9 million acres in 1988. The trend suggests a likely increase in irrigated acreage. Supplemental irrigation systems in the Midwest and Southeast will probably comprise most of the increase. Increases in irrigated acreage are, however, likely to be accompanied by less water use per irrigated acre. Better timing of water application has the potential to reduce the water demands of existing irrigation systems. Also, water conserving technology, such as low pressure center pivot and trickle irrigation systems, are likely to be employed in the future.

Another difficulty in prediction is that many issues that are of concern have only recently surfaced, and data have not been collected until recently, if at all.

Figure 3.6. Acres of Field Crops Treated with Pesticides

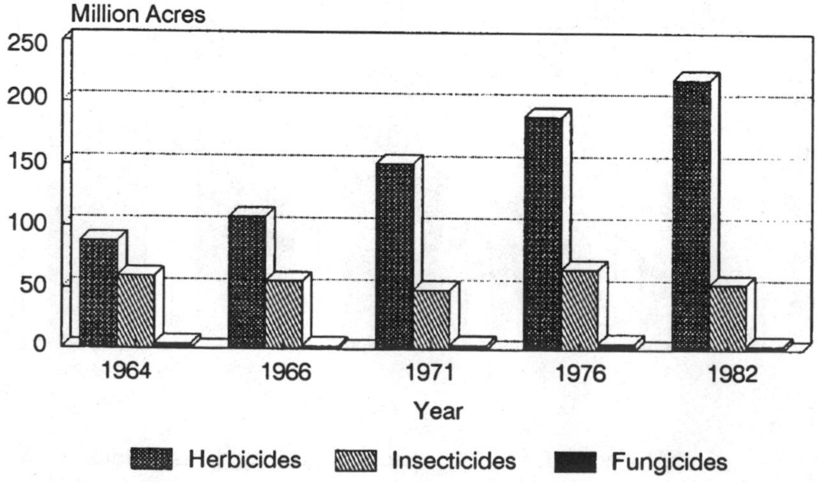

Source: USDA 1983.

Figure 3.7. Annual Fertilizer Use

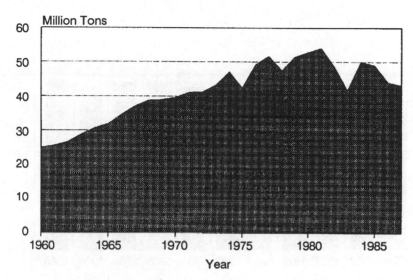

Source: National Fertilizer Development Center 1987.

A case in point is soil erosion and soil productivity, two concerns at the heart of this chapter. Reliable estimates on historical levels of soil erosion do not exist (Batie 1983). In terms of soil productivity, about the best that can be done is to employ the U.S. Department of Agriculture's crop production indices (Figure 3.10). With 1977 set as the base year, the productivity of the nation's land has increased over time. It is important to remember, however, that this increase has largely come about by substituting agrichemicals for the inherent productivity of the land. This rise in productivity in recent years must also be tempered by considering land retirement, especially CRP land, which tends to remove marginal land from production and may be biasing the crop production index upward. Even so, we feel that it is possible that this index may continue to increase over time. That increase is, however, likely to be due to the implementation of sustainable, less chemically dependent, agricultural production systems. While some individuals would make a distinction between low-input and sustainable agricultural production systems, for the purpose of this chapter, we will not make that distinction. These sustainable systems will depend more on the inherent productivity of the soil and the health (complexity) of the production environment rather than purchased chemical inputs. A major unknown in assessing the possible future path of soil productivity is biotechnology. For

Figure 3.8. Irrigated Acreage

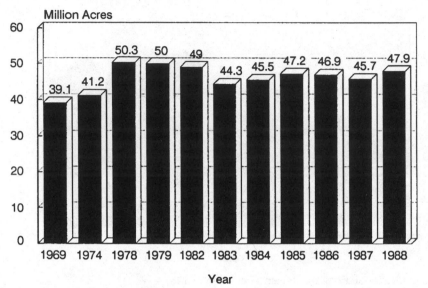

Source: National Fertilizer Development Center 1987.

Figure 3.9. Irrigation Trends

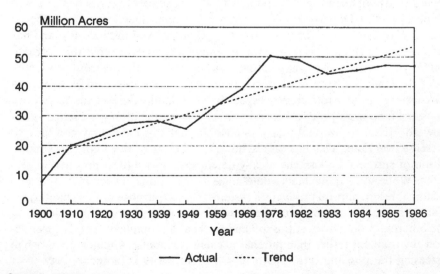

Source: USDA 1988.

cxamplc, if a nitrogen-fixing wheat or corn variety were developed, how would that influence this last projection?

Another major uncertainty influencing the entire agricultural production system relates to climatic change. Perhaps, given recent public concerns, it is most appropriate to focus on the warming effects. For example, a moderate warming could reduce the United States' grain production by two million metric tons, whereas a large warming could reduce grain production by over four times that amount.

Social and Economic Factors: Farm Program Influences

While many of the factors listed in Table 3.1 have contributed to the current structure of agriculture, it is probably true that the chief influence has been the farm programs of the last half century. The farm programs' influence on the agricultural sector has been so pervasive that it is difficult to imagine what agriculture would be comprised of, where it would be located, which inputs it would use in what quantity, what technology would be adopted, who would gain from its profits, what would be the price of its products, or how the products would be transported and distributed if there had not been any farm programs.

Still, there are some generalizations that can be made about the impact of

Figure 3.10. U.S. Crop Production Indices (1977 equals 100)

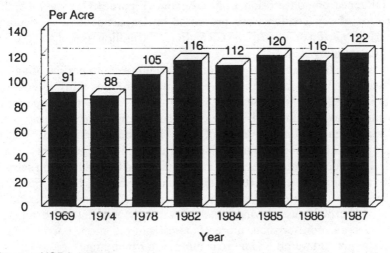

Source: USDA 1988.

agricultural policies on the current agricultural system. There are several elements of farm policy that have encouraged farmers to "monoculturally" plant more program crops, to farm cropland more intensively, and to rely more on chemicals to assure high yielding acreage. These are acreage restrictions, price support for commodity crops, and income support for farmers. (This section draws heavily from Batie 1984 and Batie 1987.)

Acreage restriction programs trace to the original farm legislation of the 1930s. With the exception of two periods of rapidly expanding production during World War II and in the mid-1970s, farmers have periodically been eligible for land retirement programs for corn, sorghum, rice, wheat feed grains, tobacco, and peanuts. Over time, variations of acreage restriction programs have been referred to as land diversions, set asides, soil banks, acreage reserves, and conservation reserves. All of the programs, with the possible recent exception of the Conservation Reserve Program (CRP) in the 1985 Farm Bill, were designed to reduce commodity surpluses; soil and water conservation goals were either secondary or used as a political expediency.

From 1969 through 1988, there has been considerable variation in the amount of cropland idled under federal programs (Figure 3.11). Beginning with 58 million acres idled in 1969, the idled acreage plummeted to 2.7 million in 1974 at the heart of the resurgence of "fence row to fence row" production. Since 1974 idled acreage has increased, until 1988, when 78.8 million acres were idled. Much of the land that has been idled in the last few years has been due to the CRP.

The CRP and U.S. Department of Agriculture programs have exerted a strong influence on soil erosion from cropland (Figure 3.12). In 1985, 164 million tons of soil erosion were prevented by Department of Agriculture efforts; it is projected that due to the CRP alone, 730 million tons of soil erosion will be prevented by 1990.

Acreage restrictions tend to encourage farmers— both participating and nonparticipating in the farm program — to use their lands more intensively. Through increased fertilizer use, increased irrigation, and increased pesticide use, farmers have dramatically increased production. For example, corn production increased from an average of three billion bushels during 1950-59 to four billion bushels during 1960-69, despite the absolute decline in corn acreage planted. The average number of acres in corn declined from 80 million acres in the 1950s to 68 million acres in the 1960s (Cochran and Ryan 1976). Fertilizer use during this same period increased by 253 percent (Duffy and Taxler 1987); pesticide and herbicide use also increased substantially. Such intensive management may mean more erosion, more chemical run-off, more percolation of chemicals to ground water, and more ground-water pumping.

It is tempting to hypothesize that increases in the intensity of the use of cropped acres would be offset by acreage retirement. While this may be true,

Figure 3.11. Cropland Idled Under Federal Programs

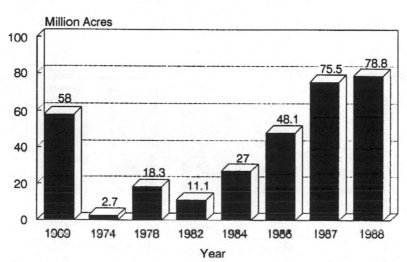

Source: USDA 1988.

there is some evidence that not all of the retired acreage would have been planted, had the program not been in effect. This phenomena is frequently referred to as "slippage." In 1973 and 1974, for example, acreage diversion requirements were first reduced and then eliminated. Commodity prices were reaching record highs, yet the amount of land returned to production did not equal the amount of land involved in prior year diversion programs. "In 1972, 230.9 million acres were planted to the seven major crops, and 61.5 million acres were listed as idled by land reserve. In 1975, no land reserve provisions were operative, yet the increase in planted acreage of the seven major crops was only 31.0 million acres" (Ericksen 1976). The implication is that approximately 30 million acres enrolled in the reserve would not have been planted even if the program had not been in effect. Thus, there was not necessarily an offsetting retirement of lands to compensate for increased intensity of use on cropped acres in response to acreage restriction programs.

Acreage restriction requirements are used in conjunction with price and income support programs. To the extent that these programs actually stabilize or increase farmer income, they also provide incentives to farm land more intensively and to specialize in program crops. The major crops historically supported by farm programs also tend to rely on chemically oriented production practices. The Department of Agriculture estimates, for example, that about 90 percent of all herbicides and insecticides are applied to only four crops: corn,

Figure 3.12. Cropland Erosion Prevented by USDA Programs

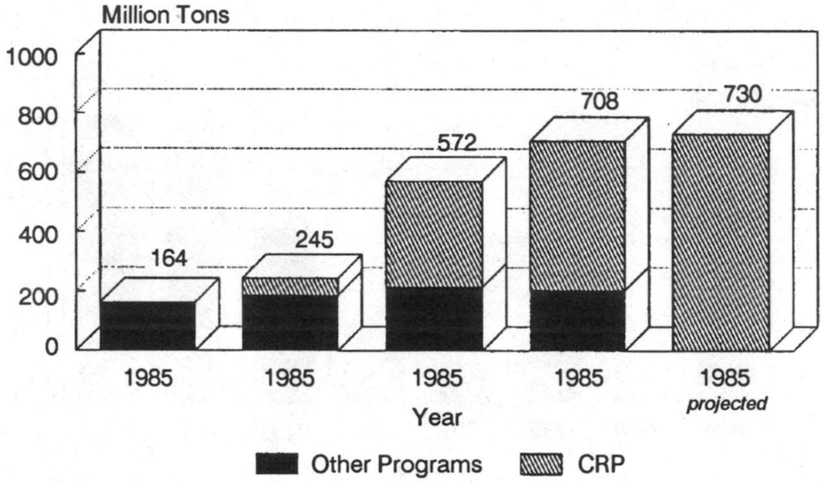

Million Tons

Source: USDA 1988.

cotton, soybeans and wheat. Corn by itself accounted for 54 percent of all herbicides and 43 percent of all insecticides (The Conservation Foundation 1986). If more program crops are planted because of the existence of price supports, it is reasonable to also conclude that more chemical use has resulted because of the farm programs.

A further consideration is that the farm programs encourage the devoting of large acreage to single crops. Thus, fertilizer-saving and pest-controlling rotations are less likely to be used. As a recent study by the American Farmland Trust noted:

> Commodity program payments made in any one year are based on yields and on the amount of land planted to program crops in previous years. Farmers usually can increase their program payments by bringing marginal land into production, then retiring the same land when government programs allow. For a variety of reasons, production control programs have created subtle incentives for farmers to abandon sod-based rotations in favor of continuous production of program crops; to plow up pasture and haylands; and to eliminate stripcropping or any other conservation system which may reduce program acreage (American Farmland Trust 1984).

Also, because most program payments are based on production, farmers have an incentive to expand operations by purchasing or renting more land. The end result is that there are far fewer and far larger farms now than a few decades earlier. The number of farms has fallen from 6.1 million in 1940 to 2.2 million today, and average size has increased from 175 acres to 441 acres per farm (U.S. Department of Agriculture 1985b). Now four percent of the nation's farms account for over half of the U.S. farm production (Reimund, Brooks and Velde 1986); and today there are only about 700,000 farms that reasonably match the description of a genuine "family farm" (Galston 1985).

The Adequacy of Future Food and Fiber Production

We have not discussed all the factors influencing future food and fiber production; to appropriately address each and their interrelationships is a book in itself. But even if we had done so we could not predict with certainty the adequacy of future food and fiber production. There is not a consensus about the probable long-run world food situation or the adequacy of the resource base; such a consensus could not be expected, given the numerous assumptions involved with any such forecasting. The assumptions concerning the demand and supply of food and fiber are open to challenge because they involve predicting the impacts on harvests of possible climatic variations, human modifications of the environment, and monocultural crop diseases. Differing opinions can result from ignorance of both biological and physical systems, as well as the social values associated with these systems. Finally, some predictions are based on an analysis of what will happen if there are no policy changes, others are based on the analysts' best guesses of probable policy and price responses to future events, and still others are worst-case scenarios (Batie, Shabman, and Kramer 1986). Thus, well-intended individuals differ concerning the validity of the assumptions and the probability of any predicted outcomes. The various analyses are best thought of not as forecasts of a knowable future, but possible alternative future scenarios— or images.

The Desirability of the Current Agricultural Production System

There is another facet to the concerns about the adequacy of future food and fiber supplies. We can look at past trends and see that today's agriculture differs greatly from that of even a few decades ago. While the number of cropland acres have been amazingly stable throughout many decades, the agriculture of today is predominantly monocultured, chemical dependent, high technology-using, and concentrated in ownership. This structure has been a concern of many for differing reasons. Some are concerned because they disapprove of concentration of ownership of the nation's land resources, or feel that such concentration has weakened rural communities and led to inappropriate numbers of farmers having to leave their chosen profession. Others are concerned because of the environmental implications of a reliance on chemicals for production. Still others are concerned because they believe that the farming practices that were encouraged directly or indirectly by the nation's farm programs have led to an agriculture that is not sustainable in the long run. Others believe that such a specialized system of production is vulnerable to sudden and unpredicted shocks such as corn blight disease or other nations' trading decisions.

New Images and New Agendas

The two components— concern over the adequacy of resources to guarantee a future food supply and concern over the current agricultural policies— have resulted in new perspectives of the current situation. These perspectives will condition new images of our future. While many perspectives remain positive, such as the virtuous family farmer exemplifying important democratic and work ethics, others are in sharp contrast: an agricultural system dominated by factory-like farms (Kohl, Shabman, and Stoevener 1987), "an international agribusiness that . . . destroys topsoil and water supplies, . . . fills the food chain with carcinogenic pesticides, herbicides, growth hormones, and antibiotics, . . . which processes the nutrients out of . . . food" (Hayden 1984). Curiously, such contrasting images can be and are held simultaneously, frequently by the same individual. We argue, however, that it is the more negative view that is gaining dominance (Batie, Shabman and Kramer 1986; Batie 1988).

Implications for Policy Design

What are the implications of the trends, conflicting perspectives, and future images for policy design? In our opinion, the answer lies not in predictions of future trends, but with adaptive planning.

Kenneth Boulding has noted, ". . . if nothing is happening, it is fairly easy to predict the future" (Boulding 1984). This is the case, for example, with many aspects of the solar system and thus we are able to predict solar eclipses with a high degree of accuracy. However, with respect to the social and complex physical systems represented by the factors detailed in Table 3.1, such precision is not only difficult, but impossible. Uncertainty is as basic to the future as it was to the past; "History is full of surprises" (Boulding 1984). Thus, while some alternative images of the future are more probable than others, accurate prediction is impossible. In this context, policy makers need to be prepared for unpleasant surprises as well as probable developments.

To ensure adequate food and fiber production, policy makers must emphasize that farmers and other members of the agricultural sector need also to be prepared. Such positioning implies an agricultural system that has flexibility (the ability to adapt goals to circumstances); robustness (the ability to absorb and adjust to surprises); and resiliency (the ability to recover from disaster) (Shabman 1988).

Critics of the current agricultural system are, we submit, basically arguing that the system is not well positioned for an uncertain future. The farm programs promote rigidity, not flexibility. The dependency on chemical agriculture, monocultures, and concentrated ownership of resources means a far less robust system than a diverse system which relies on a broader range of production techniques and has more widespread ownership and management. These same characteristics indicate the current agricultural system is far from resilient in meeting unexpected disasters such as those that might attend rapid climate changes, rapid changes in consumer demands, or diseases.

Positioning agriculture through an adaptive planning process that encompasses the need for flexibility, robustness, and resiliency requires changes from the status quo. These changes could include: 1) removal of obstacles to and provision of incentives for more sustainable agricultural production systems; 2) protection of the environment and a diverse gene pool; 3) maintenance of excess resources including "excess farmers"; and 4) a broadening of the research and policy environment to include a broad cross section of interests and clientele.

Removal of Obstacles

A "sustainable agriculture" has the potential of providing flexibility and diversity in agriculture. Not all changes to obtain a more sustainable system are necessarily desirable; however, at a minimum we argue for the removal of obstacles to and the provision of some incentives for a more sustainable agriculture. Actions could include adjustment of "base" calculations in farm programs that lock farms into historical use patterns, transition insurance for farmers experimenting with conversion to more sustainable systems, and the provision of scientific knowledge about sustainable systems.

There are many institutional barriers to adoption of more sustainable systems even where they are profitable. One is the loss of a farm's commodity base, which can be considered a valuable property right that guarantees the farmer access to farm program benefits. If switching to a more sustainable system means the loss of this base, particularly if the switch is viewed as an experiment, the costs of conversion are significantly raised. This cost may be exacerbated by the problem of transition. That is, sustainable systems are occasionally profitable, but not until three or four years after the initial conversion. If farmers do not have access to farm program benefits during this transition, they may not be able to afford the conversion.

In addition to protecting the property right to base acre calculations, policy responses could include the provision of transition insurance on yields. Such insurance could lower the risk of experimentation and transition to sustainable agriculture by protecting farmers' rights to farm program benefits during experimentation.

There are additional barriers to adoption, such as lack of knowledge about sustainable systems. While many farmers are quite knowledgeable about sustainable farming systems, they consider the available knowledge to be inadequate to undertake major changes in the way they farm. Furthermore, it is well known that farmers have varying access to the information.

Also, in order for sustainable systems to be economically viable, farmers will almost assuredly have to increase their management and time commitment. For example, scouting in an integrated pest management program will enable a farmer to reduce pesticide applications, but it does take time. It is possible that computer aided decision-making, or "expert systems," may be a partial solution to the management time dilemma which sustainable production systems may place on farmers.

There is need of improved knowledge with respect to a more diverse production system. Why is it difficult for American firms to obtain domestic oats or malting barley of sufficient quality to fulfill their needs? While some may argue that comparative advantage is the explanation, part of the answer to this question could lie with commodity programs. Specifically, oats and barley are not supported by commodity programs. Therefore, farmers have not had the incentive to grow these crops to the same extent they have corn and soybeans, nor has research been conducted on these crops in any significant amount when compared to research on crops in the commodity programs. Research and commodity program redirections appear appropriate.

Protection of the Environment and Gene Pools

A more robust system is one with diversity: environmental as well as agricultural diversity. In addition to maintaining environmental quality, actions can be taken to better protect the agricultural gene pool. Improved seed banks and the protection of endangered domestic and wild animals are possible approaches. Biotechnology that "engineers" plants and animals that require fewer chemicals, as well as broader adoption of integrated pest management, can also play important roles in developing a more robust agricultural system.

Maintenance of Excess Resources

Redundancy helps to enhance resiliency and robustness of a system. The nation, therefore, may wish to have agricultural policies that insure excess capacity: excess farmers and excess agricultural inputs in order to be able to respond to surprises. Maintenance of surplus resources suggests there will be a need for government support of farm programs; however, a restructuring is necessary to assure broad, more equitable distribution of benefits. If managed correctly, the conservation reserve program has the potential of helping to maintain excess resources. Of course, there is a balance to be struck since excess resources represent a cost. The cost is less, however, in times of surplus if the excess resources are not producing surplus commodities.

New Clientele

It is important that a broad range of interests be involved in adaptive planning. This suggests that the research and extension programs of the U.S. Department of Agriculture and land-grant institutions should embrace new clientele, such as environmentalists, international experts, and food safety advocates. We would be well advised not to constrain ourselves with rigid definitions of clientele priorities, for we know that agriculture is more than farms and that rural areas are more than agriculture (Libby 1986) and that the forces of the future will be influenced by many people outside the agricultural establishment. Changes in clientele reflect the need for changing missions. Programs need to better address the current and future effects of agricultural technology and science on the environment; farm labor wages, safety and employment; ownership patterns and property rights; food safety, quality and price; farmers' health, safety and profits; and the quality of rural life (Batie 1988).

A Final Note

As economists, we know that all things worth doing are not necessarily worth doing well. To reduce the specialization, monoculture, and chemical dependence of agriculture will be costly. The opportunity and costs of such a transition should be carefully examined, and some proposals encompassed by adaptive planning may be too expensive to implement. Our argument is not one of advocacy for any particular suggestion, but rather the importance of recognizing the process of forming images and using them to guide decisions. "While we have to be prepared to be surprised by the future, we do not have to be dumbfounded by it . . ." (Boulding 1984). By developing a robust, flexible and resilient sustainable agricultural production system the nation is more likely to be able to ensure an adequate supply of food and fiber as we move into the 21st century and beyond.

REFERENCES

American Farmland Trust. 1984. **Soil Conservation in America: What Do We Have to Lose?** Washington, D.C.: American Farmland Trust.

Batie, S. S. 1983. **Soil Erosion: Crisis in America's Croplands?** Washington, D.C.: The Conservation Foundation.

Batie, S. S. 1984. (Dec.) "Agricultural Policy and Soil Conservation: Implications for the 1985 Farm Bill." American Enterprise Institute for Public Policy Research: Occasional Paper. Washington, D.C.

Batie, S. S. 1987. "Institutions and Ground Water Quality." pp. 22-40 in Larry Canter (ed). **Proceedings of a National Symposium on Agricultural Chemicals and Ground Water Pollution Control.** Kansas City, Mo.

Batie, S. S. 1988. (July) "Agriculture as the Problem: New Agendas and New Opportunities." Southern Journal of Agricultural Economics: pp. 1-12.

Batie, S. S., and R. G. Healy, eds. 1980. **The Future of American Agriculture as a Strategic Resource.** Washington, D.C.: The Conservation Foundation.

Batie, S. S., Leonard A. Shabman, and Randall Kramer. 1986. "U.S. Agriculture and Natural Resource Policy: Past and Future." pp. 132-148 in C. Ford Runge (ed). The Future of the North American Granary: Politics, Economics, and Resources Constraints in North American Agriculture. Ames, Iowa: Iowa State University Press.

Boulding, K. 1984. "The Fallacy of Trends" National Forum 64(3): pp. 19-20.

Brewer, M. and R. Boxley. 1982. "The Potential Supply of Cropland. pp. 93-109. In P. R. Crosson (ed). The Cropland Crisis: Myth or Reality? Washington, D.C.: Resources for the Future.

Cochran, W. and M. Ryan. 1976. **American Farm Policy: 1948-73.** Minneapolis, MN: University of Minnesota Press.

The Conservation Foundation. 1982. **State of the Environment.** Washington, D.C.: The Conservation Foundation.

The Conservation Foundation. 1986. **Agriculture and the Environment in a Changing World Economy.** Washington, D.C.: The Conservation Foundation.

Council for Agricultural Science and Technology (CAST). 1988. (June). "Long-Term Viability of U.S. Agriculture." Report #114. Ames, Iowa.

Crosson, P.R., and S. Brubaker. 1982. **Environmental Effects of Trends in U.S. Agriculture.** Washington, D.C.: Resources for the Future.

Duffy, M., and G. Taxler. 1987. "Institutions and Their Effect on Agricultural Chemical Policies." Draft Manuscript. Ames, Iowa: Iowa State University.

English, B. C., J. A. Maetzold, B. R. Holding, and E. O. Heady (eds). 1984. **Future Technology and Resource Conservation.** Ames, Iowa: Iowa State Press.

Ericksen, M. H. 1976. (Sept.) "Use of Land Reserves to Control Agricultural Production." Economic Research Service ERS/USDA-635. Washington, D.C.: USDA.

Galston, W. A. 1985. **A Tough Row to Hoe: The 1985 Farm Bill and Beyond.** Roosevelt Center for American Policy Studies. New York: Hamilton Press.

Gray, L. C., O. E. Baker, F. J. Marschner, B. O. Weitz, W. R. Chapline, Ward Shepard, and Raphael Zon. 1924. "The Utilization of Our Lands for Crops, Pasture, and Forests." pp. 415-506. In Agriculture Yearbook: 1923. USDA Government Printing Office.

Hayden, F. G. 1984. A Geobased National Agricultural Policy for Rural Community Enhancement, Environmental Vitality and Income Stability. Journal of Economic Issues 18:181-221.

Ickes, H. L. et al. 1934. (Dec.) National Resources Board. Washington, D.C.: U.S. Government Printing Office.

Kohl, D. M., L. A. Shabman, and H. H. Stoevener. 1987. (July) "Extension Economists in a Changing Agricultural Economy." **Southern Journal of Agricultural Economics** 19:35-44.

Libby, L. W. 1986. "Restructuring Agricultural Economics Extension to Meet Changing Needs." **American Journal of Agricultural Economic** 68:1313-15.

Muscle Shoals, AL.Office of Technology Assessment (OTA). 1981. **Impacts of Technology on U.S. Cropland and Rangeland Productivity.** Washington, D.C.: Government Printing Office.

The National Agricultural Lands Study (NALS). 1981. Final Report, USDA and Council on Environmental Quality.

National Fertilizer Development Center for the TVA. 1987. Commercial Fertilizer, Muscle Shoals, AL.

Reimund, D., N. L. Brooks, and P. D. Velde. 1986. (May) **The Farm Sector in the Mid-1980's.** Economic Research Service, Agricultural Economics Report #548. Washington, D.C.: USDA.

Runge, C. F. 1986. **The Future of the North American Granary: Politics, Economics, and Resource Constraints in North American Agriculture.** Ames, Iowa: Iowa State University Press.

Sampson, R. N. 1981. **Farmland or Wasteland: A Time to Choose.** Emmaus, Pa.: Rodale Press.

Shabman, L. A. 1988. (July). Personal Communication, Dec. 8, 1988. (Department of Agricultural Economics, Virginia Polytechnic Institute and State University.)

Thompson, L. M. 1974. "Climate Change and World Grain Production." Prepared for the Chicago Council on Foreign Relations. Chicago, IL: Chicago Council on Foreign Relations.

United States Department of Agriculture, 1978. Department of Agricultural Economics, Statistics, and Cooperatives Service. **Changes in Farm Production and Efficiency.**

United States Department of Agriculture. 1983. Inputs Outlook and Situation. IOS-1;2.

United States Department of Agriculture. 1985a. Cropland Use and Supply Outlook and Situation Report, CUS-2.

United States Department of Agriculture. 1985b. Agricultural Statistics. 1985. Washington, D.C.: USDA.

United States Department of Agriculture. 1988. Agricultural Resources, Cropland, Water and Conservation Situation and Outlook Report AR-12. Washington, D.C.: USDA.

CHAPTER 4

Forests

Perry Hagenstein

After four centuries of settlement, forests still dominate much of our landscape. Just less than a third of the United States is forest land. In the East, the most heavily developed section of the country, the proportion is even higher, nearly 40 percent. And Canada, with a slightly greater total area than the United States, is about 44 percent forested. Its forests, east and west of the prairies, are concentrated in the southern half of the country.

The temperate and boreal forests of the United States and Canada are a major world resource. They contain much of the world's softwood timber resources outside of the Soviet Union. Hardwood forests of the United States are one of the world's major sources of temperate hardwoods for furniture and other wood products. But these forests also provide society with many other vital needs. They protect watersheds, provide habitat for wildlife and fish, are a source of people's enjoyment, affect the climate, and help maintain the productivity of our land base.

Most forest land in the United States has been affected by people in response to society's needs for resources and recreation. For example, most of the current forest land in southern New England was farmed or in pasture through much of the nineteenth century. Many of the pine stands in the South that have been logged over the past three decades grew up on abandoned cotton fields. Forest land in the eastern third of the country that has not been farmed has probably been logged, perhaps more than once. Even much of the relatively wild forest land of the West has been affected to some extent by people's activities. Changes in land use that affect forest land continue.

This chapter examines trends in forest land area and condition, timber prices, possible changes in climate, and their implications for the future. Focus is on forest lands in the United States, and to a lesser extent Canada, and their ability to supply natural resources and related uses over the coming decades. Had the examination of trends been extended to the rest of the world, the conclusions might have differed considerably.

LONG-TERM TRENDS IN FOREST AREA

Forest land is commonly defined as land that is at least 10 percent tree covered or is being regenerated to tree cover (U.S. Forest Service 1982). About 29 percent of the forest land in the United States has trees, but is not capable of growing timber at a rate (at least 20 cubic feet per acre per year) that allows it to be managed for timber production. Another five percent, mainly in parks and wilderness areas, is timberland reserved from timber harvesting. The other 66 percent, classed as "timberland," can sustain and is available for commercial harvesting (Table 4.1).

Additional land in urban areas that is partially or even largely covered by trees is not classified as forest land. Although these trees furnish a small portion of the nation's supply of timber, their contribution is not included in this analysis. Little will be said about these trees in the remainder of this paper, but they exist and can contribute to our needs in the future.

"NONCOMMERCIAL" FOREST LAND

Most of the 29 percent of the forest land that grows less than 20 cubic feet per acre per year is in the West. About half of it is in Alaska and much of the rest is on dry sites in California and the inland West. These forests are not as productive biologically as those classified as timberland. Nevertheless, they support wildlife, protect watersheds, provide forage for domestic livestock, and satisfy people's need for recreation, solitude, and dramatic landscapes. Despite slow growth rates, some of this forest land also has good timber in quantities that can be economically harvested.

The area of this "noncommercial" forest land in the 48 contiguous states has diminished by about 16 percent since 1952. Some has been converted to pasture and range for livestock, some has been cleared for urban, residential, and recreation development, and some has been cleared for reservoir sites. Some of the apparent change is probably due to changes in definitions. It seems clear, however, that there has been a downward trend in the area of this noncommercial forest land. Some of the causes of this trend, especially clearing for pasture and for reservoir sites, may have run their course.

RESERVED TIMBERLAND

The area in the contiguous states of reserved timberland—productive timberland that is in parks and other areas that have been withdrawn from timber harvesting— has tripled since 1952. The most important factor has been the designation of federal wilderness areas. An additional five million acres in southeast Alaska has also been reserved from timber harvesting. This reserved forest land, too, continues to contribute to meet needs for wildlife habitat, watershed protection, recreation, and protected natural areas. As society's needs gradually change, the trend toward the withdrawal of some forest land from timber harvesting is also likely to continue, although probably not at the same rate as during the past two decades.

TIMBERLAND

The remainder of the nation's forest land is the 483 million acres defined as timberland. This is the forest land that is suitable biologically for producing timber on a continuous basis and is presumably available for timber harvesting. It is also the forest land for which most of the information on productivity, use, and potential is available.

Had there been a pre-settlement survey of forest lands, much of our present urbanized area, especially in the East, would have been classed as timberland. Most of the farmland in the eastern third of the country and in the valleys of the Northwest would also have been classed as timberland. While there have been some surges in the timberland area, as cotton fields in the South and pastures in the North have reverted to their original forested condition, the long-term trend in timberland has been down. Since 1962, the loss of timberland has amounted to about six percent, some 32 million acres.

Table 4.1. Land Area of the United States by Class of Land and Region, 1987

(million acres)

Region	Total land	Forest Land [1]				Other land
		Total	Timber-land [2]	Reserved timber-land [3]	Other forest land [4]	
North [5]	606.7	169.8	158.3	6.8	4.8	436.9
South [6]	534.0	199.9	195.4	3.0	1.5	334.1
Rocky Mountains [7]	546.9	220.1	57.6	11.9	68.6	408.9
Pacific Coast [8]	569.7	138.1	71.8	13.3	135.1	349.6
Total	2,257.4	727.9	483.1	34.9	210.0	1,529.5

Source: USDA, 1988

DEFINITIONS OF FOREST LAND
Note: Definitions and source refer to tables 4.1 and 4.2

[1] Forest land— Land at least 10 percent stocked by forest trees of any size, including land that formerly had such tree cover and that will be naturally or artificially regenerated. Forest land includes transition zones, such as areas between heavily forested and nonforested lands that are at least 10 percent stocked with forest trees, and forest areas adjacent to urban and built-up lands. Also included are pinyon-juniper and chaparral areas in the West, and afforested areas. The minimum area for classification of forest land is 1 acre. Roadside, streamside, and shelterbelt strips of timber must have a crown width of at least 120 feet to qualify as forest land. Unimproved roads and trail, streams, and clearings in forest areas are classified as forest if less than 120 feet in width.

[2] Timberland — Forest land that is producing or is capable of producing crops of industrial wood and not withdrawn from timber utilization by statute or administrative regulation. (Note: Areas qualifying as timberland have the capability of producing in excess of 20 cubic feet per acre per year of industrial wood in natural stands. Currently inaccessible and inoperable areas are included.)

[3] Reserved timberland— Forest land that would otherwise be classified as timberland except that it is withdrawn from timber utilization by statute or administrative regulation.

[4] Other forest land —— Forest land other than timberland and reserved timberland. It includes unproductive forest land, which is incapable of producing annually 20 cubic feet per acre of industrial wood under natural conditions because of adverse site conditions such as sterile soils, dry climate, poor drainage, high elevation, steepness, or rockiness. It also includes urban forest land, which due to its location is unavailable for sustained timber harvesting.

[5] North — Includes Connecticut, Delaware, Maine, Maryland, Massachusetts, New Hampshire, New Jersey, New York, Pennsylvania, Rhode Island, Vermont, West Virginia, Illinois, Indiana, Iowa, Michigan, Minnesota, Missouri, Ohio, Wisconsin, Kansas, Nebraska, North Dakota, and South Dakota.

[6] South —— Includes Florida, Georgia, North Carolina, South Carolina, Virginia, Alabama, Arkansas, Kentucky, Louisiana, Mississippi, Oklahoma, Tennessee, and Texas.

[7] Rocky Mountain — Includes Arizona, Colorado, Idaho, Montana, Nevada, New Mexico, Utah, and Wyoming.

[8] Pacific Coast —— Includes Alaska, California, Hawaii, Oregon, and Washington.
Source: U.S. Department of Agriculture, Forest Service, 1988a. An Analysis of the Timber Situation in the United States, 1989-2040. Part I: The Current Resource Situation and Use (Draft) 530 pp.

Figures on gross changes in timberland area hide some significant information. For one thing, the shift of timberland into parks and wilderness areas has been greater than the net reduction in timberland area. There have also been some additions to the timberland category since 1952, mainly from crop and pastureland that has reverted to forest. In addition, we know that there are continuing shifts of some forest land in and out of farming.

An important factor determining the use of this land is the changing views of landowners about the appropriate use of their forest land. More than 57 percent of the timberland in the United States is privately owned by individuals, families, and businesses that have no forest products processing facilities. The bulk of these lands will continue to be forested. But the continuing expansion of our urban population outward from population centers and the growing importance of space as an amenity that people want and for which they will pay are changing the use and management of these forest lands.

The influence of an urbanized population on the forest and its uses now extends over much of the nation's timberland. While the view from an airplane may still show a primarily forest cover, the actual uses of the land are being modified by fragmentation of ownerships and changing landowner priorities. The price of timberland in much of the country now precludes buying it solely to grow timber.

CANADA'S FORESTS

Canada is an important supplier of timber products to the United States and a competitor in supplying timber products to world markets. Its softwood forests are much more extensive than those in the United States. They are, however, generally less productive because of the colder climate.

The forest land and timber situation in Canada is something of an enigma, rather like that in interior Alaska. Well-organized time-series information on the forests and timber resources are not available for much of Canada. Thus, comparisons with the United States and interpretations of the available information are hampered.

The total forest land area of Canada is nearly 50 percent greater than that of the United States. Even the apparently productive forest land area exceeds the United States timberland area by 35 percent. This gross forest area is undoubtedly decreasing somewhat as some forest land is shifted into more intensive uses. But the rate of loss of forest land to other uses and the area lost are probably not as great as those in the United States.

A significant part of Canada's timber is not economic for timber harvesting. The 653 million acres of productive forest— land that is capable of producing a merchantable stand of timber within a reasonable period— include some that are beyond the limits of current economic availability. Higher timber prices would make more of this forest land economically operable.

In contrast to the United States, most forest land in Canada is publicly owned. The highest proportions of privately owned forests are in the Maritime Provinces in eastern Canada. The proportion of public forest land, most of which is owned by the provinces, increases to the west, with about 95 percent in provincial forests in Alberta and British Columbia. The federal government owns very little forest land. No substantial effort has been mounted in Canada to change the present forest ownership pattern.

As in the United States, both commercial timberland and the remaining forest land, primarily in the North, provide resources and uses other than timber. Population presses more lightly on the land, however, than in the United States. Conflicts over the use of these forest lands seem minor compared to those below the 49th parallel, but they are growing.

LONG-TERM TRENDS IN OWNERSHIP

Ownership of forest land affects how it will be used and managed. Public owners act differently from private owners and large ownerships differ from small ownerships. Although knowing something about ownership is critical for some public and private policy decisions, our knowledge is surprisingly limited. Even information on ownership of the United States timberland base is limited.

How the United States got to its present pattern of forest land ownership helps explain the existing pattern (Table 4.2). Disposal of the public domain in the late nineteenth century established some of our basic forest land ownership that has persisted to this day. In the eastern United States west of the Appalachian Mountains, much of the public domain forest land was simply sold to private parties. Land grants to the states on entering the Union and for internal improvements also played a role. As the frontier moved west, forest land was also granted, often fraudulently, under the terms of laws intended to encourage settlement (Gates 1968). Grants to railroads and statehood grants also moved substantial areas of forest land out of federal ownership.

With the rise of the conservation movement, a substantial area of public domain forests was reserved from disposal and became the basis for our current National Forest and National Park systems. As the conservation movement prospered, the federal government acquired additional lands for both national forests and national parks. Additions to the National Forest System were greatest during the 1930s as the federal government bought worn-out farmland. This was also the time when the three Great Lake states— Michigan, Minnesota, and Wisconsin— took over large areas of tax delinquent lands that are now the basis for their extensive state and county forests.

Forest land ownership has been relatively stable since the 1940s. The federal government continues to acquire land for national forests, parks, and wildlife refuges, but the scale of acquisition is small. Its share of the nation's timberland, however, keeps falling as areas are withdrawn from possible timber

Table 4.2. Area of Timberland in the United States by Ownership and Region, 1952, 1962, 1970, 1977, and 1987

(Million acres)

Region and year	All ownerships	Public			Private		
		Total	National forest	Other	Total	Forest industry	Other
North:							
1952	158.2	31.7	10.8	20.9	126.7	13.7	112.9
1962	160.4	30.7	10.8	19.9	129.8	13.7	116.1
1970	158.1	30.8	10.9	19.9	127.4	17.2	110.1
1977	157.2	30.7	10.2	20.5	126.3	17.5	108.8
1987	158.3	32.2	10.4	21.8	126.0	16.9	109.2
South:							
1952	204.6	17.7	10.9	6.8	186.9	31.8	155.0
1962	208.7	18.0	11.2	6.8	190.7	33.6	157.0
1970	203.3	18.4	11.2	7.2	184.9	35.9	149.0
1977	198.4	18.6	11.5	7.1	179.8	36.8	142.9
1987	195.4	19.7	11.8	7.9	175.7	38.2	137.4
Rocky Mountain:							
1952	62.6	48.1	40.9	7.2	14.5	2.2	12.3
1962	63.1	48.7	41.5	7.2	14.4	2.2	12.2
1970	60.8	46.4	39.3	7.1	14.4	2.2	12.2
1977	56.5	42.1	35.5	6.6	14.4	2.1	12.3
1987	57.6	42.9	34.8	8.1	14.7	2.9	11.8

Table 4.2 continued

(Million acres)

Region and year	All ownerships	Public			Private		
		Total	National forest	Other	Total	Forest industry	Other
Pacific Coast:							
1952	83.4	55.5	32.2	23.3	27.9	11.1	16.8
1962	82.9	55.0	33.4	21.6	27.9	11.8	15.9
1970	81.8	54.6	33.2	21.4	27.2	12.3	15.0
1977	79.2	52.7	31.5	21.2	26.4	12.5	13.8
1987	71.8	41.2	28.2	13.0	30.5	12.5	18.1
United States:							
1952	508.9	152.8	94.7	58.1	356.0	59.0	297.0
1962	515.1	152.5	96.8	55.7	362.6	61.4	301.2
1970	504.1	150.2	94.6	55.6	353.8	67.6	286.3
1977	491.1	144.2	88.7	55.5	346.9	68.9	278.0
1987	483.1	136.0	85.2	50.8	347.1	70.5	276.5

Note: For definitions of timberland and regions and for source, see page 81

harvesting. The states— including some western states that have retained their original statehood grants— are neither extending considerably nor narrowing sharply their forest landholdings. The timber industry has increased its share of timberland ownership from 12 to 15 percent of the total since 1952, but the pace of its acquisitions has slowed considerably in recent years. The nonindustrial private owners' share of the total has remained nearly constant since 1952.

OWNERS' OBJECTIVES

The benefits of forest land shape ownership management decisions and they vary among the major classes of owners. We will consider three very aggregate ownership classes– firms, individuals, and society (or the public). The objectives of owners within each class vary, too, and they undoubtedly differ somewhat among regions of the country. But a simple view of their objectives probably captures the most important elements of the owners' behavior.

The objectives of firms— mainly forest products companies in the case of forest land — are perhaps the simplest. The long-run goal of the firm is to maximize profits. This usually translates into two goals for forest land. One is to provide a regular flow of income or raw materials to supply the firm's processing facilities. The other is to protect the firm's investments in processing facilities by providing, if needed, an assured raw material supply for a significant period.

Individual owners comprise the great mass of private owners who do not own processing facilities and their specific objectives vary widely. But, more and more, and especially where the forest lands are part of a holding that includes a residence, such owners appear to act to increase the value of their property. That is, they attempt to maximize the value of their assets rather than to get a steady flow of income. Decisions are typically made in terms of the whole property rather just the forest portion.

This postulated behavior of individual forest land owners accords well with the "life cycle savings theory," which argues that people accumulate wealth during their active years to provide a source of retirement income. A portion of this accumulated wealth is ultimately distributed as bequests to heirs, but most is spent during a person's life (Modigliani 1988). While many reasons for ownership are given by individual forest landowners, the life cycle savings theory is a general explanation that fits well with how they invest in, manage, and perhaps harvest their forest lands. Their management of individual forest holdings generally cannot be separated from their management of their whole property.

Public forest lands are usually managed for societal benefits. Since these are broad and changing, and since no one view dominates, conflicts arise. Where the base of public ownership is narrow, the objectives of the owners are also likely to be narrow. The result is fewer conflicts over the use and management of, say, state owned forest lands than of federally owned lands. An example is the use of Washington's forest lands to provide income for the state's trust fund for schools. While agreement with this goal is not universal among the citizens of Washington, conflicts over management are surely less than over the use of national forests.

Owners' goals have implications for the level and kind of investments in managing the land. On lands owned by forest products firms, investments in timber-growing are made to the extent that they are necessary to sustain annual flows of income or timber and to provide a back-up source of timber for their mills. In the past, pursuit of the goal of profit maximization generally encompassed all of a firm's operations. Profit maximization was a corporate goal and forest management was evaluated in terms of its place in meeting the overall corporate goal.

Emphasis in recent years on maximizing profits for profit centers within firms has changed this. The profit center approach is not inconsistent with maximizing profits for the firm as a whole, but it can lead to different allocations of investments and resources. Separating the forest and timber production profit center in a firm from the processing profit center can lead to either increased or decreased investments in forest management. The guess here is that over a period of some years it has been leading to lower levels of forest management investments. The chief investment of forest products firms in forest management has been in building average per acre timber inventories. Under financial pressures to maximize profits for the timber profit centers, the trend has been toward lowering targets for average per acre timber inventories, which is implicit in shortening timber rotations.

Individual owners are likely to invest in forest management only where this will increase the overall value of their property. Since much of the individually owned forest land is held in conjunction with some sort of residence, either permanent or seasonal, owners are likely to view their investments in the forest in relation to their potential effect on the value of the whole property, including the residence. Investments in forest management are likely only when they will add to the overall value of the property. Similarly, actions that might reduce overall property values, such as timber harvesting, are likely to be avoided even if they result in short-term gains in income.

Changes in investments in management to meet societal goals on public forest lands are apparent. The gradual reduction in national forest lands available for timber harvesting is a case in point. Another is the decreasing share of appropriations for National Forest management that are devoted to timber management. Even though the share of appropriations for recreation and wildlife has increased rather slowly over the past two decades, it *has* increased. The absolute levels of investment in most national forest resources may still be efficient. But it is clear that additional investments will be most productive if allocated to extra-market outputs of the national forests (Binkley and Hagenstein 1987).

FOREIGN OWNERSHIP

Data are scarce about a perceived increase in foreign ownership of forest land in the United States over the past decade or two. The buy-out a few years ago by Sir James Goldsmith, an English financier, of two old and large American forest products firms has been the most dramatic instance. But one or two instances such as this do not make a trend, and the picture can change quickly. Goldsmith, for example, has already sold substantial parts of his United States holdings to domestic firms.

Forest land and timber in the United States do offer foreign investors and others who have a long-term outlook an attractive place to sequester funds, however. Rates of return are not high relative to other investment opportunities, but the investments are relatively safe because of the political stability of the country and the availability of strong markets for products and forest land. Some increase in foreign investments has been noted, especially in the southeastern United States. There have also been some significant, although modest, purchases of timberland by Canadian forest products firms.

At least at current levels, foreign ownership of forest land in the United States poses no substantial problem for users or others interested in the future of these lands. There is no readily apparent difference between foreign and domestic owners in the tenure of ownership. Use of the land and investments in management appear to be consistent with those of domestic owners. Nevertheless, this is a subject on which additional information should be assembled.

TRENDS IN CONDITION OF FOREST LAND

Tracing changes in the condition of forest lands over recent years and guessing about the next few decades are based on limited information. The problem of projecting past trends into the future is compounded by the possibility that we may be at a watershed in relation to major climatic changes. The prospects of significant global warming are growing, but just how and to what extent this will affect forest conditions are still speculative.

Most of the available information on forest conditions in the United States concerns timber production on timberlands, that portion of the total forest area capable of and available for growing continuous crops of timber. Measures of overall biological productivity in relation to the land's potential and direct measures of condition in relation to uses other than timber growing are generally lacking.

Forest land conditions are affected by physical factors— precipitation, latitude, elevation, aspect. They are also affected by use— the way they have been and are being used. Perhaps the most significant factor for much of the forest land in the eastern United States has been past use for agriculture. This affects not only the current vegetative cover, but also the productivity of the land itself, at least during the first timber rotation following reversion of the land to forest.

Extended wildfire protection and insect and disease control programs during this century have led to a general improvement in growing conditions in forests. These effects are reflected in increased net annual timber growth, in increased hardwood timber inventories throughout the country, and in the increased softwood inventories everywhere but on the Pacific Coast. Only a small part of the decline in softwood inventories on the Pacific Coast, where harvest volumes still exceed growth in old-growth timber, can be attributed to losses from fire, insects, and disease.

At the same time, losses from all three causes, especially from insects and disease, continue to be high. This is a reflection in part of the age and character of the forests. But it is also a reflection of the level of effort devoted to controlling these losses. While it may not be economic to undertake more effective control measures, losses could certainly be reduced from recent levels.

Fire, insects, and disease also affect another dimension of forest productivity. To the extent that these are normal elements in the development of forests, they play a role in nutrient cycling and the development of vegetative cover. As the amount of woody material builds up under forests, the threat of serious wildfire and insect infestations also increases. Controlled use of fire can reduce fuel build-up and help in removing a potential source of insect infestations.

TRENDS IN TIMBER INVENTORIES, GROWTH, AND PRICES

Timber is one important forest output. It is an important raw material and the basis for a vital segment of the nation's economy. The Forest Service estimates that the forest industries (lumber and wood products, furniture and fixtures, paper and allied products, and gum and wood chemicals) accounted for 8.1 percent of all manufacturing employment and 7.3 percent of all value added by manufacture in 1982 (U.S. Forest Service 1988a). In many parts of the country these proportions are considerably higher.

Timber is also an integral part of the basic vegetative cover of forest lands. While timber inventory and growth statistics do not tell the whole story of the condition of the forest vegetation, they do provide a relevant picture of forest products. They also give some indication of the general health and character of the forests.

Overall timber inventories on timberland in the United States have been rising steadily since 1952. With the concurrent decline in timberland area, average per acre volumes have risen even more rapidly. In the three and a half decades from 1952 to 1987, the volume of softwood growing stock (trees larger than five inches in diameter) increased five percent. But this small total increase consisted of a 23 percent decline in the Pacific Coast region and 74, 77, and 14 percent increases in the North, South, and Rocky Mountains, respectively. The total increase in hardwood volume was 69 percent, with only small differences from one region to the next.

Interestingly, the proportion of hardwood timber in the Pacific Coast region increased from five percent in 1952 to 11 percent in 1987, suggesting that even further proportional increases are possible as the remaining old-growth inventory is depleted. This was the result of both a substantial decline in softwood volume and a 69 percent increase in hardwood volume.

Timber removals, the major component of which is commercial timber harvests, increased from 1970 to 1986 in all regions except the Rocky Mountains. The total increase was about 27 percent, which is about a 1.5 percent annual increase over that period. By 1986, the South accounted for just over half of the total removals from growing stock in the United States, up from about 45 percent 16 years earlier.

Net growth of stock timber has also increased over this period, but at about 0.8 percent, a slower rate of increase than that for removals. While net growth in all regions still exceeds removals for both hardwoods and softwoods, except for softwoods in the Pacific Coast region, the ratios are narrowing. Removals of softwoods exceed growth over large areas of the South.

One of the results of this increasing pressure on timber supplies has been higher timber prices for at least some species (Table 4.3). Timber prices (timber on the stump) were higher in 1987 in real terms (prices adjusted to eliminate the effects of general price inflation) than in 1970 for major timber species. This continues a long-term trend that goes back at least to 1920.

Softwood timber prices rose much more rapidly prior to 1960 than in recent decades, at least if the peak years for softwood prices of 1978-1981 are not considered. Annual rates of increase of 7.1 and 4.8 percent for Douglas fir and southern pine timber, respectively, from 1920 to 1960, fell to 2.3 and 0.7 percent from 1960 to 1987. And 1987 prices were considerably above those of the previous two years (Ulrich 1988). Business cycle effects are apparent in annual differences. The rapid increases in oak timber prices since 1960 (4.1 percent per year to 1987) are not typical for hardwoods generally.

Timber price statistics do not reflect all of the changes that have taken place.

Table 4.3. Average Stumpage Prices for Saw Timber Sold from the National Forests by Selected Species and Years, 1920-87

(Dollars per thousand board feet)

Year	Douglas fir [1]		Southern pine [2]		Oak, white, red, black	
	Current dollars	1967 dollars	Current dollars	1967 dollars	Current dollars	1967 dollars
1920	1.80	2.20	4.40	5.50	0	0
1925	2.10	3.90	3.20	6.00	0	0
1930	3.30	7.40	3.20	7.20	0	0
1935	1.70	4.10	4.50	10.90	0	0
1940	2.30	5.70	4.50	11.10	0	0
1945	5.00	9.20	9.30	17.00	0	0
1950	16.40	20.00	26.70	32.60	0	0
1955	28.90	32.90	32.00	36.40	0	0
1960	32.00	33.70	34.50	36.40	23.40	24.70
1965	42.60	44.10	31.70	32.80	21.30	22.00
1970	41.90	38.00	44.10	39.90	26.60	24.10
1975	169.50	96.90	57.00	32.60	29.70	17.00
1980	432.20	160.80	155.40	57.80	65.60	24.40
1985	126.20	40.90	90.70	29.40	94.50	30.60
1987	190.20	61.80	135.70	44.10	146.80	47.70

Source: USDA, Forest Service. Data for 1920-50 in An Analysis of the Timber Situation in the United States, 1952-2030. For. Res. Rep. 23, Govt. Printing Office, Washington, D.C. 499 pp. 1982. Data for 1955-86 in the U.S. Timber, Production, Trade, Consumption, and Price Statistics, 1950-86. Misc. Pub. 1460. 8lp. 1988. Data for 1987 from Forest Service records.

For one thing, the "market basket" of timber that is harvested has changed substantially since 1960 and even more markedly over a longer period. Merchantability standards are lower today than two or three decades ago. Prices paid in 1960, and even more so in 1920, bought larger and higher quality timber than in 1987. As timber supplies have become tighter, the market has responded with technological changes. Three such changes have been important.

First, the output of products per unit of timber has increased, through changes in product standards (e.g., 2 x 4s are now 1-1/2 x 3-1/2), through better processing and more effective use of logs, and through using residues from one process as inputs to another. Second, products using more readily available timber have been substituted for those using timber in short supply. Examples are woodpulp made from hardwoods instead of softwoods and waferboard made from aspen instead of plywood from Douglas fir. Finally, processing equipment, such as veneer lathes for softwood plywood that can now process very small logs, has been adapted to small timber that once was not usable.

One other factor that may affect future timber use is the growing problem of disposing of wastepaper in landfills. Wastepaper has usually made up about 20 percent of the raw material for making paper in the United States. This proportion, significantly lower than in Japan and Europe, has been determined by the relative costs of using virgin woodpulp and wastepaper.

For the largest volume categories of wastepaper, there has been little room for reducing the cost of the wastepaper to paper mills— prices are already very low. But as communities throughout the country seek alternatives to disposing waste in landfills, the prospects of subsidized recycling of wastepaper are growing. The subsidies will probably take the form of communities bearing the cost of collecting and segregating wastepaper by grades. The result will be lower costs for wastepaper as a furnish for paper production.

While these technological changes have tended to moderate timber price increases, the growing foreign markets for forest products have intensified them. The strong export market for softwood logs in the Pacific Northwest over the past 15 years as well as the restriction on exports of logs from federal lands have created a two-tier price system. Export logs and the resulting timber bring much higher prices than logs used domestically. Strong export demand has also led to higher prices for hardwood logs and lumber, mainly in the eastern states.

Export markets are likely to continue to be strong, both for western softwoods and for hardwoods. Current strong export markets for woodpulp and various paper products are also likely to continue, although they will vary more with changes in currency exchange rates. The effect of these export markets on timber prices must be weighed against the effects of domestic demand and the ability of processors to respond to raw material price increases with technological changes. Consideration must also be given to the growing ability of southern hemisphere nations to compete in world markets.

The role of softwood lumber imports from Canada has also been important in moderating timber price increases in the United States. Prior to the 1986 agreement with Canada on lumber imports, they accounted for about a third of all United States softwood lumber consumption. But even with the 15 percent Canadian excise tax on their lumber exports to the United States, which was the first step in the 1986 agreement, imports into the United States fell only slightly. This helped to slow United States timber price increases. Substantial imports of Canadian forest products are likely to continue.

Most of the recent published forecasts of future timber prices in the United States conclude that the upward trends of recent decades will continue (Binkley and Vincent 1988: U.S. Forest Service 1988c). But the persistent trend among these studies is that each succeeding report forecasts somewhat lower future prices than its predecessor. The most recent timber prices, which have remained well below 1970s levels even in a period of very high production of most forest products, suggest that even the modest upward timber price trends since 1960 are abating. As we approach the end of the nation's available original endowment of timber, we are apparently nearing a period of more stable timber prices.

Timber price increases are, of course, paid for by the consumers of forest products, both domestic and foreign. At the same time, they benefit timberland owners and encourage investments in forest management, as well as in timberland. Much of the speculative investment in timberland in recent years is based on a belief that timber prices will continue to increase. Possible future increases in timber prices would also seem to be a factor in investments by individual private forest owners, but the evidence of this is inconclusive (de Stiguer 1983).

OTHER MEASURES OF FOREST CONDITIONS

As noted, changes in timber inventories, growth, and prices indicate something about changes in forest conditions. Other broad-scale quantitative measures are lacking. Nevertheless, some indications of the direction of change are available. Most suggest a deterioration in some kinds of forest conditions.

One indication is the extent to which the public has turned to regulation of forest practices, including regulation of logging. Public regulation of forest practices is a response to a perceived deterioration in forest conditions. Several states in the North and Pacific Coast regions have adopted new or strengthened regulations since 1970 (Henly and Ellefson 1986). Most regulations are aimed at assuring regeneration of logged areas and water quality protection. In addition, federal water quality regulations affect forestry practices. These signal a national concern with at least some conditions on forest land.

Another indication is the concern over the effects of air pollution on forest health. This is recognized as a possible cause of declines in timber growth rates (U.S. Forest Service 1988b). It is also an apparent cause of mortality and other changes in forest stands throughout the Appalachians and eastern Canada. Scientists continue to worry about the possible effects of short-rotation single-species plantations on the long-term productivity of forest soils.

A third indication is the disputes over management of the national forests, especially those concerned with clear-cutting and loss of old growth timber stands. However these disputes are framed, they indicate serious concern with the condition of federal forests. National forest plans provide some sign of the extent to which forest conditions have deteriorated, or possibly will deteriorate. For example, the recent draft plan and environmental impact statement for the Gifford Pinchot National Forest in Washington project declines in populations of several indicator species (pine marten, pileated woodpeckers, and cavity excavators) for most management alternatives (U.S. Forest Service 1988c). The projected declines are directly related to habitat conditions for these species and the changes in habitat are the result of projected timber harvests. The deterioration in habitat conditions on this national forest is much the same as that reported in other national forests in that region.

These indications of a decline in forest conditions are tentative. But uncertainty with changes in forest conditions suggests the need for defining better measures of forest condition and collecting the relevant information. It is not enough to rely on interpretations and extrapolations of timber inventory and timber growth statistics.

LOSS OF FOREST LANDS

A basic change in the condition of forest land occurs when it is converted to other uses. We have relatively limited data to indicate the extent of these changes and their impacts on the availability of forests for various purposes. We have come only recently to be concerned about the loss of forest land and to take steps to limit such changes.

One such measure is zoning to maintain productive forest land. Oregon is in the forefront of other states in zoning, although the effectiveness of its approach has not yet been established. The goal of the Oregon approach is to limit development and changes in use that would disrupt use of forest land for timber production in designated zones.

The threat of disruptive development in forest areas hits hardest in regions with attractive forests and heavy tourism. Northern New England is a case in point. The recent sale of 89,000 acres of former timber industry lands in northern New Hampshire and Vermont to a developer has led to an innovative approach to assure that at least a portion of these lands will continue to be available for timber production and dispersed recreation. This approach involves joint purchase of 45,000 acres by the state of New Hampshire and the federal government. When the purchase is completed, the Forest Service will hold a conservation easement on the property, giving the public most of the advantages of a National Forest, but at a much lower cost, and control over development. This could become a model for other situations where the goal is to keep large tracts of forest land available for timber production and public recreation and to minimize the threat of major changes in use.

FORESTS AND TRENDS IN GLOBAL CLIMATE CHANGE

Studies of long-term trends in forest land area and timber inventories, growth, and prices have all been based on an implicit assumption of a climate similar to that of the historical period used as a base for the analysis. It is becoming clear that this is no longer a tenable assumption. There is a growing body of information that shows that increasing levels of carbon dioxide, chlorofluorocarbons, methane, and nitrous oxides in the atmosphere are likely to lead to long-term and important climate changes. These, and other trace gases, act much like a greenhouse by reducing the radiation of heat (infrared radiation) to space, creating the "greenhouse effect."

Carbon dioxide, the most important of the greenhouse gases, is formed by the burning of fossil fuels and the burning or decomposition of plants and trees. In response to large increases in burning fossil fuels, which began with the start of the industrial revolution around 1860, and the associated massive deforestation of many regions of the world, the concentration of carbon dioxide in the atmosphere has grown by about 25 percent. Most of this increase has taken place since 1940.

The concentration in the atmosphere of chlorofluorocarbons, synthesized chemical compounds unknown before the 1930s, has nearly doubled in the last decade. This build-up is linked to economic growth and seems likely to continue as the world gross product rises. The concentration of methane in the atmosphere has roughly doubled in the last 200 years and it is currently rising about one percent per year. This is largely the result of human activities and particularly rice culture, agriculture generally, cattle and sheep raising, and the use of oil and natural gas. Nitrous oxide, chiefly from fossil fuel combustion and fertilizer denitrification, has been increasing in concentration in the atmosphere by about 0.2 percent per year.

The most authoritative current estimates indicate that with a doubling of carbon dioxide in the atmosphere, average global temperatures are likely to increase 5.4 degrees Fahrenheit (plus or minus 2.7 degrees) by some time in the next century. The general impacts of global warming have received wide publicity. They include melting of the polar ice caps, with rising sea levels and flooding of low-lying coastal areas as a consequence, and changes in global wind directions that will bring about an increase in the extent of tropical rainbelts and reduced precipitation in the zone from 30 to 40 degrees latitude. Impacts are likely to be most severe in the middle and higher latitudes— average temperatures may rise by as much as 18 degrees Fahrenheit in the higher latitudes.

Significant shifts in the regional climate trends around which variations in the climate of the continental United States and Canada take place are likely. These shifts and the reduced precipitation in the mid-latitude continental regions are significant for forests in the two countries.

One study explored the kind of changes that might take place in the southeastern United States (Miller, Dougherty, and Switzer 1987). It concluded that the probability of summer drought in the central parts of this region would markedly increase. Summer and fall rainfall would decrease; average temperatures would rise in the summer by 3 to 4 degrees Fahrenheit, while winter and spring precipitation would rise and be accompanied by an increase in run-off. Changes in the coastal regions would not be as great. The study indicated that rainfall would remain relatively stable in Pennsylvania and New Jersey, but that there would be a major warming trend in the winter— from 11 to 18 degrees Fahrenheit.

The study also examined the prospective impacts of these kinds of climate changes on the range of loblolly pine, the major commercial species of the southern United States. It would expand north and northeast into Pennsylvania and New Jersy and shrink in the western part of its current range. The total area of its range would expand, but overall productivity would be lower because a larger part of the new range would be on highlands with lower productivity.

A similar study of six major western species showed significant climate and range changes (Leverenz and Lev 1987). Estimated average temperature increases varied from less than four degrees Fahrenheit on the southern California coast to more than 11 degrees in Arizona, New Mexico, southern Colorado, and southern Utah. In general, average projected temperatures increased from west to east and from north to south. As a result, the projected range of ponderosa pine increased in California and the Cascade Mountains in Oregon, but decreased on the east slope of the Rockies from Canada to Mexico. The Douglas fir maintained most of its commercially significant range, but decreased on southern and coastal sites and on the east slope of the Rockies. Western hemlock range decreased in northern Idaho and east of the Willamette Valley, but increased along the Oregon coast. Western larch range generally increased, although there were decreases in area in Oregon and Washington. There were no substantial effects on the range of lodgepole pine. The Engelmann spruce declined in acreage over its whole range.

In addition to expected changes in the range of timber species, other widespread impacts from global warming are likely. They include an increase in the probability of drought and an associated increase in damage from fires and pests. There will also be greater extremes of temperature, precipitation, and wind over large areas of forest land. On the other hand, increased carbon dioxide concentrations could increase tree growth and improve the efficiency with which trees use water.

Global warming could also cause substantial shifts in the ranges of many important commercial tree species and associated decreases in timber growth. This would probably be accompanied by dislocations in forest products production, and in the communities that are now dependent on such production, as wood supplies become more distant from established processing facilities.

Global warming is a problem that requires global solutions. But forests in the United States could make a modest contribution to ameliorating the problem while effective approaches are developed and applied. Forests act as a "carbon sink" as they grow and use carbon dioxide from the atmosphere and accumulate carbon in woody parts of the trees. There are some opportunities in the United States for increasing net growth and accumulating more carbon in trees. This could, to a degree, offset some of the annual additions to atmospheric carbon dioxide from burning fossil fuels.

Information prepared as part of the Forest Service's current assessment of the renewable resources situation shows economically plausible opportunities to increase net annual merchantable timber growth by 9.1 billion cubic feet (U.S. Forest Service 1988d). About three-quarters of these opportunities are on private nonindustrial forest lands. Most opportunities— seven billion cubic feet — involve regeneration of timber stands. Some 4.9 billion of the seven billion cubic feet would come from regenerating, with site preparation, existing non-stocked or cut-over commercial forest lands. In addition, there are about 22 million acres of cropland and pasture, including nearly eight million acres of highly erodible cropland, that are suitable for growing trees. If planted to pine, these lands, which are marginal for crops and pasture, would produce about 2.1 billion cubic feet annually of net timber growth.

These net growth estimates are for portions of trees that are suitable for making forest products. Additional carbon would be accumulated in branches, tops, and other nonmerchantable parts of these trees. Where land now devoted to crops or pasture is planted to trees, the "carbon sink" amounts to all of the carbon accumulated in the planted trees. On the other hand, regenerating nonstocked or cut-over land would in part replace carbon now stored in nonmerchantable trees on these lands.

Most of these nonstocked and cut-over lands are already growing woody materials, in some cases at rates approaching the maximum for the sites in question. But if these lands were regenerated to potentially merchantable timber, there generally would be a net increase in the accumulation of carbon in trees because the planted trees grow faster (i.e., accumulate and store carbon faster) than the plants that now occupy the sites. Allowance must be made for the potential additions to atmospheric carbon from the disposal of woody material during site preparation.

The potential increased removal of carbon dioxide from the atmosphere resulting from planting marginal crop and pasture land to trees is on the order of 100 million tons per year. The net effects on carbon storage of regenerating currently nonstocked and cut-over land are uncertain, but could well be of the same order. The subsequent net removal of atmospheric carbon dioxide from these two actions would amount to some five to 10 percent of the carbon dioxide going into the atmosphere each year in the United States from burning fossil fuels. The Forest Service estimates the total capital investment needed to respond fully to potential economic opportunities to increase timber growth to be about $15 billion.

Investments of this magnitude in management opportunities will also have important implications for future timber supplies, if the timber is to be harvested when it becomes merchantable. And these investment opportunities are economic, in the Forest Service's parlance, only if the timber is to be harvested. To the extent that merchantable parts of harvested trees go into solid wood products, such as lumber, and are used in permanent structures, they, too, will store carbon. The carbon in logging residues and some products is likely to be returned to the atmosphere as these materials decompose.

Investing in increased timber management opportunities in the United States will not reverse the trends toward global warming. It can, however, slow the rate of warming somewhat and, if done in concert with other actions, provide some added time to respond to the challenge posed by the "greenhouse effect."

CONCLUSIONS

The loss of forest land in the United States as defined in Forest Service surveys is not alarming in itself. It does not pose a major threat to future timber supplies, nor does it substantially threaten future supplies of other resources and uses of forest land. What is of more concern is the dividing of large forest tracts into smaller tracts.

This subdividing of forest land holdings is not captured fully in Forest Service statistics. But it exists and, if unchecked, will lead to significant reductions in future timber supplies, upward pressure on prices for forest products, loss of some natural amenities, and less forest land available for such recreation as hunting and fishing. The threat of subdividing comes from rapid development in some forested parts of the country, speculation in forest land, and pressure from Wall Street to maximize short-term returns on forest industry lands.

Increases in timber inventories and net annual growth in recent decades indicate some improvements in the condition of forest land in the United States. But other indications suggest some deterioration of other forest conditions. We know far too little about the effects of major changes in forest cover, nutrient cycling, and the effects of air pollution to be sanguine about the future condition of our forests. Major efforts are needed to improve our basic understanding of forest processes, not just in relation to timber production, but in relation to the whole range of expectations we hold for these lands.

Improvements in technology and alternatives to depleted sources of wood as a raw material have slowed the rate of increase in timber prices. Continued technological improvements and shifts to use of more hardwoods will tend to hold down future timber price increases despite some losses in our effective timberland base. There are significant opportunities to increase timber supplies and hold down price increases even more. But this provides little encouragement for forest landowners to continue to hold forest land in the face of increases in the value of their land for other uses.

Global atmospheric warming poses a significant, although uncertain, threat to the future productivity and use of forest land in the United States. Shifts in the ranges of important timber species and in their average growth rates are possible during the first half of the next century. Ameliorating the degree of atmospheric warming will require action on many fronts, but forestry could play a part, just as forest depletion has played a part in the warming itself.

Investments in what appear to be plausible timber management opportunities from a social viewpoint could offset in a modest way some of the effects of burning fossil fuels. This would occur as a result of increased timber growth rates and the accumulation of additional woody material in forests. One result would be to give some additional time to address the root causes of global climate changes.

REFERENCES

Binkley, Clark S., and Perry R. Hagenstein. 1987. Economic analysis of the 1985 RPA Program. Journal of Forestry 85:11:25-28.

Binkley, Clark S., and Jeffrey R. Vincent. 1988. Timber prices in the U.S. South: past trends and outlook for the future. Southern Journal of Applied Forestry 12:1:15-18.

de Stiguer, J. E. 1983. The influence of incentive programs on nonindustrial private forestry investment. Royer, Jack P., and Christopher D. Risbrudt, eds., Nonindustrial Private Forests: A Review of Economic and Policy Studies. School of Forestry and Environmental Studies, Duke University. pp. 157-164.

Gates, Paul W. 1968. Pages 536-561 in History of Public Land Law Development. Government Printing Office, Washington D.C. 828 pp.

Henly, Russell K., and Paul V. Ellefson. 1986. Pages 2-3 in State Forest Practice Regulation in the U.S.: Administration, Cost, and Accomplishment. Station Bulletin AD-SB-3011, University of Minnesota Agricultural Experiment Station. 154 pp.

Leverenz, Jerry W., and Deborah J. Lev. 1987. Effects of carbon dioxide-induced climate changes on the natural ranges of six major commercial tree species in the western United States. In: Shands, William E., and John S. Hoffman (eds.). The Greenhouse Effect, Climate Change, and U.S. Forests. Conservation Foundation, Washington D.C. pp. 123-155

Miller, W. Frank, Philip M. Dougherty, and George L. Switzer. 1987. Effects of using carbon dioxide and potential climate change on loblolly pine distribution, growth, survival, and productivity. In: Shands and Hoffman (eds.). pp.157-187.

Modigliani, Franco. 1988. The role of intergenerational transfers and life cycle saving in the accumulation of wealth. Journal of Economic Perspectives. American Economic Association. pp. 15-40.

Ulrich, Alice H. 1988. Page 28 in U.S. Timber Production, Trade, Consumption, and Price Statistics, 1950-86. U.S. Forest Service Misc. Publication No. 1460. 81 pp.

United States Forest Service. 1982. Page 496 in An Analysis of the Timber Situation in the United States: 1952-2030. Forest Resource Report No. 23. Washington D.C. 499 pp.

United States Forest Service. 1988a. Page 167 in Draft: An Analysis of the Timber Situation in the United States: 1989-2040. Part I. 281 pp. and appendices.

United States Forest Service. 1988b. p. 151 in The South's Fourth Forest: Alternatives for the Future. Forest Resource Report No. 24. Washington D.C. 512 pp.

United States Forest Service. 1988c. Appendix B in Proposed Land and Resource Management Plan, Gifford Pinchot National Forest, Appendices — Draft Environmental Impact Statement.

United States Forest Service. 1988d. Draft: An Analysis of the Timber Situation in the United States: 1989-2040. Part II, chapters 6-11.

CHAPTER 5

Rangelands

Thadis W. Box

Rangelands have been central to the development and well-being of this country for more than 200 years. Without natural forage for draft animals and milk stock, the first Europeans could not have survived. As the country developed, "range" became the romantic center of the very culture of the American West.

The term "rangeland" is American in origin, often evoking images of cowboys and horses on western plains and mountains. However, the deserts of North Africa, the steppes of China, the tundra of Russia, and the swamps and marshes of Florida are all rangelands. The word means not so much a place or use as a kind of land. Rangelands are those areas of the world which are, by reason of physical limitations, unsuited to cultivation or intensive forestry. Too hot, too dry, too cold, too rocky or too high for growing crops, they provide forage for free ranging livestock and wild animals. Rangelands are most often thought of as arid lands. However, other factors may prohibit cultivation or intensive forestry. Shallow soils, rough topography, poor drainage, cold temperatures, or low soil fertility may be as important as aridity in preventing intensive agricultural use. Rangelands are important for a variety of reasons in addition to grazing. They produce wood, water, incense, and other products for human enjoyment. They may also be a source of nuts, berries, tubers, and other food products for direct human consumption. Vast open rangelands are increasingly important as a place for people to enjoy outdoor recreation. Their remoteness, scenery, and open space attract more people each year. These lands are also an important source of biological diversity. They are critical to the understanding of large ecosystems, and a key to the overall environmental improvement of the world's land base. However, their isolation also makes rangelands a target for disposal of unwanted material from more humid areas. Hazardous waste, nuclear residue, and other potentially harmful substances are finding their way to rangeland sites.

America has nearly a billion acres of rangeland, some of the world's most productive. Most of the earth's surface is grazed by some animal, but about 5.5 billion acres of grazing land are in developing countries. Of these, at least half are rocky, poorly drained, and cold, making them marginal for farming, but supporting forage that provides the basis for the livestock industry. They are also the major source of fuelwood for cooking in many developing countries.

The importance of rangelands is often determined by cultural factors. Primitive societies value food from wild plants and the opportunity to hunt wild animals. Countries with pastoral economies value forage for domestic livestock and wood for fuel. In crowded, developed countries such as those of North America, the most important products may be water and recreation. In Texas, ranchers often earn more for selling their hunting privileges than they do leasing their land for grazing. The White Mountain Apache Tribe in Arizona sells hunting privileges for trophy elk. At $7,000 to $10,000 each, the waiting list for people wanting to harvest the animals is several years. As economies become more complex and populations increase, wilderness and waste disposal become increasingly important. Despite these differences the historical and present value of rangeland is predominately for the production of forage for wild and domestic animals.

HISTORY OF RANGE USE IN AMERICA

Grazing is a natural process on rangelands. Long before man domesticated the first animal, since the end of the Ice Age, the American ranges were grazed. Horses, camels, giant bisons, and antelope-like grazers and browsers roamed the American continent. These animals became extinct and were replaced by the buffalo, deer, elk, and wild sheep found when the first European arrived less than five hundred years ago. Since the plant communities evolved under grazing (Box and Malechek 1987), foraging animals can be used for environmental enhancement or to promote stability.

History of Livestock Use
The first livestock were brought to America by Spanish explorers in the early 1500s. Coronado, in his search for the seven cities of Cibola, brought sheep to the Zuni and other native Americans. Herds of wild cattle built up around the Spanish missions in the Southwest before the United States was formed. But the complete stocking of the American West occurred as part of the growth and development of our new country. To settle the land, to develop the resource, to tame the wilderness were seen as good and honorable goals.

When the white settlers brought their domestic herds and flocks, they found plant communities that were the result of past grazing pressures. Individual plant species had developed mechanisms that allowed them to survive and produce while being grazed (Box and Malechek 1987). The settlers and investors came from humid areas. They did not understand the limitation of the arid and semi-arid ranges (Box 1978). In the mid-1800s, gold in California and "unlimited" grass on the open ranges lured people west. Almost every state experienced the upheaval described by H.L. Bentley in Texas:

> Old men, middle-aged men, and young men representing every sphere of life, were eager to give up enterprises with which they were familiar and go into the "cow business." Every state in the United States was represented in the single state of Texas; and in every county in the State recognized as stock country. Englishmen, Scotchmen, and indeed men from most of the countries of Europe, were rushing to get a foothold, "a range right," and herds of cows to make them rich in a hurry, eating "free grass" (Bentley 1898).

These men saw the American rangelands as similar to the lush green pastures of home. But the ranges they found were not the same. The semi-arid and arid lands needed different management than the swards and heaths of Scotland. Rainfall was poorly distributed, and droughts were common.

Weather records in the western United States have been kept for a little more than 100 years, but tree ring studies show that severe droughts occurred in every century for the last 1,200 years. Records indicate that in the drought of 1778, forage was so scarce that when the Zuni villages in New Mexico sent aid to the Hopi villages in Arizona, horses of the party sent to aid the Hopies could not survive. It is likely these droughts, combined with grazing by native animals, caused continuous vegetative change prior to the introduction of domestic livestock.

The livestock industry began its expansion in one of the major droughts. Tree ring studies show the years from 1880 to 1905 as one of the driest periods on record. Don Biggers (N.D. Franks) of Colorado City, Texas, gives one colorful account of the effects of weather on the early livestock industry:

> In the winter of 1884 began a series of the most disastrous years ever known in the cattle history . . . When a blizzard would sweep over the country the cattle would drift before it, and it was then no uncommon sight to see great herds of cattle rolling southward, nothing to eat, nothing to drink, pelted by sleet and covered with snow; while around them the pittiless [sic] blizzard seemed to howl in fiendish glee.

> The winter of 1886 was very severe, and in the spring of
> 1887 occurred, beyond a doubt the awfullest [sic] die-up
> ever known in the United States. From the Canadian
> borders to the Rio Grande the range country was covered
> with carcasses . . . When the blizzards came, the cattle
> would drift south until they came to the southern line of
> fence. Unable to go further they would move back and
> forth, pressing close to the fence or standing in clusters,
> suffering from the cold, hunger, and thirst and trampling
> out every vestage [sic] of grass. One would fall or lie down
> and others would tumble over it, and soon there would be
> a heap of dead along the line of fence. I saw one instance
> and heard of many others, where, for a distance of two or
> three hundred yards, the heaps of dead bodies were higher
> than the fence. Over these bodies the snow drifted and
> sifted between them soon forming a solid, frozen mass over
> which hundreds of living cattle walked, tumbled over the
> fence and drifted away. This awful spectacle was to be re-
> produced in 1894 (Franks).

The record indicates that American ranges were generally overgrazed and
depleted by the beginning of the 20th century (Box and Malechek 1987).
Livestock numbers increased throughout the West and were high during the last
half of the 19th century. The last two decades of the century were the driest since
record-keeping began (National Oceanic and Atmospheric Administration
1985) and one of the driest periods in the past 1,500 years. During this time the
major arroyo (gulch) formation occurred in the American Southwest (Cooke
and Reeves 1976). Although the tendency has been to blame the increased
erosion on grazing, the record suggests other causes as well. Recent geomor-
phological and climatic literature shows that droughts sufficiently severe to
cause near barren landscapes have often occurred and that episodes of severe
erosion similar to the 1880s and 1890s occurred prior to the introduction of
domestic livestock (Cooke and Reeves 1976; Graf 1983; Wells 1987).

Comparison of pictures taken in Wyoming in the mid-19th century and in
1970s show that riparian areas were more actively eroding before livestock
introduction than they are today (Johnson 1987). It has been estimated that
more than 67 million bison, elk, deer, antelope, and native sheep grazed the
western ranges before domestic animals were introduced (Seton 1927). These
numbers were probably as high as those of the domestic animals that were
associated with the rapid decline of the western range and the destruction of
riparian habitat.

Regardless of the multiple causes of range deterioration, drought and grazing were major factors in the decline of range condition in the late 19th century.

In the 1890s the U.S. Botanical Survey sent Assistant Agronomist J.G. Smith to inspect the West. He wrote:

> There has been much written in the last 10 years about the deterioration of the ranges. Cattlemen say the grasses are not what they used to be, that the perennial grasses are disappearing, that their place is being taken by the less nutritious annuals. This is true to a very marked degree in every section of the grazing country (Smith 1895).

Agronomist Smith discussed both the condition of the range and the situation facing the cattle industry. He underscored the problem of people from humid areas who did not understand the drought-prone West:

> The present shortage of cattle all through the West is due to the fact that ranges were stocked up to the limit that they would carry during the series of exceptionally favorable years preceding the years of drought. Then followed the bad years when the native perennial grasses did not get rain enough to more than keep them alive. The cattle on the breeding grounds of the West and Southwest died by the thousands of thirst and starvation (Smith 1895).

Within the first half century of grazing with domestic livestock, the American ranges had changed from an area "where the buffalo roamed" to one plagued by drought and filled with livestock.

The Acreage and Ownership of Rangeland Today

Rangelands today represent 34 percent or about 770 million acres of the total land area of the United States (Joyce 1988). Large areas of this nation's forests (32 percent of the total land base) and a considerable amount of cropland in conservation reserve are managed as rangeland. In total, almost half of our country's land, over one billion acres, is rangeland.

More than half of the nation's rangeland is privately owned. Some 43 percent is in federal ownership (Joyce 1988). The remainder is owned by state and local governments.

In the early years of our country, the vision was to have all land owned and developed by private citizens. In the late 1800s, leaders recognized a need to set aside public lands for special purposes. They created national parks, set aside forest reserves, and in 1905 established a system of national forests. The remainder of the land continued as "open range" on the public domain until 1934, when the Taylor Grazing Act was passed.

Today the public rangeland is managed largely by the Bureau of Land Management and Forest Service under specific acts of Congress that require management for multiple uses. Congress has reaffirmed that these lands will continue in public ownership.

Private rangelands are managed by the people who own them. Landowners are supported by technical assistance from the Soil Conservation Service and the Extension Service. Land-grant universities and federal research labs provide information for both public and private managers.

The Development of Range Management

Range management is a new science, arising from roots in ecology and tempered by practical animal husbandry, forestry, and botany. A hundred years ago, ecology had not yet emerged. Therefore, not only has range management had to develop its approach in this century, but the basic science from which it draws its strength is still maturing. Range management, in fact, has contributed to the establishment of ecology as a separate science.

The field of range management began as cattlemen settled the West. Although some expressed concern for the problem of overgrazing before the turn of the century, the scientific management of rangelands is only decades old. Landowners viewed undergrazing as a waste of forage. Few recognized harm to the range through overgrazing.

The art and science of range management was mostly art in the early days. Stocking rates were set by people calling on past experience. Much of that experience either came from the humid east or was influenced by the popular ideas that the grass was "unlimited" in its ability to produce.

During the last three decades of the 1800s, while most of America's ranges were being used heavily, a small group of scientists, mostly botanists, were observing the process. Although they were primarily interested in collecting and describing the individual plants, their notes recorded their observations on the effects of grazing. At the same time, animal scientists and economists were describing the livestock industry. These accounts, coming from different disciplines and written for different reasons, were not usually connected. There was no unifying theory or body of knowledge to bring them together.

The concept of succession finally supplied the needed theory. In the following decade, a number of universities and professional botanists enlarged and developed the concepts of ecology. The first formal course in range management was taught around 1914. By World War I, courses dealing with range management were taught in agriculture, botany, animal husbandry, forestry, and perhaps other departments. Content of the courses generally included plant identification, forage value of plants, livestock management, survey methods, improvements (fencing, water, corrals, etc.), and, depending upon the department, forestry, soils, agronomy, or animal husbandry.

Two landmark publications appeared in 1919. The first was James T. Jardine and Mark Anderson's *Range Management on the National Forests*. This was more than a handbook for managing national forests. For the first time it pulled together the literature and practices that had developed in the fledgling field. It formed the basis for a profession. Sampson's paper on plant succession in relation to range management brought the new science of ecology front and center and gave a theoretical basis for describing and predicting community change (Sampson 1919).

The next 30 years saw the early ideas tested and the profession develop. From the beginning there had been a philosophical difference between people in range management. One group was concerned with *protection* of the resources. These were predominantly people with botany or forestry backgrounds whose emphasis was on plants. They were centered, though not exclusively, in the Forest Service. The other major group was concerned with *productivity*, primarily of animal products. These people were usually trained in animal husbandry or economics and usually found in the Bureau of Animal Industry, Agricultural Extension, etc.

In some agencies, such as the Indian Service, this difference between plant and animal oriented people often caused conflicting reports and options on the same data. This philosophical conflict in range management was highest during the 1920s and gradually lessened as data became available that showed productivity over the long run is related to protection of the plant and soil resource. The concept of sustained yield embraces both.

The development of scientific tools that would allow quantification of data helped to solidify philosophical concepts and give scientific merit to rangeland management. The demand for range graduates increased. In 1943, L.A. Stoddart and A.D. Smith published the first edition of the classic range management text (Stoddart and Smith 1943). With its publication, range management became a science as well as an art. The fortunate timing and high quality of the textbook caused it to be used as the basic document for training the growing number of range students following World War II. Few range people have not used it, or its revisions, as their basic text.

Because of the growing need for identity, a movement began in the late 1940s to form a professional society. In 1948 the American Society of Range Management was formed in Salt Lake City. The following year the first issue of the *Journal of Range Management* was published. Range management had become a profession.

Since 1947, range management has matured into a science-based profession. Today the Society for Range Management has over 5,500 members worldwide, publishes two journals, accredits universities to teach range management, and certifies consultants competent to do professional range management work.

CONDITION OF AMERICAN RANGELAND

"Range condition" is a term professional range management people use to describe the health of the range. The concept and procedures determining the health of the range have changed through time, and even range professionals are occasionally hard pressed to reconcile range condition statements in certain surveys. The lay public is sometimes completely confused by the apparently conflicting information coming from different sources. This confusion has served as a platform for extremists to condemn livestock grazing as the only cause for range deterioration or to defend the status quo as the best way to manage the public ranges. Thus, the concept of range condition has come under fire by environmentalists and livestock producers alike.

A number of techniques for determining range condition have been used over the years. Basically, they fall into three categories: 1) reporting forage production variability around some mythical average year (range condition, for example, is 55 percent of normal due to low rainfall this year); 2) estimates of the range to produce forage for animal products, emphasizing the abundance, palatability, and nutrition of various plants for livestock production; and 3) estimates measuring the deviation of the present range from some "ideal" range, usually the ecological climax.

Changing Concepts in Range Condition

The first to report range conditions were agriculturalists and climatologists. In a normal year, range conditions were considered good; in a low rainfall year, they were poor; in a high rainfall year, excellent. These subjective estimates of productivity continue in weather communications even today, but do not form the basis of range condition as used by professional range people.

Jardine and his co-workers conducted the first professional range surveys in 1910. His "reconnaissance method" did not report range condition *per se*. It determined range types, mapped them, and estimated plant density (cover) by species. These data were used to calculate forage acres, which when used with forage acre factors and forage acre requirements were used to calculate carrying capacity. A subjective estimate of range health, using such things as plant vigor and erosion, was used to make adjustments in carrying capacity.

The Jardine, or plant density, method was later modified and more elaborate score cards constructed. Almost all had the value of forage for livestock as their base, with plants being classified as desirable, intermediate, or less desirable. As time went on more emphasis was placed on stability of the landscape or multiple use values of the land, and less on the value of the forage for livestock.

Today, almost all range condition methods are based on some measure of the deviation from an ideal range. These fall primarily into two groups. One measures a deviation from some ideal "potential" productivity. The techniques for this method include the artificial reconstruction of an "ideal" range to produce products society desires. Such attributes as plant composition, soil, and erosion are sampled and reported as a deviation from the ideal.

More often, the deviation from an ecological ideal, or climax, is the measure of range condition. The ecological basis for range condition is found in the early writings of Clements, but it was not articulated and used until much later. In the 1920s, Sampson taught that the story of the range could be read in the plants. J.E. Weaver, L.A. Stoddart, and others used ecological criteria in judging range. However, it was not until E. J. Dyksterhuis published his paper "Condition and Management of Rangeland Based on Quantitative Ecology" in 1949 that the range profession really accepted the "deviation from climax" basis for range condition. Today, virtually all United States land management agencies use some modification of the quantitative ecology method for determining range conditions.

The Society for Range Management has a committee working to help standardize range condition terms and concepts. All major land management agencies have committees and task forces working to make their data more understandable to lay audiences. However, the data that are available from past assessments were done with a variety of techniques, often working from very different philosophical bases. To really understand what a range condition report means, it is necessary to know when it was made, the techniques used, and the purpose for which the assessment was made.

The first national assessment of rangeland was made in 1936 (U.S. Senate 1936). More of a political document than a biological survey, it reported the range in stages of depletion rather than in range condition (Table 5.1). National forests were judged to have the least depletion; the public domain the most. Private ranges were more variable and intermediate between the major public land categories. The private lands (including Indian lands) and national forest lands had improved since 1905; the public domain had deteriorated (Table 5.2).

No national assessments of range conditions were made from 1936 until 1966. During the early 1960s, Congress was considering changing the laws governing the public lands. A Public Land Law Review Commission was established. The Review Commission staff contracted with Pacific Consultants to evaluate the condition of the nation's rangelands. Pacific Consultants did not make on-the-ground surveys, but compiled data from various sources. Although the accuracy of the data has been questioned, their report has to be used as one of the benchmarks against which change is measured.

In 1972, the Forest Service made an estimate of the condition of federal

Table 5.1.   Percent Depletion of Rangelands by Ownership in 1935

Ownership	Percent by Depletion Class			
	Moderate Depletion	Material Depletion	Severe Depletion	Extreme Depletion
Federal				
NationalForests	45.5	40.0	12.0	1.5
Indian Lands	6.6	35.8	54.0	3.6
Public Domain	1.5	14.3	47.9	36.3
Other Federal	2.0	21.2	50.1	26.7
All Federal	46.1	26.4	38.1	19.4
State and County	7.1	47.4	37.0	8.7
Private	11.7	36.9	36.4	15.0

Source: Senate Document #199, 1936, adapted from Box, Dwyer and Wagner 1976.

Table 5.2.   Trends in Range Forage Depletion from 1905 to 1935

Land Control	Percent of Land by Trend Class		
	Improved	Declined	Unchanged
National Forests	77	5	18
Indian Lands	10	2	15
Public Domain	2	93	5
Other Federal	7	81	12
State and County	7	88	5
Private	10	85	5

Source: Senate Document #199, 1936, adapted from Box, Dwyer and Wagner 1976.

ranges. Again, it appears that much off-the-shelf data from old surveys were used. More recently, Congress has directed the Forest Service and the Soil Conservation Service to report the condition of public and private rangeland, respectively, at least once each decade. These laws have led to range condition reports at least every five years. Unfortunately, the agencies released the reports at different times, using different techniques and differing formats. This contributed to each private interest group using the agency's data to make whatever point is favorable to them. Confusion continues, or perhaps has increased, because of the variable reporting system.

Current Range Conditions

I believe that the American range is in the best condition that it has been in this century. This view is primarily based on my review of historical reports and our collective experience. This does not mean that the job of restoring the range from the past abuses has been completed. There are still many areas in need of management. It does indicate that the range can be improved with good management and favorable climatic conditions.

In the past two years there have been a number of attempts by the management agencies, oversight agencies, and professional organizations to evaluate range condition. These include the periodic reports of the Soil Conservation Service, the Bureau of Land Management, and the Forest Service. Linda A. Joyce recently summarized the agency reports in preparation for the Resources Planning Act report required by Congress (Joyce 1988). Oversight reports by the Environmental Protection Agency (Kuch 1988) and the General Accounting Office (General Accounting Office 1988b) have been recently distributed. A committee from the Society for Range Management is making an independent report (Ruyle et al. 1988).

In general, the oversight agencies make a pessimistic interpretation of the data (Table 5.3). For instance, the Environmental Protection Agency states: "Over 60 percent of the range and pasture land is classified as in fair or poor condition, after long periods of overgrazing. Range quality on public grazing lands continues to be far below that of private lands. High erosion rates are associated with the loss of critical plant cover" (Kuch 1988). The General Accounting Office report concludes that the federal management agencies lack reliable, up-to-date data on range condition but that stocking rate exceeded carrying capacity on 18 percent and 21 percent of the Bureau of Land Management's and Forest Service's respective allotments (General Accounting Office 1988b).

Livestock agencies and farm organizations tend to look at the same data and say that 78 percent of the land is in fair or better condition. Only a small amount, less than a fifth, is in poor condition. The condition of America's ranges becomes a classic case of looking at a half-filled glass: one sees it as half full, the other as

Table 5.3. Condition of Rangelands in the United States

	Excellent	Good	Fair	Poor
Private[a]	4	31	47	17
National Resources Land (BLM)[b]	4	30	41	18
National Forests[c]	15	31	38	15

Source: Joyce 1988.

[a] Data from Soil Conservation Service 1987 report.
[b] Data from Bureau of Land Management 1987 report.
[c] Data from United States Department of Agriculture 1986 report.
Data are reported as deviation from a potential natural community and are not directly comparable to the others.

half empty. Regardless of the perception, there are at least two real issues that need better understanding before the confusion will diminish: 1) the quality of the data themselves, and 2) the condition (or seral stage) that is to be chosen as a target for management.

Much has been said about the differing techniques and methods of collecting data. These differences are confusing even to professionals, and the Society for Range Management has a continuing committee to try to standardize terminology and technique. Data that are confusing to professionals become next to impossible for laymen and lead to misinterpretation and honest differences of opinion. Even more alarming is the revelation that the condition of more than a fourth of our rangeland is simply unknown, that another 40 percent of the data reported is more than 10 years old, and that more than half of grazing allotments do not have management plans (Bureau of Land Management, 66 percent; Forest Service, 27 percent) (General Accounting Office 1988a). Until the agencies can collect sound data for each specific site, it will be impossible to discover the real condition of America's rangeland.

Second, even if good data were available, we will continue to get disagreements about range condition until a management objective is determined for each site. The agency reports are now careful to point out that range classified as excellent, good, fair, or poor is not directly comparable to those classified as potential natural community, late seral stage, mid-seral stage, and early seral stage. This confuses the layman and is actually begging the question. All agencies now use a system based on ecological deviation from an ideal. The question is really what stage, or condition, is best for society. Let us look briefly at one stage: the fair or mid-seral stage.

People with an environmental or protection philosophy tend to lump this stage with poor, therefore unacceptable. People with a production philosophy may accept it as a desirable condition. Many of our wildlife species (mule deer in winter, bob white quail, Rio Grande turkey, sage grouse) are more productive when their rangeland habitat is in fair condition range than when it is rated excellent. Some forest products, some livestock ranges, and even cover to protect soil may be better on some sites under fair range condition than under excellent.

This leads me to two major points about range condition: 1) range condition, and the ultimate management of the range, is site specific. While I have been discussing condition in terms of national averages, it is the management of specific range areas that is important in improving condition. 2) The value of the land for society will depend upon the management objectives set and the land's ability to produce what society wants. Range in low seral stages may be more valuable to society than climax or excellent ranges.

Regardless of what society wants, or the system used to classify ranges, it is most important to know the trend of the range. The direction and speed of movement from one seral stage to another will dictate the specific management policies.

TRENDS IN RANGELAND CONDITIONS

I believe that the trend for rangelands, on the average, has been upwards over a number of decades and that the range is in the best condition of this century. This is my professional opinion and cannot be well documented with specific surveys and reports. We may consider available data, however.

The drought period of the 1880s continued over most of the West until about 1905. All classes of land were probably denuded and in poor condition when the rains started. Table 5.2 reports the perception of professional land managers of the trend between 1905 and 1936. Forest Service lands probably reached their lowest condition shortly after the turn of the century and have been in an upward trend since that time. Private lands and the public domain probably reached their lowest condition during the dust bowl days of the 1930s.

The trend since 1936 has apparently continued upward to the present time (Table 5.4). The only nationwide data available are from broad, general surveys based more on opinion than on fact. Each survey could be questioned for accuracy. We do not defend the absolute percentages in the table, but the changes are sufficiently large so that we are comfortable in forming a professional opinion on several areas of average trend of United States ranges.

First, the trend since 1905 is generally toward improvement of American

Table 5.4. Percentages of Federal Land in Three Condition Classes. [a]

	Percent by Condition Class		
	Good or Excellent	Fair	Poor or Bad
1936 [b]	16	5	58
1966 [c]	18	49	33
1972 [d]	18	50	32
1984 [e]	36	30	30
1986-87 [f]	40	40	16
1988 [g]	32	31	11

[a] All data are rounded to the nearest percentage point.

[b] Data adapted from depletion categories to Senate Document #199 (1936). Moderate Depletion was used to present good condition; Material Depletion, Fair condition; Severe and Extreme Depletion, poor or bad condition.

[c] Data adapted from Pacific consultants (1968).

[d] Data from Forest Report No. 19, United States Department of Agriculture Forest Service (1972).

[e] Data from Bureau of Land Management, Proc. 50th Anniversary Taylor Grazing Act (1984).

[f] Data interpolated from 1986 and 1987 Forest Service and Bureau of Land Management Reports. Numbers do not add to 100 percent because of ca. 4 percent unknown.

[g] Data from General Accounting Office (1988). Data do not equal 100 percent because of ca. 26 percent unknown

rangelands. The upward trend started first on national forest lands and much later on private lands and on the public domain.

Second, the shift has been to improve the mythical "average" range by about one condition class (poor ranges are now fair; fair ranges, good). The amount of poor range has diminished steadily.

Third, over three fourths of the range has seral stage with adequate plant cover and species composition to make continued improvement if good management is practiced.

Fourth, the upward trend has occurred in a period of average or better rainfall. Widespread droughts occurred in the 1930s and the 1950s, but the past decade has been a period of extremely favorable rainfall.

Management agencies now report over half of the nation's rangeland to be stable (Table 5.5). About a sixth is improving and another sixth declining. It is not possible to tell from the reports how much land is purposefully being held in a stable condition to meet management objectives and how much is stable because management has not obtained the desired response. Certainly, the sixth that is declining needs attention.

Another disturbing statistic is that the trend is not known on 12 percent of the national forests and 26 percent of the national resource lands. When this is

Table 5.5. Trends in Rangeland Condition in the United States

	Up	Stable	Down	Unknown
Private Lands [a]	16	69	15	0
National Resources Lands				
Bureau of Land Management Estimates [b]	15	64	14	7
General Accounting Office Estimates [c]	20	47	7	26
National Forests				
Forest Service Estimates [d]	44	42	14	0
General Accounting Office Estimates [c]	30	49	9	12

[a] Soil Conservation Service 1987 data reported by Joyce (1988).

[b] Bureau of Land Management 1987 data.

[c] General Accounting Office 1988 data.

[d] United States Department of Agriculture Forest Service 1987 data.

combined with the range in decline, it means that proper management attention is not being given to at least a fourth to a third of the rangeland.

Possible Future Trends

No one can accurately predict the future trends on rangeland. We do know that the trend will depend largely on the weather, the management of the land, and the policies directing management.

Much of the western rangeland is now in drought conditions. Some areas are suffering the most severe moisture stress since the 1930s. Studies have shown that good or excellent range condition can deteriorate to poor in the absence of grazing from drought alone (Weaver and Albertson 1956; Branson 1985). Individual plant species respond differently to drought or combinations of drought and grazing pressure (Box 1967; Chamrad and Box 1965), causing plant composition changes even in a short drought. Therefore, it is highly likely that range condition will decline and the trend will be down because of the current drought. If the drought continues, major losses in condition could occur throughout the rangelands.

While the level of management is important at any time, it becomes critical in drought periods. About two-thirds of the Bureau of Land Management allotments and a fourth of the Forest Service allotments do not have allotment management plans. An additional 16 percent of Bureau of Land Management allotments and 31 percent of those managed by the Forest Service are over a decade old (General Accounting Office 1988b). The agencies do not have personnel or budget to correct the situation. Combined, the agencies have only about 1,400 people to manage rangelands. This means that on the average, each person is responsible for about 22 allotments or about 191,000 acres. In addition, professional range people are diverted to write environmental impact statements, develop mine reclamation plans, and other duties that prevent them from doing the range management job. If the understaffing continues, the future trend of federal ranges is likely to be down.

The people, through congressional acts, have stated that the public ranges will remain in public ownership and that they will be managed for multiple use. However, funds and personnel to manage those lands have been withheld in favor of defense and other issues. After examining the budgets for natural resource management since 1982, Frederic H. Wagner concluded: "Policies have reversed with 1) reductions in renewable-resource-management funds and manpower while minerals and energy have grown, 2) a shift in management responsibilities from the Bureau of Land Management to the land users, and 3) an attitudinal tilt toward commodity uses and a hardening attitude toward noncommodity uses. The result appears to be declining monitoring and management of renewable resources, advertent or inadvertent lack of enforcement of regulations applied to commodity users, and extremely low morale among the renewable resources management staff," (Wagner 1984). The recent General Accounting Office reports on rangelands (General Accounting Office 1988a) and riparian systems (General Accounting Office 1988b) show that the agencies do not have funds or personnel to gather basic management data on the public lands. Professionals in the field do not believe they have the backing of the Administration to implement grazing reductions or riparian habitat improvement. If the current policy on management of natural resources continues, the trend in rangeland condition will likely be downward.

As with the public land commitment, the funds for range research, the Soil Conservation Service, the Extension Service, and others who assist private landowners have declined. Unless funds for their support is available, private rangeland will not have the basic support needed.

TOWARD A SUSTAINABLE FUTURE

Traditionally, rangelands have been used primarily for grazing and the production of livestock products. Some 370 million Animal Unit Months of livestock grazing are produced on the nation's private rangelands and another 29.4 million on public rangelands (Joyce 1988). Virtually all of the feeder livestock in this country spend part of their lives on native forage. Therefore, the traditional range use for livestock grazing will continue. However, it will likely share the range with other multiple uses.

The use of both private and public ranges for purposes other than livestock is growing. Several national conferences have been held in the past few years to highlight these changes (United States Department of Agriculture Soil Conservation Service 1985; Ft. Keogh Research Symposium 1987). These new uses are gaining favor because of economic, aesthetic, and environmental conditions.

Wild animals used the rangelands long before domestic animals arrived, but management of rangelands for wildlife yield is relatively new. Today, most ranches in Texas derive income from the wildlife on the land. Private ranchers in other states are fast realizing that management for wildlife can be profitable. Public concern for wildlife has caused agencies managing the public lands to put more emphasis on the wild animals in the forest and rangelands. Not only are economically important wildlife, such as game animals, a management target species, but non-game animals and endangered species are now considered in the management of the ranges.

Recreation, from dispersed camping to intensively managed bed-and-breakfast hotels, is depending more and more on rangeland. The solitude of the open spaces, the remote locations, and the lack of commercial development have a special attraction to many. Management for recreation will become more important.

Water yield from rangeland is one of the most valued products of rangeland.

Watershed protection and stability are important to those who live downstream from rangelands. The remoteness of many ranges makes them targets for places to dispose of the wastes nobody wants.

With the multiple demands being made upon them, very few ranges will be managed for single uses in the future. The mix of range goods and services will depend upon their ecological potential, their location and proximity to users, and the policies of our nation.

Laws on endangered species, wilderness, grazing fees, food prices, etc., will set the parameters for the management of the nation's rangelands. The economic viability of the private rancher and the funds appropriated to the public agencies will be major factors in the future condition of America's rangeland.

CONCLUSION

Rangelands are an important renewable national resource. Their size alone, around half of the land of the United States, makes them important. Every American has a stake in the productivity of the land. Their food supply, recreation opportunities, water, and wildlife depend on the health of the range.

The range is in the best condition in a hundred years, but there are crucial areas that deserve special management attention to make them better. The trend has been toward better ranges for many decades. This trend is in danger of being reversed by a natural drought and negligent governmental policies.

If America's rangelands are to fulfill their potential for the people, we must have a national commitment to invest in them. They can continue to improve and provide more for society, or they may be allowed to deteriorate. We as a people must make that choice.

REFERENCES

Bentley, H. L. 1898. Cattle ranges of the Southwest: A history of the exhaustion of pasturage and suggestions for its restoration. U. S. Dept. Agr. Farmers Bul. 72.

Box, Thadis W. 1967. The influence of drought and grazing on mortality of five West Texas grasses. Ecology 48: 654-656.

Box, Thadis W. 1978. The Arid Lands Revisited. 100 years since John Wesley Powell. Utah State University. Honor Lecture. 30 pp.

Box, T. W., D. D. Dwyer, and F. H. Wagner. 1976. Unpublished report on the condition of the Western Rangelands. Council on Environmental Quality, Washington, D. C.

Box, Thadis W. and John C. Malechek. 1987. Grazing on American Rangelands. Western Sheep Task Force. Denver, Colorado. 32 pp.

Branson, Farrel A. 1985. Vegetation changes on western rangelands. Soc. Range Manage. Range Monograph. 2: 76 pp.

Chamrad, A. D. and T. W. Box. 1965. Drought associated mortality of range grasses in South Texas. Ecology 46:780-785.

Clements, F. E. 1916. Plant Succession. Carnegie Institute of Washington. Pub. 242.

Cooke, R. U. and R. W. Reeves. 1976. Arroyos and environmental change in the American Southwest. Oxford, Clarendon Press, Oxford, U.K. 213 pp.

Cowles, H. C. 1899. The Ecological Relations of the Vegetation on the Sand Dunes of Lake Michigan. Bot. Gazette. 29:95-391.

Dyksterhuis, E. J. 1949. Condition and Management of Rangeland Based on Quantitative Ecology. J. Range Manage. 2:104-115.

Franks, Lou (pseudonym Don Biggers). No date. History that will never be repeated. Colorado City, Texas. pp. 22-25.

General Accounting Office. 1988a. Rangeland management. GAO/RCED-88-80. U.S. Govt. Printing Office, Washington, D.C. 72 pp.

General Accounting Office. 1988b. Public rangelands. GAO/RCED-88-105. U.S. Govt. Printing Office, Washington, D.C. 85 pp.

Graf, W. L. 1983. The arroyo problem-paleohydrology and paleo-hydraulics in the short term, in Gregory, G. K., ed., Background to paleohydrology. John Wiley and Sons. New York. pp. 279-302.

Jardine, J. T. and M. Anderson. 1919. Range Management on the National Forests. U.S. Dept. Agr. Bul. 790:1-98.

Johnson, Steve. 1987. Allan Savory: Guru of False Hopes and an Overstocked Range. High Country News: Apr. 27, 1987.

Joyce, Linda A. 1988. An assessment of the forage situation in the United States-1989. Draft Tech. Dept. USDA Forest Service.

Kuch, Peter. 1988. Natural resources for the 21st century. EPA Dept. Washington, D.C. 125 pp.

National Oceanic and Atmospheric Administration. 1985. National weather records summaries. National Oceanic and Atmospheric Administration, Charlotte, North Carolina.

Neilson, Ronald P. 1986. High-resolution climatic analysis and southwest biogeography. Science 232: 27-33.

Ruyle, George, T. Box, D. Merkel, W. Peterson, R. Williamson, and J. Newman. 1988. Assessment of rangeland condition and trend of the United States 1987. SRM Pub. Affairs Committee Report. Unpublished.

Sampson, A. W. 1919. Plant Succession in Relation to Range Management. U.S. Dept. Agr. Bul. 791.

Sampson, A. W. 1923. Range and Pasture Management. John Wiley and Sons. New York.

Seton, E. T. 1927. **Lives of Game Animals Vol. III.** Hoofed Animals. Doubleday and Co., Inc. New York.

Smith, J. G. 1895. Forage conditions in the prairie regions. **U.S.** Dept. **Agr.** Yearbook, Washington, D.C. 322 pp.

Stoddart, L. A. and A. D. Smith. 1943. **Range management.** McGraw-Hill, New York.

Stoddart, L. A. and A. D. Smith. 1955. **Range management.** McGraw Hill, New York. 2nd edition.

Stoddart, L. A., A. D. Smith, and T. W. Box. 1975. **Range Management.** McGraw-Hill, New York. 3rd edition.

U. S. Senate. 1936. The western range. **Senate Document 199,** U.S. Congress, Washington, D. C.

Wagner, Frederic H. 1984. Progress and problems, 1934-1984, in improvement of wildlife habitat. Proc. 50th Anniversary of Taylor Grazing Act. Grand Junction, Colorado. pp. 51-58.

Weaver, J. E. and F. W. Albertson. 1956. **Grasslands of the Great Plains.** Johnsen Publ. Co. Lincoln, Nebraska.

Wells, S. G. 1987. A Quantitative Analysis of Arroyo Development and Geomorphic Processes in the Zuni River Drainage, West-Central New Mexico. Unpublished Report. University of New Mexico. 550 pp.

CHAPTER 6

Wetlands

Billy Teels

The values of wetlands— such as flood control, ground and surface water purification, sediment control, and fish and wildlife habitat — have been only recently recognized for their contributions to public health and welfare. In recent years a number of newly enacted state and federal wetland laws have echoed growing public sentiment for wetland protection. Currently, there are approximately 90 million acres of vegetated wetlands in the lower 48 states which receive various forms of protection, depending on wetland type, locality, and purpose for conversion.

Within the last 200 years, 30 to 50 percent of these wetlands have been converted to other uses as a result of activities such as agriculture, mining, forestry, oil and gas extraction, and urbanization (Office of Technology Assessment 1984). According to a recent federal survey, a net amount of approximately 11 million acres of wetlands in the lower 48 states were converted to these uses between the mid-1950s and mid-1970s. This amount was equivalent to a net loss each year of about 550,000 acres, or about 0.5 percent of the remaining wetlands. Approximately 80 percent of actual losses involved draining and clearing inland wetlands for agricultural purposes (Frayer et al. 1983).

Currently, wetland protection efforts such as Section 404 of the Clean Water Act of 1977, the Wetland Conservation provision of the Food Security Act of 1985, and the North American Waterfowl Management Plan are being implemented to improve the condition of the nation's wetlands and reduce wetland loss. The United States Department of Interior Fish and Wildlife Service has taken on the major responsibility of conducting an inventory of the nation's wetlands to project wetland status and trends. This chapter: presents information on wetland status and trends assembled from data collected by the Fish and Wildlife Service; addresses current accomplishments under the previously listed wetland protection efforts; and briefly discusses the effects and adequacy of these programs.

STATUS AND TRENDS

Historical Attitudes Toward Wetlands

From colonial times until recently, people have regarded wetlands as nuisances, wastelands, habitats for pests, and threats to public health. Wetlands have been drained, cleared, filled, exploited for resources, and altered in every conceivable way. They have been everything but appreciated. In colonial times settlers believed that flooding rivers were uncivilized and had to be controlled. George Washington and Thomas Jefferson joined one of the nation's earliest corporations, the Dismal Swamp Canal Company. The company was to build a canal which would drain the Dismal Swamp, a wetland in North Carolina and Virginia, for agricultural purposes. It completed the drainage canal in 1794 (Brande 1980).

The philosophical, intellectual, and scientific opinion of the time was that wetlands were of limited value. With the idea of fee simple absolute ownership, and the desire of individuals and the government to convert all unproductive lands into improved income-producing lands, it is not surprising that in 1849 Congress passed the first of the Swamp Acts to provide financial support for the drainage of western wetlands. The United States Department of Agriculture and land grant colleges also promoted land drainage. In 1912, Charles G. Elliott, chief of drainage investigations for the Department of Agriculture, wrote: "More than 70,000,000 acres of unreclaimed land await the touch of the engineer and the intelligent activity of the ambitious and enterprising farmer" (Elliott 1912).

Historical Wetlands

It is impossible to determine the actual acreage of wetlands that existed at the time of European settlement. A 1954 publication entitled "Engineering for Agricultural Drainage" stated that there originally was a total of 216 million acres of potential agricultural land that could be benefited by drainage, 53 million acres of which had already been drained (Roe and Ayres 1954).

In the early 1950s it became apparent to the Fish and Wildlife Service that drainage of wetlands was having an adverse impact on wildlife habitat. Information was needed on the distribution, extent, and quality of the remaining wetlands in relation to their value as wildlife habitat. The Fish and Wildlife Service placed primary emphasis on identifying wetlands considered susceptible to drainage or other land use changes that destroyed wildlife habitat (Shaw and Fredine 1956). Through the use of aerial photographs, topographic maps, geodetic survey charts, United States Forest Service maps, soils maps, federal and state land-use maps, county highway maps, and state fish and game biologists, the Fish and Wildlife Service completed the inventory in June 1954. All of the north central United States and the southeastern states were inventoried. In the rest of the country the inventory efforts were restricted to physiographic regions where good waterfowl habitats were most abundant. It was estimated that 90 percent or more of all wetlands used significantly by waterfowl were inventoried. The Fish and Wildlife Service published the results of the 1954 inventory as a national report (Shaw and Fredine 1956). It has been one of the most influential documents used in the protection of wetlands. The report noted the gross acreage, general distribution, and the relative importance to waterfowl of the 75 million acres of wetlands included in the inventory.

The first comprehensive, statistically reliable effort to estimate the size of the nation's wetlands was completed in 1982 by the Fish and Wildlife Service National Wetlands Inventory Project. This study, entitled "Status and Trends of Wetlands and Deepwater Habitats in the Conterminous United States," produced numbers on the total acreage of wetlands in the contiguous 48 states, their rate of disappearance over a 20-year interval, and the general cause for the losses.

In the mid-1970s, wetlands covered approximately five percent of the land surface of the contiguous United States (Frayer et al. 1983). Palustrine wetlands (inland freshwater wetlands) accounted for 93.7 million acres, of which 49.7 million were forested, 28.4 million were emergent, 10.6 million were scrub/ shrub, 4.4 million acres were small shallow ponds, and 0.6 million were in various other minor categories. Estuarine wetlands accounted for 5.2 million acres, of which 3.9 million were emergent wetlands, 0.6 million were mangrove and other estuarine scrub/shrubs, and 0.7 were intertidal non-vegetated areas. Of the original 215 million acres of wetlands, only 99 million acres still remained by the mid-1970's in the contiguous United States— a loss of 54 percent.

Between the mid-1950s and the mid-1970s, approximately 11 million acres of wetland were lost, while two million acres of new wetland were created. Thus, in that 20-year interval, a net loss of 9 million acres of wetland occurred. This acreage equates to an area about twice the size of New Jersey. Annual net wetland losses averaged 458,000 acres; of this, 440,000 acres were palustrine losses and 18,000 acres were estuarine wetland losses. This annual net loss equals an area about half the size of Rhode Island. Agricultural development was responsible for 87 percent of recent national wetland losses. Urban development and other development caused only eight percent and five percent of the losses, respectively (Tiner 1984). Other significant losses are outlined in the following paragraphs (Wilen 1985).

Recent Data
Recent data on wetland losses are site-specific and limited. Examples of wetland losses in various states are provided in Table 6.1, and a summary of coastal wetland losses is presented in Table 6.2.

Although many people believed that the conversion of bottomland hard-woods had essentially stopped by the mid 1970s, this apparently was not true. The Forest Service data indicate there were 6.9 million acres of bottomland hardwoods in 1982, a loss of 740,000 acres in approximately eight years. The bottomland hardwood region of the lower Mississippi alluvial plain is important for wintering waterfowl; the prairie pothole region is important for waterfowl breeding.

The Emergency Wetlands Resources Act of 1986 (P.L. 99-645) directs the Secretary of Interior, through the director of the Fish and Wildlife Service, to produce, by September 30, 1990 (and at ten-year intervals thereafter), a report to update and improve the information contained in the Fish and Wildlife Service 1982 report (Frayer et al. 1983). The act also requires the Fish and Wildlife Service to produce, by September 30, 1998, National Wetlands Inventory maps for the remainder of the contiguous United States and, as soon as practicable, wetland maps for Alaska and noncontiguous portions of the United States. Currently wetland maps are available for 60 percent of the contiguous states and 16 percent of Alaska.

WETLAND PROTECTION AUTHORITIES

Section 404, Clean Water Act, as Amended (P.L. 100-4)

The goal of the Clean Water Act (CWA) is to "restore and maintain the chemical, physical, and biological integrity of the nation's waters." The Clean Water Act provides for regulation and management of a variety of activities that affect water quality, from both point and non-point sources of pollution. Section 404 establishes a regulatory program to control the impact of the discharge of dredged or fill material from a point source to waters of the United States. The Army Corps of Engineers administers the regulatory program by evaluating permit applications under guidelines developed by the Environmental Protection Agency. The guidelines provide environmental standards for permit decisions and include the following policy statements: "Fundamental to these Guidelines is the precept that dredged or fill material should not be discharged into the aquatic ecosystem, unless it can be demonstrated that such a discharge will not have an unacceptable adverse impact either individually or in combination with known and/or probable impacts of other activities affecting the ecosystem of concern . . . filling operations in wetlands, are considered to be among the most severe environmental impacts covered by these guidelines."

From these two policy statements it is clear that the purpose of the Clean Water Act Section 404 regulatory program is to protect waters of the United States by carefully controlling the discharge of dredged or fill material. It is equally clear that the discharge of such material into special aquatic sites, including wetlands, is strongly discouraged. Indeed, the program is an aquatic habitat (including wetlands) protection program. Unfortunately, the law does

Table 6.1. Examples of Wetland Losses in Various States

State or Region	Original Wetlands (acres)	Today's Wetlands (acres)	Percent of Wetlands Lost	Source
Iowa's Natural Marshes	2,333,000	26,470	99	Bishop (1981, unpublished)
California	5,000,000	450,000	91	U. S. Fish and Wildlife Service (1977)
Nebraska's Rainwater Basin	94,000	8,460	91	Farrar (1982)
Mississippi River Alluvial Plain	24,000,000	5,200,000	78	MacDonald et al. (1979)
Michigan	11,200,000	3,200,000	71	Michigan Dept. of Nat. Res. (1982)
North Dakota	5,000,000	2,000,000	60	Elliott, U. S. Fish and Wildlife Service (unpublished)
Minnesota	18,400,000	8,700,000	53	University of Minnesota (1981)
Louisiana Forested Wetlands	11,300,000	5,635,000	50	Turner and Craig (1980)
Connecticut Coastal Marshes	30,000	15,000	50	Niering (1982)
North Carolina Pocosins [1]	2,500,000	1,503,000	40	Richardson et al. (1981)
South Dakota	2,000,000	1,300,000	35	Elliott, U. S. Fish and Wildlife Service (unpublished)
Wisconsin	10,000,000	6,750,000	32	Wisconsin Dept. of Nat. Res.(1976)

[1] Only 695,000 acres of pocosins remain undisturbed; the rest are partially drained, developed, or planned for development.

Source: Tiner 1984.

not regulate all activities that can destroy wetlands such as draining, clearing, and chemical pollution. Thus, the Clean Water Act provides an imperfect wetland protection program.

Wetland determinations. Historically, one of the most controversial aspects of the program has been wetland delineation. Under Section 404, the Corps regulates the discharge of dredged or fill material into waters of the United States. Typically, the landward extent of waters of the United States occurs at the wetland-upland boundary. In steep-banked situations and along saltwater wetlands this line of demarcation is relatively easy to determine. However, in fresh-water situations where the elevation changes slowly, it is often very difficult to determine the wetland-upland boundary. The Environmental Protection Agency has the ultimate authority to determine the extent of jurisdiction under the Clean Water Act; however, the Corps makes the vast majority of the determinations.

The Corps and the Environmental Protection Agency have an identical definition of wetlands: "The term wetlands means those areas that are inundated or saturated by surface or ground water at a frequency and duration sufficient to support, and that under normal circumstances do support, a prevalence of vegetation typically adapted for life in saturated soil conditions." However, the technical guidance that each agency uses to implement this definition is slightly different. Since the technical guidance is not mandatory and is somewhat complex, some variability among field offices occurs.

To further confuse the situation, the Department of Agriculture Soil Conservation Service also delineates wetlands pursuant to its authority under the Food Security Act of 1985. The Soil Conservation Service uses a virtually identical definition of wetlands, but yet another technical method. An intense effort to resolve these differences is currently the focus of a work group comprised of the Environmental Protection Agency, the Corps, the Soil Conservation Service, and the Fish and Wildlife Service. The goal of this effort is to reconcile the three technical approaches and produce a single joint methodology.

Resolution on the methodology will not eliminate all problems. However, it will bring a sorely needed element of consistency to the process of determining wetland boundaries. There is tremendous variation in the physical nature of wetlands across the nation. This is exemplified by the variability between such types as southeast bottomland hardwood forests, western riparian wetlands, New England bogs, and Alaskan tundra. Developing a manual that accurately delineates wetlands in such a variety of ecosystems is a great challenge.

Federal definitions and the three federal technical approaches to delineating wetlands are based on three parameters: vegetation, soils, and hydrology. While the hydrologic regime is vital, it is very difficult to accurately quantify. As a result, the technical methods rely more heavily on vegetation and soils. Each

Table 6.2. Summary of Coastal Wetland Losses in the Contiguous United States

State	Coastal Shoreline (miles)	Historical Coastal Wetlands (acres)	Present Coastal Wetlands (Acres)	Wetlands Lost (percent)
ATLANTIC COAST				
Maine	3,478	NA	135,000	NA
New Hampshire	131	NA	10,000	NA
Massachusetts	1,519	NA	90,000	50
Rhode Island	384	NA	6,966	NA
Connecticutt	681	NA	15,000	NA
New York	1,850	NA	1,640	NA
Pennsylvania	89	NA	1,640	11
New Jersey	1,792	363,000	289,500	20
Delaware	381	98,000	89,800	8
Maryland	3,190	175,000	165,000	6
Virginia	3,315	243,000	236,000	3
North Carolina	3,375	NA	175,725	NA
South Carolina	2,876	NA	504,500	NA
Georgia	2,344	NA	626,921	NA
GULF COAST				
Florida	8,426	1,184,344	1,169,344	1
Alabama	607	NA	39,700	NA
Mississippi	359	15,000+	8,594	43
Louisiana	7,721	2,445,000	1,885,000	23
Texas	3,359	1,153,000	553,026	52
WEST COAST				
California	3,427	381,000	114,000	70
Oregon	1,410	NA	117,100	NA
Washington	3,026	145,000	72,725	50
GREAT LAKES				
All States	11,240	NA	167,660	NA

Source: Dahl unpublished.

of the technical methods for delineation has a routine and comprehensive approach. The routine method is for relatively straightforward determinations, while the comprehensive method is for more complex situations.

Wetland delineation is a vital aspect of the permit process under Section 404, since it describes the geographic extent of the area regulated. The Corps does the vast majority of the determinations. The Environmental Protection Agency intervenes when it has determined that a special case involving difficult technical issues or policy implications exists. The agency infrequently makes such determinations, but often provides input to the Corps. The Corps conducts several thousand wetland delineations each year.

Number of permits issued. The Corps receives an average of 14,000 permit requests per year; of these, they issue approximately 10,000 permits per year and deny approximately 500 requests. The remainder are determined to be covered by some form of general permit, do not involve a regulated activity, or are withdrawn by the applicant. Of the 10,000 permits issued, approximately 8,500 involve Section 404 (the Corps also regulates activities under other authorities, which accounts for the remainder). A majority of the permits issued include modifications to the original permit application in response to environmental concerns raised by the Corps, the Environmental Protection Agency, or other federal or state agencies. In addition to these "individual" permits involving a public notice and an individual evaluation, the Corps estimates that approximately 80,000 activities are undertaken each year that are authorized by nationwide permits. Nationwide permits are a form of general permit intended to authorize activities that are similar in nature and involve only minimal cumulative or individual adverse environmental impacts. Under another form of general permit known as regional permits, the Corps authorizes approximately 20,000 activities per year. These permits involve activities with similar criteria as are applicable to nationwide permits, but on a regional basis.

Examples of activities authorized by general permits include bank stabilization of 500 feet or less provided no wetlands are impacted, minor road crossings involving less than 200 cubic yards of fill material below the ordinary high water line, and backfilling of seismic drill holes. Activities authorized by individual permits include such activities as site development fills, causeways, bank stabilization that involves fill in wetlands, and disposal of dredged material (for example, sidecasting of excavated material during construction of ditches to drain wetlands for agricultural conversion). Although more common recently, it remains uncommon for any development to occur in a wetland without filling first.

State and Local Authorities

Several states and some local governments have tried to bridge the regulatory void created by the limitations of Section 404 of the Clean Water Act. The state is close to the resource and has a vested interest in protecting its assets.

Where a state determines that the federal program is not adequately protecting a wetland, the state may implement its own program. Similarly, local governments have a vested interest in their wetland resources. Local governments have zoning authority as one of their most effective means of protecting wetlands. If a local government is made aware of the values of wetlands in maintenance of water quality and flood prevention, it may become interested in using its zoning authority to protect the wetland areas.

States can assume the Section 404 program from the federal government for certain waters in their states (all waters, including wetlands, that the Corps determines are not navigable for purposes of Section 10 of the Rivers and Harbors Act of 1899). In some states, this is a majority of the waterbodies and wetlands while in other states it is not. For example, coastal states typically can assume less than 50 percent of the program. Lack of funding discourages states from assuming the Section 404 program, and only one state (Michigan) has done so to date. The Environmental Protection Agency expects that a total of five to 10 states will assume Section 404 by 1995. In lieu of assumption, several states have developed wetland regulatory programs which often regulate a broader range of activities than does Section 404. These authorities are most effective when administered in a joint process with the Corps' regulatory program. Some states, such as Massachusetts, Connecticut, Florida, and Oregon, have strong wetland protection regulatory programs for all waters. Other states, such as Maryland, Virginia, and North Carolina, only have strong coastal programs, although each state is working on state inland wetland legislation.

States also have authority under Section 401 of the Clean Water Act and under Section 307 of the Coastal Zone Management Act in the case of coastal states, to certify whether a proposed activity complies with state water quality standards, or is consistent with the state's coastal zone management plan, respectively. Both of these actions by the state apply to activities regulated by the federal government and give the state an effective veto of the proposed activity. Coastal states have used their Section 307 authority effectively to protect wetlands for a number of years. Conversely, most states have not effectively used their Section 401 certification authority. The Environmental Protection Agency is now encouraging states to more fully use this authority and is preparing some guidance for the states.

Many states (Florida and New Jersey, for example) also have active acquisition programs to purchase or obtain easements on valuable natural resources. States use a variety of taxing authorities to obtain funds and typically prioritize the areas for aquisition.

"Swampbuster," Food Security Act of 1985 (P.L. 99-198)

As previously discussed, agriculture has contributed to greater than 80 percent of the nation's total wetland loss. A prime factor contributing to wetland losses for agricultural production were incentives provided by the Department of Agriculture to bring land into crop production through its various commodity programs. By allowing farmers to include crops produced on converted wetlands as part of their base acreage for various farm support programs, the Department of Agriculture in effect encouraged the loss of wetlands. The same incentives to produce agricultural commodities also contributed to commodity surpluses and depressed farm prices.

On December 23, 1985, the Food Security Act and its Wetland Conservation ("Swampbuster") provision was signed into law with the purpose of reducing wetland losses due to agricultural conversions (Titles XII, L., P.L. 99-198).

Under the Swampbuster provision, certain Department of Agriculture program benefits are withheld from persons who plant an agricultural commodity (annual crop) on wetlands converted after December 23, 1985 (the date the Food Security Act was enacted) unless otherwise exempted by the same authority. Programs covered are federal price and income supports, disaster payments, crop insurance, Farmers Home Administration loans, Commodity Credit Corporation storage payments, farm storage facility loans, and other programs under which payments are made with respect to agricultural commodities. About 80 percent of the nation's two million farmers participate in these programs.

The majority of Soil Conservation Service wetland determinations made to date are clustered in the upper Midwest. Of the total wetland determinations made since the Act, 27,399 have been reported from Minnesota, and 24,405 from North Dakota, so that these two states have made about half of the wetland determinations to date. A total of 57,183 converted wetland determinations have been made nationwide since "Swampbuster," comprising 57,139 acres.

The Soil Conservation Service has set a goal of December 31, 1991, to inventory wetlands on farms that have requested federal benefits where there is cropland or other areas with a high potential for conversion. Plans are to use a team wetland mapping approach to inventory wetlands in areas where potential for conversion is highest (for example, Prairie Pothole Region, Lower Mississippi Valley, Atlantic Coastal Plain, Central Valley of California, and so forth). A similar approach has already been taken in the Red River Valley of Minnesota and North Dakota, and is partly responsible for the large number of wetland determinations currently reported in those two states.

The team approach uses a two-to-four-person team to interpret office information such as Soil Conservation Service soil surveys, Agricultural Stabilization and Conservation Service color slides, eight-inch-per-mile black and white photos, and color infrared photography to make wetland determinations using collateral information such as National Wetland Inventory maps, state wetland maps, and United States Geological Survey topographic maps. The Soil Conservation Service, in consultation with the Fish and Wildlife Service, develops mapping conventions which are followed by the team in the mapping process. The teams are located in local Soil Conservation Service offices, and inventories are conducted on a county basis until all the priority wetlands are identified. Final determinations are made only after verification of the team's effort by the Soil Conservation Service district conservationist.

The Soil Conservation Service makes other wetland determinations as part of the process for self-certification by producers participating in Department of Agriculture programs. Before receiving such benefits, producers must certify their intent concerning improving drainage on wet areas or bringing new land into crop production. If the producer responds positively to either of these points, the Soil Conservation Service will make a wetland determination.

Other provisions of the Food Security Act are also being used to protect or enhance wetlands. Although currently wetlands cannot be entered into the Conservation Reserve Program unless they are part of a highly erodible field or are themselves highly erodible, wetlands can be created or restored on eligible lands under the shallow water area practice (CP-9). Through the sixth Conservation Reserve Program sign-up, approximately 2,500 acres of wetland have been created or restored through the CP-9 practice. An additional 7,500 acres of wetland have been restored on or adjacent to Conservation Reserve Program lands through assistance from the Fish and Wildlife Service.

Sections 1314 and 1318 of the Food Security Act authorizes the Farmers Home Administration to place conservation easements on Farmers Home Administration inventory property prior to resale as farmland, and to place conservation easements on certain Farmers Home Administration borrower properties in return for debt forgiveness. Through consultation with the Fish and Wildlife Service under the Food Security Act Section 1314 and Executive Order 11990, approximately 1,100 easements have been proposed for Farmers Home Administration inventory lands which includes over 100,000 acres of wetland to be restored, improved, or protected. Although the Food Security Act Section 1318 has yet to be fully implemented, approximately 118,000 delinquent borrowers may be affected by this provision which will provide yet another opportunity for wetland protection through conservation easement.

The North American Waterfowl Management Plan

After years of coordination and planning, the North American Waterfowl Management Plan was signed on May 14, 1986. This represented the beginning of an innovative international partnership in waterfowl and wetlands conservation that recognizes the international importance of the waterfowl resource.

During its 15-year planning horizon, the plan directs public and private involvement in a comprehensive endeavor to restore waterfowl populations to levels of the 1970s. It lists population goals for 37 species of ducks, geese, and swans. It sets population objectives for ducks at 62 million breeders and a fall flight of 100 million birds, a level common in the 1970s. The plan also lists objectives for geese and swans. Objectives for dabbling ducks include 8.7 million breeding mallards, 6.3 million breeding pintails and a wintering population index of 385,000 black ducks in the Atlantic and Mississippi flyways. Objectives for some diving ducks are 760,000 breeding redheads and 578,000 breeding canvasbacks. For geese, the objective is a post-hunting season level of six million for all populations except resident giant Canada geese, which probably number one million continentally (Nelson 1988).

The plan identifies the most important waterfowl breeding, staging, and wintering areas in the two countries and calls for their conservation and management. Partners in the plan intend to protect or enhance more than six million acres of prime waterfowl habitat in both the United States and Canada, enough to achieve the plan's population goals.

Achieving the Waterfowl Management Plan's population and habitat goals will guarantee that duck hunters, naturalists, and North America as a whole will continue to benefit from waterfowl and wetlands. A fall flight of 100 million birds will mean that about 2.2 million duck hunters could harvest 20 million ducks annually. Birdwatchers will continue to derive hours of enjoyment from observing waterfowl. Other species of fish and wildlife that depend on wetlands for food or shelter will also benefit. The plan will guarantee that North America gains strong values from wetland ecosystems, which serve as pollution filters, flood controls, and groundwater rechargers.

The plan does not replace the Flyway Council System or related federal and provincial cooperative management systems now in place, nor does it alter processes used in each country to establish waterfowl harvest regulations. Instead, it is implemented through regional "joint ventures" or teams of United States federal, state, and Canadian provincial agencies, and private conservation organizations.

In the United States, there are six joint ventures: the Atlantic Coast, California's Central Valley, Great Lakes/St. Lawrence Basin, Gulf Coast, Lower Mississippi Valley, and the Prairie Potholes and Parklands (Patterson and Nelson 1988).

The Atlantic Coast Joint Venture extends from Maine to South Carolina. It focuses on protection and enhancement of 60,000 additional acres of water-fowl habitat— 50,000 in the United States and 10,000 in Canada. Black duck migration and wintering habitat is a special concern here. Private landowners will also be encouraged to enhance their lands for waterfowl conservation.

California's Central Valley, a critical wintering area for waterfowl of the Pacific Flyway, is the site for the Plan's Central Valley Joint Venture. Partners in this joint venture intend to protect or enhance 80,000 additional acres in this unique ecosystem. Agricultural lands and other privately owned tracts are also targeted for improvement through cooperative ventures.

In the Great Lakes/St. Lawrence Basin Joint Venture, the goal is to protect or enhance 70,000 acres of waterfowl breeding and migrating habitat. Many wetland acres in this region have already been lost to industry, agriculture or urbanization. Initial plans for this joint venture include more than 10,000 identified acres in the United States and 50,000 acres in Canada to be improved and acquired for waterfowl conservation. On both sides of the border, planners are taking a new look at these goals and will likely redefine this venture to a larger operation.

The Gulf Coast Joint Venture focuses on waterfowl wintering habitat in the vast coastal marshes of the Gulf of Mexico from Texas to Florida. In this joint venture, 386,000 acres will be preserved, restored, or enhanced.

The Lower Mississippi Valley Joint Venture extends from the bottomland swamps of southern Illinois through the hardwood forests of the great rivers of the South. This region is prime habitat for wintering waterfowl. Partners in this joint venture will preserve, enhance, or restore 300,000 acres, in addition to enhancing habitats on private lands.

The Prairie Pothole Joint Venture targets prairie wetlands and their associated uplands for duck breeding habitat. This area has been heavily affected by agriculture. Partners in this joint venture project intend to preserve, protect, or enhance 4.7 million acres of duck breeding habitat— 1.1 million acres in the United States and 3.6 million acres in Canada's Prairie Habitat Joint Venture.

In Canada, four joint ventures have been organized: the Arctic Goose Joint Venture, the Black Duck Joint Venture, the Eastern Habitat Joint Venture, and the Prairie Habitat Joint Venture.

The Arctic Goose Joint Venture addresses populations of Arctic nesting geese in Canada. The Black Duck Joint Venture analyzes population problems of the Black Duck in both Canada and the United States. Partners in these two "species joint ventures" will work to determine limiting factors for populations and develop creative management strategies.

To meet the acreage and population goals as set forth in the plan, six basic strategies are being used. First, the partners in the plan are offering financial incentives to urge the farming community to protect waterfowl habitat. Second, plan participants are encouraging local governments and public land management agencies to regulate land use to prevent wetland destruction. A third method is acquisition of a limited number of unique areas that support large waterfowl populations or populations that are in severe decline. Fourth, partners in the plan are working to intensify management on public lands to increase productivity for waterfowl. Fifth, partners are encouraging public works projects, such as dam construction, to mitigate or prevent further habitat loss. Finally, plan participants are using educational campaigns to raise awareness about soil and water conservation and other wetlands issues.

A program this ambitious will be expensive to implement. Estimates for the 15-year implementation of the habitat components of the plan are 1.5 billion dollars. The plan will cost far more than the current United States and Canadian federal budgets for waterfowl conservation. Because large governmental budget increases are unlikely in the near future, private organizations and individuals who enjoy waterfowl are being asked to contribute part of the funds needed for the plan. The plan states that 75 percent of the funds should come from United States sources.

Status of implementation. Since the May 1986 signing, participants have taken decisive steps to implement the North American Waterfowl Management Plan. An international committee, the North American Waterfowl Management Plan Committee, was established in September 1986. This group has 12 members, six from the United States and six from Canada, who are coordinating work between the countries. The group will monitor and update the plan at five-year intervals, coordinate current work, and review new proposals and joint ventures.

The United States Implementation Board, a coalition of national conservation organizations and private foundations, was established on June 2, 1988. Organizations represented on the Board are: Ducks Unlimited, National Audubon Society, National Wildlife Federation, National Association of Conservation Districts, American Forest Foundation, International Association of Fish and Wildlife Agencies, The Wildlife Society, The Nature Conservancy, National Rifle Association, National Fish and Wildlife Foundation, Izaak Walton League, North American Wildlife Foundation, Wildlife Management Institute, American Farmland Trust, Land Trust Exchange, and Berry B. Brooks Foundation. The board has established action committees for fundraising, legislation, communications, and agricultural liaison to provide support in these areas.

At the grassroots level, the United States joint venture projects have working teams organized and led by Fish and Wildlife Service "joint venture coordinators." The coordinators are developing detailed plans with state and project goals. These plans will identify how the joint venture objectives will be met and who is sharing the responsibilities. The coordinators have also formed steering and technical committees to guide the progress of the joint ventures.

Already, projects at the state and local level are underway. In the Gulf Coast Joint Venture, private landowners are becoming active. Rice farmers have agreed to manage their lands as mini-refuges for wintering waterfowl, restricting hunting, and leaving water on the flooded fields throughout the winter months.

In the Central Valley Joint Venture, the National Fish and Wildlife Foundation has worked with the California Waterfowl Association to develop cooperative funding for a pilot project to offer incentives to farmers who leave rice and other grain stubble on fields for wintering waterfowl.

Partners in the Gulf Coast and Lower Mississippi Valley Joint Venture are encouraging landowners to restore wetlands that were drained and used for cattle grazing or cultivation of cereal grains. Work is proceeding on salt-water intrusion problems in the marshes along the Gulf Coast.

In the Prairie Pothole Joint Venture, lands are being acquired in the flooded watershed of Lake Thompson in South Dakota, an area that promises to be prime waterfowl habitat when the planned wetland restoration project is completed. Partners are contracting with landowners who agree to modify their farming practices to accommodate ducks, geese, and other water birds in the Lake Thompson project.

In all of the joint ventures, new enthusiasm is developing for putting more effort into existing programs. This includes ongoing acquisition and extension programs at the state and federal levels.

Private businesses are becoming active in the plan. For example, a large timber company has signed an agreement with the partners of the Gulf Coast Joint Venture that stipulates that the company will alter its logging practices, plant nesting cover on timber lands, and install nesting structures.

Overseeing implementation of the plan is the United States Office, established in the Twin Cities, Minnesota, during December 1987. The United States Office was formed to coordinate projects with Canada and Mexico and to direct implementation of the plan in the United States. The United States Office staff is also working to build support for the plan from other federal agencies, the national conservation community, and the public at large.

Several federal agencies are participating, or have discussed participating, in the plan. The Department of Defense, under the provisions of the Sikes Act, has offered to manage military lands for better waterfowl production. They are currently evaluating 30 military installments in 12 states for potential under this agreement, which will be funded by the Department of Defense through 1993. The Department of Agriculture Forest Service has a new 1.3 million dollar program called "Taking Wing." The Department of Interior Bureau of Land Management will begin work with the plan under the Prairie Pothole Joint Venture. Other federal agencies, including the Tennessee Valley Authority, the Soil Conservation Service, and the Farmers Home Administration, are more directly in the plan. To coordinate participation in the plan, an interagency working group is forming which will be comprised of the principal federal land management agencies.

In Canada, early implementation of the plan centered around the Prairie Habitat Joint Venture, which comprises the prairie provinces of Alberta, Saskatchewan, and Manitoba. The Prairie Habitat Joint Venture's Quill Lakes Project, located in southern Saskatchewan, has been Canada's "First Step Project." This is a fast-track effort to protect and enhance vital habitats in the Quill Lakes region, one of Saskatchewan's significant waterfowl production areas.

A matching grant program, initiated by the International Association of Fish and Wildlife Agencies, provided funding for the First-Step Project. In the

United States, twelve states, the National Fish and Wildlife Foundation, and Ducks Unlimited have raised four million dollars for this project. United States funding will be matched by Canadian organizations.

Pilot projects have been developed for the prairie provinces of Manitoba and Alberta. Partners in the Eastern Habitat Joint Venture have also identified priority areas and projects.

To make the plan a truly continental effort, United States and Canadian partners are seeking participation from Mexico. In March 1988 the three federal wildlife directors of Canada, the United States, and Mexico signed a working agreement.

Key participants in the North American Waterfowl Management Plan have identified three areas of concern for the near future: fundraising at all levels, legislative support at the state and national levels, and improved information and education.

The North American Waterfowl Management Plan is one of the most innovative natural resource management programs ever attempted, representing the conservation community's best and perhaps last chance to save our precious waterfowl resource. The plan's success depends upon creativity, commitment, and international cooperation. It is the conservation challenge of the remainder of the 20th century.

Tax Reform and Additional Laws

In addition to the Food Security Act, Section 404 of the Clean Water Act, and the North American Waterfowl Management Plan, the mid-1980s brought four other federal laws which strengthen the nation's commitment to wetland conservation. The Tax Reform Act of 1985 eliminates the deduction for most drainage expenses and eliminates the capital gains benefit on appreciation of the value of converted wetland. Both changes will reduce incentives to drain. The Water Resources Development Act of 1986, which authorized new Corps flood control and navigation projects, places more emphasis on the mitigation of wetland losses than any previous water bill.

The Emergency Wetlands Resources Act of 1986 refines several wetland protection programs. Most notable are increases in funding for wetland acquisition by the Fish and Wildlife Service. Finally, the Water Quality Act of 1987 authorizes grants to state and local governments for control of non-point water pollution. The ability of wetlands to enhance water quality will be considered in implementing this new authority.

Non-regulatory/Non-governmental Activities

There are a number of non-regulatory activities carried out by non-governmental groups across the country to protect wetlands. Many of these are acquisition programs. The Nature Conservancy has acquired millions of acres of land, including wetlands, often as a holding action until a government agency can purchase the land. Another active acquisition group is the Land Trust Exchange and member local land trusts. These private groups acquire property for a variety of purposes, including preservation of important landscapes (often including wetlands), conservation easements, and selective development. Frequently, the land trusts protect the most valuable portions of the landscape through selective development.

Other conservation groups such as the National Wildlife Federation, Sierra Club, and their local chapters also acquire certain areas that are of environmental importance. Ducks Unlimited is an international organization that develops and preserves vast acreages in Canada, primarily for waterfowl production. During recent years they have expanded their habitat program in the United States. In addition, substantial wetland acreage has been protected and managed, for waterfowl production, by both the Fish and Wildlife Service and the states.

Acquisition is not the only approach taken by non-governmental groups to protect wetlands. Local community groups have organized to protect a given wetland through educating the local leaders and property owners. When a strong constituency develops for protecting an area, it is usually listened to. Groups such as "Adopt a Wetland" have also been organized to clean up and manage a particular site.

Some farmers have also become involved in protecting wetlands both for their natural resource value and for economic benefit. During the severe drought of 1988 in the north central plains, the farmers who fared the best were those who had kept some of their acreage as wetland. They were able to graze their cattle longer and produce a modest hay crop. Other farmers are learning that keeping a percentage of wetlands on their land has other benefits, such as providing a source of predators to control rodents and even moderating the temperature in the immediate vicinity of the wetland enough to save crops during cold snaps.

CONCLUSION

As recently as 1984, federal policies and programs did not deal consistently with wetlands use. In fact, they affected wetland use in opposing ways (Office of Technology Assessment 1984). Since that time legislative and other attempts have been made to more closely align federal policies relating to wetlands. The Food Security Act of 1985 reduced incentives for wetland conversion for agricultural purposes, which had accounted for more than 80 percent of the nation's wetland loss. The Tax Reform Act of 1985 eliminated the deduction for most drainage expenses and eliminated the capital gains benefits on appreciation of the value of converted wetland.

Correspondingly, policies regulating wetland loss and wetland acquisition have been strengthened. The Water Resources Development Act of 1986, which authorized new flood control and navigation projects, places more emphasis on mitigation of wetland losses than any previous water bill. The Emergency Wetlands Resources Act of 1986 reinforced a number of the Fish and Wildlife Service wetland authorities, most notably the increased funding for wetland acquisition. The Clean Water Act of 1987 expanded the authority of federal, state, and local governments for wetland protection through increased funding for programs regulating wetland loss.

Efforts are currently under way to merge federal wetland delineation methods used by the Fish and Wildlife Service, the Environmental Protection Agency, the Corps, and the Soil Conservation Service, to enable a unified federal approach to identify wetlands. Other forms of federal cooperation include consultation between the Department of Agriculture agencies and the Fish and Wildlife Service for wetland protection under the Food Security Act, including development of rules and regulations, and operational procedures. Cooperative wetland acquisition and protection are major components of the North American Waterfowl Management Plan. It is clear, at least within the federal establishment, that efforts are underway to establish consistent wetland policies and create a better public understanding of government's role in wetland protection.

In 1984, the best available information indicated that the wetland conversion rate was approximately 300,000 acres per year. A question of utmost concern is whether the rate of wetland conversion has slowed with the implementation of the new and expanded wetland protection programs of the mid-1980s. The answer to that question is difficult to determine because recent data on this subject are site-specific and limited. However, at the recently held symposium, Protection of Wetlands from Agricultural Impacts (Stuber 1988), it was a general consensus that wetland drainage for agricultural purposes hasn't been significantly reduced. In fact, general observations were that there had been recent increases in wetland drainage particularly in the prairie pothole region. That consensus suggests that recent wetland protection authorities, particularly those addressing agricultural drainage, such as "Swampbuster," are not working effectively. However, because the mid-1980s wetland authorities are so recent, it is difficult to assess their effectiveness at this time. As with all new government programs, implementation lags somewhat. As we continue to study and analyze wetlands data gathered by the National Wetland Inventory, we will be able to determine the efficiency of these programs.

A looming question is whether the current set of wetland protection authorities are adequate even if properly implemented. For example, Section 404 of the Clean Water Act regulates only the discharge of dredged or fill material onto wetlands. Actions such as excavation, drainage, clearing, and flooding of wetlands that do not involve a discharge are not covered by Section 404 and are not regulated by the Corps. Yet such activities were responsible for the vast majority of inland wetland conversions between the mid-1950s and the mid-1970s. Correspondingly, another major federal wetland drainage deterrent, "Swampbuster," addresses only the conversion of wetland for the purpose of producing agricultural commodities. Persons who do not participate in Department of Agriculture programs are not affected by the authority, nor are program participants who drain wetlands, but do not produce an annual crop. At best, Section 404 and "Swampbuster" deal with wetland protection only indirectly. There are no other federal authorities which address wetland conversion in a more direct fashion. This raises the question: can we expect adequate wetland protection without federal authorities designed specifically for that purpose?

There is no way to predict whether new legislative mandates will be enacted to further protect wetland or their values. However, assuming existing authorities remain in place and improved implementation occurs, it is reasonable to expect that the rate of wetland conversion will decline. In fact, there has already been a decline in the rate of loss since the 1960s and 1970s. National Wetland Inventory data suggest that the highest rate of wetland loss since the turn of the century occurred in the 1960s and 1970s, with an average annual rate of loss of 478,000 acres. In the 1970s the rate slowed to about 300,000 acres per year, due to declining rates in agricultural drainage and perhaps government programs that regulate wetland use (Office of Technology Assessment 1984). It follows that the increased regulation and disincentives for wetland conversion along with the increased funding and program emphasis for wetland acquisition since the mid-1980s would contribute to even greater decline in the rate of wetland loss.

In addition, economic changes in the early 1980s have lowered the demand for agricultural products. The most discussed problem in agricultural land use is no longer the possibility of future shortages but the reality of current excess capacity. Projections of future developments made for the draft second Resources Conservation Act appraisal suggest that, barring any unforeseen events (such as changes in climate or massive disruption of historic trends), the shortages of productive capacity that seemed possible just a few years ago are not likely to occur. The change in outlook is based on relatively constant agricultural demands and considerable increases in productivity that agricultural researchers now believe will be achieved in both crop and livestock production (U.S. Department of Agriculture 1987).

Currently, there are approximately 421 million acres of cropland in the United States. Projections are that by the year 2030, the nation's demand for food and fiber could be met on as few as 220 million acres to as high as 347 million acres of cropland (U.S. Department of Agriculture 1987). Acknowledging that wetland conversion for agriculture is the primary factor in the loss of wetland, the future projections for agricultural products suggest that wetland drainage for agricultural production should be greatly diminished.

Despite favorable land use projections and recently enacted wetland protection mandates, there will still be incentives to drain. Wetlands can be excellent cropland, pastureland, and urban land if properly drained and treated. Wetland monitoring and evaluation must be employed in the future to continually define wetland status and trends. The need for additional federal, state, and local authorities to protect wetlands must continually be assessed based on status and trend analyses. Finally, private, state, and federal institutions must continue to improve cooperative efforts to recognize wetland values and develop effective working relationships to preserve our valuable wetland resource in the 21st century.

REFERENCES

Bishop, R.A. 1981. Iowa's wetlands. Proc. Iowa Acad. Sci. 88(1):11-16.

Brande, J. 1980. Worthless, valuable or what? An Appraisal of Wetlands. Journal of Soil and Water Conservation, 35(1):12-16.

Dahl, Thomas E. 1988. Wetland Losses in the Coastal United States. Unpublished report. USDI Fish and Wildlife Service, Washington, D.C. 55 pp.

Elliott, C.G. 1912. Engineering for land drainage. John Wiley and Sons, New York, New York.

Farrar, J. 1982. The Rainwater Basin: Nebraska's Vanishing Wetlands, Nebraska Game and Parks Commission. 15 pp.

Ferrigno, F., L. Widjeskog, and S. Toth. 1973. Marsh destruction. N.J. Pittman-Robertson Report. Project W-53-R-1, Job I-G. 20 pp.

Frayer, W.E., T.J. Monahan, D.C. Bowden, and F.A. Graybill. 1983. Status and trends of wetlands and deepwater habitats in the conterminous United States. 1950s to 1970s. Dept. of Forest and Wood Sciences, Colorado State University, Ft. Collins, Co. 32 pp.

Fruge, D.W. 1982. Effects of wetland deterioration on the fish and wildlife resources of coastal Louisiana. In D.F. Boesch (ed). Proceedings of the Conference on Coastal Erosion and Wetland Modification in Louisiana: Causes, Consequences, and Options. U.S. Fish and Wildlife Service. FWS/OBS-82/59. pp. 99-107.

Great Lakes River Basin Commission. 1981. Wetlands. Great Lakes Communicator (June) Vol. 11(9).

Haddock, J.L. and L.W. DeBates. 1969. Report on drainage trends in the Prairie Pothole Region of Minnesota, North Dakota and South Dakota. U.S. Fish and Wildlife Service, Minneapolis, Minnesota. 8 pp.

Hardisky, M.A. and V. Klemas. 1983. Tidal wetlands natural and human-made changes from 1973 to 1979 in Delaware: mapping techniques and results. Envir. Manage. 7(4): 1-6.

Kentucky Department of Fish and Wildlife Resources. 1983. February 23 letter from C.E. Kays, Commissioner to B. Wilen, U.S. Fish and Wildlife Service. 2 pp.

MacDonald, P.O., W.E. Frayer, and J.K. Clauser. 1979. Documentation, Chronology, and Future Projects of Bottomland Hardwood Habitat Loss in the Lower Mississippi Alluvial Plain. Vol.I: Basic Report. U.S. Fish and Wildlife Service, Ecological Services, Vicksburg, Mississippi. pp. 1-33.

Michigan Department of Natural Resources. 1982. Michigan's Wetlands. Lansing, MI. 47 pp.

Nelson, H.K. 1988. Status Report on U.S. Implementation of the North American Waterfowl Management Plan. Transactions of the 78th Annual Meeting of the International Association of Fish and Wildlife Agencies. Toronto, Ontario, Sept. 1988.

Office of Technology Assessment. 1984. Wetlands: Their Use and Regulation. U.S. Government Printing Office, Washington, D.C. 208 pp.

Patterson, J.H. and H.K. Nelson. 1988 Progress in Implementing the North American Waterfowl Management Plan. Transactions of the 53rd North American Wildlife and Natural Resources Conference (1988). Wildlife Management Institute, Washington, D.C. pp. 24-28.

Redelfs, A.E. 1983. Wetlands values and losses in the United States. M.S. Thesis. Oklahoma State University, Stillwater. p. 143

Richardson, C.J., R. Evans, and D. Carr. 1981. Pocosins; an ecosystem in transition. In C.J. Richardson (ed). Pocosin Wetlands. Hutchinson Ross Publishing Co., Stroudsburg, Pennsylvania. pp 3-19.

Roe, H.R., and Q.C. Ayres. 1954. Engineering for agricultural drainage. McGraw-Hill Book Co., New York, N.Y.

Shaw, S.P., and C.G. Fredinc. 1956. Wetlands of the United States. Fish and Wildlife Service, U.S. Department of Interior, Washington, D.C., Circ. 39. 67 pp.

Stuber, P.J. (Symposium Coordinator) 1988. Proceedings of the National Symposium on the Protection of Wetlands from Agricultural Impacts. Fish and Wildlife Service, U.S. Department of Interior, Washington, D.C. Biological Report, 88(16). 221 pp.

Tiner, R.W. 1984. Wetlands of the United States: Current status and recent trends. Fish and Wildlife Service, U.S. Department of the Interior, Washington, D.C. 59 pp.

Tiner, R.W. 1987. Mid-Atlantic Wetlands: A disappearing natural treasure. Fish and Wildlife Service, National Wetlands Inventory, U.S. Department of Interior, Newton Corner, Mass. p. 28.

Turner, R.E. and N.J. Craig. 1980. Recent area changes in Louisiana's forested wetland habitat. Proc. of the Louisiana Acad. Sci. Vol. XL III: pp. 61-68.

United States Department of Agriculture. 1987. The Second RCA Appraisal (Review Draft). U.S. Government Printing Office. 351 pp.

United States Department of Interior and Environment Canada. 1986. North American Waterfowl Management Plan. Washington, D.C. 1988.

United States Fish and Wildlife Service. 1977. Concept Plan for Waterfowl Wintering Habitat Preservation. Central Valley California. Region 1, Portland, Oregon. 116 pp. plus appendices.

United States Fish and Wildlife Service. 1982. Agricultural resources and wetland changes 1972-1980, Palm Beach County, Florida. National Wetlands Inventory, St. Petersburg, Florida. Unpublished mimeo. 8 pp.

University of Minnesota, Center for Urban and Regional Affairs. 1981. Thematic Maps: Presettlement wetlands of Minnesota and available wetlands for bioenergy purposes. Prepared for Minnesota Energy Agency.

Weller, M.W. 1981. Freshwater Marshes: Ecology and Wildlife Management. University of Minnesota Press. 146 pp.

Wilen, B.O. 1985. Status and trends of wetlands and deepwater habitats in the conterminous United States, 1950s to 1970s. Proceedings of Fifth International Waterfowl Symposium, Feb. 15-17, 1985. Kansas City, Missouri. pp. 32-42.

Wilen, B.O. (in press). Status and trends of U.S. wetlands and deepwater habitats. Proceedings of the International Forested Wetlands Resource: Identification and Inventory Sept. 19-22, 1988, Baton Rouge, Louisiana, 41 pp.

Wisconsin Department of Natural Resources. 1976. Wetland Use in Wisconsin: Historical Perspective and Present Picture. Division of Environmental Standards, Water Quality Planning Section. 48 pp.

Wooten, H.H., and L.A. Jones. 1955. The history of our drainage enterprises in water, The Yearbook of Agriculture, USDA, Washington, D.C. pp. 147-156.

CHAPTER 7

Water Resources

Kenneth D. Frederick

NATURE OF THE RESOURCE

The hydrological cycle makes water a truly renewable resource that can be used and re-used almost indefinitely. Driven by energy from the sun, water constantly circulates from the seas, lakes, and streams (through evaporation) or the plants (through transpiration) to the atmosphere and back to the earth (through precipitation). Regardless of how much we use it, the quantity of water in the cycle remains essentially unchanged. Moreover, the evaporative process removes salts and other impurities that may be acquired as water precipitates out of the atmosphere, infiltrates through the soil, mixes with impure surface and ground waters, or is used to sustain or enrich life on the planet.

The quantities of water involved are enormous. Approximately 40,000 billion gallons per day of water vapor pass in the atmosphere over the conterminous United States. On an average day more than 10 percent of this vapor condenses and precipitates as rain, snow, or hail. Average annual precipitation is nearly 30 inches. Approximately two-thirds of the 4,200 billion gallons per day of precipitation is returned to the atmosphere through evapotranspiration; the remaining 1,400 billion gallons comprise the renewable water supply of the conterminous United States which flows into the nation's lakes, rivers, ground-water aquifers, and eventually the oceans (United States Geological Survey 1984).

These renewable supplies represent only part of the water potentially available for use. Much larger quantities of fresh water are stored in the nation's surface and ground-water reservoirs. Nearly 150,000 billion gallons (about 450 million acre-feet) are stored in large (50 acre-feet or more) reservoirs, and at least 200 times this amount are stored in aquifers within 2,500 feet of the surface (United States Water Resources Council 1978).

Although human activities have negligible impact on the quantity of water

143

in the entire system, they have major impacts on the usable supply and its potential value for meeting human needs. Timing, location, reliability, and quality are important dimensions of the potential value of supplies. Investments in dams, reservoirs, and conveyance facilities that help control the timing and location of the water increase supplies while reducing potential damages from floods and other unusual hydrologic events. On the other hand, many activities have negative or highly uncertain impacts on supplies. Our lakes and streams are degraded when they are used as waste disposal sites; water resources may also be degraded by wastes initially deposited on the land or in the atmosphere. For instance, air pollution resulting from automobile, power plant, and factory emissions initiates chemical processes that increase the acidity of precipitation and, consequently, of our lakes. And chemicals left on the land from farming or other activities are likely to travel by water into surface or ground-water reservoirs. Moreover, human-induced changes in land use, vegetation, and, most ominously, the climate can alter the hydrologic cycle itself. (For examples see United States Geological Survey 1984.)

WATER USE

Water provides many valuable services. Some are provided without ever removing water from a stream or reservoir. Indeed, instream uses such as hydropower production, recreation, navigation, and fish and wildlife habitat depend on maintaining stream flows and lake levels. Offstream uses include withdrawals from a ground or surface water source for public, agricultural, domestic, commercial, industrial, mining, and thermoelectric activities. Most of the water withdrawn for these activities is subsequently returned to a source where it can be re-used. Consumptive use is the portion that is withdrawn and not returned to a usable ground or surface water source. Even when water is not consumptively used, the quality, location, and timing of the available supply are altered, usually adversely, by the withdrawal.

Two activities, irrigation and thermoelectricity (water used in the production of electric power generated with fossil fuel, geothermal, or nuclear energy), dominate offstream water use (See Table 7.1). Irrigation alone accounted for 40 percent of the fresh-water withdrawals and 80 percent of the consumptive use. Thermoelectric uses accounted for 39 percent of the fresh water and 92 percent of the saline-water withdrawals. However, since most of the water used to produce thermoelectric power is available for re-use, this activity accounted for less than five percent of the consumptive use of fresh water. No other activity accounted for more than a small percentage of the nation's offstream water use. Domestic use— which includes drinking, food preparation, bathing, washing clothes and dishes, flushing toilets, and watering lawns and gardens— accounted

Table 7.1. Offstream Water Use for the Forty-eight Conterminous States by Sector, 1985

(billions of gallons per day)

Category of Use	Withdrawals		Consumptive use	
	Fresh	Saline	Fresh	Saline
Public use and losses [a]	3.8			
Domestic	23.9		5.6	
Commercial	6.8		1.2	
Irrigation	135.9		73.7	
Livestock	4.3		2.4	
Industrial	27.9	3.5	4.2	1.0
Mining	2.7	0.8	0.7	0.3
Thermoelectric	130.4	53.0	4.3	1.8
Total [b]	336.3	57.3	92.1	3.1

[a] Public supply, which refers to water withdrawn by public and private water suppliers and delivered to multiple users, totaled 35.8 bgd in 1985. The quantities delivered to domesic, commercial, industrial, and thermoelectric uses are included along with self-supplied withdrawals under their respective categories of use. The residual which is referred to as public use and losses includes water for firefighting, street washing, municipal parks, swimming pools, and losses in the collection and distribution system.

[b] The figures may not add to totals due to independent rounding.

Source: Wayne B. Solley, Charles F. Merk, and Robert Pierce, **Estimated Use of Water in the United States in 1985**, U.S. Geological Survey Circular 1004 (Washington, D.C., GPO, 1988).

for seven percent of fresh-water withdrawals and six percent of consumptive use. Fresh water for industrial processing, washing, and cooling accounted for eight percent of withdrawals and five percent of consumptive use.

SUPPLY PROBLEMS

A comparison of national offstream water use and the average renewable supply provides no indication of actual or potential water supply problems. Fresh-water withdrawals from both ground and surface sources totaled 336 billion gallons per day, less than one-quarter of the 1,400 billion gallons per day of renewable supply. Consumptive uses were less than seven percent of the average renewable supply.

This comparison, however, masks important considerations. First, water problems are local or regional in nature and there are vast regional differences in the use and supply of water. Second, water demands are both time- and location-specific, and seasonal as well as annual variations in precipitation pose problems for matching demands with available supplies. Third, water use in some regions depends on nonrenewable ground-water stocks. Fourth, both economic and environmental costs of developing additional supplies for offstream use have increased sharply in recent decades. Fifth, although instream water demands are difficult to quantify, they are large, growing, and often highly competitive with withdrawal and other instream uses. And sixth, the quality of some supplies has deteriorated to the point that the water is of little value, and the threats to the quality of the nation's waters are growing.

Regional Differences

Average annual precipitation varies widely by region. Although the average is 30 inches, average annual precipitation is less than 20 inches in about one-third of the nation and in some desert areas is only a few tenths of an inch. At the other extreme, some locations in Hawaii receive nearly 400 inches of rainfall per year (U.S. Geological Survey 1986).

Runoff, "precipitation that falls on land and eventually reaches stream channels, lakes, ponds, or wetlands" (U.S. Geological Survey 1986), provides a better measure than precipitation of a region's usable renewable supply. Nationally, annual runoff amounts to about one-third of precipitation; the rest is quickly evaporated and transpired. But the rate of loss through evapotranspiration differs widely among regions depending on a number of factors including temperature, topography, and the quantity and timing of the precipitation. Although potential evapotranspiration can exceed 70 inches per year in arid and semiarid regions, actual losses are limited by available precipitation. Annual runoff in such areas may be 1 inch or less unless rainfall is concentrated in a few large storms. In contrast, in some small basins in the eastern United States runoff exceeds 40 inches per year (U.S. Geological Survey 1986).

There are also major regional differences in water use. Daily per capita fresh-water withdrawals in 1985 ranged from 152 gallons in Rhode Island to 22,200 gallons in Idaho. Relative differences in per capita consumptive use of fresh water between these two states (24 versus 5,264 gallons per day) are even greater. While these states represent the extremes, they reflect broad regional differences as to offstream water use. Per capita fresh-water withdrawals averaged 2,214 gallons per day in the 17 western states, more than twice the average for the 31 eastern states. Average per capita consumptive use was 1,005 gallons per day in the West, more than eight times the level in the East (Solley et al. 1988).

Comparisons of water supply and use data for states or regions reveal a striking fact— offstream water use tends to be much higher in the areas with the lowest levels of precipitation and runoff. For instance, even though the 17 western states receive only about one-fourth the rainfall per acre, their withdrawals are nearly double and their consumptive use is nearly 10 times the per capita use in the East (Frederick 1986). This inverse relationship between precipitation and water use is largely attributable to regional differences in the relative importance of irrigation and water prices.

Variability of Supply

The 1,400 billion gallons per day of renewable water supply for the conterminous 48 states as well as the regional runoff figures which make up this total are long-term averages based on past hydrological conditions. Actual runoff on any given day is likely to differ greatly from the average as a result of both seasonal and annual variations.

Seasonal Variations

Rivers tend to have seasonal-flow patterns characteristic of their particular geographic region. The seasonal changes can be very large; the ratio of maximum to minimum stream flow within a normal year can exceed 500 to 1 (U.S. Water Resources Council 1978). In areas where temperatures generally remain above freezing, seasonal run-off corresponds closely to precipitation. For the southern Pacific coastal region, this implies heavy flows during the winter months (about 70 percent of the flow of the Cuyama River near Santa Maria, California comes in February and March). In Florida, precipitation and runoff are highest in the summer and early fall (nearly 70 percent of the flow of Fisheating Creek at Palmdale, Florida is from July to October). In contrast, in the higher latitudes and altitudes, runoff comes largely from the spring melting of snow and ice (more than 60 percent of the runoff in the Boise River near Twin Springs, Idaho comes from April to June) (U.S. Geological Survey 1986).

Large unregulated seasonal variations in run-off may result in flood damages during peak flows and shortages during low-flow periods. In some cases, however, seasonal variations can be favorable such as when high runoff coincides with the peak demand for irrigation water.

Annual Variations

Changing weather patterns produce uncertainty and fluctuations in annual precipitation and temperatures. These fluctuations result in even larger percentage changes in runoff, especially in arid and semiarid areas where relatively small changes in precipitation can lead to large changes in runoff. For example, a 20 percent increase in annual precipitation might increase runoff by 150 percent in a region with 20 inches annual rainfall and by 30 percent in a region with 50 inches (U.S. Geological Survey 1986).

Variations in annual stream flow are usually expressed in terms of the flow that is expected to be exceeded in a certain percentage of years. The ratio of very high flows (those exceeded in only five of every 100 years) to very low flows (those exceeded in 95 of every 100 years) is one indication of annual variability. The ratio for the conterminous 48 states is 2.9. But among the 18 water resource regions the ratio varies from 22.0 in the Rio Grande to 1.4 in the lower Colorado (U.S. Water Resources Council 1978). Moreover, inter-annual changes in the run-off for any given month are generally greater than the annual changes because monthly precipitation and temperature vary widely among years.

The magnitude and uncertainty of the variations create management problems. Storage helps even out and, thereby, increases the dependable flow of water and reduces the risk of flooding. Yet, as is noted in the next section, there are obstacles to increasing dependable supplies with additional dams and reservoirs. Furthermore, there may be conflicts between managing the existing storage to protect against drought or floods. For instance, filling a reservoir early in the high runoff season provides maximum protection against subsequent drought but leaves minimum capacity to prevent flooding.

Ground-Water Use

As noted above, the amount of water in the nation's aquifers (bodies of unconsolidated materials such as sand, gravel, and soil that are saturated with water and sufficiently permeable to produce water in useful quantities) far exceeds the annual levels of water use and even the renewable supply. Aquifers are either confined (that is, overlain by layers of impermeable material) or unconfined. Since confined aquifers receive little or no recharge, the water in them is essentially a stock resource which can be depleted through pumping. Most ground-water pumping, however, is from unconfined aquifers which are an integral part of the hydrologic cycle. Indeed, seepage from unconfined aquifers supplies about 30 percent of the nation's stream flow, and these aquifers are recharged by the downward percolation of precipitation, snowmelt, or water from streams, canals, and reservoirs (U.S. Water Resources Council 1978). Recharge and discharge rates vary with seasonal and annual changes in runoff and precipitation as well as with withdrawals from ground and surface waters. Under natural conditions an equilibrium is established in which long-term discharge equals long-term recharge.

Pumping disrupts an aquifer's natural equilibrium. As water is withdrawn, ground-water levels decline. This decline causes the rate of natural discharge from the aquifer to fall and it may cause the rate of recharge to rise. If the rate of pumping is not too high, a new equilibrium is established in which pumping is balanced by the new natural discharge and recharge rates. On the other hand, if pumping exceeds the natural adjustments, the ground-water table falls until economic or other factors lead to a decline in the rate of pumping.

Ground-water mining can go on for decades in some areas. However, as the quantity of fresh water stored in an aquifer declines, one or more of several factors will eventually reduce the rate of pumping. A declining ground-water table results in higher pumping lifts and lower well yields, both of which result in higher pumping costs. Long before the water is gone, rising costs will reduce and eventually eliminate the mining. Other areas may be less well suited to long-term ground-water mining. For instance, in coastal as well as some inland areas the fresh water may be replaced by the intrusion of saline water. Even though there may be no net loss of water, deterioration in its quality may make the aquifer unusable for most purposes. Alternatively, as water is withdrawn, the materials making up the aquifer may become compacted resulting in an irreversible loss of storage capacity and subsidence of the land surface.

Ground water is the source of more than one-fifth of the nation's fresh-water withdrawals. It has become a principal source of supply in many areas rather than just a supplemental source to maintain levels of use during dry periods. Consequently, significant ground-water mining is occurring in many areas of the nation, especially in the West. Ground-water storage in the Mississippi, Missouri, and four other western water resource regions was depleted at a rate of 18.2 billion gallons per day as of 1980. Depletion as a percentage of consumptive use was 37 percent in the Texas-Gulf water-resource region, 33 percent in the Arkansas-White-Red, and 19 percent in the Colorado (U.S. Geological Survey 1984). In 1983 ground-water levels declined from six inches to over five feet under more than 14 million irrigated acres in 11 states. This acreage amounted to about 45 percent of the total under irrigation in these states, and this excludes about two million acres in the Texas High Plains that had been taken out of irrigation since the mid 1970s largely because of declining ground-water levels (Sloggett and Dickason 1986).

The *National Water Summary 1983* listed saline-water intrusion as a problem in thirty-four states (U.S. Geological Survey 1984). Important drinking and irrigation supplies are at risk in many of these states. Perhaps the most serious situation is on Long Island where the drinking water of millions of people is threatened. With the imposition of temporary pumping restrictions more than 40 years ago, salt-water intrusion is hardly a new problem. These early actions, however, have not kept the problem from becoming more serious or the restrictions from becoming more extensive. Limitations on ground-water use imposed in 1986 are likely to severely curtail development in several Long Island counties, but they are not likely to eliminate further damage to the aquifer from saline intrusion. Seven New Jersey counties, the Florida cities of Miami, Tampa, and Jacksonville, and California's southern and central coasts were also among the listed problem areas. In California's Central Valley, the nation's most productive agricultural area, pumping threatens to draw an extensive underlying saline water body up into the valley's fresh-water aquifer.

Land subsidence stemming from ground-water pumping results in a permanent loss of storage capacity. Although this loss does not preclude future pumping from an aquifer, the damages that often accompany subsidence make it prudent to regulate ground-water use in subsidence-prone areas. Likely effects of subsidence include structural damage to buildings, roads, bridges, buried cables, well casings, and increased susceptibility to flood damage in coastal areas that sink below sea level. Areas in California (the Santa Clara and Central valleys), Nevada (the city of Las Vegas), and Texas (the Houston-Galveston area) are among those reporting costly subsidence problems (U.S. Geological Survey 1984).

Sinkholes, which usually result from a sudden collapse of the underlying rock after it has been dissolved and weakened by circulating water, develop from natural processes. There is evidence, however, that ground-water pumping can accelerate their development. Human activities are suspected of contributing to the formation of sinkholes in Alabama, Florida, Georgia, Tennessee, Pennsylvania, and Missouri; the linkages between sinkholes and pumping are particularly strong in Florida. Although their impacts are localized, sinkholes can involve major property damage as well as loss of life (U.S. Geological Survey 1984).

Rising Costs

Long-term average runoff (1,400 billion gallons per day for the conterminous 48 states) is the theoretical upper limit for sustainable supply. An enormous amount of storage capacity without any attendant increase in evaporation losses would be needed to approach this limit. With the reservoir capacity as of 1975, only about 675 billion gallons per day of this limit were actually available in 95 years out of 100 (U.S. Water Resources Council 1978).

About 450 million of the 1,200 million acre-feet potential reservoir capacity estimated to exist in the conterminous 48 states has been developed (U.S. Geological Survey 1984). The high costs of developing additional storage, the losses in capacity due to siltation, and the increased evaporation that accompanies surface storage all suggest that increases in secure water supplies will be slow in coming. Both the economic and the environmental costs of developing new supplies have risen sharply in recent decades, and further increases appear inevitable for several reasons.

The best reservoir sites were developed first. Consequently, successive additions to a basin's storage capacity generally require larger and larger investments in dams. A study of decadal changes in reservoir storage capacity per unit volume of dams for the 100 largest dams in the United States illustrates this application of the law of diminishing returns. The average reservoir capacity (in acre-feet) produced per cubic yard of dam declined from 10.4 in the 1920s and earlier to 2.1 in the 1930s, 0.52 in the 1940s, 0.45 in the 1950s, and 0.29 in the 1960s (U.S. Geological Survey 1984).

The quantity of water controlled by a unit of storage is also subject to the law of diminishing returns. As W.B. Langbein (1959) demonstrated, "each successive increment of control (safe yield) requires a larger amount of reservoir storage space than the preceding increment." Moreover, because evaporation increases along with the surface area of the reservoirs, at some point the gains from additional storage are more than offset by increasing evaporation losses. The Colorado Basin, which has reservoir capacity equivalent to 403 percent of annual renewable supply, is already close to the point of diminishing net yields (U.S. Geological Survey 1984).

The opportunity costs of (that is, the benefits forgone by) storing and diverting water are rising due to both supply and demand pressures. On the supply side, as withdrawals reduce stream flow and make the resource scarcer, the marginal values of the remaining flows increase. Demand for the services provided by instream flows is also increasing as a consequence of population and income growth and the increasing importance being given to environmental values.

High economic and environmental costs have slowed the rate of construction of surface reservoirs for meeting municipal, industrial, and agricultural water demands. Yet, an estimated 1.4 to 1.5 million acre-feet of storage capacity is permanently lost each year due to the filling of lakes and reservoirs with sediment (Guldin 1988). Between 1970 and 1980 available storage declined from the equivalence of 216 to 201 days of withdrawals. This decline, the first in the six decades for which records are available, implies an increased risk of deficiencies for offstream use (U.S. Geological Survey 1984).

Instream Uses
Assessing the adequacy of water resources solely in terms of meeting offstream uses ignores some potentially valuable instream uses. Until recently, however, most water planners and western water law did just that. Only within the last two decades have concerns over instream water values emerged as an important consideration in water development decisions.

The earliest state water laws were based on the common law doctrine of riparian rights, which gives owners of land adjacent to a lake or stream rights to use water bordering their property. The rights are inseparable from the land and limited to uses that do not unduly inconvenience other riparian owners. By protecting the interests of downstream riparian landowners, this doctrine also provides some protection to instream flows.

The riparian doctrine was an obstacle to developing secure supplies for offstream use in regions where there are few streams and their flows are uncertain. Development in the arid and semiarid western states depended on being able to divert assured supplies of water beyond riparian lands. Thus, the 17 western states abandoned or at least modified the riparian doctrine in favor of the doctrine of prior appropriation. Appropriative rights are acquired by withdrawing water from a stream and putting it to a beneficial use. Priority in use is based on the principle of "first-in-time, first-in-right." Even though enjoyment of the beauty of free-flowing streams and the fish and wildlife habitat they support may have been the earliest uses of many western streams, water rights were not granted to protect such uses.

In fulfilling its responsibility to maintain navigation on the nation's waterways, the federal government provided some protection for the flows of the larger rivers. But it has only been within the last two decades that any of the western states have modified their laws to provide for instream rights. Interest in as well as the legal means of protecting instream values has grown rapidly in the 1980s. Minimum stream-flow legislation has been adopted or proposed in several states. Some courts have recognized the Public Trust doctrine as a means to reconsider the legality of water withdrawals that threaten aquatic environments, the preservation of which is in the public interest (Scott 1986). And most importantly, the National Environmental Policy Act of 1969 requires that environmental considerations be taken into account in planning and constructing new water projects. As a result, environmental values are now an important and sometimes even the deciding factor in water development decisions.

The first comprehensive effort to evaluate the nation's instream flow conditions and needs was undertaken as part of the Second National Water Assessment. Instream-flow need was defined as "that amount of water flowing through a natural stream channel needed to sustain the instream values at an acceptable level." The relevant values included "fish and wildlife population maintenance, outdoor recreation activities, navigation, hydroelectric generation, waste assimilation (sometimes termed water quality), conveyance to downstream points of diversion, and ecosystem maintenance that includes freshwater recruitment to the estuaries and riparian vegetation and flood-plain wetlands" (U.S. Water Resources Council 1978). But there was no attempt to estimate the values that would be gained from a given stream flow or to estimate how the values might be affected by changes in the flow. This would have been a truly monumental and probably an impractical task. Instead, the assessment implicitly assumed the complementary relationship among all instream uses and focused on quantifying the minimum flow needs of two dominant uses— navigation and fish and wildlife. Since the fish and wildlife use was dominant in all subregions, this became the proxy for all instream uses. In spite of its shortcomings, this analysis provided some useful insights as to the adequacy of the nation's rivers to meet the combined instream and offstream uses.

Total water use, defined as the sum of consumptive use and estimated minimum instream needs, was estimated at about 86 percent of average annual stream flow as of 1975 (U.S. Water Resources Council 1978). As noted earlier, however, national aggregates and annual averages mask important considerations in evaluating the adequacy of supplies. In four western water resource regions estimated total water use actually exceeded the average renewable supply. Further disaggregation suggests total water use exceeded the mean annual stream flow in 24 western water-resource subregions covering an area from central and southern California through Nevada, most of Arizona, New Mexico, eastern Colorado, and the western sections of Texas, Oklahoma, Kansas, and Nebraska (Frederick and Hanson 1982). For the time being, the depletion of ground-water stocks are generally meeting the shortfalls. Eventually, however, water use will drop into line with long-term renewable supply.

Water Quality
The adequacy of supplies to meet the varied demands placed upon them depends on the quality as well as the quantity of the resource. Water is rarely pure; all ground and surface water naturally contains minerals dissolved from soil and rock, and even precipitation usually contains impurities picked up in the atmosphere. Fortunately, very few uses require pure water and the natural concentrations of minerals (commonly referred to as salts) and other contaminants in the nation's rivers, lakes, and aquifers are generally within acceptable ranges for most uses. Anthropogenic factors, however, contribute a wide variety of contaminants (including toxics, bacteria, nutrients, biochemical oxygen demand, sediment, and salts) which have reduced and in some cases destroyed the utility of important water supplies.

Deterioration of the quality of streams and lakes can threaten human health, the viability of aquatic systems, and the ability of the resources to support activities such as irrigation and recreation. In extreme cases water bodies that were once coveted as sources of scenic beauty can be converted into malodorous eyesores. Contamination of ground water, which is used for drinking by more than half of the nation's population, poses major health risks that can be very expensive to remedy.

Water quality might be defined and evaluated in several ways — the effluents discharged into a water body; the chemical, physical, and biological attributes of the water; the ability of the water to serve designated uses; and the socioeconomic benefits and costs associated with using the water for specific uses. Assessments of the quality of the nation's waters vary depending on the approach taken (United States General Accounting Office 1986a). The following discussions of surface and ground-water quality draw primarily on the Environmental Protection Agency's *National Water Quality Inventory: 1986 Report to Congress* (1987). This national inventory is based on state reports assessing whether or not their water resources are capable of fulfilling the uses the state has designated for them.

Surface-Water Quality

Results of the 1986 *National Water Quality Inventory* (summarized in Table 7.2) suggest that water quality was sufficient to support the designated uses in roughly three-fourths of the assessed river miles, lake acres, and estuaries. Nearly one-fifth of the assessed waters were capable of only partially supporting the designated uses, and seven percent were too contaminated to support any of the designated uses.

Shortcomings of the underlying data provided by the state reports pose problems for interpreting these results. The measure of quality depends first on the use assigned to a particular water resource and then on the reporter's judgment as to how well this use is being fulfilled. Furthermore, there are inconsistencies and incomplete coverage in the reporting. For instance, only 21 percent of the nation's rivers, 32 percent of the lakes, and 55 percent of the estuaries were covered in the 1986 inventory. The Environmental Protection Agency suggests "that since States generally focus their monitoring resources on waters most likely to have problems — e.g., urban waters or those that are intensively used for recreational purposes — the remaining unassessed water may be of better quality" (U.S. Environmental Protection Agency 1987). There

Table 7.2. Degree to Which the Quality of the Nation's Rivers, Lakes, and Estuaries Support Their Designated Uses

(as a percent of the total assessed miles of rivers, acres of lakes, and square miles of estuaries) [a]

	Rivers	Lakes	Estuaries
Fully supporting	74	73	75
Partially supporting	19	17	18
Not supporting	6	7	7
Unknown	1	2	0.3

[a] The assessed water bodies as a percentage of the nation's totals were 21% of the rivers, 32% of the lakes, and 55% of the estuaries.

Source: U.S. Environmental Protection Agency, **National Water Quality Inventory: 1986 Report to Congress**, EPA-440/4-87-008 (Washington, D.C., November 1987).

are no data to test this hypothesis. If correct, however, it implies that the percentages in Table 7.2 overstate the relative magnitude of the nation's surface water-quality problems.

Where the resources were impaired, the states identified the primary source of the pollutants (Table 7.3). Nonpoint sources such as runoff from farms, streets, construction and mining sites, and other locations lacking a single discharge point, were the principal problem on 65 percent of the rivers and streams, 76 percent of the lakes and reservoirs, and 45 percent of the estuaries and coastal waters that failed to support their designated uses. Point sources, which are primarily municipal waste water and industrial discharges, were identified as the principal problem for 27 percent of the rivers and streams, nine percent of the lakes and reservoirs, and 34 percent of the estuaries and coastal waters. Natural sources were the predominant problem for 12 percent of the impaired lakes and reservoirs, and other or unknown causes were listed for 18 percent of the impaired estuaries and coastal waters.

Current concerns over nonpoint pollutants stem in part from the fact that the nation's past clean-up efforts have been overwhelmingly focused on reducing point sources while little has been done to curb nonpoint pollutants. When the

Table 7.3. Primary Pollution Sources in the Nation's Water Resources That Failed to Fully Support Their Designated Uses as of 1986

(In percent) [a]

	Point Sources			Nonpoint Sources	Natural	Other
	Industrial	Municipal	Combined Sewers			
Rivers and Streams	9	17	1	65	6	2
Lakes and Reservoirs	1	8	0.03	76	12	3
Estuaries and Coastal Waters	8	22	4	45	3	18

[a] The percentages are derived from weighted averages based on miles of rivers and areas of lakes and estuaries.

Source: U.S. Environmental Protection Agency, **National Water Quality Inventory: 1986 Report to Congress**, EPA-440/4-87-008 (Washington, D.C., November 1987).

Federal Water Pollution Control Act Amendments of 1972 (commonly known as the Clean Water Act) became law, discharges of industrial and municipal wastes through pipes and ditches into surface waters were viewed as the primary threat to the nation's waters and they became the principal target of the initial clean-up efforts. The 1972 Act established the construction grants program which mandated and assisted in developing and implementing waste-water treatment management plans and practices. Although grants to municipalities were first authorized in 1956, it was not until the Clean Water Act authorized grants of up to 75 percent of construction costs that the federal government became the dominant funder of municipal waste-water treatment plants. Federal expenditures for these facilities grew from less than $2 billion prior to 1972, to $37 billion from 1972 to 1985 (U.S. General Accounting Office 1986b). Including the expenditures of state and municipal governments and industry, the nation has spent more than $100 billion in the last fifteen years to limit and treat industrial and municipal wastes (Smith et al. 1987).

Although costly, these efforts brought some significant reductions in point-source pollutants. For instance, in the decade following enactment of the Clean Water Act, municipal biochemical oxygen demand loads declined an estimated 46 percent and industrial biochemical oxygen demand loads declined at least 71 percent even though population and inflation-adjusted gross national product increased by 11 and 25 percent respectively (Smith et al. 1987). Nevertheless, point sources are still significant sources of biochemical oxygen demand, bacteria, nutrients, toxics, and other pollutants (U.S. Environmental Protection Agency 1987), and it has been estimated that an additional $118 billion are needed through the end of this century for the construction of municipal treatment plants (Smith et al. 1987).

In spite of the past successes and the remaining problems, support for federal grants has dwindled. Although previous investments did reduce point-source discharges, little is known about their effects on water quality or the social benefits they produced (U.S. General Accounting Office 1986a). Moreover, by distorting the investment decisions of municipalities, subsidies provided under the construction grants program reduced the effectiveness of the nation's investments in treating municipal waste water. A Congressional Budget Office study concluded that the subsidies resulted in larger, more sophisticated plants than would have been built in their absence. Where the municipalities were forced to bear more of the costs, local involvement and pressure to reduce costs were greater, construction periods were shorter, reserve capacity was lower, technologies were simpler, and re-use of effluents was more innovative. Reducing the maximum subsidy from 75 to 55 percent of capital costs in 1985 was expected to reduce the capital costs for secondary waste-water treatment plants by an average of 30 percent (Congressional Budget Office 1985). The 1987 Clean Water Act amendments provide for phasing federal construction grants out by 1994. The 1987 Act authorizes an additional (and allegedly final) $18 billion for construction of sewage treatment facilities and establishing a revolving fund to assist financing future projects.

Another reason for disillusionment with the construction grants approach is that it no longer addresses the principal sources of the nation's surface water-quality problems. As noted in Table 7.3, nonpoint sources are now the major obstacle to restoring the nation's surface waters to their designated uses. Nonpoint contaminants include the conventional pollutants such as nutrients, sediment, oxygen-demanding materials, and salts as well as toxics such as pesticides, organic chemical compounds, and heavy metals. These contaminants emanate from countless diffuse activities, most of which make no intended use of water resources. By definition, there is no specific point where these sources can be intercepted and treated before they pollute a stream or lake. Furthermore, the problems as well as their solutions, at least those so far adopted, usually involve land-use rather than water-use practices.

Nonpoint sources are more difficult to deal with than point sources. Yet, as of 1981 nonpoint pollution had only received one percent of federal funding for water pollution control (Copeland and Zinn 1986). The limited funding that was available was spent in support of the 208 planning process (specified in section 208 of the 1972 Clean Water Act Amendments) which called for developing area-wide plans to identify nonpoint sources of pollution and to set forth procedures and methods (including land-use requirements) to control them to the extent feasible. Federal funding for this planning process, which was not viewed as a great success, was terminated in 1980 and not reestablished until passage of the Water Quality Act of 1987 (Carriker and Boggess 1988).

Agriculture is probably the most pervasive and predominant source of nonpoint pollution (Copeland and Zinn 1986). Reducing erosion— which produces sediment and related nutrients in water bodies where they contribute to eutrophication, siltation, and other problems— has been the focus of past efforts to control agricultural nonpoint pollution. However, the U.S. Department of Agriculture's efforts to curb erosion have always emphasized the productivity effects rather than the water-quality effects of erosion. Despite studies that indicate the water-quality damages far exceed the productivity losses associated with cropland erosion (Crosson 1986), productivity remains the top priority of the Soil Conservation Service. In 1988, however, water quality was elevated to the number two priority of the Soil Conservation Service's conservation program.

The Rural Clean Water Program established under the 1977 amendments to the Clean Water Act was the first U.S. Department of Agriculture program to specifically link soil conservation with water quality. This program provided federal cost sharing to farmers agreeing to implement best management practices, defined as one or more practices that would improve water quality.

This program, however, was never well funded, and the limited funds were not targeted to areas where they might make the greatest contribution to water quality.

The Conservation Reserve Program and other conservation provisions of the 1985 Farm Bill represent the most recent and ambitious approaches to curbing agricultural nonpoint pollution. Under the Conservation Reserve Program, 40 to 45 million acres of highly erosive land could be withdrawn from crop production by the early 1990s. A Resources for the Future study (Gianessi et al. 1988) concludes that relatively little of the 20 million or so acres placed in the reserve as of mid-1987 were in areas where they would make an important contribution to improving water quality. In an encouraging move, filter strips on cropped lands bordering rivers, streams, lakes, and large wetlands were made eligible for the Conservation Reserve Program in February 1988. These strips are a potentially important tool for controlling agricultural runoff into surface waters (Caulkins 1988). Nevertheless, in the absence of targeting to areas where they will have the greatest impacts, expenditures on erosion control through the Conservation Reserve and Rural Clean Water programs will probably produce low returns in improved water quality per dollar invested.

Withdrawal or offstream uses of water affect quality in two ways. First, reducing the quantity of water in a stream reduces its capacity to assimilate wastes or dilute naturally-occurring pollutants such as salts that get washed into streams. Second, the portion of the water withdrawn that is not consumptively used carries salts, sediment, and other contaminants on its return to a usable body of water.

Thermoelectric plants and irrigators, the two largest offstream water users (Table 7.1), have very different impacts on water quality. Thermoelectric plants use most of the water for cooling and then return about 97 percent of the amount withdrawn. The return flows are warmer than the withdrawals. Since warmer water holds less oxygen and is of generally lower quality, the higher temperatures can adversely affect an aquatic ecosystem. Irrigation, on the other hand, returns less than half of the water withdrawn and accounts for about 80 percent of the nation's consumptive use of water. Water quality is adversely affected by both the resulting stream-flow depletion and the contaminants delivered in the return flows. As noted above, agricultural runoff, which can come from dryland as well as irrigated lands, is a major source of nonpoint pollution. However, salinity associated with irrigation, especially in arid and semiarid regions, warrants separate consideration.

High and rising salinity levels stemming in part from irrigated agriculture have diminished the quality of some of the West's major rivers, including the Colorado, Rio Grande, and San Joaquin. Irrigation water carries salts, and the concentrations increase as water evaporates, is transpired by plants, and passes over saline soils. For instance, salt levels in the Colorado River Basin rise 11-to 15-fold as the river flows from its headwaters in the Rocky Mountains to downstream users in Southern California and Mexico. About 55 percent of the downstream salt concentrations are estimated to result from natural sources, 37 percent from irrigation, and most of the rest from reservoir evaporation and transbasin diversions (Young and Horner 1986).

Agricultural, municipal, and industrial water users are all adversely affected by the high downstream salt concentrations. High salt levels reduce yields, limit the crops that can be grown successfully, and force farmers to adopt more sophisticated and costly management practices. Average annual agricultural damages in California's Imperial Valley have been estimated at $46,000 per milligram per liter in the range from 800 to 1,100 per milligram per liter. Adverse effects of high salt levels on municipal and industrial users include scaling of metal pipes, accelerated depreciation of appliances and fabrics, and higher expenditures for soap and detergents. Aggregate household damages from salinity in the Lower Colorado River have been estimated at seven times the level of agricultural damages (Young and Horner 1986).

Acid precipitation is another pollutant of some of the nation's surface waters. Although precipitation is, of course, a nonpoint pollutant, the origins of the acids can be traced back to both point sources (sulfur dioxide emissions from coal-burning electric utilities) and nonpoint sources (nitrogen oxide emissions from automobiles). The impacts of human activities on surface-water acidity remain an item of considerable controversy. There is mounting evidence, however, that human sources are contributing to high lake acidity in New York State, New England, as well as some other areas and that acidity is having adverse impacts on aquatic ecosystems in these areas (Guldin 1988).

Ground-Water Quality

The United States has very large ground-water resources suitable for drinking, and so far only a very small fraction of them are known to have been contaminated to the point that they fail to meet state and federal drinking-water standards. Nevertheless, scientists view ground water as one of the nation's most threatened resources, and there are good reasons for concern. The potential sources of contamination are ubiquitous and the pollutants are often hazardous. Moreover, the most heavily used aquifers are often the most seriously threatened. Yet, because of technical difficulties and high costs, monitoring of ground water tends to be infrequent or nonexistent. Consequently, for some of those relying on ground water for drinking— including more than half the nation's total population and 97 percent of its rural population— questions of water safety persist. And once an aquifer is contaminated, it is very expensive and difficult to clean. In many cases, the only practical solutions will be to either write the aquifer off as unusable for most purposes and find an alternative water source or to control the source of the pollution and then wait (in some cases centuries) for natural flushing to restore its quality.

Aquifers may be divided into three categories for purposes of examining their susceptibility to contamination. Since confined aquifers receive little or no recharge, the quality of their water is relatively unaffected by the quality of the surface water or most land-use practices. Consequently, lands overlying confined aquifers have environmental advantages as sites for activities such as feedlots that would threaten ground-water supplies in other areas. However, confined as well as unconfined aquifers can be exposed to a variety of pollutants by drilling to tap their water resources, to mine underlying oil and gas reserves, or to inject wastes into deep geological strata. Contamination of usable ground-water sources can result if the design, construction, placement, operation, or abandonment of such wells is faulty.

Because unconfined aquifers have no impermeable cover, they can be easily contaminated by percolation from overlying lands or interconnections with surface waters. A wide range of activities including careless disposal of wastes, runoff of agricultural chemicals and road salts, and leaks and spills of chemicals, radioactive substances, or other pollutants can degrade the utility of these aquifers.

The third category comprises unconfined coastal aquifers which are also susceptible to salt-water intrusion when pumping exceeds recharge. Since coastal areas are among the nation's most populated and industrialized, their aquifers often face the dual threats of salt-water intrusion and contamination from surface activities.

Septic and underground storage tanks were the most commonly cited major sources of ground-water contamination in the Environmental Protection Agency's 1986 *National Water Quality Inventory* (1987). This result is not surprising since they represent millions of potential sources of pollutants. There are about 20 million domestic on-site waste-disposal systems in the United States. Septic systems are the most common of these, but all have the potential for contaminating ground-water with nitrates, phosphates, pathogens, inorganic contaminants, cleaners, or other toxics that might be poured into household drains. In 1980, as many as one-third of all septic systems may have been operated in a manner that threatened ground-water quality (The Conservation Foundation 1987). Since the 1950s, there has been a rapid increase in the use of underground tanks for storing a variety of liquids such as fuel, acids, metals, solvents, chemicals, and chemical wastes. An estimated 1.5 million of these contain hazardous substances or petroleum products; the petroleum industry alone has been estimated to have as many as 350,000 leaking tanks. The tanks are generally made of carbon steel with no protection from corrosion and have a life expectancy of only 15 to 20 years. Leaks from these tanks have grown rapidly in recent years and are likely to continue to grow (The Conservation Foundation 1987).

Agricultural activities were the third most commonly cited source of groundwater contamination in Environmental Protection Agency's 1986 inventory. About 400 million acres are planted to crops each year in the United States, and agricultural chemicals are applied to most of these lands. Some of these chemicals end up in the ground water. In the absence of national data on the levels of contamination from agriculture, Nielsen and Lee (1987) have used available data sources to identify the areas where ground water is most likely to be affected by agricultural activities. Regions particularly susceptible to pesticide contamination are the Eastern Seaboard, the Gulf Coast, and the Upper Midwest; those most susceptible to nitrate contamination are the Great Plains, portions of the Northwest, Southwest, and Corn Belt; and the locations most likely to have problems with both contaminants are portions of the Corn Belt, Lake States, and Northeast. The 19 million people drinking water from private wells are at the greatest risk from these activities. Private wells tend to be much shallower and, thus, much more readily contaminated than those used by public water systems. Moreover, private wells are generally unregulated and the least likely to be monitored. Nielsen and Lee estimated that it would cost about $1.4 billion for just a first-time monitoring of the wells servicing the nation's households.

On-site and municipal landfills, abandoned waste sites, surface impoundments, and oil and gas brine pits are also high on the Environmental Protection Agency's 1986 inventory list of the 16 major sources of ground-water contamination. Depending on which estimate is used, from 42 to 55 percent of the nation's hazardous waste is managed in surface impoundments and landfills. Until recently, management in this form usually meant dumping the waste into unlined pits or lagoons with no barrier between the waste and ground water other than the soil (McCarthy and Reisch 1987). The Hazardous and Solid Waste Amendments of 1984 require double liners and leachate collection systems for all new land disposal facilities and retrofitting of previously existing sites. These amendments, which will cost billions of dollars to implement, will reduce but not eliminate an important threat to ground water. Pollutants from unlined or inadequately lined landfills and impoundments will continue leaching into ground water for the indefinite future. In recognition of the long-term problem and the need to target scarce technical skills and funds, the Environmental Protection Agency has placed the worst sites (based on an evaluation of the relative hazards posed to human health and the environment) on their National Priorities List for long-term remedial action. As of July 1, 1988 more than 1,177 "Superfund" sites, mostly landfills and surface impoundments, were on the final and proposed list (*Environmental Reporter* 1988).

Other major sources of ground-water contamination listed in the Environmental Protection Agency's 1986 inventory are salt-water intrusion, other landfills, road salting, land application of sludge, regulated waste sites, mining activities, underground injection wells, and construction activities. Although these are all viewed as important problems in some parts of the country, space limitations prevent any discussion or quantification of these threats. Nevertheless, the preceding discussion could support a conclusion that ground water is an endangered resource. Although the supplies that are known to have been contaminated are a small fraction of the total, it is disconcerting to know that the fraction tends to increase with more sophisticated and extensive monitoring. Even where the water is currently suitable for drinking, this provides no guarantee for the future. And even if all new sources of pollution could be eliminated today, contaminants will continue to be leached into some ground-water supplies for decades to come. Uncertainties as to what is now or might in the future be in the ground water diminish its value as a resource.

MAJOR TRENDS

Past changes in total withdrawal and consumptive uses followed similar patterns; they increased at a generally declining rate from 1950 to 1980 and then declined over the next five years. (This discussion is based on estimates of offstream water use for five year intervals from 1950 to 1985 in Solley et al. 1988.) Per capita offstream use peaked in the mid-1970s.

Underlying the trends in the national aggregates are some significant differences in the growth of the various categories of water use. Public supplies and rural domestic and livestock uses increased throughout the 35 year period while industrial and irrigation use declined in recent years. The available data suggest that self-supplied withdrawals for industrial, commercial, and mining uses declined by more than 30 percent from 1980 to 1985. Although these data may overstate the actual magnitude of the decline, significant reductions in these uses were achieved through improved plant efficiencies and increased reuse. Thermoelectric withdrawals increased at gradually declining rates from the mid-1960s to 1980 and then declined nearly 10 percent during the first half of the 1980s (Solley et al. 1988).

Irrigation is the sector most strongly affected by changes in the costs and availability of water. Nationally, irrigated acreage declined in the last decade. In some of the West's more water-scarce regions, the decline started much earlier. The annual rate as well as the absolute level of growth of irrigated acreage in the West has declined steadily since 1950. Principal factors underlying this decline are the increasing competition for limited water supplies, the rising cost of developing new surface-water supplies, and the increasing cost of ground water use resulting from the depletion of stocks and rising energy costs. As the largest and generally lowest value users, irrigators have become important suppliers for the West's growing domestic, industrial, and commercial demands. These trends have led to concerns over the future of irrigation and the general viability of rural communities in the West. Water transfers from agriculture to other uses will continue both as irrigators find it more profitable to sell water rights than to continue irrigating and as groups seeking to increase their use of water find agricultural water the least expensive and in some cases the only source. Some farm communities will certainly decline and perhaps disappear as a result of these transfers. Nevertheless, for the foreseeable future, the overall impacts of these trends on western agriculture will be minor. Because irrigation currently accounts for about 90 percent of the consumptive use of water in the West, large percentage increases by non-agricultural users can be met with relatively small declines in irrigation use. Moreover, there are opportunities for increasing the returns to irrigation water through improved management, switching to higher-value crops, and other changes (Frederick 1988). As water becomes more costly, irrigators can be expected to make increasing use of opportunities that have the potential to produce large increases in the value of agricultural output per unit of water.

Irrigation also accounts for more than 25 percent of the value of agricultural production in the Southeast and Delta States (Day and Horner 1987). In some of the more intensively irrigated areas of these agricultural production regions, water has become an important constraint. For most of the humid East, however, economic factors largely unrelated to the cost of water are the principal constraints to the expansion of irrigated agriculture.

Instream users get what is left in the rivers and lakes after providing for offstream uses. These water bodies may provide a variety of services, some of which are not competitive in their demands for water. For instance, providing enough water for navigation is likely to be sufficient to meet most of the recreation and fish and wildlife demands. On the other hand, hydropower generation and waste disposal are likely to be competitive with uses such as recreation, fish habitat, and navigation.

With the exception of hydroelectric power generation, there are no estimates of instream water use. Water used for generating hydroelectric power followed a pattern not unlike that of overall withdrawal uses. Hydroelectric use increased 200 percent from 1950 to 1975, remained unchanged from 1975 to 1980, and then declined six percent from 1980 to 1985 (Solley et al. 1988).

Many factors have influenced past trends in water use. Demand for all uses tends to grow with population and income. Actual use, however, is constrained by cost and available supply. When supplies are abundant or can be expanded with little increase in cost, water use tends to grow more or less in step with the growth of the economy. Where water is scarce, competition among uses develops and intensifies as the economy expands. Scarce resources in our society are generally allocated based on the willingness to pay of the competing users.

But this is rarely the case for water. The outcome of the competition for scarce water supplies is usually determined more by the legal structure, historical use, and administrative decisions rather than by current economic considerations.

Historically, the competition has been heavily tilted in favor of offstream users. While withdrawal users may pay the costs of transporting and treating water, they do not pay for the water itself. Furthermore, even the delivery and treatment costs are often subsidized either directly (as with federally supplied irrigation water) or indirectly (through subsidized power for pumping and average-cost pricing). Average-cost pricing in the water industry has been used to justify investments in new supplies for which the marginal costs of the water far exceed the marginal benefits to the users. And as noted earlier, state water law has only recently started to recognize instream water rights in the West.

Past neglect and abuse of instream flows have imposed high costs on the nation in the form of depleted and polluted rivers and lakes. The growing scarcity of water together with recent efforts to provide for the growing demands for instream water uses are important factors underlying the sharp decline in the growth of offstream water use.

CLIMATE CHANGE

The planning, construction, and operation of water facilities has traditionally assumed that future levels and patterns of precipitation, runoff, and evapotranspiration would be similar to past experience. (This section draws extensively on Frederick and Gleick 1989.) The prospect of global climate change, however, raises questions about this assumption. A greenhouse warming, which is now viewed as virtually inevitable by most climate modelers, could have major impacts on both the supply and demand for water. Higher temperatures and atmospheric concentrations of carbon dioxide and other trace gases are likely to alter precipitation patterns, evapotranspiration rates, the timing and magnitude of runoff, and the frequency and intensity of storms. The nature of these impacts on specific regions, however, is unknown and difficult to estimate from existing climate models which have only coarse spatial resolution and simplistic hydrologic characterizations. Within a given region, likely changes in average annual precipitation associated with a 1.5 to five degrees Celsius increase in average global temperatures (the range of likely impact by the middle of the next century) are on the order of plus or minus 20 percent.

The hydrologic uncertainties associated with a greenhouse warming are compounded since relatively small changes in precipitation and temperature can have much larger effects on the volume and timing of runoff, especially in arid and semi-arid areas. For example, one study suggests that an increase in temperature of two degrees Celsius accompanied by a 10 percent decrease in precipitation would result in an estimated 17 to 28 percent decrease in runoff within the Great Basin. On the other hand, a similar temperature change combined with a 10 percent increase in precipitation would result in an estimated 20 to 35 percent increase in runoff (Flaschka et al. 1987). In California's Sacramento Basin an increase in temperature of two degrees Celsius with no change in precipitation would increase winter runoff by nearly 10 percent, but would decrease summer runoff by 22 percent (Gleick 1987). Moreover, changes in temperature and rainfall would alter the demand for water, especially for irrigation.

The uncertainties and long-term nature of the problem complicate the task of developing and implementing feasible and effective policies for abating and adapting to the hydrological impacts of climate change. Investments in infrastructures become riskier as the underlying hydrology becomes less certain. Building for changes that never materialize or failing to build facilities for changes that do occur are both costly prospects. The prospect of climate change, however, should not obstruct the development of effective water policy. The supply and demand for water will continue to change regardless of whether or not there is a greenhouse warming. A prudent strategy for adapting— regardless of whether these changes are the result of climatic change, the vagaries of the hydrologic cycle, or changes in demand— would provide increased incentives (that more closely reflect the social costs of the various water uses) to conserve and would increase the flexibility to allocate scarce resources to their highest value and most vulnerable uses on a timely basis.

SUPPLYING FUTURE WATER DEMANDS

Water has become a scarce resource, and it is sure to become scarcer as demands for water and the services it provides grow and as valued supplies are degraded or lost through contamination or depletion. Except for periods of floods and some relatively remote and undeveloped areas, supplies must be allocated among competing uses.

Scarcity alone, however, is not cause for alarm and it need not result in crises or even shortages. All economic goods and resources are scarce, and the primary purpose of our economic system is to allocate these goods and resources among competing uses. Allocation decisions are usually made through the operation of markets and the incentives provided by prices. High prices encourage producers to increase supply or to employ less costly and more abundant inputs, and they encourage consumers to reduce use. Where markets operate effectively, they produce an efficient allocation of resources while keeping the quantities demanded in equilibrium with the quantities supplied. Competitive prices provide a measure of scarcity and help avoid shortages. (For a discussion of the concepts of efficiency as applied to water resources, the problems of developing effective water markets, and some of the distortions in the pricing of municipal and agricultural water, see Frederick and Kneese 1988.)

Water is an exception, however, as productive markets and competitively determined prices are rare for water resources. The nature of the resource makes it difficult to establish the conditions required for such markets. Clearly defined and transferable property rights are a necessary condition for the smooth operation of markets. Such rights are difficult to establish for water resources that are fugitive over time and space or stored in common property aquifers. Moreover, if markets are to produce socially efficient exchanges and appropriate price signals, buyers and sellers must bear the full costs and benefits of using or exchanging the property. Water transfers commonly result in externalities or third-party effects that would not be taken into account in an unfettered market exchange.

The absence of effective markets in an environment of increasing resource scarcity places considerable pressure on public policies and management practices to avoid shortages and misuse of resources. Opportunities for managing water supplies and demands in the next decade or so are examined briefly below.

Supply-Side Management

Traditionally, planners gave priority to offstream uses and sought to build additional dams, reservoirs, wells, and other infrastructures to provide for projected withdrawal uses during all but the most extreme drought periods. It was assumed that these uses would grow roughly in step with population and income. Projections of offstream use were treated as virtual necessities to be provided regardless of cost; the possibility of limiting use through higher prices was essentially ignored. This structural approach may have been appropriate when the costs of developing new supplies were low and stream flows were sufficient to meet all demands. For reasons discussed above, however, such conditions no longer exist. Sharply rising costs and increasing values placed on instream uses have curbed the growth of new supplies. Planners are being forced to explore alternative ways to help keep supply and demand in balance.

Unfortunately, alternative or unconventional water sources are not likely to have more than a minor impact on the nation's water supplies for the foreseeable future. In selected areas, however, there may be opportunities for achieving modest increases in usable supplies.

There are vast quantities of saline water in the oceans and aquifers, and increasing amounts of waste water are generated by municipal and industrial users. The technology exists to upgrade these waters but the costs of doing so are high relative to current water prices. Barring major reductions in energy costs and unexpected technological developments, desalinization of sea water will remain too expensive for all but the most water-scarce regions and high-value uses. The economics of desalting brackish waters with salt concentrations well below those found in the oceans and of recycling municipal and industrial waste waters are much more promising. As water becomes scarcer and more expensive, it seems likely that both the use of low-quality supplies and investments in upgrading supplies will rise. Surprisingly, use of recycled waste water is actually five percent lower now than it was in 1960 (Guldin 1988). This trend should soon be reversed as additional supplies become more expensive and difficult to acquire. Although some people may find recycled waste water an unacceptable substitute for fresh drinking water at almost any price, waste water (with less extensive treatment than is required to achieve drinking-water standards) can be used to irrigate golf courses, public roadways, and perhaps crops. Some industrial and agricultural users have also found they can make do with lower quality and that doing so may be more profitable than paying treatment costs.

Vegetation can also be managed to reduce evapotranspiration and increase runoff. Removing plants that thrive along streams, including those that use large amounts of water and those of low value, can increase flows. Moreover, forests can be managed for higher water yields and to produce a more favorable timing of runoff (Guldin 1988). Conflicts may exist, however, between managing a forest for increased water yields or for other objectives such as timber production or recreational opportunities.

Harvesting rainfall by diverting water to fields or cisterns is an ancient technology that has been used sparingly in the West. Although some promising opportunities for harvesting may still exist, this technology will not have a significant impact on western water supplies.

More exotic and controversial options involve use of icebergs and weather modification. The availability of enormous quantities of fresh water trapped as polar ice has raised the possibility of towing icebergs for use in the arid southwestern coastal communities. A combination of technical, economic, environmental, and legal problems has dampened, if not extinguished, proposals for such uses of icebergs in the United States.

Purposeful weather modification, especially through winter cloud seeding, was once viewed as a promising way of augmenting precipitation and runoff. Although seeding is done commercially in some ski areas, the technology remains controversial after more than 40 years of research. The general pessimism regarding the potential of this technology is reflected in the elimination of funding in fiscal year 1989 for the Bureau of Reclamation's weather modification program. Even if the technology were established and the economics were favorable, other obstacles might prevent any extensive adoption of weather modification. For instance, legal objections might be raised by downwind residents who believe seeding would divert precipitation from their lands or by towns that get stuck with the costs of increased snowfall that benefits downstream users with increased runoff during the following spring and summer.

As its water becomes scarce, a region often looks for imports. Transfers do not add to total supplies, but they can move water from low- to high-value uses. In the 1960s, large-scale water transfers from as far away as Alaska and northern Canada were proposed as long-term solutions to the problems stemming from the natural aridity of the Southwest and the High Plains. Interest in such projects waned as the magnitude of their economic and environmental costs became clearer. More modest interbasin transfers, however, have been a regular part of water development in the United States. But even relatively small transfers are becoming difficult to arrange because very few regions are now willing to depart, at least without compensation, with their water. As instream water values increase, approval of an interbasin transfer will depend on prospective importers being willing and able to compensate exporting regions for the opportunity costs of the water. The institutional bias that has given offstream users an advantage in the competition for water does not extend to interbasin transfers. Only relatively high-value users are likely to be able to afford the full costs of a transfer, especially when water is transported uphill or over long distances out of its natural channels. On the other hand, the possibility that a greenhouse warming could produce unprecedented change, leaving some areas with much more and others with much less water, could make interbasin transfers politically and economically more attractive in the more distant future.

In view of the high financial and economic costs of developing new water supplies and the limited prospects for expanding supplies through unconventional means, the best means for increasing the effective supply of water may lie with improved management of the existing infrastructure. Opportunities for increasing effective water yields have been demonstrated in the District of Columbia metropolitan area where joint operation of the systems of three principal water-supply agencies increased drought-condition water yields by over 30 percent. The infrastructure required to produce a similar increase in safe yield would have cost between $0.2 to $1.0 billion. Studies suggest that important benefits could also be gained through improved management in other regions with very different hydrologic characteristics (U.S. Geological Survey 1986). Achieving these gains, however, will not be easy and will require removing institutional obstacles stemming from the separate ownership of facilities, multi-state jurisdictions, and restrictive water laws.

Demand-Side Management
Implications of the previous section are that aggregate water supplies will expand slowly at best and perhaps not at all. In contrast, demands for both instream and offstream water uses will continue to grow with population and incomes. Water use will, of course, be limited by available supply. The way scarce supplies are rationed among competing uses will determine the benefits derived from these resources and whether the future will be characterized by shortages and periodic crises or, hopefully, by a relatively uneventful adaptation

to ever-changing conditions. The absence of effective water markets and efficient pricing policies leaves the outcome in doubt.

There are two basic approaches to managing demand — a regulatory or command-and-control approach which relies on government restrictions to allocate resources and limit use, and a market approach which relies on prices to provide incentives to conserve and allocate resources to their best uses. Elements of both approaches are employed for water.

Regulatory measures are almost always employed to curb use during extreme events and to restrict the disposal of wastes into water bodies; they are commonly used to allocate water among competing uses. The large and rapid changes in supplies that characterize extreme droughts are not handled well by markets. Command-and-control measures are employed in these cases. Temporary drought-emergency measures are likely to start with appeals for voluntary conservation and, if necessary, move on to restrictions on non-essential uses such as lawn watering and car washing.

A somewhat more controversial application of the regulatory approach is to impose water-conserving standards on appliances, showerheads, toilets, and other items. The widespread adoption of such items can provide for sizable reductions in water use at relatively little social cost. Proponents of the regulatory approach argue that unacceptably large increases in water prices would be required to encourage both manufacturers to produce products that use little water and consumers to purchase them. An unwillingness to allow prices to rise to reflect the full costs of developing new supplies as well as a skepticism about the impacts of price on use have led several communities to adopt water-conserving standards.

The command-and-control approach has dominated efforts to achieve water-quality objectives. Nevertheless, the high costs of past efforts to improve water quality and the failure to achieve all the legislatively established objectives are reasons for considering how economic incentives might be employed to more efficiently achieve cleaner water. As noted earlier, federal subsidies have distorted past incentives for treatment of municipal wastes. Adoption of effluent charges set to approximate damages and use of marketable discharge permits would encourage polluters to develop and adopt more cost-effective alternatives for reducing discharges. And research suggests that improved on-farm irrigation, which can be encouraged by charging farmers prices that more nearly reflect the full costs of their water use, is the most cost-effective way of reducing salt loading, agricultural chemicals, and other pollutants attributable to irrigation drainage in the western United States (Frederick 1987).

Markets and pricing incentives could also be more extensively and effectively employed to facilitate transfers among competing uses and to provide incentives to conserve. Currently, the laws, administrative procedures, subsidies, and pricing policies often limit the ability to transfer resources among alternative uses and discourage conservation. Government policies at all levels contribute to the problems. Federal agencies have been eager to divert and tame the nation's rivers but their projects may not result in an improved use of scarce water. Political considerations often replace economic criteria in project selection; environmental impacts tend to be understated; inefficiency and distorted incentives are commonly a by-product of the subsidies, pricing policies, and restrictions placed on the use of federally supplied water; and instream uses are likely to be ignored or undervalued in the planning and management of federal projects. The diversion of federal tax revenues to local communities is often the biggest attraction of these projects to their local sponsors.

State law and administrative procedures establish the framework that determine individuals' rights to use and transfer water that is not explicitly encumbered by federal law. Many of these laws and procedures restrict transfers to different uses and locations. All western states permit transfers under some conditions if third-party interests are not impaired, and in recent years some of these states have adopted measures to facilitate marketing. Gaining approval of a proposed transfer, however, often involves costly and time-consuming judicial or administrative procedures, the outcome of which is uncertain. Transfers can be even more difficult to arrange in the East where the riparian doctrine, which ties water rights to ownership of the riparian lands, is the basis of state water law.

Both state and municipal governments influence water use through their regulation of water suppliers. The urban water industry has traditionally treated water as a necessity, the use of which is not responsive to price. Utilities focus on providing what they consider to be the necessary supply at the lowest cost. Water rates are set just high enough to cover a firm's average costs and a "fair" return to investors. Since the costs of developing new water supplies have risen sharply over time, this pricing policy means that consumers pay much less for the new supplies than society pays to supply them. Average-cost pricing of water has two perverse implications— consumers have less incentive to conserve than is socially desirable, and utilities invest in supplies that cost more than they contribute to social welfare. (For a more extensive discussion see Frederick and Kneese 1988.) In Denver and some other cities residential water use is not even metered, a fact that leaves consumers with essentially no incentive to conserve.

The evidence that water use is responsive to price is overwhelming. Water demand studies suggest that the price elasticity of demand (that is, the percentage change in use prompted by a given percentage change in price) varies considerably geographically and among types of use. A conservative estimate of the elasticity for indoor domestic use, which is one of the least responsive water uses, would be -0.25. This suggests a doubling of water rates would result in a 25 percent decline in this use. Outdoor domestic uses such as watering lawns and gardens are much more responsive to price, and the percentage change in outdoor use is likely to exceed the percentage price change (Gibbons 1986).

Irrigation, the largest consumptive use of the nation's water, is also one of the more sensitive to water costs. Consequently, there is considerable latitude for influencing water use through improved price incentives.

The obstacles to developing effective water markets and pricing policies are great, and fully competitive markets will be an unattainable goal in most cases. As previously noted, the nature of the resource argues for some governmental input to adjust for common-property and third-party problems, to provide for public goods, and to prevent monopolistic pricing by water suppliers. Nevertheless, much can and should be done to facilitate voluntary transfers and to eliminate some of the perverse impacts of existing laws and policies. The states can do more to establish transferable property rights in water and to facilitate consideration of the third-party impacts of transfers. The federal government could assist by permitting transfers of federally supplied water and by quantifying Indian water rights and making them transferable. And both public and private suppliers could move toward marginal-cost pricing of water. Such changes will help ensure that the quantities of water demanded are kept in line with available supplies as supply and demand conditions change over time.

SOME FINAL THOUGHTS

The case for increased marketing and marginal-cost pricing of water is based on efficiency considerations. The objective of increasing the total size of the social pie may be important but it is clearly not the only, and rarely even the most important, concern of policymakers. Thus, it is useful to consider some of the more commonly raised objections to proposals for marketing and marginal-cost pricing.

In principle, a larger pie suggests everyone could be made better off. In practice, some groups would be worse off, and it is often suggested that irrigators would be one of those groups. Irrigators are the only group for which water constitutes a significant portion of total production costs. Consequently, they would be expected to make major adjustments to higher water prices. As noted earlier, however, irrigators have many opportunities to conserve without abandoning agriculture and the overall impacts on the sector would be limited because large increases in municipal and industrial water use can be met with small percentage reductions in irrigation water use. Moreover, as the owners of most of the water rights in the arid parts of the country, irrigators would be among the major beneficiaries of water markets. If it were deemed desirable to protect rural communities that are economically dependent on irrigation, there are better ways to do this than by locking scarce water resources into low-value and inefficient uses.

Marginal-cost water pricing has been dismissed on several grounds. The industry traditionally argues that marginal-cost pricing would not curtail use because water use is not sensitive to price. This argument, however, is belied by the evidence (Gibbons 1986). Other objections to marginal-cost pricing are that it would produce huge profits for utilities and impose severe hardship on low-income families. These concerns are valid, but they can be dealt with through a combination of taxes and innovative rate-setting policies that still preserve the incentives of marginal-cost pricing. (For a discussion of how this might be achieved for municipal water supplies see Frederick and Kneese 1988.)

Another objection to markets is that private decisions will under-allocate water for instream uses such as recreation and fish and wildlife habitat. Currently, the protection afforded instream flows by state and federal law is unsystematic and, at least in the West, prejudicial to instream uses. Ideally, instream values would be systematically evaluated and compared with offstream alternatives. Water markets might facilitate such a comparison because market prices would provide an indication of the opportunity costs of reserving or purchasing water for instream uses. By making these costs explicit, a community would be in a better position to make rational and defensible decisions regarding the use of its waters.

Institutional change should take equity as well as efficiency implications into account. However, greed and short-sightedness may be the principal obstacles to major water-policy reform. Water policy has been a costly and relatively ineffective instrument for helping the urban poor, the small farmer, or any other specific group. The interests of the poor are not well served by policies that provide billions of dollars in subsidies for water projects of questionable merit or that reduce the total national product by preventing water from flowing to its highest-value uses. Interests in the West are not well served by policies that create and preserve pockets where water is virtually free while adding to the scarcity in the rest of the region. The interests of the nation are not served by lax environmental policies that permit the deterioration of water quality. Nor are the interests of the nation served by ill-conceived regulations that lead to costly, ineffective remedies (Frederick 1984).

On the other hand, the national interest would be served by policies that encourage conservation, discourage abuse, and facilitate voluntary transfers of scarce water resources. Indeed, such policies are needed to ensure that high-quality water will be available in our homes and businesses at the turn of a tap as well as in our lakes and streams. While the costs of leaving a tap on will rise, it will be a small price to pay for protecting the quality and ensuring the continued availability of a precious resource.

REFERENCES

Carriker, Roy R. and William G. Boggess (1988). "Agricultural Nonpoint Pollution: A Regulatory Dilemma," Forum for Applied Research and Public Policy, vol. 3, no. 2, Summer 1988, pp. 63-70.

Caulkins, Peter (1988). Chief, Water Economics Branch, Office of Policy, Planning and Evaluation, United States Environmental Protection Agency. Personal communication.

Congressional Budget Office (1985). Efficient Investments in Wastewater Treatment Plants (Washington, District of Columbia, GPO, June).

Conservation Foundation (1987). Groundwater Protection— Groundwater: Saving the Unseen Resource and A Guide to Groundwater Pollution: Problems, Causes, and Government Responses (Washington, District of Columbia, The Conservation Foundation).

Copeland, Claudia and Jeffrey A. Zinn (1986). "Agricultural Nonpoint Pollution Policy: A Federal Perspective," Congressional Research Service, 86-191 ENR, TD 420 U.S. B (Washington, District of Columbia, December 1).

Crosson, Pierre R. (1986). "Soil Erosion and Policy Issues," in Tim T. Phipps, Pierre R. Crosson, and Kent A. Price, editors, Agriculture and the Environment (Washington, District of Columbia, Resources for the Future, 1986).

Day, John C. and Gerald L. Horner (1987). United States Irrigation: Extent and Economic Importance, Economic Research Service, Agricultural Information Bulletin no. 523 (Washington, District of Columbia, GPO, September).

Environmental Reporter (1988), vol. 19, no. 9, p. 310.

Flaschka, I.M., C.W. Stockton, and W.R. Boggess (1987). "Climatic Variation and Surface Water Resources in the Great Basin Region" in Water Resources Bulletin 23, pp. 47-57.

Frederick, Kenneth D. (1984). "Current Water Issues" in Journal of Soil and Water Conservation, March-April, vol. 39, no. 2.

Frederick, Kenneth D., editor (1986). Scarce Water and Institutional Change (Washington, District of Columbia, Resources for the Future).

Frederick, Kenneth D. (1988). "The Future of Irrigated Agriculture" in Forum for Applied Research and Public Policy, vol. 3, no. 2, Summer, 1988, pp. 80-89.

Frederick, Kenneth D. (1987). "Discussion of the Mineral Water Quality Problem from Irrigated Agriculture" in Tim Phipps, Pierre R. Crosson, and Kent A. Price, editors, Annual Policy Review 1986: Agriculture and the Environment (Washington, District of Columbia, Resources for the Future).

Frederick, Kenneth D. and Peter H. Gleick (1989). "Water Resources and Climate Change," in the proceedings of a workshop Controlling and Adapting to Greenhouse Warming, held in Washington, District of Columbia, June 14 and 15, 1988.

Frederick, Kenneth D. with James C. Hanson (1982). Water for Western Agriculture (Washington, District of Columbia, Resources for the Future).

Frederick, Kenneth D., and Allen V. Kneese (1988). "Western Water Allocation Institutions and Climate Change," Discussion Paper Series No. RR88-02 (Washington, District of Columbia, Resources for the Future).

Gianessi, Leonard, Henry Peskin, Tim Phipps, Cynthia Puffer, and Pierre Crosson (1988). "Analysis of the Effects of the Conservation Reserve Program on the Quality of the Nation's Waters," unpublished paper (Resources for the Future, January).

Gibbons, Diana (1986). The Economic Value of Water (Washington, District of Columbia, Resources for the Future).

Gleick, Peter (1987). "Regional Hydrologic Consequences of Increases in Atmospheric CO_2 and Other Trace Gases" in Climatic Change 10, pp. 137-161.

Guldin, Richard W. (1988). An Analysis of the Water Situation in the United States: 1989-2040: A Technical Document Supporting the 1989 RPA Assessment (Washington, District of Columbia, United States Forest Service), in draft.

Langbein, W.B. (1959). "Water yield and reservoir storage in the United States." United States Geological Survey Circular 409, 5 pp. Cited in United States Geological Survey, 1984, p. 30.

McCarthy, James E. and Mark E. Anthony Reisch (1987). Hazardous Waste Fact Book, Congressional Research Service Report 87-56 ENR (Washington, District of Columbia, January 30).

Nielsen, Elizabeth G. and Linda K. Lee (1987). "The Magnitude and Costs of Groundwater Contamination from Agricultural Chemicals: A National Perspective," Economic Research Service, Natural Resource Economics Division, Staff Report AGES870318 (Washington, District of Columbia, June).

Scott, Lisa LaBelle (1986). "The Public Trust Doctrine— A Tool for Expanding Recreational Rafting Rights in Colorado," University of Colorado Law Review (Spring): 625-637.

Sloggett, Gordon and Clifford Dickason (1986). Ground-water Mining in the United States, Economic Research Service, Agricultural Economic Report Number 555 (Washington, District of Columbia, GPO).

Smith, Richard A., Richard B. Alexander, and M. Gordon Wolman (1987). "Water-Quality Trends in the Nation's Rivers" in Science, vol. 235, March 27, pp. 1607-1615.

Solley, Wayne B., Charles F. Merk, and Robert R. Pierce (1988). Estimated Use of Water in the United States in 1985, U.S. Geological Survey Circular 1004 (Washington, District of Columbia, GPO).

United States Environmental Protection Agency (1987). National Water Quality Inventory: 1986 Report to Congress, EPA-440/4-87-008 (Washington, District of Columbia, November).

United States General Accounting Office (1986a). The Nation's Water: Key Unanswered Questions About the Quality of Rivers and Streams, PEMD-86-6 (Washington, District of Columbia, September).

United States General Accounting Office (1986b). Water Quality: An Evaluation Method for the Construction Grants Program— Methodology, PEMD-87-4A, Vol. 1 (Washington, District of Columbia, December).

United States Geological Survey (1984). National Water Summary 1983— Hydrologic Events and Issues, Water-Supply Paper 2250 (Washington, District of Columbia, GPO).

United States Geological Survey (1986). National Water Summary 1985— Hydrologic Events and Surface-Water Resources, Water Supply Paper 2300 (Washington, District of Columbia, GPO).

United States Geological Survey (1988). National Water Summary— Hydrologic Events and Ground-water Quality, Water Supply Paper 2325 (Washington, District of Columbia, GPO).

United States Water Resources Council (1978). The Nation's Water Resources 1975-2000: Second National Water Assessment, vol. 1 (Washington, District of Columbia, GPO).

Young, Robert A. and Gerald L. Horner (1986). "Irrigated Agriculture and Mineralized Water," in Tim T. Phipps, Pierre R. Crosson, and Kent A. Price, editors, Agriculture and the Environment (Washington, District of Columbia, Resources for the Future, 1986), pp. 77-116.

CHAPTER 8

Wildlife

Jack Ward Thomas

In the United States there are some 3,000 vertebrate wildlife and fish species (Flather and Hoekstra, in press). This number of species and the lamentable fact that there are no ongoing, standardized regional or national inventories make examination of trends in wildlife populations and habitats difficult (Hirsch et al. 1979). Using the best data available, this overview of trends will discuss groups of species, resources dedicated to wildlife conservation, recent legislation, and the trend toward holistic management of natural resources.

GOVERNMENTAL RESOURCES DEDICATED TO WILDLIFE WORK

The trend in financial resources allocated to carry out governmental tasks associated with wildlife is one measure of the value that society places on wildlife. Examination of the money allocated to wildlife-related work during 1950 to 1988 (Figure 8.1) indicates, on average, a sustained and significant increase. Personnel employed by state and federal agencies to carry out wildlife-related functions increased in number in a similar, though less dramatic, pattern. There have been parallel increases in the amount of funds expended and the number of wildlife workers employed in the private sector (Dumke, Burger, and March 1981; White 1987). Wildlife has become an indicator for a healthy environment, a significant concern for a modern industrialized state that values its past and its vision of the future, and a symbol for an evolving culture that increasingly understands that it cannot exist independently of nature and of natural resources (Brokaw 1978).

There are some success stories in the management of those species that are known as big game. Trends and circumstances for other species such as waterfowl and song birds are not so encouraging. All in all, this is an upbeat story of past successes, of threats to wildlife recognized and faced, and a call for renewed effort to retain wildlife as part of the American heritage and dreams for the future.

POPULATION TRENDS AND HABITAT STATUS

The species that first stirred widespread public interest in wildlife conservation were the big game species pursued by hunters for recreation and the procurement of meat (Schmidt and Gilbert 1978). It is these species on which the most widespread data base exists. Some current data are based on questionnaires sent to each of the states, the United States Department of Agriculture Forest Service, the Bureau of Land Management, the United States Department of Interior National Park Service, and the United States Fish and Wildlife Service. Forty-two states responded. The National Park Service could not provide information on wildlife numbers nor on the resources devoted to wildlife. As examples, the trends in population for four species (Figure 8.2), white-tailed deer (*Odocoileus virginianus*), black bears (*Ursus americana*), elk (*Cervus elaphus*), and pronghorns (*Antilocarpa americana*). The figures also reveal the dramatic importance of the national forests and Bureau of Land Management lands as habitat for most big game species. (See pages 196-199.)

Waterfowl

Waterfowl are well-studied migratory birds which have produced an extensive body of literature, much of which is reviewed in Bellrose (1980). The class is divided into ducks, geese, and swans. The 41 species that are hunted are addressed here.

Ducks. Since 1955, the United States Fish and Wildlife Service and Canadian Wildlife Service have conducted operational aerial surveys annually during the spring and summer in major duck nesting areas to assess habitat conditions, population size, and production (U.S. Department of the Interior 1988).

Although changes in habitat conditions influence distribution on the breeding grounds, the proportional breeding in Canada and the United States is relatively constant. Within the area surveyed in May, about 65 percent of most species of ducks breed in Canada, 12 percent in Alaska, and 23 percent in the five north-central states. Generally, 85 percent of diving ducks breed in Canada and Alaska. Seventy percent of mallards (*Anas platyrhynchos*) breed in Canada. Some 40 percent of blue-winged teal (*Anas discors*) nest in the contiguous United States. Approximately 85 percent of black ducks (*Anas rubripes*) breed in Canada as do most ring-necked ducks (*Aythya collaris*). Wood ducks (*Aix sponsa*) breed more commonly in the United States than in Canada.

Trends from 1955 to 1988 indicate oscillations in breeding populations around a mean of 36 million (Figure 8.3). Populations were high during the mid-

Figure 8.1. Trends: Budgets

(State in 1988 dollars)

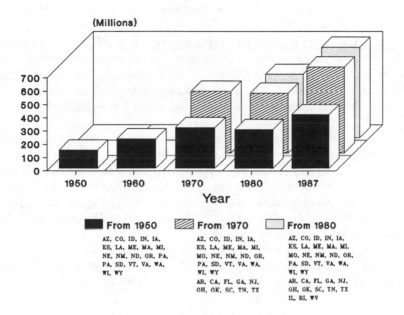

From 1950	From 1970	From 1980
AZ, CO, ID, IN, IA, KS, LA, ME, MA, MI, NE, NM, ND, OR, PA, PA, SD, VT, VA, WA, WI, WY	AZ, CO, ID, IN, IA, KS, LA, ME, MA, MI, MO, NE, NM, ND, OR, PA, SD, VT, VA, WA, WI, WY AR, CA, FL, GA, NJ, OH, OK, SC, TN, TX	AZ, CO, ID, IN, IA, KS, LA, ME, MA, MI, MO, NE, NM, ND, OR, PA, SD, VT, VA, WA, WI, WY AR, CA, FL, GA, NJ, OH, OK, SC, TN, TX IL, RI, WV

(Federal in 1988 dollars)

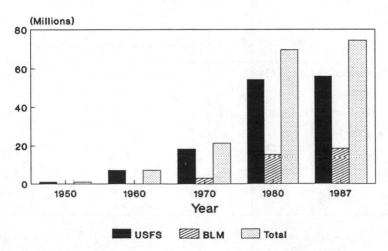

1950s and declined in the early 1960s due to drought conditions in the prairie-parkland region. Populations increased during the late 1960s and early 1970s and remained high throughout the 1970s. Severe drought in some areas affected productivity during the early 1980s, and breeding populations reached record lows in 1985. (See page 200.)

Geese. Most breed in arctic and subarctic regions of Alaska and Canada, with more than 20 major nesting areas for more common species. Population objectives are identified in the North American Waterfowl Management Plan. Because it is not practical to census all populations throughout this vast and remote area, fall and winter surveys provide the major information on population trends.

Table 8.1 summarizes indices relative to population and management goals in the North American Waterfowl Management Plan. The nationwide trend in winter counts of overall populations of Canada (*Branta canadensis*) and snow geese (*Chen caerulescens*) has been steady or upward since the 1960s. Exceptions are the decline of cackling (*B.c. minima*) and dusky Canada geese (*B.c. occidentalis*). Populations of "resident" or giant Canada geese that nest in the lower 48 states have grown considerably.

Snow geese (including Ross' [*C. rossii*], greaters, lessers, and the blue color phases) totaled over two million in 1987— well above numbers of the 1950s and 1960s. Annual counts of white-fronted geese (*Anser albifrons*) averaged 270,000

Table 8.1. North America Goose Population Indices and Management Goals

Species	1987-1988	Stable	Recent Trend (1980-1988) No. Populations			Population Index goal (2000)
			Increasing	Decreasing	Unknown	
Canada Goose	3,037,757	7	7	2	0	3,029,000
Snow Goose	2,366,217	0	3	2	0	1,615,000
Ross' Goose	100,000	0	1	0	0	100,000
White-fronted Goose	297,926	1	1	1	1	620,000
Brant	269,600	1	0	1	0	309,000
Emperor Goose	65,700	0	0	1	0	150,000

birds during 1983-87, well above the average of 192,000. Populations outside of Alaska appear to be doing well. In Alaska, white-fronted geese nest principally on the Yukon-Kuskokwim Delta. The 1987 population was approximately 130,600, substantially below the objective of 300,000. Generally, all populations of geese nesting on the Yukon-Kuskokwim Delta declined since the late 1960s, including black brant (*Branta bernicla*) and the emperor goose (*C. canagica*) (which occurs only in Alaska). Recent extensive research and management efforts have been put forth to restore numbers (U.S. Department of the Interior 1987).

Atlantic brant (*B. bernicla*) made a gradual strong recovery from a series of severe winters and reduced productivity during the late 1970s. More birds were seen on eastern coastal wintering grounds in 1985 than had been seen since 1971. Only 21,900 black (Pacific) brant were recorded during the 1988 United States winter survey. In recent years, most black brant have wintered on mainland Mexico and at Baja California, which accounts for the fewer birds observed in the United States. Because of this change the birds are now censused in Mexico. When these counts are included, the 1988 winter survey placed the population at 138,600, well below the objective of 185,000.

Swans. The tundra swan (*Cygnus columbianus*) breeds in Alaska and northern Canada and winters principally in coastal areas of the Atlantic and Pacific flyways. Its breeding habitat is relatively secure and pristine. Wintering habitat has been lost and degraded in some areas. However, swans have adapted to changing conditions and in some places are now upland field feeders.

Surveys to measure rangewide abundance of breeding swans are not practical. This has not been a problem, as the birds can be censused on the wintering grounds. Most swans winter in coastal marshes and estuaries of the Atlantic and Pacific flyways where numbers have increased over the years, and, in 1987, totaled 147,000, well above the 35-year average of 114,000.

Habitat Requirements

Ducks. The amount and quality of duck habitat have decreased substantially as wetlands have been converted to agricultural use. Remaining wetlands have produced fewer ducks in recent years due to dry conditions in the prairie pothole region. Associated upland nesting areas have diminished in amount and quality, concentrating nests where they are more vulnerable to predation. As a consequence, the capacity of North America's wetlands to produce and winter ducks has been greatly reduced. Despite significant governmental and private efforts, the outlook for coming years is for a continuing reduction in the supply of ducks.

Geese. Most geese nest in remote areas of the arctic and subarctic regions that have not been affected seriously by development. Goose production varies with climatic conditions (U.S. Department of the Interior 1988), but the nesting habitat base remains stable and secure.

Some Canada geese nest in the lower 48 states. In the Intermountain West, the recent rise of the Great Salt Lake has covered much of the Lake's marshlands and destroyed nesting habitat. However, most nesting habitat in southern Canada and the lower 48 states are in satisfactory condition.

While loss and degradation of wetland habitats have been detrimental to ducks and to waterfowl in general, habitat conditions for geese are generally satisfactory. Most breeding habitat is stable and secure, and geese have adapted to changes in migrational and wintering habitats. Currently high population levels suggest that numbers have not been limited by habitat.

Anticipated Trends

Ducks. Populations have been declining since 1970. The mallard breeding population was at 10 million in 1970, eight million in 1980, and 6.5 million in 1988. Pintails went from seven million to five million to 2.5 million over the same time intervals. In 1985, the fall flight index for all ducks was at 62 million, the lowest on record. It increased to 73 million in 1986 and 74 million in 1987, then dropped to 66 million in 1988. The 1988 breeding stocks approximate those of 1986 and 1987 with a distinct prospect of further reductions in the spring of 1989. Recovery of habitat to more normal conditions is unlikely over one year; recruitment in 1989 probably will not be high. Ducks are now at very low levels with reduced ability of populations to respond to increased surface water compared to previous decades.

Destruction of nesting habitat has been widespread over the prairies and parklands with long-term and continuing conversion of grassy and bushy areas and pond margins to agriculture. Even when water conditions return to average, ducks will be limited in recruitment capability. When surface water is scarce, the situation for ducks is not promising. This situation in 1988 and beyond is grim and reflects the cumulative consequences of years of habitat destruction aggravated by severe and prolonged drought.

Any recovery in duck numbers will require at least several years of good climatic conditions plus the large-scale habitat management measures proposed in the North American Waterfowl Management Plan. Without significant governmental and private efforts both the near and long-term outlook is for a continuing, perhaps irreversible, reduction in numbers of ducks.

Geese. The complexity of management increases each year, due to difficulties in harvest allocation between political entities involved. Harvest is a sensitive biological and political issue because: 1) most managers recognize a direct relationship between harvest and subsequent population numbers, and 2) differential harvest rates are partly responsible for changing distributions.

Many populations have increased to levels above management objectives. Changing distributions during the fall and winter are creating political conflict, however. Problems are caused, simultaneously, by excessive and inadequate population numbers. Managers achieve harvest allocation with difficulty, in the absence of coordinated national and international programs.

Necessary changes in management strategies at the national and international level include: 1) development of long and short term population, harvest, and distribution goals for recognized populations consistent with the North American Waterfowl Management Plan, and 2) implementation of monitoring programs (inventory, banding, and harvest) on the breeding grounds of the major goose populations to provide essential data for harvest management decisions.

Swans. Population levels are not expected to change significantly for tundra swans. A carefully regulated harvest will continue.

FURBEARERS

Furbearers include about 40 species ranging from the smallest carnivore in North America, the least weasel (*Mustela nivalis*), to the largest, the brown bear (*Ursus arctos*). Although most furbearers are carnivores, also included are the only marsupial native to North America, the Virginia opossum (*Didelphis marsupialis*), several native rodents including the beaver (*Castor canadensis*) and muskrat (*Ondatra zibethica*), and one exotic rodent, the nutria (*Myocastor coypu*). The thread that binds this diverse group is their fur, valuable for garment manufacture and the basis for a commercial industry.

The fur industry has been viable for nearly 400 years, since its initiation in 1490 as an offshoot of the North Banks codfishing industry (Ray 1987). The beaver was the most highly sought species. Then a shift in fashion from use of beaver in the 1830s, coupled with a decline in beaver numbers, depressed the fur industry. Even so, commercial interest in furbearers, particularly raccoon (*Procyon lotor*) and muskrat, continued until the outbreak of the war between the States in 1861 (Ray 1987). In this century, harvest of furbearers increased rapidly as the industry diversified.

The best known furbearer, the beaver, was severely reduced throughout much of its North American range by 1900 (Novak 1987); it was extirpated from 11 states (primarily in the northeast) due to habitat destruction and over-harvest (Deems and Pursley 1978). Restoration efforts in the 1940s and 1950s were successful and beavers were reintroduced into portions of at least 20 states. By the mid-1970s numbers approached 15 million (Hill 1987).

Furbearers that were dramatically reduced or eliminated from large portions of their range, primarily due to habitat destruction, were fisher (*Martes pennanti*), marten (*M. americana*), river otter (*Lutra canadensis*), sea otter (*Enhydra lutris*), wolverine (*Gulo luscus*), lynx (*Lynx canadensis*), wolf (*Canis lupus*), and swift fox (*Vulpes velox*) (Deems and Pursley 1978). Most of these species have been successfully reintroduced, and other native and exotic species have been widely introduced into non-native habitats where they have established viable populations (Deems and Pursley 1978).

Habitat Requirements

Furbearers occupy nearly every portion of North America. However, those of greatest commercial value are north temperate species— those that live in climates cold enough in winter to require a hair coat with a thick layer of fur fibers. The best of 18 major vegetation zones in North America for furbearers, based on the number of species present, are the coniferous forest, northeastern mixed forest, and Pacific Coast forest of the northern United States and southern Canada (Allen 1987), which demonstrate high diversity in vegetational structure. Zones with less structural diversity generally have fewer furbearers.

Even in these zones, habitat diversity is key to furbearer abundance. For example, one group of furbearers (including beaver, muskrat, river otter, mink [*Mustela vison*], raccoon, and nutria) require wetlands— ponds, rivers, estuaries, or shorelines. Vegetative structure, plant species diversity, water quality and permanence, and surrounding land use and quality all influence the value of wetlands as furbearer habitat. Elimination of debris and structural diversity along shorelines, and in and adjacent to wetland areas and waterways, has been shown to reduce habitat values (Allen 1987). Similarly, agricultural or forest management practices that reduce habitat diversity can degrade habitat quality.

Management of furbearers on public lands is a state responsibility, with the exception of marine mammals (including the sea otter) and some endangered species which are managed by the federal government. On private lands furbearers are typically managed by default, favored by practices that enhance habitat diversity and reduced by monoculture management, over-grazing by livestock, and draining or alteration of waterways (Allen 1987).

Most federal management efforts are driven by the goals of preserving endangered species, ensuring the persistence of management indicator species, or controlling predators to protect agricultural interests. State agencies and private interests are involved most often in maintaining optimal yields of commercial or recreational products. Management of populations also involves limiting certain furbearer populations to protect human health and safety resulting from animal-borne diseases such as rabies (MacInnes 1987) or to prevent damage to livestock or crops. Management of furbearer habitats is a holistic approach that features the existence of furbearers as one of the interacting portions of a healthy environment.

Virtually all commercially valuable furbearer populations have recovered from overharvesting. Annual harvests in the 1980s are down only 20 percent from all-time high harvest levels of the 1940s (Obbard et al. 1987). Although some furbearers are classified as threatened or endangered (for example, black-footed ferret [*Mustela nigripes*], wolf, swift fox), such circumstances have resulted primarily from habitat destruction rather than overharvest (Obbard et al. 1987). Populations of the five most commonly currently harvested furbearers (muskrat, raccoon, nutria, opossum, and beaver) have demonstrated general population stability, with slight fluctuations due to wetland habitat conditions (Linscombe, in Flather and Hoekstra, in press). Muskrats and mink have shown general declines in some areas due to declines in the amount of wetland habitat (Sisson-Lopez, in Flather and Hoekstra, in press).

Several social issues have impacts on furbearer management. One of those is opposition to trapping, based on reservations about steel leg-hold traps or animal-rights objections to killing furbearers to produce clothing (Kellert 1981). Opposition to leg-hold traps has taken the form of prohibitive legislation, although recent referenda to ban such use in Ohio and Oregon failed (Gentile 1983). Opposition to killing furbearers is widespread, particularly among urban citizens (Kellert 1981).

Nuisance animal control has also a major influence on furbearer management and covers a wide range of issues, from coyote (*Canis latrans*) predation on livestock (Andelt 1987), to damage to property or concerns for human health and safety in urban and suburban areas (Williams and McKegg 1987). Coyotes will continue to cause problems with livestock operations and adapt to a wide range of control techniques (Andelt 1987). The trend away from generally applied coyote population control toward selective nonlethal and lethal methods will continue (Andelt 1987). Many problems associated with nuisance wildlife in urban and suburban areas can be addressed through programs of public information and education, combined with spot control in specific areas (Williams and McKegg 1987, de Almeida 1987). Programs that involve trappers and others in resolving such nuisance wildlife complaints have been developed (Williams and McKegg 1987).

The expense of manufacture of fur garments had restricted demand and insulated the fur market from economic conditions until demand for fur garments increased markedly in North America and Europe in the late 1960s and spread to the Far East in the 1970s with development of a manufacturing industry in Hong Kong (Shieff and Baker 1987). The increase in markets did not prevent recent decline in the industry, however; the average real price per pelt received by trappers declined 50 percent between 1979 and 1985, and total real value declined by 75 percent. Trapper numbers then declined by nearly 35 percent between 1980 and 1985 (Linscombe, in Flather and Hoekstra, in press). However, if demand steadies, habitat losses and restrictions on harvest due to anti-trapping sentiments may limit supplies and send pelt prices up (Flather and Hoekstra, in press). Stable markets are expected over the next 12 years (Shieff and Baker 1987).

BIRDS

Approximately 700 species of birds breed in the United States (American Ornithologists' Union 1983). Little or nothing is known about population trends for about half of those species. The annual Breeding Bird Survey coordinated by the U.S. Fish and Wildlife Service since 1966 provides data for 375 species (Robbins et al. 1986; Droege and Sauer 1987). In an analysis of trends through 1979, Robbins found that 22 percent of 230 species or species groups increased significantly and only 13 percent decreased significantly in abundance (Flather and Hoekstra, in press). A more recent analysis, covering 1966 to 1987 (Droege and Sauer 1987), showed that of 347 species with data sufficient for analysis, 60 increased, 63 decreased, and 224 did not change in abundance. (Values are based on computer printouts of trends shown by the North American Breeding Bird Survey, U.S. Fish and Wildlife Service, supplied by S. Droege, August 29, 1987.)

Range Expansion

Range expansion is a factor in population increases. Spectacular examples are introduced exotic species such as ring-necked pheasants (*Phasianus colchicus*), European starlings (*Sturnus vulgaris*), and house sparrows (*Passer domesticus*). Such events sometimes occur naturally, as in the spread of cattle egrets (*Bubulcus ibis*) throughout the conterminous United States. Since the first detection of the birds in Florida 40 years ago, Robbins (1986) reported that more cattle egrets are now recorded during Breeding Bird Surveys than all other species of herons and egrets combined. Even endemic species sometimes undergo range expansion, as with the brown-headed cowbird (*Molothrus ater*) in response to the spread of livestock and the fragmentation of forests.

Such events sometimes have serious, negative consequences not easily anticipated from an introduced species' life history in its native environs. For example, starlings compete with native songbirds for nesting cavities, consume large quantities of grain in cattle feedlots, and create disturbances and large accumulations of feces when they roost in enormous flocks in urban settings. The cowbird's strategy of nest parasitism on other songbirds is thought to be partially responsible for the endangerment of some species (summary in Rothstein et al. 1980). "The Hawaiian Islands have had more bird introductions (162 species) and more exotic species established (45 definitely established, 25 probable) than any other area on earth" (Scott et al. 1986). Competition for food and the introduction of avian diseases are factors in the decline and extinction of many native Hawaiian birds.

Introduction of parrots and their allies is another example of a matter for concern. At least five of these species have been successfully introduced in Florida and at least four in California (American Ornithologists' Union 1983). Parrots eat fruit and seed and may become serious threats to certain agricultural crops. This has not gone unnoticed, with efforts underway to control populations of the monk parakeet (*Myiopsitta monachus*) in several eastern states (American Ornithologists' Union 1983). It is time to decide whether control measures should be implemented for other introduced parrots before populations get too large to control.

Long-Term Environmental Changes

Birds evolved in a milieu of annual variation in weather conditions and changes in food supplies which cannot be controlled. Resulting population fluctuations are normal and generally not threatening. Yet threatening declines in populations, sometimes ending in extinction, usually do result from long-term changes in environments including build-up of toxic chemicals, introduction of exotic parasites and diseases to which a species has not evolved resistance, or introduction of more efficient competitors or predators. Probably the most common threats to bird populations, however, are extensive, long-term changes in habitats resulting from human activities including: 1) draining and/or filling of wetlands; 2) destruction of native riparian vegetation; 3) conversion of natural grasslands and shrublands to cultivated fields and urban and suburban developments; and 4) fragmentation of forests, particularly old-growth forests.

Major wetland and riparian conversions occurred before monitoring of bird populations began making assessment of population changes of species dependent on wetlands or riparian habitats possible. About 41 percent of the wetlands were drained and converted to crops and pasture by 1968; and Roe and Ayers' (1954) estimate of the original wetlands suggests a 54 percent decline by the mid-1950s. Despite efforts to restore wetlands, the downward trend continues (summary in Flather and Hoekstra, in press). For example, Frayer et al. (1983) described an 8.4 percent decline from 1954 to 1974. Only 12 percent of the remainder is classed as high-quality for waterfowl (Bellrose 1980), and the process continues.

Additional factors are affecting populations of some species that breed in wetlands. For example, the Breeding Bird Survey shows that Franklin's gulls (*Larus pipixcan*) declined at a mean annual rate of 14.9 percent for the past 21 years— a cumulative decline of 97 percent. Similarly, black tern (*Chlidonias niger*) numbers dropped 80 percent, common terns (*Sterna hirundo*) 65 percent, and American avocets (*Recurvirostra americana*) 50 percent in the same period. These declines were well in excess of equivalent declines in wetlands, indicating that other factors were involved. Perhaps inputs of agricultural chemicals are reducing the quality of wetlands on which these and other wildlife species depend (Grue et al. 1986, 1988).

Recent estimates indicate that 70 to 90 percent of native riparian habitat has been eliminated (summary in Ohmart and Anderson 1986) with 98 percent lost in the Sacramento Valley of California (Smith 1977), 95 percent in Arizona (Warner 1979), and 90 to 95 percent of the cottonwood-willow riparian type in the Rocky Mountains/Great Plains region (Johnson and Carothers 1981). Ohmart and Anderson (1986) concluded that as the cottonwood-willow "community type becomes extirpated from the West Coast eastward, at least 10 bird species will be lost . . ." Western riparian wetlands are among the nine most critical problem areas to receive emphasis in protecting vanishing habitats (Flather and Hoekstra, in press). With wholesale conversion of riparian habitats that support some of the richest and abundant bird assemblages, it is understandable that a high proportion of riparian-dependent species, such as Least Bell's vireo (*Vireo bellii pusillus*), are listed as threatened, endangered, and sensitive species (Johnson 1978). Although once widespread and abundant throughout California, this vireo no longer occurs in northern portions of that state (Goldwasser et al. 1980).

Conversion of range lands to crop production are related to declines of grassland birds (Robbins et al. 1986). For example, lark buntings (*Calamospiza melanocorys*) declined at an average, annual rate of 2.8 percent from 1966 to 1987— perhaps a total decline of 45 percent in 21 years. Similarly, grasshopper sparrows (*Ammodramus savannarum*) declined 50 percent, lark sparrows (*Chondestes grammacus*) 41 percent, and field sparrows (*Spizella pusilla*) 55 percent during the same 21-year period.

There has been a general decline in abundance of neotropical migrants that breed in eastern hardwood forests. Studies have documented the absence of many species of neotropical migrants from small, isolated forest patches (for example, see review and summary in Whitcomb et al. 1981).

C.S. Robbins and his colleagues (publication in preparation) found that 12 of 51 species (23.5 percent) of neotropical migrants in the eastern United States had negative population trends from 1966 to 1978. Thirty-eight species (74.5 percent) showed positive trends (18 significant). From 1978 to 1987, however, 38 species showed negative trends (15 significant) and 12 had positive trends (four significant). The difference between median trends was also significant. Trends of 28 species changed from positive to negative between periods, eight involving changes from significant positive to significant negative trends. On the other hand, only seven species showed a pattern of decline from 1966 to 1978 followed by an increase from 1978 to 1987, and only one involved a change from a significant negative to a significant positive trend.

Population trends of permanent residents and short-distance migrants did not parallel the pattern shown by neotropical migrants. Six of 13 (46 percent) permanent residents had positive trends in both periods, but none showed a pattern of increase from 1966 to 1978 followed by a decline from 1978 to 1987. Median trends were not significantly different between periods. Three species of short-distance migrants had increasing trends from 1966 to 1978, followed by a decline from 1978 to 1987; eight short-distance migrants had positive trends before 1979, and six had positive trends after 1978. Short-distance migrants increased (not significantly) in median trend between periods.

The causes of population declines among neotropical migrants that breed in eastern hardwood forests cannot be ascertained from available data. The fact that long-distance migrants are now found breeding primarily or solely in relatively large forest stands suggests that smaller remnants of forest are less suitable for these migrants. However, Verner (1984) asserts that a comparison of trends among different assemblages of birds can provide insights about cause-and-effect relationships. If this is true, the fact that populations of permanent residents and short-distance migrants did not decline, while those of long-distance migrants did, indicates that problems probably exist somewhere on the migration routes or wintering grounds of the long-distance migrants.

SMALL MAMMALS

For this section, "small mammals" are terrestrial species no larger than hares and porcupines (*Erethizon dorsatum*); viz., shrews and moles; bats; pikas, rabbits and hares; and rodents (except beaver, *Castor canadensis*, which is a furbearer). Weasels and other mustelids in the "small" size range are excluded here, because they are considered in the section on furbearers. About 250 species of small mammals occur in the United States (Burt and Grossenheider 1952).

Long-term monitoring of small mammal populations has not been done, probably because small mammals are inconspicuous, relatively nonvocal, and mostly nocturnal. The effort needed to obtain statistically reliable estimates of population trends is extraordinarily costly. Thus, the few species with quantitative assessments of population changes are based on occasional studies restricted geographically. Nonetheless, certain patterns emerge, indicating habitat types in which long-term changes will likely have significant, negative impacts on populations of many species. In addition, available data clearly show an urgent need for special attention to an entire mammalian taxo— the bats (Order Chiroptera).

The Plight of Bats

Only five of 37 bat species are on the Federal list of Threatened and Endangered Species, but probably others should be listed. For example, migratory populations of Brazilian free-tailed bats (*Tadarida brasiliensis*) have harmful levels of DDE in their fat (Geluso et al. 1981). Summer populations of these bats at Carlsbad Caverns, New Mexico, were estimated at 8.7 million in 1936 (Allison 1937) but only at 200,000 in 1973 (Altenbach et al. 1979) —— a decline of 98 percent. Similarly, at Eagle Creek Cave, Arizona, summer numbers of these bats dropped from an estimated 25 million in 1964 (Cockrum 1969) to an estimated 600,000 in 1970 (Reidinger 1972)—— also a decline of 98 percent. Geluso et al. (1981) speculated that the ban on use of DDT in the United States has not benefited these migratory populations of bats, either because they continue to accumulate DDT where it is still used in the bats' foraging areas in Mexico, or because illegal use or excessive pre-ban accumulations continue to be a problem where the bats forage in the United States.

Jones (1971) reported declining populations of 22 bat species in the United States, and a later survey indicated that all phyllostomatid bats were declining (Jones 1976). Williams (1986) proposed special concern for six species and one subspecies of bats in California— more than 25 percent of those recorded in the state.

In addition to pesticides, other factors such as habitat destruction, roost disturbance, and public ignorance influence population declines of bats. Better management of human activities in roost caves and education of the public about the role of bats in the regulation of insect populations are measures that could contribute to recovery of bat populations.

Long-Term Environmental Changes

As with birds, small mammal populations respond to short-term weather changes and food supply, but such factors are normal and unlikely to be of concern. Not surprisingly, however, long-term habitat changes create problems for small mammals. For example, Williams (1986) identified 36 species or subspecies in California facing threats to population maintenance. Thirty-two of these are small mammals, and habitat loss was identified as a concern in 28 cases. Seven taxa are impacted by loss of riparian habitat; four for wetlands; four for salt marsh; six for grassland/desert scrub; two for grasslands; two for thickets; and one each for sagebrush, fir forests, and conifer/sage habitat.

The loss of riparian habitats has occurred on such a massive scale that it constitutes a threat to most wildlife species that depend on them. Evidence from Williams' (1986) California study shows this to be the case for small mammals in that state, and the pattern is probably similar elsewhere— particularly in arid regions. A study in disturbed and undisturbed riparian habitats in mixed-conifer forests of southwestern Oregon showed "a differentially high use of riparian habitat by small mammals. Harsh perturbations of this habitat radically affect the presence and abundance of many species. Riparian leave strips were found to support small-mammal communities comparable to undisturbed sites" (Cross 1985). A study of conifer forests in the western Sierra Nevada suggested that many species of small mammals, even typically upland forms, depend on riparian areas as refuges during unusually hot, dry, or cold weather (D. F. Williams, personal communication, 1984). In any case, heroic efforts are needed to save existing riparian habitat and to re-establish native riparian vegetation on a large scale in areas where it has been removed (for example, see Anderson and Ohmart 1985; Swenson and Mullins 1985). Similar concerns apply to wetlands, grasslands, and shrublands converted to agricultural uses or overtaken by urban sprawl and industrial parks.

Forest fragmentation and removal of old-growth forests is a problem for small mammals. Two factors negatively impact populations: loss of habitat and fragmentation of habitat into patches too small to support some species and too isolated to permit effective dispersal of animals among patches. For example, Gottfried (1979) recorded seven (average 5.8) species of small mammals on four "mainland" forest plots of 74 acres or more, but no more than three (average 1.6) species in any of 10 isolated patches of forest (0.02 to 0.16 acres, average 0.11 acres) surrounded by cornfields in eastern Iowa. The isolated woodlots were separated from "mainland" sources of small mammals by distances ranging from 0.05 to 1.79 miles, but only patch size contributed significantly to variation in the number of species. Larger patches had more species than small ones, and no patch smaller than 0.12 acres had more than 1 species of small mammal. Matthiae and Stearns (1981) reported similar results in 22 isolated forest patches in Wisconsin and we found a significant correlation between patch size and number of species in these data.

THE ENDANGERED SPECIES ACT OF 1973

Extinction is not a new phenomenon, but the impacts of a rapidly growing and developing human population have caused the premature disappearance of many animal and plant species. In 1966, this led Congress to pass the first in a series of federal laws intended to protect imperiled wildlife. A stronger law replaced it in 1969, followed by the Endangered Species Act of 1973, widely considered among the strongest, most comprehensive wildlife conservation laws ever enacted. It provides powers to protect animal and plant species listed as endangered or threatened, conserve their habitat, and bring about their recovery. The U.S. Fish and Wildlife Service holds responsibility for terrestrial and fresh-water species, and authority for most marine species rests with the National Marine Fisheries Service.

Listing Protection
Except as authorized by Congress, wildlife is under state jurisdiction. Listing a species as endangered or threatened gives the U.S. Fish and Wildlife Service or the National Marine Fisheries Service authority to perform conservation activities on its behalf, including preservation of habitat and institution of a recovery plan.

These controls are sometimes enough to lead to a species' recovery. For example, in the 1960s, the American alligator (*Alligator mississippiensis*) was jeopardized by overexploitation for the exotic leather market. After receiving protection, the alligator recovered to the extent that it was delisted and some states have instituted hunting seasons. Threats facing most listed species are more difficult to resolve.

As of August 1, 1988, 317 animals and 187 plants were listed as endangered or threatened and 2,485 plants and 1,506 animals identified as candidates for future listing. Candidates fall into two categories: the first describes the 881 plants and 86 animals for which "substantial" information exists to support listing; the second contains the 1,604 plants and 1,420 animals for which information exists showing that listing is *possibly* appropriate.

The U.S. Fish and Wildlife Service estimates that 2,000 to 2,500 species from both categories will qualify for protection. Some 50 are listed annually.

Appropriations enacted for listing actions were $2.8 million in fiscal year 1984, $3.2 million in fiscal year 1985, $3.1 million in fiscal year 1986, $3.5 million in fiscal year 1987, and $3.2 million in fiscal year 1988. Considering a five percent inflation rate, this represented a 16 percent decline in resources for this activity from fiscal years 1984 to 1988.

If a federal agency finds that a planned action may adversely affect a listed species, it must consult with the U.S. Fish and Wildlife Service. Such activities include water projects; issuance of permits for wetland modification; changes in land management practices; resource use and development (mining, logging, grazing, oil/gas production) that occur on public lands or require a federal permit; and federal funding for construction. When consultations are initiated early in the planning process, solutions are usually developed that achieve project objectives and avoid threats to listed species and their habitat.

Over the past nine years, the U.S. Fish and Wildlife Service has conducted more than 60,000 such consultations, and the numbers are growing each year. Most consultations have been informal and quickly accomplished. As most federal agencies are becoming more aware of responsibilities under the Endangered Species Act, a growing number of potential impacts on listed species are avoided.

Appropriations for consultations were $2.8 million in fiscal year 1984, $2.8 million in fiscal year 1985, $2.6 million in fiscal year 1986, $3.1 million in fiscal year 1987, and $2.9 million in fiscal year 1988. Considering a five percent inflation rate, this represented a 21 percent decline in available resources over the period of fiscal 1984 to 1988.

The goal of the Endangered Species Act is restoration of listed species so that they are secure, self-sustaining components of their ecosystems, no longer in need of special protection. The Endangered Species Act requires the U.S. Fish and Wildlife Service to implement recovery plans for each native endangered and threatened species which set recovery goals and identify protection, research, and management needs.

Research on endangered species is increasing. In Hawaii, for example, palila (*Loxioides bailleui*) populations are monitored to determine its possible recovery after the removal of feral sheep that were overgrazing its habitat. Propagation studies are proceeding for the whooping crane (*Grus americana*), the Puerto Rican parrot (*Amazona vittata*), and other rare wildlife. Large numbers of Apache trout (*Salmo apache*), masked bobwhites (*Colinus virgini-*

anus ridgwayii), and some other listed species have been raised in captivity and released. Cuttings from the one known Knowlton cactus (*Pediocactus knowltonii*) population have been transplanted to a second site in New Mexico.

Despite some successes, propagation docs not guarantee recovery. Diseases have struck facilities housing whooping cranes and black-footed ferrets. Depleted gene pools are a concern. Some species do not breed readily in captivity or require special environmental conditions not yet understood. Other problems may be encountered when species are released into the wild.

Reintroduction, a practice clouded by other problems, can be controversial. As an example, in 1975 the red wolf (*Canis rufus*) became extinct in the wild when the last few were captured to prevent genetic swamping by an expanding coyote population. The wolves bred in captivity, but it was difficult to find an area whose residents were willing to accept a reintroduction. In 1982 Congress authorized the designation of "experimental populations" which can be managed with more flexibility than previously allowed, making such reintroductions more palatable.

Some form of habitat enhancement and/or protection is important in recovery plans. Federal agencies are required to conserve the habitat of listed species. Agreements with state agencies and similar agreements or conservation easements with private landowners are sometimes possible. Organizations such as The Nature Conservancy have been helpful in making these arrangements. In some cases, purchases of particularly important and vulnerable habitat have been made.

Approximately $4.4 million was enacted for recovery actions in fiscal year 1984, $5.9 in fiscal year 1985, $6.0 in fiscal year 1986, $6.4 in fiscal year 1987, and $7.5 in fiscal year 1988 (excluding research and law enforcement). Considering a five percent inflation rate, this represents an increase of 40 percent in funds available for recovery from fiscal year 1984 to fiscal year 1988. These funds supported 190 recovery actions for 100 listed species. About 10 recovery actions per listed species are needed, on average, to achieve recovery goals.

LEGISLATIVE IMPACTS ON WILDLIFE AND FISH RESOURCES — THE FOOD SECURITY ACT

An important development in legislative policy that has potential to improve the quantity and quality of wildlife habitat is the 1985 Food Security Act (also known as the Farm Act). The Food Security Act encourages agricultural producers to address soil erosion, enhance water quality, and restore wildlife habitat by integrating a conservation dimension into farm support programs.

A key provision is the Conservation Reserve Program that pays farmers to retire highly erodible croplands and filter strip areas adjacent to streams, lakes or reservoirs from commodity production for a minimum period of 10 years. In addition to annual rental payments, farmers receive technical assistance and cost-sharing for establishing protective vegetative cover.

The goal is to retire up to 45 million acres of highly erodible land. As of February 1988, 25.5 million acres enrolled in 239,409 contracts. Texas led with more than five million acres; Montana, North Dakota, Kansas, Minnesota, Colorado, Iowa, and Missouri each have more than two million acres; Nebraska, South Dakota, Oklahoma, Idaho, and Washington have more than one million acres.

The Conservation Reserve Program has diverted 1.6 million acres to trees, with 73 percent being planted to pine in Georgia, Mississippi, Alabama, and South Carolina. Only about 5,200 acres have been established as windbreaks or shelterbelts in the Great Plains. Nearly seven million acres have been returned to native grasses and another one million acres have been planted to native grasses, legumes, and shrubs. About 2,500 acres of shallow water areas have been created and another 16,100 acres protected as filter strip areas for wetlands.

The Conservation Reserve Program's potential for increasing wildlife was demonstrated by the 1956 Soil Bank Program which peaked in 1960, when more than 28 million acres of grassland and woody cover were established. The abundance of pheasants (Berner 1987) and other grassland wildlife species increased significantly as a result.

With 1.8 million acres in the Soil Bank, pheasant numbers in South Dakota went from a population of 4-6 million birds to 8-11 million (Dahlgren 1967). A 250 percent increase in nonresident hunters, who contributed $10 million annually to South Dakota's economy, was documented (Erickson and Wiebe 1973).

Studies are underway to document vegetative and wildlife responses to the Conservation Reserve Program in the Midwest, Northern Great Plains/Intermountain, Southern Great Plains, and Southeast.

Wildlife benefits could be expanded by converting annual set-asides to multi-year set-asides as authorized by the Food Security Act. Without multi-year planning, farmers are reluctant to invest in long-term vegetative cover that would provide soil, water, and wildlife benefits on set-aside lands. As a result, most annual set-asides, about 47.5 million acres annually since 1985, are unseeded or lightly seeded. Moreover, U.S. Department of Agriculture policies requiring farmers to disc the little cover available on annual set-aside acreages reduce nesting success of wildlife species (Berner 1988).

Three other provisions of the Food Security Act offer potential by discouraging further degradation or destruction of habitat. These provisions deny benefits to farmers who drain wetlands or bring previously unplowed erodible land into commodity crop production; they also require farmers who are tilling highly erodible croplands to develop plans to protect soil, water, and wildlife.

Agricultural conversion has been a most pervasive cause of wetland habitat loss and wildlife decline. Such habitat loss to agriculture between the mid-1950s and mid-1970s was 12 million acres (U.S. Department of Agriculture 1987). Since then, the rate of drainage is as much as 400,000 acres (87 percent of the annual wetland loss) each year (Heimlich and Langner 1986). About 5.2 million acres of the 71 million acres of remaining nonfederal palustrine wetlands have a medium to high potential for agricultural conversion (Heimlich and Langner 1986), of which two million acres fall within the six wetland regions identified as critical for wildlife (Tiner 1984). Agricultural drainage within one region, the prairie potholes, is the major factor leading to waterfowl population declines (Bellrose 1980).

Properly administered, and in combination with tax code reform that eliminates fast write-off of wetland drainage costs, the act should reduce rates of wetland habitat conversion to agriculture and help maintain populations of wetland wildlife.

A final conservation provision established by the Food Security Act author-izes the Farmers Home Administration to establish 50-year or longer conserva-tion easements on land held in inventory; as well, easement provisions can be used to lower the debt of farmer borrowers. Conservation easements protect valuable wetlands, highly erodible uplands, threatened or endangered species habitats, and other natural or cultural features. The U.S. Fish and Wildlife Service works to protect and enhance 80,000-100,000 acres of habitat through conservation easements on more than 1,100 land parcels now in Farmers Home Administration inventory. Another estimated 150,000 acres is subject to review by the Fish and Wildlife Service. Additional opportunities for securing conser-vation easements through debt restructuring exist on much of the estimated five million acres of farm land qualifying for Farmers Home Administration loan servicing.

Overall, a wide variety of wildlife— birds, mammals, reptiles, amphibians, and fish — will be affected favorably by the protection and enhancement of wetland, woodland and upland habitats through the conservation provisions of the 1985 Farm Act (Berner 1988; Robinson 1987).

Other laws enacted since 1965 that have great potential for positive impacts on wildlife include, among others, the Endangered Species Act of 1973, Forest and Rangeland Renewable Resources Planning Act of 1974, the Multiple-Use Sustained Yield Act of 1960, the National Environmental Policy Act of 1976, the Public Rangelands Improvement Act of 1978, the Sikes Act, the Soil and Water Resources Conservation Act of 1977, and the North American Waterfowl Plan.

HOLISTIC MANAGEMENT

Wildlife species and their habitats do not exist independently of other species, resources, and uses. All species are dependent to some degree on each other and no "free lunch" exists in nature or in human affairs. Every activity has a price (or trade-off) in both ecologic and economic senses. Holistic resource management attempts to recognize these trade-offs and guide decisions toward societal benefit.

Holistic management involves application of knowledge about all species and their environments into an integrated management approach. It is largely still an unrealized ideal. The alternative scenario is separation of management into component parts. The latter scheme is attractive in that all variables are judged to react to manipulation of the one variable in question. Most academic structures, educational approaches, on-the-job training, and the human tendency to simplify reinforce this traditional approach to resource management.

Traditional resource management is functional— foresters manage trees, hydrologists manage water, and wildlife specialists manage wildlife. Multiple resource management, on the other hand, has been consistently aligned with mitigation procedures and documentation of impacts rather than with applied concepts of multiple objectives and joint products.

The answers to many questions about the cumulative effects of human action on ecosystems and interactions among ecosystems are presently not understood. Management approaches must adapt to new sets of driving variables. Past approaches are not sufficient to guide management decisions in the 21st century, and natural resource managers know this. The management of resources, however, depends on the state of human knowledge and the willingness of the traditional interest groups to cooperate.

Too often, the human view of wildlife has lacked altruism. Society's goals and values have reflected the use and availability of wildlife. The value of wildlife is based in a perception that changes with degrees of wildlife availability, knowledge about wildlife, and a sense of its importance. This value exists only to the extent it is recognized and acted upon. As society's values change, resource management adjusts. If management fails to adjust, the availability of resources will be increasingly unsatisfactory to society.

When management is out of step with society's demands and values, litigation and legislation occur. Holistic management attempts incorporation of societal views, as they become known, through management rather than through Congress or the courts. Under holistic management, political and managerial decisions should build on objective and encompassing knowledge concerning interactions, consequences, and cumulative effects.

Holistic management also has economic aspects because it requires knowledge of interactions among resources and uses. Decisions based on single or dominant use alone are not appropriate under holistic management. Provision for the plethora of wildlife species, most not valued in traditional markets, requires decisions not guided by traditional economic theory.

Traditional economic approaches to decision-making in situations using multiple resources and resulting in multiple products require prices or values on each. When all products and resources are valued and their production relationships known, it is possible to determine a course of action where marginal cost is equal to marginal revenue for all outputs, resulting in the most efficient production mix.

However, the application of multiple input, multiple output economic theory is difficult to apply even with as few as three outputs and three inputs with known prices involved in an analysis. Expanding this economic theory to holistic natural resource management guided by the maxim that "everything is related to everything else" produces a situation not presently capable of empirical derivation, particularly when some inputs and outputs, such as wildlife, are not valued in markets. Reality forces the use of relatively simplistic relationships, assumptions, and conservative estimates to compensate.

Truly holistic management may not be achievable with today's technology, but limiting ourselves to single or dominant use based on tradition or shifting political pressures is clearly not in society's best interest in the long run. Wildlife resources and their habitats will continue to increase in value and yet not be exchanged in markets. The challenge is to observe the actions and reactions of society to management actions and alternatives and consider the value of all products in the decision process. The presence or absence of a market does not dictate the presence or absence of value.

SUMMARY

Examination of the information presented here leads to some overall conclusions. Management has shown the greatest success among species (such as most big game species and some threatened and endangered species) for which habitat existed in some abundance. With proper management practices, species with severely reduced populations could respond to protection, reintroduction into suitable habitat from which they had been extirpated or which was previously unoccupied, reduction of competition, and population manipulation.

The species that are in trouble— and there are probably many more than we currently recognize— tend to be species whose habitats have been declining in amount and quality. We are entering into an era in natural resource management that will require a more holistic approach, implying the need for knowledge and application of community ecology. The ongoing planning operations of the U.S. Forest Service and other land management agencies have revealed how lacking and inadequate our understanding of community ecology (including the human aspects of economic analysis) are to assure long-term viability of the ecosystems that provide the renewable natural resources on which civilization relies.

Resources going into the research and development needed to provide the understanding necessary to move to the holistic management of renewable natural resource are woefully inadequate. And, at the rate ecosystems are being altered, time is obviously short.

Figure 8.2. Trends: White-Tailed Deer Populations

(State reports)

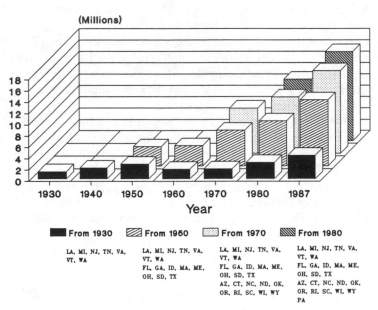

From 1930   **From 1950**   **From 1970**   **From 1980**

LA, MI, NJ, TN, VA, VT, WA	LA, MI, NJ, TN, VA, VT, WA	LA, MI, NJ, TN, VA, VT, WA	LA, MI, NJ, TN, VA, VT, WA
	FL, GA, ID, MA, ME, OH, SD, TX	FL, GA, ID, MA, ME, OH, SD, TX	FL, GA, ID, MA, ME, OH, SD, TX
		AZ, CT, NC, ND, OK, OR, RI, SC, WI, WY	AZ, CT, NC, ND, OK, OR, RI, SC, WI, WY
			PA

(Federal Reports)

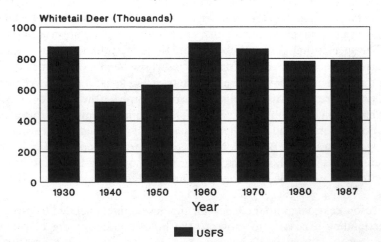

USFS

Figure 8.2 continued. Trends: Black Bear Populations

(State reports)

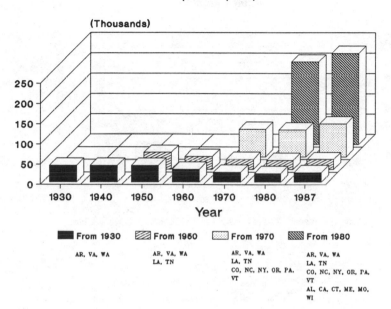

From 1930	From 1950	From 1970	From 1980
AR, VA, WA	AR, VA, WA LA, TN	AR, VA, WA LA, TN CO, NC, NY, OR, PA, VT	AR, VA, WA LA, TN CO, NC, NY, OR, PA, VT AL, CA, CT, ME, MO, WI

(Federal Reports)

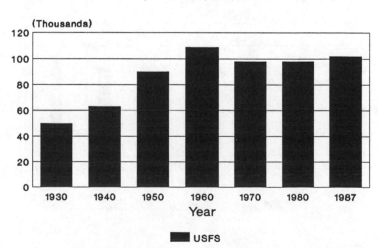

USFS

Figure 8.2 continued. Trends: Elk Populations

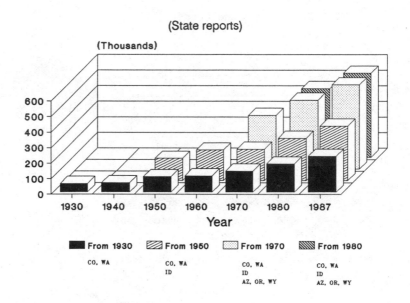

(State reports)

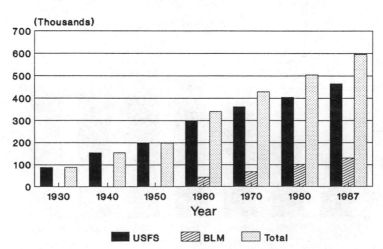

(Federal Reports)

Figure 8.2 continued. Trends: Pronghorn Populations

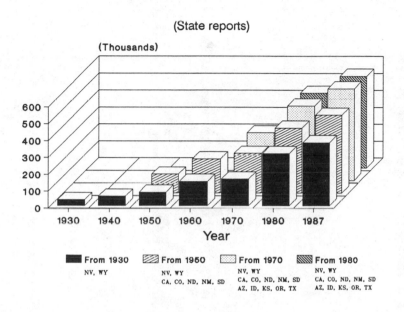

(State reports)

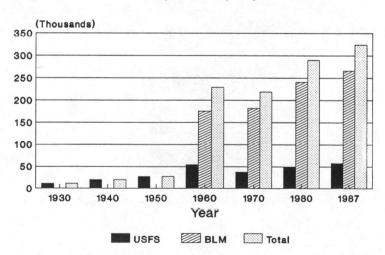

(Federal Reports)

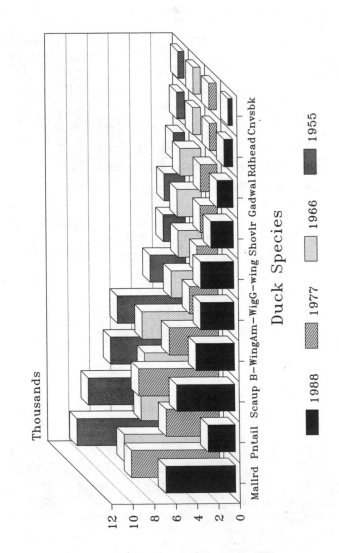

Figure 8.3. Breeding Population Estimates 10 Species of Ducks — 11 Year Intervals

Source: USDI, 1988: North American Waterfowl Management Plan

REFERENCES

Allen, A.W. 1987. The relationship between habitat and furbearers. Pages 164-179 in M. Novak, J.A. Baker, M.E. Obbard, and B. Malloch, eds. **Wild furbearer management and conservation in North America.** Ministry of Natural Resources, Ontario, Canada. 1150 pp.

Allison, V.C. 1937. Evening bat flight from Carlsbad Caverns. **Journal of Mammalogy.** 18:80-82.

Altenbach, J.S., K.N. Geluse, and D.E. Wilson. 1979. Population size of *Tadarida brasiliensis* at Carlsbad Caverns in 1973. pp. 342-358 in H.H. Genoways and R.J. Baker, eds., Biological Investigations in the Guadalupe Mountains National Park, Texas. National Park Service, Proceedings and Transaction, Series No. 4.

American Ornithologists' Union. 1983. **Check-list of North American Birds.** Sixth edition. American Ornithologists' Union. Allen Press, Lawrence, Kansas. 877 pp.

Andelt, W.F. 1987. Coyote predation. Pages 128-140 in M. Novak, J.A. Baker, M.E. Obbard, and B. Malloch, eds. **Wild furbearer management and conservation in North America.** Ministry of Natural Resources, Ontario, Canada. 1150 pp.

Anderson, B.W. and R.D. Ohmart. 1985. Managing riparian vegetation and wildlife along the Colorado River: Synthesis of data, predictive models, and management. pp. 123-127 in R.R. Johnson, C.D. Ziebell, D.R. Patton, P.F. Ffolliott, and R.H. Hamre, tech. coords., Riparian Ecosystems and Their Management: Reconciling Conflicting Uses. Forest North American Riparian Conference, Tucson, Arizona, 16-18 April 1985. Gen. Tech. Rep. RM-120. Fort Collins, CO: U.S. Department of Agriculture, Forest Service, Rocky Mountain Forest and Range Experiment Station.

Bellrose, F.C. 1980. **Ducks, Geese and Swans of North America.** Wildlife Management Institute. Stackpole Books, Harrisburg, Pennsylvania. 540 pp.

Berner, A.H. 1988. The 1985 Farm Act and its implications for wildlife. **Audubon Wildlife Report 1958/1989.** Academic Press. San Diego, CA. pp. 437-465.

Berner, A.H. 1987. Federal pheasants: impact of federal agricultural programs on pheasant habitat, 1934-85. In W.R. Edwards and G. Burger, eds., **Symposium on Pheasants: Symptoms of Wildlife Problems on Agricultural Lands.** 49th Midwest Fish and Wildlife Conference, North Central Chapter of the Wildlife Society.

Brokaw, H.P. (editor). 1978. Wildlife and America. Council on Environmental Quality. Washington, D.C. 532 pp. 151-155 in M. Novak, J.A. Baker, M.E. Obbard, and B. Malloch, eds. Wild furbearer management and conservation in North America. Ministry of Natural Resources, Ontario, Canada. 1150 pp.

Burt, W.H. and R.P. Grossenheider. 1952. **A Field Guide to the Mammals.** Houghton Mifflin Co., Boston, Massachusetts. 200 pp.

Cockrum, E.L. 1969. Migration in the guano bat, *Tadarida brasiliensis*. pp. 303-336 in J.K. Jones, Jr. ed., **Contributions in Mammalogy.** University of Kansas. Museum of Natural History Miscellaneous Publication No. 51.

Cross, S.P. 1985. Responses of small mammals to forest riparian perturbations. pp. 269-275 in R.R. Johnson, C.D. Ziebell, D.R. Patton, P.F. Ffolliott, and R.H. Hamre, tech. coords., Riparian Ecosystems and Their Management: Reconciling Conflicting Uses. First North American Riparian Conference, Tucson, Arizona, 16-18 April 1985. Gen. Tech. Rep. RM-120. Fort Collins, CO: U.S. Department of Agriculture, Forest Service, Rocky Mountain Forest and Range Experiment Station.

Dahlgren, R. B. 1967. What happened to our pheasants in 1966? **South Dakota Conservation Digest.** 34(4):6-9.

de Almeida, M.H. 1987. Nuisance furbearer damage control in urban and suburban areas. pp. 996-1006 in M. Novak, J.A. Baker, M.E. Obbard, and B. Malloch, eds. **Wild furbearer management and conservation in North America.** Ministry of Natural Resources, Ontario, Canada. 1150 pp.

Deems, E.F., Jr., and D. Pursley. 1978. North American furbearers: their management, research and harvest status in 1976. University of Maryland Press, College Park, Maryland. 171 pp.

Droege, S. and J. Sauer. 1987. Breeding Bird Survey - Administrative Report to Cooperators - 1987. U.S. Fish and Wildlife Service, Laurel, Maryland. 6 pp.

Dumke, R.T., G.V. Burger, and J.R. March. 1981. Wildlife management on private lands. LaCrosse Printing Co., La Crosse, WI. 576 pp.

Erickson, R.E. and J.E. Wiebe. 1973. Pheasants, economics and land retirement programs in South Dakota. Wildlife Society Bulletin. 1:22-27.

Flather, C.H. and T.W. Hoekstra. [In press] An Analysis of the Wildlife and Fish Situation in the United States: 1989-2040. Gen. Tech. Rep. WO-xxx. Washington, D.C: U.S. Department of Agriculture, Forest Service. xx p.

Frayer, W.E., T.J. Monahan, D.C. Bowden, and F.A. Graybill. 1983. Status and trends of wetland and deepwater habitats in the conterminous United States, 1950's to 1970's. Colorado State University, Department of Forest and Wood Sciences, Fort Collins, Colorado. 32 pp.

Geluso, K.N., J.S. Altenbach, and D.E. Wilson. 1981. Organochlorine residues in young Mexican Free-tailed Bats from several roosts. American Midland Naturalist. 105:249-257.

Gentile, J.R. 1983. The evolution and geographic aspects of the anti- trapping movement: a classic resource use conflict. Ph.D. diss., Oregon State University, Corvallis, Oregon. 145 pp.

Goldwasser, S., D. Gaines and S.R. Wilbur. 1980. The Least Bell's Vireo in California: a de facto endangered race. American Birds. 34:742-745.

Gottfried, B.M. 1979. Small mammal populations in woodlot islands. American Midland Naturalist. 102:105-112.

Grue, C.E., M.W. Tome, G.A. Swanson, S.M. Borthwick, and L.R. DeWeese. 1988. Agricultural chemicals and the quality of prairie-pothole wetlands for adult and juvenile waterfowl— what are the concerns? Pages 55-64 in Proceedings of the National Symposium on Protection of Wetlands from Agricultural Impacts, P.J. Stuber, coord. Biological Report No. 88 (16). U.S. Department of Interior, Fish and Wildlife Service.

Grue, C.E., L.R. DeWeese, P. Mineau, G.A. Swanson, J.R. Foster, P.M. Arnold, J.N. Huckins, P.J. Sheehan, W.K. Marshall, and A.P. Ludden. 1986. Potential impacts of agricultural chemicals on waterfowl and other wildlife inhabiting prairie wetlands: An evaluation of research needs and approaches. Transactions of the North American Wildlife and Natural Resources Conference. 51:357-383.

Heimlich, R.E. and L.L. Langner. 1986. Swampbusting: wetland conversion and farm programs. Econ. Rept. No. 551, Econ. Res. Serv., U.S. Dept. of Agriculture, Washington, D.C. 34 pp.

Hill, E.P. 1987. Beaver restoration. pp. 281-285 in Kallman, H., C.P. Agee, W.R. Goforth, J.P. Linduska, S.R. Hillebrand, N. Rollison, W.J. Savannah, W.T. Nebel, S.A. Exum, and G. Gallo. Restoring America's Wildlife: 1937-1987. U.S. Department of Agriculture, Fish and Wildlife Service, Washington, D.C. 394 pp.

Hirsch, A., W.B. Krohn, D.L. Schweitzer, C.H. Thomas. 1979. Trends and needs in federal inventories of wildlife habitat. Trans. N. Am. Wildl. Nat. Res. Con. 44:340-359.

Johnson, R.R. 1978. The lower Colorado River: a western system. pp. 41-55 in R.R. Johnson and J.F. McCormick, tech. coords., Strategies for Protection and Management of Floodplain Wetlands and Other Riparian Ecosystems. Proceedings of a Symposium. Gen. Tech. Rep. WO-12. Washington, D.C.: U.S. Department of Agriculture, Forest Service.

Johnson, R.R. and S.W. Carothers. 1981. Southwestern Riparian Habitats and Recreation: Interrelationships and Impacts in the Rocky Mountain Region. Eisenhower Consortium Bulletin. Fort Collins, CO: U.S. Department of Agriculture, Forest Service, Rocky Mountain Forest and Range Experiment Station.

Jones, C. 1976. Economics and Conservation. Biology of Bats of the New World Family Phyllostomatidae, Part I. The Museum, Texas Tech University, Special Publications. 10:133-145.

Jones, C. 1971. The status of some populations of North American bats. Paper presented at the Symposium on Bat Research, Albuquerque, New Mexico, 26-27 November 1971.

Kellert, S.R. 1981. Trappers and trapping in American society. pp. 1971-2003 in J.A. Chapman and D. Pursley, eds. Proceedings of the Worldwide Furbearer Conference, Frostburg, Maryland. 2056 pp.

MacInnes, C.D. 1987. Rabies. Pages 910-929 in M. Novak, J.A. Baker, M.E. Obbard, and B. Malloch, eds. Wild furbearer management and conservation in North America. Ministry of Natural Resources, Ontario, Canada. 1150 pp.

Matthiae, P.E. and F. Stearns. 1981. Mammals in forest islands in southeastern Wisconsin. Chapter 5. pp. 55-66 in R.L. Burgess and D.M. Sharpe, eds., Forest Island Dynamics in Man-Dominated Landscapes. Springer-Verlag, New York, NY.

Novak, M. 1987. Beaver. Pages 283-312 in M. Novak, J.A. Baker, M.E. Obbard, and B. Malloch, eds. Wild furbearer management and conservation in North America. Ministry of Natural Resources, Ontario, Canada. 1150 pp.

Obbard, M.E., J.G. Jones, R. Newman, A. Booth, A.J. Satterthwaite, and G. Linscombe. 1987. Furbearer harvests in North America. pp. 1007-1034 in M. Novak, J.A. Baker, M.E. Obbard, and B. Malloch, eds. Wild furbearer management and conservation in North America. Ministry of Natural Resources, Ontario, Canada. 1150 pp.

Ohmart, R.D. and B.W. Anderson. 1986. Riparian habitat. Chapter 9. pp. 169-199 in A.Y. Cooperrider, R.J. Boyd, and H.R. Stuart, comps. and eds., Inventory and Monitoring of Wildlife Habitat. U.S. Department of Interior, Bureau of Land Management, Washington, D.C.

Ray, A.J. 1987. The fur trade in North America: an overview from a historical geographical perspective. pp. 21-30 in M. Novak, J.A. Baker, M.E. Obbard, and B. Malloch, eds. Wild furbearer management and conservation in North America. Ministry of Natural Resources, Ontario, Canada. 1150 pp.

Reidinger, R.F., Jr. 1972. Factors influencing Arizona bat population levels. Ph.D. dissertation. University of Arizona, Tucson. 172 pp.

Robbins, C.S., D. Bystrak, and P.H. Geissler. 1986. The Breeding Bird Survey: Its First Fifteen Years, 1965-1979. Resource Publication 157. U.S. Department of Interior, Fish and Wildlife Service, Washington, D.C. 196 pp.

Robinson, A.Y. 1987. Saving soil and wildlife: the promise of the Farm Act's conservation title. Izaak Walton League of America Bulletin. 63 pp.

Roe, H.B. and Q.C. Ayers. 1954. Engineering for agricultural drainage. McGraw Hill Book Co., New York, New York. 501 pp.

Rothstein, S.I., J. Verner, and E. Stevens. 1980. Range expansion and diurnal changes in dispersion of the Brown-headed Cowbird in the Sierra Nevada. Auk. 97:253-267.

Schmidt, J.L. and D.L. Gilbert (editors). 1978. Big game of North America: ecology and management. Stackpole Books, Harrisburg, PA. 498 pp.

Scott, J.M., S. Mountainspring, F.L. Ramsey and C.B. Kepler. 1986. Forest Bird Communities of the Hawaiian Islands: Their Dynamics, Ecology, and Conservation. Cooper Ornithological Society. Studies in Avian Biology 9. 431 p.

Shieff, A. and J.A. Baker. 1987. Marketing and international fur markets. Pages 862-877 in M. Novak, J.A. Baker, M.E. Obbard, and B. Malloch, eds. Wild furbearer management and conservation in North America. Ministry of Natural Resources, Ontario, Canada. 1150 pp.

Smith, F. 1977. A short review of the status of riparian forests in California. pp. 1-2 in A. Sands, ed., Riparian Forests in California: Their Ecology and Conservation. Institute of Ecology, Publication 15. University of California. Davis, California.

Swenson, E.A. and C.L. Mullins. 1985. Revegetating riparian trees in Southwestern floodplains. pp. 135-138 in R.R. Johnson, C.D. Ziebell, D.R. Patton, P.F. Ffolliott, and R.H. Hamre, tech. coords., Riparian Ecosystems and Their Management: Reconciling Conflicting Uses. First North American Riparian Conference, Tucson, Arizona, 16-18 April 1985. Gen. Tech. Rep. RM-120. Fort Collins, CO: U.S. Department of Agriculture, Forest Service, Rocky Mountain Forest and Range Experiment Station.

Tiner, R.W., Jr. 1984. Wetlands of the United States: Current status and recent trends. National Wetlands Inventory, U.S. Fish and Wildlife Service, Washington, D.C. 59 pp.

United States Department of Agriculture. 1987. The second RCA appraisal: soil, water and related resources on nonfederal land in the United States — analysis of condition and trends. Washington, D.C. 377 pp.

United States Department of the Interior. 1987. 1987 status of waterfowl and fall flight forecast. United States Fish and Wildlife Service. Washington, D.C. 40 pp.

United States Department of the Interior. 1988. Final Supplemental environmental impact statement: issuance of annual regulations permitting the sport hunting of migratory birds. United States Fish and Wildlife Service. Washington, D.C. 339 pp.

Verner, J. 1984. The guild concept applied to management of bird populations. Environmental Management. 8:1-14.

Warner, R.E. 1979. California riparian study program: Background information and proposed study design. Planning Branch, California Department of Fish and Game, Sacramento, California. 177 pp.

Whitcomb, R.F., C.S. Robbins, J.F. Lynch, B.L. Whitcomb, M.K. Klimkiewicz, and D. Bystrak. 1981. Effects of forest fragmentation on avifauna of the eastern deciduous forest. Chapter 8. pp. 123-205 in R.L. Burgess and D.M. Sharpe, eds., Forest Island Dynamics in Man-Dominated Landscapes. Springer-Verlag, New York, New York.

White, R.J. 1987. Big game ranching in the United States. Wild Sheep and Goat International. Mesilla, NM. 355 pp.

Williams, D.F. 1986. Mammalian species of special concern in California. California Department of Fish and Game. Wildlife Management Division Administrative Report 86-1. 112 pp.

Williams, O. and J. McKegg. 1987. Nuisance furbearer management programs for urban areas. pp. 156-163 in M. Novak, J.A. Baker, M.E. Obbard, and B. Malloch, eds. Wild furbearer management and conservation in North America. Ministry of Natural Resources, Ontario, Canada. 1150 pp.

CHAPTER 9

Fisheries

William G. Gordon

A little more than 15 years ago, Americans concerned about the future of marine resources united to bring about extended fisheries jurisdiction for the United States in its offshore waters. Their efforts led in 1976 to passage of the Magnuson Fisheries Conservation and Management Act. Implementation of this act has led to almost total replacement of foreign fishing by American fishermen within the United States 200 nautical mile Exclusive Economic Zone. However, despite 12 years under the act many major stocks of fish and shellfish remain at low levels of abundance. Even in fresh-water environments such as the Great Lakes there have been drastic changes in populations of desirable fresh species. Scientists and fishery managers speculate that the causes range from overfishing and short-term habitat changes to long-term environmental changes. Whatever the cause, the available living aquatic resources within the jurisdiction of the United States are limited and will not satisfy the demands for quality recreational fishing and the needs of the American consumer by the year 2000.

This chapter forecasts the future needs for recreational and commercial fisheries. It also gives an overview of the status of fisheries by region and comments on the outlook for these fisheries by the year 2000.

STATUS OF RECREATIONAL FISHERIES

The National Survey of Fishing, Hunting, and Wildlife Associated Recreation, conducted at five-year intervals by the United States Fish and Wildlife Service, shows fishing as the premier outdoor recreational activity in the United States. Over the 30 years that the report has been produced, the data have shown a steady increase in the percentage of the population that fishes. The rate of participation increased more quickly during the first 15-year period of the report, from 1955 to 1970 (3.1 percent per year compounded). The data presented in the 1980 and 1985 reports indicated that the rate is slowing, but a

205

1.8 percent increase was measured during that period. This rate of increase still exceeded the 1.3 percent increase per year of the population of the United States.

The rapid expansion in fishing participation between 1960 and 1975 correlated with a boom in the construction of large (500 acres and larger) reservoirs. An estimated 239,000 acres of new reservoirs were added nationwide each year from 1960 to 1970. Between 1970 and 1980 large new additions of reservoir acres (39,000 acres per year) were followed by slower growth in fishing participation between 1980 and 1985. In numbers, the 1985 National Survey reports that 46.4 million Americans (one in four) age 16 and over participated in the recreational fishing in this country (Table 9.1). These anglers spent 976.6 million days and $28.1 billion pursuing their sport. The majority, 39.8 million, were fresh-water fishermen who fished 827.9 million days, an average of 21 days per angler. Additionally, 13.7 million anglers spent 155.2 million days salt-water fishing, an average of 11 days per salt-water angler.

Table 9.1. Anglers, Days of Participation and Days Per Fisherman, by Type of Fishing During 1985 [1]

Type of Fishing Opportunity	Participants (millions)		Days of Participation		Days per Fisherman
	Number	Percent	Number	Percent	
Total, all fishing [2]	46.4	100	976.6	100	21
Total, fresh-water	39.8	86	822.9	84	21
Fresh-water, except Great Lakes	38.4	83	785.9	80	20
Great Lakes	3.2	10	46.4	5	12
Total, salt-water	13.7	30	155.2	16	11

[1] These data were taken from the draft document entitled "1985 National Survey of Fishing, Hunting, and Wildlife-Associated Recreation."

[2] Since many anglers enjoy more than one type of fishing the total sum of anglers fishing different water types are greater than the total (46.4 million) for all fishing. Source: Titus 1988.

In short, recreational fishermen heavily use aquatic fishery resources today and, if continued growth is to be realized, we must become more conscious of their needs. Significant growth of fishing occurred as a result of tremendous development of manmade ponds and reservoirs. These developments for the most part have ceased so that continued opportunities for anglers must come from other sources. Over the next several decades recreational fishing partici- pants are projected to grow at the rate of two to four percent annually. By the turn of the century about 84 million Americans could be expected to participate in recreational fishing.

CONSUMPTION AND PRODUCTION

Annual per capita consumption of fish and shellfish from commercial sources has reached 15.4 pounds, a record level. The growth in per capita consumption has come largely in the fresh and frozen category, which has almost doubled since 1960. Per capita consumption is expected to grow and although growth at the six to seven percent rate of recent years is probably unrealistic, simply maintaining present per capita consumption at expected population levels will require significant new supplies of fish and shellfish products (Table 9.2).

The United States supply of fish and shellfish products is derived from United States landings and from imports. In 1987, commercial landings (edible and industrial) by United States fishermen at ports in the 50 states was 6.9 billion pounds (3.1 million metric tons) valued at $3.1 billion. Commercial landings by United States fishermen at unloading points outside the 50 states were 4.1 billion pounds (1.9 million metric tons) valued at $454 million. The total import value of edible and nonedible fishery products was a record $8.8 billion in 1987. Imports of edible fishery products (product weight) were a record 3.2 million pounds (1.5 million metric tons). Imports of nonedible products were valued at $3.1 billion (also a record value). Overall the United States supply of edible fishery products (domestic landing plus imports round weight equivalent) was a record 10.6 billion pounds (4.8 million metric tons) in 1987. Exports of edible and nonedible fishery products of domestic origin were $1.7 billion in 1987– also a record. Imports reflect a change upward of six percent from 1986.

In 1986, the most recent year for which data are available, world commercial fishery landings were 92.2 million metric tons. Global production from wild fisheries appears to have peaked and most fishery scientists and managers believe production will remain within the 90-100 million metric ton level. Fluctuations will occur as a result of natural events, changes in management practices and harvesting efficiencies, but no major increases are forecast. Thus the United States and the world must meet needs through wise stewardship of natural resources and by moving more aggressively to aquaculture.

Table 9.2. United States Annual Per Capita Use of Commercial Fish and Shellfish 1960-1987

Year	Civilian Resident Population (July 1)	Per Capita Consumption			
		Fresh and Frozen [1]	Canned [2]	Cured [3]	Total
1960	178.1	5.7	4.0	0.6	10.3
1961	181.1	5.9	4.3	0.5	10.7
1962	183.7	5.8	4.3	0.5	10.6
1963	186.5	5.8	4.4	0.5	10.7
1964	189.1	5.9	4.1	0.5	10.5
1965	191.6	6.0	4.3	0.5	10.8
1966	193.4	6.1	4.3	0.5	10.9
1967	195.3	5.8	4.3	0.5	10.6
1968	197.1	6.2	4.3	0.5	11.0
1969	199.1	6.6	4.2	0.4	11.2
1970	201.9	6.9	4.5	0.4	11.8
1971	204.9	6.7	4.3	0.5	11.5
1972	207.5	7.1	4.9	0.5	12.5
1973	209.6	7.4	5.0	0.4	12.8
1974	211.6	6.9	4.7	0.5	12.1
1975	213.8	7.5	4.3	0.4	12.2
1976	215.9	8.2	4.2	0.5	12.9
1977	218.1	7.7	4.6	0.4	12.7

Table 9.2. Continued

Year	Civilian Resident Population (July 1)	Per Capita Consumption			
		Fresh and Frozen [1]	Canned [2]	Cured [3]	Total
1978 (4)	220.5	8.1	5.0	0.3	13.4
1979 (4)	223.0	7.8	4.8	0.4	13.0
1980 (4)	225.6	8.0	4.5	0.3	12.8
1981 (4)	227.7	7.8	4.8	0.3	12.9
1982 (4)	229.9	7.7	4.3	0.3	12.3
1983 (4)	232.0	8.0	4.8	0.3	13.1
1984 (4)	234.8	8.5	4.9	0.3	13.7
1985 (4)	237.0	9.0	5.1	0.3	14.4
1986 (4)	239.4	9.0	5.4	0.3	14.7
1987 (4)	241.5	*10.0	5.1	0.3	*15.4

[1] Fresh and frozen fish consumption from 1910 to 1928 is estimated. Beginning in 1973, data include consumption of artificially cultivated catfish.
[2] Canned fish consumption for 1911 to 1920 is estimated. Beginning in 1921, it is based on production reports, packer stocks, and foreign trade statistics for individual years.
[3] Domestic landings data used in calculating these data are preliminary.
*Record.
Note: These consumption figures refer only to consumption of fish and shellfish entering commercial channels, and they do not include data on consumption of shellfish and those caught recreationally, which since 1970 is estimated to be between 3 to 4 pounds (edible meat) per person annually. The figures are calculated on the basis of raw edible meat, i.e. excluding bones, viscera, shells, etc. U.S. Department of Agriculture (USDA) consumption purchased in retail stores. USDA estimates the net edible weight to be about 70-90 percent of the retail weight, depending on the cut and type of meat. From 1970 through 1980 data were revised to reflect the results of the 1980 Census.
Source: National Marine Fisheries Service.

Within the United States' jurisdiction some stocks are increasing, some are stable, while many important regional resources are declining. By region, the following details the status of resources.

NORTHEAST ATLANTIC AREAS FISHERIES

The passage of the Magnuson Fisheries Conservation and Management Act brought extreme optimism to American fishermen, processors, and investors. The large quantities of fish formerly caught by the foreign vessels would now be caught by Americans; huge profits were the thought of the day. New boats replaced old boats, bigger boats replaced smaller boats, and some fishermen built a second or even a third boat. The United States consumer was not interested in mackerel, large herring or red hake and the silver hake market was small. The New England fishery was a traditional groundfish fishery of cod, haddock and a few species of flounders along with a shellfish fishery of scallops and lobsters. Effort therefore increased on the traditional groundfish species. The number of vessels in the otter trawl fishery doubled from 825 in 1977 to 1,620 by 1983.

The number of days fished increased 73 percent from 1976 to 1986, with almost a 100 percent increase in the Gulf of Maine, 57 percent increase on Georges Bank, and 83 percent in Southern New England. The average size of the fishing vessels also greatly increased. New electronic equipment could now be purchased and the wheelhouses bristled with new technology. The fishing power of these larger vessels increased by a considerable amount. With this large increase in fishing effort, catches increased as well. In the Gulf of Maine, bottom trawl landings increased by 41 percent from 1976 to 1983. On Georges Bank and in southern New England, landings increased by 83 percent (1976 to 1982) and 94 percent (1976 to 1984) respectively.

The fishing of many species increased heavily in just a few years. Catches doubled or more than doubled in the Gulf of Maine for American plaice (dabs), gray sole (witch flounder), winter flounder, white hake, cusk, Atlantic wolffish, and haddock.

Fishing mortality increased so greatly during this period of time that 40 to 50 percent of the fishable populations of some groundfish were landed annually. Large numbers of smaller fish were also discarded. Such large increases in fishing mortality caused the population abundance of many groundfish species to decline sharply. As a result, catches started to decrease in the early 1980s and still continue today. The decrease in groundfish landings during this period (1983 to 1987) was about 31 percent for the Gulf of Maine, 55 percent for Georges Bank (1982 to 1987), and 28 percent (1984 to 1987) for southern New England. The decline in abundance is actually much worse for some species. Table 9.3 shows the percentage decline from 1977 to 1987 for each of nine stocks

Table 9.3. Percentage Declines in Abundance for 1977 to 1987, Estimates of MSY, 1977 Catch and 1987 Catch for Principal Groundfish and Flounders off New England

Species/Stock	1977-1987 Decline in Abundance (percent)	MSY (000 tons)	1977 Catch (000 tons)	1987 Catch (000 tons)
Atlantic Cod (Georges Bank)	53	35	27.4	34.0
Haddock (Georges Bank)	76	47	10.8	6.3
Yellowtail Flounder (Georges Bank)	85	16	9.5	2.7
Pollock (Gulf of Maine, Georges Bank and Scotian Shelf)	42	55	41.2	67.0
Silver hake (Southern Georges-middle Atlantic)	72	Unk.	61.3	9.9
Redfish (Gulf of Maine-Georges Bank)	71	14	13.2	2.0
Winter Flounder (Georges Bank)	68	Unk.	3.6	2.6
American plaice (Gulf of Maine-Georges Bank)	80	Unk.	7.3	3.8
Witch flounder (Gulf of Maine-Georges Bank) 1977-1987	89	Unk.	3.4	3.4

Source: Titus 1988.

of the traditional groundfish species off New England along with the Maximum Sustainable Yield, 1977 catch and 1987 catch.

The haddock stock on Georges Bank had fair to good recruitment in 1977 and 1980 (from the 1975 and 1978 year classes) but they were rapidly fished out. Large year classes also appeared in Atlantic cod. Those in 1982 and 1983 were fairly dominant and were still providing good catches in 1988 in both the Gulf of Maine and on Georges Bank (Anon. 1988). In 1986, for example, the three-year-old cod from the 1983 year class accounted for half of the catch of cod from Georges Bank.

Large year classes of yellowtail flounder in recent years also created some temporary optimism. On Georges Bank, the yellowtail flounder hatched in 1978 yielded increased landings in the early 1980s before the population declined to all-time record lows in 1985 and 1986. In southern New England, the yellowtail flounder born in 1980 and 1981 were the most numerous in recent years and yielded increased landings during 1982 to 1984 before the population again declined to very low levels.

High fishing pressure, therefore, reduces the abundance of fish populations so quickly that the fisheries have had to depend on these spurts of recruitment. The problem, of course, in these high-mortality fisheries is that as the spawning population becomes smaller and smaller, large year classes occur less and less often.

There are some stocks of fish off New England and the middle Atlantic that are not declining, although the catch has increased on many and fishing mortality is too high on some to allow the catches to continue. Some examples are summer flounder (*Paralichyhys dentatus*), ocean pout (*Macrozoarces americanus*), white hake, Atlantic herring (Gulf of Maine stock), mackerel, butterfish (*Peprilus triacanthus*), dogfish (*Squalus acanthias*), and several skates (*Raja* spp).

Prospects for the Future
Overfishing can affect fish stocks in two most obvious ways. First, there is the direct reduction of abundance of an individual resource in the ecosystem for a considerable period of time. The length of time the resource is depressed depends to a certain degree on the presence and shape of any stock recruitment relationship and the chance interactions with environmental conditions that would produce strong year-classes despite small spawning stocks. This kind of effect could, however, be expected to be reversible over a fairly short time period, depending on the relationship of that species with others in the ecosystem. Second, there is the potential disruption of normal competitive predator-prey interrelationships which could alter the structure of the ecosystem and result in a change in species composition and dominance. Fishing can cause these interrelationships to rapidly change and be in a constant state of disequilibrium and unlike any normal species mixture observed in the past. Changes in

these interrelationships might be expected to be of a longer term, somewhat semi-permanent in nature.

In the first instance, there are examples of fish stocks off the New England coast that have been greatly reduced but have produced good recruitment after a period of time; some of them have recovered. The haddock stock on Georges Bank, for example, was overfished and greatly reduced in abundance in 1965 and 1966. The first good year-class in 10 years recruited in 1977 and spawned for the first time in 1978. Good recruitment again resulted from this spawning. In this case, however, these two year-classes were rapidly fished out and it was 1985 before another hint of a good year-class occurred. It was also fished out and this stock has not recovered.

Many stocks will continue to decline for the next five to 10 years, even if fishing is reduced or non-existent. The last good year-classes have been poor, assuring that the stock will continue to decline unless fishing is greatly reduced well into the 1990s. By the year 2000 we can expect to see opportunities for recovery for many offshore stocks in the form of scattered good recruitment. If this recruitment can be protected there could be rebuilding of some stocks by the year 2010. Stocks of fish that spawn inshore, or that use inshore areas for nursery grounds, however, may take even longer to rebuild when fishing pressure is relaxed. River herring (alewife, *Alosa pseudoharengus*) and blueback herring (*Alosa aestivalis*), American and hickory shad (*Alosa sapidissima* and *Alosa mediocris*), and striped bass (*Morone saxatilis*) declined during the 1970s and have not recovered. Habitat problems are much more severe in the inshore areas and there is no question that the physical environment has played a role in delaying recovery of these stocks even when fishing has been reduced.

In several places off the New England coast, further ecosystem changes have been initiated by fishing. The first example has become very clear. As the abundance of groundfish declined in the late 1970s and early 1980s, some species that were not heavily fished increased in abundance, so that the overall abundance on Georges Bank remained at a fairly high level. Dogfish, winter skate and little skate increased greatly in abundance, apparently taking advantage of the decrease in competition for food.

In 1963 on Georges Bank, 55 percent of the fish were gadoid species (cod, haddock, and hakes) and only 24 percent were skates and dogfish. In 1986, the gadoids had declined to 11 percent and skates and dogfish had increased to 74 percent. During the last eight years on Georges Bank, the abundance of both skates and dogfish increased greatly. Skates and dogfish are also major predators on other fish, and can seriously reduce the abundance of species in the same system.

In the North Sea, fishing pressure on similar populations of gadoids has remained relatively constant from 1977 to 1985. This is thought to be because skates and dogfish are heavily fished in the North Sea, and they can be easily fished down because of their very low reproductive rates. Since 1983, landings of skates have dramatically increased in New England, but the same cannot be said for dogfish.

Skates and dogfish are not expected to completely replace the traditional groundfish, but some degree of replacement is occurring because of removals by fishing. Even when good year-classes of cod, haddock and others occur again, heavy fishing may be required on skates and dogfish before the rebuilding of cod, haddock, etc. can be realized.

The rebuilding of the populations of the traditional groundfish species off New England is not simple, nor can it be done in a short period of time. There is even some question about whether mortality (fishing effort or catches) can be reduced even as the stocks collapse. One reason for this is that when the gross revenue per vessel since 1977 by vessel class is given in catches, they have increased in 1986 and 1987. One of the greatest reasons for this has been the prices paid to fishermen. Over the period of 1978 to 1987, the prices paid to fishermen for groundfish in New England rose sharply but the major increase occurred after 1983 for most groundfish as abundance reached record lows. A second reason why mortality is difficult to control in some species is the increase in recreational fishing. Recreational landings of many species of fish and shellfish harvested in marine waters off the northeast United States equal or exceed the commercial landings.

The standard procedure for reducing effort or mortality on fish stocks has been to push the fishing effort into other areas or onto underutilized species. But there are no new areas to conquer. In fact, a recent debate with Canada on the ownership of Georges Bank cost the United States access to a large amount of scallops and to cod and haddock during spawning times. There are a few under-utilized species and the United States is making limited progress diverting fishing to these. The great opportunity is in fishing for mackerel and herring. The mackerel stock has rebuilt to 1.6 million metric tons in 1987 which could sustain a total United States and Canadian catch of 325,000 tons annually (Anon. 1988). The future of the United States fishery off the northeast coast is with these ocean stocks.

Another factor to be considered by managers is the effect of the environment on the productivity of fishery resources. The influence of temperature has been suggested as a principal factor in controlling abundance levels of fish stocks on the continental shelves of the northwest Atlantic off the Canadian Maritimes and the northeastern United States (Dow 1977; Sutcliffe et al. 1977). There is no question that marine resources are tuned to their environment and changes in that environment will affect production, whether it is the physical environment such as water temperature and toxic wastes or the biological environment such as changes in species composition, predation, competition, or abundance.

Indirect deterioration of the inshore habitat of those species that are estuarine dependent is especially important to consider. Many species in the middle Atlantic area and south are estuarine dependent, and the quantitative effect of declining inshore habitat quality has not yet been calculated. The general condition of Boston Harbor, the PCB's in New Bedford harbor, the pollution gradient in Long Island Sound, the waste dumping in the New York Bight (which is only now moving offshore), the recent mortalities of our marine mammals and the strange items washing up on our beaches remind us of the habitat problems that we will have to face in the next century.

Overall, it is clear that the catching capacity of the United States fishing fleets is now excessive. Extrapolation of abundance indices produces alarmingly low numbers for many species by the year 2000. Better utilization of the presently unmarketed species of dogfish, winter skate, and little skate will be required to increase the commercial yields. Yet for the ecosystem to produce at its best, management will have to rebuild a considerable number of the traditional overfished stocks. These stocks are now so depressed that rebuilding will require significant reductions in fishing effort and short-term economic losses.

If management officials of New England and the Mid-Atlantic continue a strategy that maintains the fish stocks at low levels, the living marine resources will be at a disadvantage when questions of the multiple use of the marine environment are decided. Waste disposal is one use of the marine environment; catching fish is another. If those responsible for managing fish stocks are not concerned about low stock sizes, then it is difficult to argue against other uses of the environment such as waste dumping or coastal development. With continued low abundance, fishing will gradually decline and access to the ocean will gradually diminish as coastal development occupies the available space. Under these circumstances, even if stocks did recover, the fishing fleets could not rebuild.

In the future, the issues at focus will change from balancing conservation and utilization of the resources to protecting the resources from the harmful effects of other uses of the marine environment.

ATLANTIC HIGHLY MIGRATORY FISHERIES

Of the diverse fishes of the open oceans, the large, highly mobile predators are, perhaps, the most familiar to people. These fish range throughout the ocean without restriction. Within a single season an individual fish may pass through the waters of several nations or may not venture into waters of national jurisdiction at all. Some, such as blue marlin, prefer the deep ocean. Others, such as white marlin, albacore tuna and bigeye tuna, tend to frequent waters of the continental shelves as well as the open ocean, but do not enter coastal waters. Sailfish, swordfish, bluefin tuna, and other tunas, however, roam without great regard for location, following food concentrations and making seasonal migrations from the deep oceans to coastal waters.

Within the Atlantic, blue marlin are known to migrate from the United

States coast to the eastern tropical Atlantic, although little is known about their rates of movement. White marlin and sailfish are known to migrate northward and southward; however, transatlantic migrations are, as yet, not documented. Bluefin tuna are known to move extensively in the east Atlantic and Mediterranean Sea, along the North American Coast, and between the east and west Atlantic traveling as many as 6,200 miles (10,000 kilometers) in 50 days, approximately 124 miles (200 kilometers) per day from the Florida Straits to the Norwegian coast. Albacore tuna are also known to make extensive transatlantic movements. The extent and rate of migrations are not well-known for many billfishes and tunas. However, as information from marking experiments accumulate, results seem to consistently indicate that these fishes tend to roam the entire Atlantic rather than restricting their movements to small geographical areas.

Some of these populations have been fished through the ages. Bluefin tuna were exploited in the Mediterranean Sea by the Phoenicians more than 4,000 years ago and Romans in A.D. 2 recorded annual trap catches similar to recent ones. Swordfish were also caught in the Mediterranean by the ancient Romans and Greeks. The development of mechanized fishing methods, however, have increased the exploitation of these resources. The use of purse seine vessels in tuna fisheries began in the early 1900s and spotter aircraft were in use by the 1930s.

The Pacific purse seine fleet moved into the tropical Atlantic in the 1960s. Although the Pacific fleet left by the late 1970s, their presence was replaced by a European based purse seine fleet of similar size. Intensive purse seine fisheries for juvenile tunas, particularly yellowfin and bigeye, currently exist.

Distant water Asian longline fleets entered the equatorial Atlantic in 1956, then expanded their operations over the entire Atlantic by mid-1960s. The early fishery was carried out by vessels without deep freezer capability, thus fishing was directed at species that could be sold at canneries in the Atlantic. By the early 1970s older longline vessels were replaced by those with modern freezing capability, so fishing was redirected at species that were valuable as sashimi (bluefin tuna, bigeye tuna, marlin). Many of the older vessels still operate in the Atlantic, however, fishing for albacore and yellowfin tuna as well as other species that can be landed and sold fresh. Today, multinational swordfish longline fleets also exploit the entire Atlantic with large modern vessels, mechanized fishing gear, and satellite oceanographic information.

Big game sport fishing for Atlantic tunas and billfish has flourished in recent years, particularly along the coasts of industrialized nations of Europe, the United States, and in the Caribbean Sea. Fishing tournaments in these areas are now commonplace and the number of such sportfishing activities is rapidly increasing.

Current catches of these large tunas in the Atlantic are substantial, about

3,000,000 metric tons annually. Atlantic catches of marlins and sailfish are not, as yet, well monitored; however, available information indicates such catches are also substantial— at about 30,000 to 40,000 metric tons or more annually— and seem to be increasing.

Abundance Trends

Although little is known of the abundance of the highly migratory large fishes of the Atlantic, some species, particularly those of high commercial value or sport fishing interest, have been studied. Estimated numbers of bluefin tuna in the west Atlantic and swordfish in both the north and south Atlantic are available and, in addition, indices of relative abundance have been developed from fisheries statistics for several other species. There is some indication that the abundance of south Atlantic albacore and white marlin in the northwest Atlantic may be decreasing. East Atlantic yellowfin abundance also decreased steadily each year from the early 1970s until the purse seine fleet moved to the Indian Ocean in 1985; those vessels are now gradually returning to the Gulf of Guinea and abundance has begun to decrease once again. As yet, there is no solid indication that the abundance of blue marlin, bigeye, or North Atlantic albacore has been or is now seriously impacted by exploitation; however, more comprehensive efforts may well change our current understanding of those resources. Even with our current level of knowledge, it could be difficult to suppose that the overall level of abundance of large, highly migratory fishes in the Atlantic is constant or increasing.

The Future

Recent human activities have already impacted these populations of oceanic creatures to a degree. As technical knowledge increases ability to access and occupy the deep ocean, it seems certain that the abundance of these large predators will be affected just as the westward advance of civilization affected the abundance of North American animal populations.

The pattern of terrestrial animal populations has often been an initial pronounced decrease from exploitation (usually commercial hunting), than further decreases from habitat destruction caused by pollution, farming practices, or the construction of buildings, water impoundments, access roads, etc. Of these two causes, habitat destruction has proved to be the lethal one in the long term.

This pattern may be slightly different for the oceanic environment, however, at least in the near future. It seems unlikely technological advances will be significant enough to enable construction activities (oil exploration, sea bed mining) to occur in the deep ocean to any extent for several decades, although pollution from marine dump sites may occur. However, some populations of whales that were decreased substantially by hunting do not appear to have recovered significantly even though exploitation ceased several years ago. It seems most likely, then, that increased exploitation of the highly migratory resources will be the major determinant of their abundance, at least in the next few decades.

Since these fishes typically migrate through the open ocean as well as the jurisdictional waters of several nations, the management of their exploitation is not within the ability of any single coastal state. In an attempt to avoid a tragedy of the commons, the International Commission for the Conservation of Atlantic Tuna was formed in 1969 to achieve the maximum sustained yield from these resources. The commission meets annually in multinational political framework to determine if regulations are necessary and, if so, the extent of such restrictions. The scientific bases for various national fishing policies and the enforcement of fishing restrictions is the responsibility of each member nation.

The ability of this and similar commissions to control the abundance of these resources has often been questioned and, perhaps, with some justification. It would seem prudent, however, to question the mechanism of regulation rather than the effectiveness of a particular commission. Most fisheries regulatory agencies, both international and domestic, are based on the idea that the entities harvesting the common resource have a direct interest in maintaining the populations at the most productive level of abundance and, therefore, a group of such interests interacting within a political mechanism is its best custodian. Experience seems to indicate that such may not be the case. Often, it appears that the prime objective of the separate members is to remove as much as possible as soon as possible until abundance is so low that harvesting becomes economically infeasible and that fisheries management organizations offer a political arena for accomplishing that end.

As the world population grows and the need for food becomes greater, pressure to exploit the large, highly migratory tunas and billfishes will increase into the 21st century. Unless significant advances are made in multinational fisheries' regulation mechanisms, the future of these resources seems uncertain. Although populations are unlikely to be hunted to extinction, abundances may well decrease far below their current levels. Clearly the well-being of these resources in the 21st century is a multinational responsibility.

PACIFIC COAST BOTTOM FISHERIES

As in the Atlantic, fish stocks off the west coast of the United States were subjected to heavy fishing pressure by foreign nationals prior to the Magnuson Fisheries Conservation and Management Act. Vessels from Japan, the Soviet Union and Korea overfished various stocks during the late 1960s and early 1970s.

By 1976 foreign fleets had drastically reduced the size of some important groundfish stocks (Pacific ocean perch and sablefish) or contributed through high incidental catch levels toward the decline of other important resources such as the Pacific halibut. The bilateral agreements in force prior to the Magnuson Fisheries Conservation and Management Act left the United States with little control of the fish harvest off Alaska. Additionally, it was difficult to assess the condition of the fishery resource. The United States government had no means of independently collecting fishery data and had to rely on information submitted by the fishing nations at bilateral meetings. Usually the only information submitted was the quantity of catch. An exception was Japan, which submitted extremely detailed catch and effort data to the United States under provisions of the International North Pacific Fisheries Commission.

The sparse catch and biological data made it difficult to estimate the current status and trends in exploited populations. In some cases, such as with Pacific ocean perch and yellowfin sole, it was clear that over-fishing had occurred and catch reductions were needed to rehabilitate the stock; in other cases, such as sablefish and pollock, declines were evident, but the causes and biological significance were not as clear and a consensus on quotas and bilateral management action was difficult to achieve.

When fisheries jurisdiction was extended to 200 miles in 1977 under terms of the Magnuson Fisheries Conservation and Management Act, interim fisheries management plans were adopted for the Bering Sea-Aleutian Islands and Gulf of Alaska. These plans sought to remedy two decades of overfishing. First, foreign fishing was sharply curtailed for overexploited stocks of Pacific ocean perch, sablefish, and herring. For pollock and yellowfin sole, species that were not depleted and seemed to be improving, catch levels agreed to under bilateral agreements were reduced to allow continued rebuilding of these stocks. The allowable catch of some healthy stocks was also reduced to protect halibut stocks that had been affected by high incidental catch rates.

Foreign access to groundfish resources in the North Pacific was only slightly curtailed following the establishment of jurisdiction over the 200 mile Exclusive Economic Zone. The overall catch level was reduced from pre-Magnuson Fisheries Conservation and Management Act levels in order to protect clearly depleted or overfished stocks, and some of the species formerly harvested by the foreign fleets were allocated to United States fishermen (i.e. Tanner crab and herring). Even with foreign catch reductions, the United States fishing industry in Alaska did not have infrastructure to exploit and process the large resource available within the new Exclusive Economic Zone. As a consequence the foreign fisheries were able to continue to fish under the terms of the Magnuson Fisheries Conservation and Management Act, although United States fisheries requests were given first preference. Foreign fisheries were only allowed to harvest that part of the established quota that was in excess of the harvesting capacity of the United States fishing industry.

The "fish and chips" amendment to the Magnuson Fisheries Conservation and Management Act in 1980 began the removal of the foreign fisheries from the Alaskan Exclusive Economic Zone and sped the development of domestic fisheries. In the Gulf of Alaska, the catch was taken almost exclusively by foreign trawlers prior to 1970. In 1980, following two years of limited operation, joint-venture operations took approximately 76 percent of the total trawl catch of pollock and displaced the foreign trawl fishery as the major fishery component. While foreign processors continue to receive and process the landings in joint-venture fisheries, United States trawlers have displaced foreign trawlers in the harvesting of fish off the Pacific.

These rapid changes in the participants in the fishery has had a profound effect on the management regime. From 1977, when the Magnuson Fisheries Conservation and Management Act went into effect, until the early 1980s management efforts were directed at reducing perceived "overfishing" and reducing the catch by foreign fisheries of species of interest to United States fishermen such has crabs, halibut and herring. Catch levels were reduced or held constant and efforts were made to transfer catches to joint-ventures or domestic fishermen. There was a concerted effort by most of the fishing industry to remove foreign effort.

Early joint-venture fisheries between United States and foreign partners were encouraged and regulation was minimal. In fact, they were often exempted from conservation-oriented regulations— such as time-area closures and incidental catch restrictions— that were applied to the foreign fisheries. However, as the joint-venture fleet grew in size, conflicts began to develop between joint-venture fishermen and solely domestic fishermen such as crab, halibut, sablefish and herring fishermen. Generally these conflicts have focused on incidental catches in the joint-ventures of species allocated to other fishermen. For the most part, these have been gear related: trawlers versus pot fishermen and trawlers versus longline fishermen. However, conflicts related to access to fishing grounds and fish are arising between and within United States trawler groups. Under the current law, domestic fishermen and processors are given a preference over joint-venture groups to harvest fish from the Exclusive Economic Zone. This issue is currently being worked out and allocative schemes such as fishing periods and areas are being experimented with.

The Magnuson Fisheries Conservation and Management Act has greatly improved our knowledge of the resource and the quality of assessments and management advice. Most of the improvement has come about primarily as a result of the United States Foreign Fisheries Observer program, which was expanded with the passage of the Magnuson Fisheries Conservation and Management Act. That act stipulated that foreign fishing vessels must accept observers while engaged in fishing activities within the United States Exclusive Economic Zone. Observers were placed onboard foreign fishing vessels in order to provide estimates of catch levels, to ensure that allocations were not exceeded, and to collect biological data from the catch such as information on species, length, weight, and age composition. The United States observer program off Alaska started in 1972, when United States-Japan-Soviet Union bilateral agreements allowed the placement of a limited number of observers on trawlers in the Bering Sea to obtain data on incidental catch rates. A 1975 agreement with the Soviet Union allowed observers aboard Soviet vessels in 1975. In 1977, the first year of mandatory observer coverage, less than 20 percent of the foreign vessels operating had observers on board. However, observer coverage increased sharply in the early 1980s when the Magnuson Fisheries Conservation and Management Act was amended to require 100 percent observer coverage of foreign fishing vessels.

The fisheries observer program has greatly improved the quality of data available from the commercial fisheries. Gross catch and effort data were replaced by data detailing catch by location, duration, depth, catch of target and non-target species, discards and biological measurements. The observer program also insured compliance with regulations prohibiting retention of salmon, halibut and crabs.

The U.S. National Marine Fisheries Service's Northwest and Alaska Fisheries Center increased the scope of trawl surveys in the late 1970s to provide independent estimates of standing stock and population trends to the North Pacific Fisheries Management Council. Limited surveys are conducted annually and large scale surveys are conducted triennially.

A new trend now developing in the Alaskan fisheries is the "Americanization" of the groundfish fishery, wherein all fish are caught and processed by United States fishermen and processors. Currently, there is great activity in building catcher-processing vessels and floating and shore-based processing facilities. Despite these dramatic changes, fishing effort, indirectly measured as the number of trawlers, has remained relatively constant.

It is likely that the groundfish fisheries off Alaska will continue to undergo major evolution over the next decade. Factors such as markets and the availability of substitute species in other fisheries may have a significant impact on the economic viability of any one fishery, however. We assume that the groundfish fishery will continue to shift to total domestic fishing and processing.

There is currently a surplus in catching capacity in most Pacific fisheries since the high earning potential has induced most of the Bering Sea crab fleet and others to convert or build new vessels for trawling. Several domestic catcher-processor vessels have entered the fishery and more are under construction. Floating processors are also entering the fishery or are under construction. Several shore-based processing plants have been opened in recent years and several others are proposed. These developments in the fishery are very important in determining future levels of harvest, but it is currently unclear how management authorities will respond to increasing catch capacity.

Overall, the Magnuson Fisheries Conservation and Management Act has benefited the conservation of groundfish stocks off the Pacific and resulted in restoration of depleted species such as Pacific ocean perch. The presently abundant fish stocks are attributable to a reduction and control of foreign catch and a period of above average recruitment in many species.

Yet as the groundfish fishery is rapidly becoming a domestic fishery— a process that will be completed before the year 2000— a new set of problems is arising. The number of vessels has grown to the point that seasons as short as a few weeks have to be set on fisheries that were fished all year in the past. There is also increasing competition among user groups with petitions for special allocations. With the strong competition for a common resource, domestic fishermen are reluctant to provide fisheries information or allow observers on their vessels for fear that the information collected will be used to reduce their allocation or fishing time.

In short, the successful Americanization of the groundfish fisheries may negate the recent advances in knowledge of the resource because observers are not required on domestic vessels. The only provision for collecting data is a voluntary program, and a very limited number of domestic vessels have taken observers on board. As a result of these facts, the advances of recent years may be reversed unless the observer program is expanded to include sampling of the major portion of the domestic catch. If this critical problem is not addressed, future fishery assessments and management advice will become increasingly unreliable.

The success of the Magnuson Fisheries Conservation and Management Act for conservation of groundfish resources awaits the response of the management system to strong pressures from the domestic fishing industry. If the system can resist industry in the face of downturns in stock production on issues of stock conservation, then the Magnuson Fisheries Conservation and Management Act will be judged to be truly beneficial for the conservation of groundfish resources and the year 2000 will see reasonably stable, highly efficient and productive fishing.

ESTUARINE AND COASTAL AREAS

Estuaries and their associated coastal waters are the most productive region of the world's oceans. Enriched by nutrients from the land, mixed by tides and currents, and saturated by sunlight, they provide food, shelter, and spawning grounds for many of our fisheries. Unfortunately, increased population pressures along the coast have resulted in water quality degradation, habitat destruction, and overfishing. Paralleling these changes, we have seen dramatic declines over the last century in many of our estuarine-dependent species such as oysters, soft-shell clams, sturgeon, and striped bass, particularly in areas such as the Chesapeake Bay. This downward trend is occurring nation-wide even with the pollution control, wetlands protection, and fisheries management efforts of the last two decades. It is evident that we are incrementally destroying our estuarine and coastal fisheries

The nation's estuaries and coastal waters are vitally important to both our commercial and recreational fishing industry. Estuarine-dependent species comprise more than 70 percent of our United States commercial catch, with a value of $5.5 billion. The relative proportion is higher in areas such as the Gulf of Mexico (98 percent) and the South Atlantic (94 percent). Seven of the most valuable United States commercial fisheries — Gulf shrimp, sockeye salmon, menhaden, pink salmon, oyster, South Atlantic shrimp, and blue crabs — are dependent upon estuaries for habitat, food, and shelter. Our estuaries and coastal waters are also important to the recreational fishing industry. Every year, federal, state, and local governments spend billions of dollars to provide recreational opportunities in coastal counties. Recreational fishing, the nation's number one sport, contributes approximately $13.5 billion per year to the economy (National Oceanic and Atmospheric Administration 1987).

Although the estuarine environment is extremely valuable in terms of its productivity, it is also valued as a center for industrial, commercial, residential, and recreational activities. More than 70 percent of our population lives in coastal states, and 53 percent of the population lives and works within 50 miles of the coast (National Oceanic and Atmospheric Administration 1987). High population densities occur in the Northeast, Great Lakes, and California regions. By 1990, 75 percent of the population will live along the coast (National Oceanic and Atmospheric Administration 1987). Much of this projected growth will occur along the relatively pristine Gulf and Southeast coasts.

The ever-increasing population pressures along the coast will continue to jeopardize our valuable estuarine and coastal fisheries. The major threats are: 1) nutrient enrichment, 2) toxic contamination, 3) habitat alteration, and 4) fishing pressures.

Since population growth and associated development are expected to continue, these four major threats to the coastal and estuarine environment will not disappear in the next century. The threat can be addressed through concerted efforts to control the loadings of point and nonpoint source discharges of toxics and pathogens, habitat management, and interstate fisheries management. There is another threat facing us with which we have very little experience in controlling, however, and that is the prospect of global climate change and a rising sea level.

Nutrient Enrichment

Nitrogen and phosphorus are plant nutrients which stimulate the growth of plankton in estuarine and coastal waters. These regions can become over-enriched with nutrients from sources that include sewage effluent, agricultural run-off, atmospheric deposition, and bottom sediment releases. Algal production in enriched waters can reach nuisance proportions and result in oxygen depletion of bottom waters caused by the decomposition of organic matter associated with algal blooms.

Fish and shellfish living in bottom waters are vulnerable to periodic episodes of low levels of dissolved oxygen, known as hypoxia, and in the most polluted waters, to extended periods of no oxygen, or anoxia. Besides affecting local populations, oxygen depletion could limit the excursions of migratory fish and crustaceans up and down estuaries and in coastal waters. Many populous coastal areas suffer from oxygen depletion, including Long Island, New York Bight, Chesapeake Bay, Louisiana (west of the Mississippi), and the Gulf of Mexico.

Another effect of nutrient enrichment is a potential shift in species composition from larger to smaller forms of algae. Filter feeding fish and shellfish may require a certain size range of plankton on which to feed. Consequently, a shift to smaller species can limit the amount of available food and can reduce recruitment, abundance, and ultimately fisheries production. Researchers in the Chesapeake Bay area suggest that the recent declines in oyster production could be, in part, related to the reduced abundance of preferred plankton species. These species are relatively large and may be less numerous due to rising cyanobacteria and nanoplankton populations (Houde 1987).

Besides small-celled plankton, blooms of "red-tide" algae can be stimulated by nutrient enrichment. Certain red-tide species are toxic to fish, weakening or killing them. Others cause health problems, including paralytic shellfish poisoning in humans who have consumed contaminated shellfish and respiratory problems for people who come in contact with or simply are near contaminated waters. Red-tide organisms do not always affect the health of fish. A subtropical red-tide organism was carried to the coastal waters of North Carolina by a filament of the Gulf Stream in October 1987, and resulted in a four-month bloom, closing the harvest of shellfish from Pamlico Sound between November 1987 and February 1988 and causing an estimated loss of $25 million to the local economy (Tester et al. 1988).

Two major sources of nutrient loads to coastal waters— sewage treatment plant discharges, and agricultural and urban runoff— have been studied in detail over the past decade. Processes controlling nutrient loads from two other major sources— atmospheric deposition and benthic releases— are not as well understood. Preliminary estimates of the loading of nitrogen oxides from atmospheric dryfall and wetfall throughout the Chesapeake Bay basin suggest that atmospheric deposition is a major source of nitrogen (Fisher et al. 1988). Trends in atmospheric nitrogen loads will increase as motor vehicle traffic and the use of coal for fuel and electricity increases. Very little is known about the factors regulating the releases of nutrients from bottom sediments or trends in loads from this source.

As coastal population levels increase, we can expect to see nutrient enrichment problems in most of our bays and estuaries. It is probable that the duration and extent of low-oxygen conditions will increase, shifts in algal species composition will become accentuated, and red tide events will occur more frequently. To reverse the trend, point and nonpoint source nutrient controls, such as advanced sewage treatment and agricultural best management practices, must be implemented in targeted areas. Integrated watershed management programs, like the Chesapeake Bay nutrient reduction plan, will have to be initiated throughout our coastal and estuarine waters.

Toxic Contamination

Like nutrients, toxins enter coastal waters from a variety of sources and cause a range of effects on marine communities and human health. The major sources are industrial discharges (either direct discharge or indirect discharge by way of a municipal wastewater treatment plant), nonpoint source loadings from agricultural run-off, urban run-off, ground-water seepage, and atmospheric deposition. Some toxins, such as heavy metals, occur naturally at very low concentrations, but like nutrients, their levels in the coastal environment have become enriched near populated areas. Toxic organic chemicals are in smaller concentrations relative to heavy metals, but are still found at levels high enough to exhibit toxicity to marine and estuarine organisms and to pose health risks to seafood consumers.

The impacts of toxic contamination of our marine and estuarine environments include direct and indirect effects. Areas of extremely high concentration of toxics, such as sections of Boston Harbor, Puget Sound, or Baltimore Harbor, are devoid of benthic (sea bottom) communities. Levels in bottom sediments are high enough to cause acute toxicity to organisms, preventing their survival. Adjacent to these "hot spots" are areas with elevated concentrations which can limit colonization of the benthic environment, reduce fecundity and raise juvenile mortality. Chronic toxicity is a problem in these areas. Finfish found in these areas often have lesions and tumors.

Other regions may not have high levels of toxicants accumulated over time because the fish have consumed organisms from contaminated areas. In the case of migratory coastal species such as striped bass and bluefish which have consumed toxicants, the dangers of bioaccumulation have led to public health advisories. Another indirect effect of toxicants is a potential shift in plankton species composition, as smaller-celled species appear more tolerant to waters containing small amount of toxics. This shift could threaten the availability of suitable food for filter feeding finfish and shellfish. Furthermore, since the plankton community is the foundation of the productivity of estuaries, toxic contaminants could indirectly affect fisheries production through basic alteration of the fisheries-dependent food chain.

The collection and storage of information on toxic chemicals in estuarine and coastal waters is not sufficient to describe past trends. The National Status and Trends Program was begun by the National Oceanic and Atmospheric Administration in 1984 to monitor toxics in fish and shellfish tissue and in bottom sediments. The data presently available from this program illustrate existing patterns of toxic concentrations at approximately 150 locations in the United States. Data from 1984 show concentrations of a large category of toxic organic chemicals, known as polynuclear aromatic hydrocarbons, found in sediments. The northeast stations show relatively higher levels than other coastal regions, with the exception of San Diego Harbor, Elliott Bay in Puget Sound, and San Pedro Canyon, California. A similar pattern was found for DDT residues and PCB's (National Oceanic and Atmospheric Administration 1987). Pathogens harmful to humans include red-tide organisms and those associated with sewage contamination such as hepatitis. The shellfish diseases Dermo and MSX, on the other hand, pose no threat to the health of oyster eaters but cause significant mortalities in contaminated oyster beds.

The installation of sewage treatment facilities has reduced levels of fecal coliform bacteria, the indicator of sewage contamination, in many regions, but even well-operated plants can have overflows or bypasses during periods of high rainfall. Unfortunately, even where sufficient sewage treatment facilities are in place, shellfish areas are subject to pathogens from other sources such as failing septic tanks, discharges from marine vessels, waterfowl and wildlife, and storm water run-off.

It will be difficult in the future, with increasing development along coastal areas, to keep and maintain the sewage treatment capacity and performance in line with population growth. We can probably expect continued contamination of shellfish growing waters in areas of high population density. It is also likely that shellfish-growing waters in relatively pristine areas will be vulnerable to contamination by sewage pathogens as the areas become populated. We could see significant increases in outbreaks of hepatitis, gastroenteritis and other pathogenic illnesses. Stronger point source and nonpoint source control efforts will be required to reduce this threat.

Habitat Alteration

In ecological terms, our wetlands and submerged aquatic grasses are indispensable to our estuarine and coastal fisheries. They provide shelter for larval and juvenile fish and shellfish. They moderate concentrations of nutrients and other chemicals which could indirectly affect fisheries production (e.g. algal blooms, oxygen depletion, changes in plankton diets, etc.). They also support the detrital food web upon which many critical life stages of coastal fisheries depend.

The quality of these habitats and their abundance have taken a nose-dive in the last century due to a range of alterations that include losses in acreage and reductions in functional values of marshes, mangrove swamps, and submerged aquatic vegetation. Alterations also include the disturbance of bottom sediments due to dredging, filling, and contamination by toxic chemicals and pathogens. Habitat for most estuarine and coastal species is defined by salinity and temperature gradients and circulation patterns; changes in these fundamental physical characteristics have major effects on the distribution and abundance of estuarine-dependent species and can be influenced by both natural climatic and geophysical variability (e.g. precipitation and land subsidence) and human-induced variability (e.g. fresh-water flow diversions and consumption, sedimentation, sea level rise).

The continental United States supported approximately 11 million acres of coastal wetlands in 1780. More than 50 percent of these wetlands were gone by the mid-1970s. With the exception of Louisiana, national, state, and local wetland protection laws have reduced such drastic loss rates in most areas. However, the predominant trend is still gradual loss of wetlands habitat.

Submerged aquatic vegetation habitats are also important to our estuarine and coastal fisheries. These grasses have virtually disappeared in many sections of the East Coast. For example, submerged aquatic vegetation abundance in Chesapeake Bay between 1965 and 1980 dramatically declined. In a survey of more than 600 stations in the Maryland portion of the bay, the percent of stations vegetated with submerged aquatic vegetation dropped from 28.5 percent in 1971 to 4.5 percent in 1982. This dramatic decline in both distribution and abundance has been attributed to light limitation caused by nutrient-induced algal growth in the water column and increased sediment turbidity (Flemer et al. 1983).

Looking toward the future, recent investigations into the effects of sea level rise on coastal ecosystems suggest that the distribution of existing wetlands and submerged aquatic vegetation will be shifted inland and upstream due to inundation and increasing salinities in the 50 to 100 years (Titus 1988). The coastal areas in the Gulf of Mexico will be most vulnerable. Table 9.4 summarizes the projected losses and, in some areas, gains in wetland acreage due to increasing sea levels, using low and high estimates, for the coastal regions of the United States under two conditions: 1) existing coastal developments are "defended" with levees, bulkheads and similar structures which would prevent the inland migration of wetlands, and 2) no structures are put along the shorelines, allowing relatively unimpeded access to shallow water as sea level rise. The projections are frightening.

Preventing additional losses in the abundance and quality of wetlands and submerged aquatic vegetation habitats will not be sufficient to reverse the declining trends in estuarine-dependent fisheries production. Net gain policies will be needed to restore these habitats upon which the fisheries depend for their food, shelter, and survival. Restoration efforts such as replanting must be integrated with the management of the full range of habitat requirements including water quality. Also, major changes in the physical environment that sustains coastal wetlands and submerged aquatic vegetation (i.e. reductions in fresh-water inflow, rising sea levels, and resulting increases in salinities) should be factored into our management efforts. In summary, we must strengthen our habitat protection efforts, such as the national Section 404 wetlands protection program, and manage our coastal environments as integrated functional units.

Fishing Pressures

More than two-thirds of our commercial and recreational fish species are dependent upon estuarine or coastal waters throughout their life or during a critical life stage. It is, therefore, not surprising that we find many of our most productive fishing grounds in these areas. In fact, shellfish such as oysters and soft-shelled clams are concentrated within certain salinity and depth zones of the estuary. Finfish, on the other hand, often concentrate along density fronts in the coastal waters. Adult anadromous fish can be found highly concentrated in spawning streams during the spring. With the knowledge of these behavioral patterns and advanced fishing gear, it is very easy to decimate a population by overfishing.

The dramatic decline of several major fisheries since the late 1800s and early 1900s has in large measure been due to overfishing. For example, Maryland's oyster harvest from the Chesapeake Bay has declined 90 percent over the last century with the most significant reductions occurring at the turn of the century when harvesting pressures were at their peak. Similarly, Columbia River Basin salmon and steelhead have decreased 75 to 84 percent and chinook salmon have decreased by 90 percent from estimated pre-development levels. Although the initial dramatic declines can be clearly attributed to overfishing, water quality degradation and habitat alteration have become very important contributing factors in preventing recoveries of the populations (National Oceanic and Atmospheric Administration 1987).

With the increased demand for seafood, it is probable that fishing pressures will intensify in the future. The restoration and protection of our estuarine and coastal fisheries will require aggressive management actions. In fact, fisheries management actions taken in recent years have encouraged the recovery of stocks such as salmon and striped bass in selected areas. For example, landings of the East Coast striped bass population dramatically decreased 60-80 percent since their peak in the early 1900s; however, recent studies suggest that their numbers are now increasing due to fishing controls. Approximately 90 percent of the striped bass population used to originate in Chesapeake Bay with the remainder of the population originating in the Hudson River. Recent data suggest that today approximately 50 percent of the striped bass originate in the Hudson and 50 percent in Chesapeake Bay. The increase in the Hudson River population is due in part to the fact that it has been closed to commercial fishing since 1976, and in 1986, there was a ban on striped bass fishing in New York. In the Chesapeake Bay area, Maryland put in place a striped bass moratorium in January 1985, when it was apparent that fishing mortality had effectively eliminated all but one relatively abundant year class— 1982. The moratorium appears to be protecting this critical year class which represents the future

Table 9.4. Projected Changes in Coastal Wetlands: 1980-2100

REGION	1980	2100			
		Defend Shore		Abandonment	
A. Wetland Area (sq. km)		low	high	low	high
New England	60	58	22	58	22
Mid Atlantic	454	277	0	366	66
South Atlantic	913	652	208	954	420
Florida	598	596	357	770	517
N.E. Gulf Coast	736	672	520	685	544
Mississippi Delta	1509	298	45	298	45
Chenier Plain, TX	299	190	0	258	49
Californian Prov.	265	174	0	263	218
Columbian.	12	11	9	127	133
TOTAL	4846	2928	1161	3779	2014
B. Percent Loss (gain)					
New England		-3	-63	-3	-63
Mid Atlantic		-39	-100	-20	-85
South Atlantic		-29	-77	+4	-54
Florida		-0.3	-40	+29	-14
N.E. Gulf Coast		-9	-29	-7	-26
Mississippi Delta		-80	-97	-80	-97
Chenier Plain, TX		-36	-100	-14	-84
Californian Prov.		-35	-100	-1	-18
Columbian.		-8	-25	+958	+1000
TOTAL		-40	-76	-22	-58

Source: Titus 1988.

spawning stock of the fishery. It is evident that aggressive fisheries management efforts can help restore stocks.

Future Management Needs

Although it is always difficult to predict the future, past trends suggest that our estuarine and coastal ocean system will continue to deteriorate as population pressures increase. It will be difficult to reverse this trend, for there is no "single culprit" and no "quick fix." We must also recognize that our estuarine and coastal waters are complex interrelated ecosystems. If one part of the system is perturbed through natural or man-induced events, all parts are affected. In order to restore and protect our estuarine and coastal fisheries, our management strategies must be comprehensive and built on a strong legislative foundation that recognizes a total ecosystem perspective.

Over the past two decades, the United States Congress passed several major environmental and resource related acts relevant to estuarine and coastal resources, including the Clean Water Act, Coastal Zone Management Act, and the Fisheries Conservation and Management Act. Recent amendments to these Acts further strengthened their ecosystem perspective. We now have many of the tools and innovative approaches that could be utilized to halt the deterioration of our coastal environment. Effective use of these tools will require a long-term commitment at all levels of governments with strong public and private sector participation.

The challenge before us is to develop an ecosystem approach to managing our estuarine and coastal ocean environment. An approach is needed which recognizes that both the natural and man-made rules of the game will be changing. The climate will be warmer, due to natural trends and the "greenhouse effect"; sea level will rise due to melting glaciers; rainfall patterns will change; and much of the coastal continental United States will experience decreased river flows due to reduced precipitation and excessive water consumption. Pollutant concentrations in our rivers and estuaries will increase due to excessive waste production and decreased dilution by fresh-water inflow. Coastal habitats will dramatically change as more people demand waterfront property. Lastly, fishing and aquaculture efforts will intensify to meet the increased demand for seafood. To meet this challenge, we need to build on existing programs, implement new approaches and develop the predictive capability that will enable us to make mid-course corrections as we move through the treacherous waters that lie ahead.

GREAT LAKES

The Great Lakes, with 95,000 square miles of surface, stretch 800 miles east to west and 500 miles north to south. They provide drinking water for 26 million of the 35 million people living in the Great Lakes Basin and support 55 million angler days annually with an annual economic impact of between $2 and $4 billion. Fish, wildlife, and water quality and quantity assessment and management are shared by the Province of Ontario, eight Great Lakes states, and the federal governments of Canada and the United States. Two tribal authorities also share in the fish and wildlife management.

The clear need for cooperative arrangements in water and fishery management were met by the federal governments through 1) the 1909 Boundary Waters Treaty which created the International Joint Commission (IJC) and led to the 1972 Water Quality Agreement between the two countries and 2) the 1955 convention on Great Lakes Fisheries, which created the Great Lakes Fishery Commission (GLFC). Working together the governments, industries, and municipalities have reduced the point source discharges in the Basin and effected remarkable improvement in tributary stream and Great Lakes water quality since the late-1960s when effluent quality and quantity were at their worst.

Concerns for Great Lakes commercial fisheries existed as early as the 1830s, as overfishing, damming of tributary spawning streams, and environmental changes associated with clearing of the forests for agriculture effected great changes in what had been a a slowly evolving fish fauna. The commercial fisheries enjoyed their peak in the 1920s to 1940s and then declined both because of the above factors and because of the invasion of the sea lamprey into the upper three lakes.

The lamprey, native to the Atlantic Ocean, attaches to fish and feeds by extracting body fluids. The invasion of the sea lamprey provided the final incentive to establish the Great Lakes Fishery Commission, which has been able to bring the sea lamprey under reasonable control through its agents, the United States Fish and Wildlife Service, and Fisheries and Oceans Canada.

Tribal Involvement

There has been great friction between management agencies, the public, and native Americans as the latter attempt to exercise their treaty rights in large ceded areas of the Great Lakes. Since the mid-1970s there have been confrontations over netting interfering with recreational fishing, arguments over quotas of fish to be harvested, and accusations that the tribes take more than their total allowable and incidental catches. The tribal authorities have developed very good biological staffs and assessment capabilities and established law enforcement teams. Recently, the tribal authorities agreed to sign a joint strategic plan. As their capabilities increase, the tribes and the tribal fishermen will become outstanding stewards of the fishery resource.

Contaminants

Some species and sizes of Great Lakes fish accumulate residues of chemical contaminants from the water, sediments, and their food that exceed tolerances for unlimited consumption by humans. The council of Great Lakes Governors has instructed their public health, environmental quality, and natural resource agencies to develop uniform public healthy advisories for the lakes which can clearly understood by the public. There is a lack of data to accurately develop the advisories and, also, great differences of opinion on the criteria necessary for development of consumption guidelines to protect against cancer risk and reproductive abnormalities. There is great need for experimental work to provide information on risk, and a greater need for the epidemiological studies which will demonstrate if there are any ill effects among humans who consume Great Lakes fish.

Much of the fishery management success to date has been bioengineered through sea lamprey control, artificial replacement of native stocks by stocking, introduction of Pacific salmon, water quality and habitat improvement, and application of knowledgeable regulations controlling harvest. There are controversies about the desirability of striving for self-sustaining stocks vs. the "easy way" of put-grow-take. Hatcheries in the northern Great Lakes are currently plagued by epezootic epitheliotropic disease, a new affliction, perhaps viral, which has decimated lake trout production. This has brought home to the fishery manager that we must not create a fishery totally dependent on hatchery production or we will have some very lean fishery years. This threat to the fishery is extremely serious and deserving of a massive research effort to seek a cure or hatchery management practices which can moderate the effects. In the future, control of fish diseases in hatcheries and aquaculture facilities will be of greatly increased importance.

The Future

The 21st century will see further demands upon the Great Lakes water and water-dependent resources. Population will continue to grow and dependence upon the Great Lakes for water supply will grow in disproportion to such increases. Water dependent recreational uses— tourism, boating, fishing, swimming— will increase significantly. Fishing both recreationally and commercially will find growing conflicts with other users of water and space.

INLAND FISHERIES

In addition to the Great Lakes there are thousands of miles of non-tidal rivers and streams, thousands of acres of small lakes and reservoirs that support substantial fisheries. Although commercial fisheries exist in many such areas, the predominance of fishery activity is now recreational.

Today, one in every four Americans includes recreational fishing in their lifestyle. However, although the rate of growth of those participating in fishing has declined during the past five years, both the catch rate and the average size of fish caught have declined in recent decades, and almost all of the popular species in the marine waters of the United States are now fished above the capacity to replace themselves.

Other factors affecting the earlier dynamic increase in fishing participation can be found in small pond construction, which thrived under United States Department of Agriculture policies in effect during the 1950s and 1960s and which has since slowed considerably. This has resulted in the curtailment of new and productive fisheries habitat needed to offset the continued increase in fishing demand.

Although fish are a renewable resource, their resiliency is limited by their continuing competition with mankind. Maintaining the viability of over 2,200 species of finfish in this nation continues to be a difficult problem. At various times in their life histories, fish can be exposed to a variety of negative impacts such as overharvest, degraded water quality, physical obstacles imposed by power and navigation structures along their migratory pathways, and generalized habitat degradation due to mining, logging, or assorted other land use activities. A few examples of how various human activities have impacted various fish species on a national scope are illustrative of the problems fresh water fishery resources will increasingly face in the future.

In the Pacific Northwest, Pacific salmon and steelhead have suffered major impacts due to construction of hydroelectric, irrigation, and flood control dams. The first dams built along the Columbia River and its tributaries were constructed in the early 1900s to control floods and provide water for irrigation. The Federal Power Act of the 1920s and the New Deal Era of the 1930s embodied a vision of hydropower development that resulted in the construction of 55 dams. By the 1970s all were in place; hardly any major stream of the 260,000-square-mile watershed was left untouched. Simultaneously, the accessible habitat for natural spawning shrank by more than half, from approximately 163,000 square miles to about 73,000 square miles. By this time, the situation had become critical for some salmon and steelhead runs . . . and too late for others. Some stocks disappeared completely.

During the past several years, freshwater fishery resources have seen additional impact from dam development as a result of passage of the Public Utility Regulatory Policy Act of 1978 and the Energy Security Act of 1980. These acts provided significant incentives to develop small hydroelectric power by providing a guaranteed market and price. The resulting volume of applications to develop small hydropower projects overwhelmed federal and state resource managers. Agencies responsible for project review were disadvantaged in at least three ways: 1) there was a large number of applications to be reviewed at one time; 2) there was often little information available on the types of streams or projects under consideration; and 3) the federal incentive program made no allowances for the degree of environmental impact.

Progress has been achieved during this period to protect and mitigate for fish resources impacted by these small hydroelectric projects but only through intensive discussions, extensive interagency cooperation, and significant litigation.

The Atlantic sturgeon provides another example of how severely a fish species can be negatively impacted by human activities. The heyday for the Atlantic sturgeon fishery was about 1880, when millions of pounds were caught annually. Three reasons are generally cited for decline: overexploitation of an easily caught fish, damming of many coastal rivers which blocked their spawning migrations, and degradation of habitat by dredging and filling.

There are also success stories in enhancing inland fishery resources in the United States. Rainbow trout are an example of a qualified fish management success story. In North America this species was originally found only in the far western states, British Columbia and a small area of northwestern Mexico. Today, its distribution is much wider, with populations expanded inward into Canada, and many parts of the central United States, the Great Lakes Basin, the Appalachians, and southwestern Mexico. This expansion in range is not a testimony to increasing habitat, but a testimony to the effectiveness of modern fish culture technology. Through periodic stockings, anglers are provided a relatively stable source of catchable size rainbow trout in lakes and streams. The introduction of rainbows has resulted in some self-establishment and natural reproduction. However, this generally has been minimal, and the public demand is so high that fishery agencies continue to stock catchable size rainbows.

Negative impacts on fishery resources are not always related to land and water development pressures; sometimes the threats are biological. A continuing area of great concern is the potentially catastrophic impact to fish resources resulting from the introduction, whether intentional or unintentional, of nonnative fish or other aquatic organisms. This is a problem for which fishery managers can share much of the blame. The first known introduction of aquatic organisms into North American waters, ornamental goldfish, occurred three centuries ago. Some of the earliest fishery management efforts in the United States focused on the introduction of the common carp (*Cyprinus carpio*) and German brown trout (*Salmo trutta*). While most would call the introduction of brown trout a success story, many feel that the carp introduction was a mistake of gigantic proportions. However, concern about the introduction of aquatic organisms existed only since the late 1960s. Nevertheless, not all is well and the future will likely show additional impacts from generally unrecognized sources.

The result of all these impacts has been more than suppression of commercial or recreational fish production. It has meant extinction of species. Presently the United States Fish and Wildlife Service lists 71 species of fish as endangered or threatened, with approximately 10 percent of these being game fish. In addition, another 148 species are candidates for evaluation as endangered or threatened species, with approximately 13 percent of these being game fish.

For most anglers, studies indicate that there is a threshold level of angling success, below which they will stop fishing and pursue alternate activities. While the inherent responsibility of the professional natural resources managers in the 21st century may not be to provide an acceptable fishing experience for an ever increasing number of anglers, the perceived success of aquatic management programs could very well continue to be judged by the catch-rate criteria. Factors other than maximized protein landings on a sustained basis (maximum sustained yield) should be used to evaluate future fishery management programs. Ultimately the key to success in the 21st century will be to maximize the number of healthy fisheries, to promote the catch-and-release fishing experience, and to elevate the role of aquaculture as the source of quality fish protein.

A problem with maintaining freshwater fishery resources and their attendant fisheries lies with the failure of reservoir research programs to provide the needed management technologies to maintain the productivity of aging reservoirs. Although ponds and reservoirs will have to accommodate the bulk of the fishing pressure in the 21st century, little is being done to determine how productivity can be increased and maintained. Rather than respond to the need for an expanded reservoir research program, the United States Fish and Wildlife Service dropped its entire reservoir effort. While the time honored bass/forage fish format for ponds management has provided a fishery potential for these waters, the problems associated with keeping the species balanced are ongoing. New species and methodologies are needed in order to realize the tremendous potential of these smaller impoundments.

OVERALL PROJECTIONS

A continuing and pervasive problem to be faced in the 21st century is maintenance of water quality. Sport fishing currently represents a 25-billion-dollar-a-year industry and employs over 1 million people. The industry serves the nation's approximately 60 million anglers. The prosperity of the industry is linked inseparably to an attractive, abundant supply of sport fish which, in turn, is dependent on the quality, and productivity of the nation's streams, lakes, reservoirs, ponds, estuaries, and oceans.

Yet the waters in the natural resource banks will face increasing competition from growth and development in the 21st century. An honest forecast would have to conclude that the resource base, in spite of a valiant stand, will slowly be eroded as the socioeconomic realities of population shifts and increases occur. The natural resource manager will be constantly faced with accomplishing more with less, and new innovative management technologies will have to be used instead of the traditional management techniques of the 20th century. Even the most innovative methodologies will be dependent on the ability of the resource lobby to fight on equal terms with the developers. The need to rehabilitate or even re-create "natural habitats" as mitigation for loss of prime habitat in developing areas will be the order of the day.

The upward trend of seafood demand in the United States likely will continue. Recent projections by the U.S. Department of Agriculture indicate that by the year 2000, per capita seafood consumption in this country may increase five percent to 17 percent above the 1986 base. This would boost per capita consumption to between 15.5 pounds (7.0 kg) and 17.2 pounds (7.8 kg), up from 15.4 pounds (7.0 kg) in 1987. By these measures, supplies of edible seafood products for the total United States market will need to increase by 18 to 31 percent during the relatively few years remaining in this century.

Prospects are not good for drawing upon traditional sources of supply to meet future growth in demand for seafood in the United States. Catch trends for the United States and the world at large indicate that favored target species are being fished at or close to their biological limits. Certain stocks have been overfished.

The possibility of increasing United States fishery supplies through imports is limited. The same restrictions that limit United States landings limit world landings. While in any given year, it may be possible to increase a particular country's supply of fish products through imports, this is accomplished at the expense of supply in other countries as shipments are diverted from the weaker to the stronger markets.

Pending shortages in the supply of seafoods are a matter of concern for United States fishery managers in both industry and government. They are asking, and are being asked, questions such as the following: 1) Can future increases in demand for seafood products be met, in part, by aquaculture? 2) Will the additional supplies come from domestic or foreign sources? 3) What future role will be played in the United States seafoods market by domestic capture fisheries and domestic aquaculture?

It is the salmon and shrimp markets which are most likely to first be affected by competition between capture fisheries and aquaculture, and they provide some indications of trends.

Salmon Production

Historically, the world supply of salmon has come from catches of wild salmon in the oceans or in river systems where salmon return to spawn. Salmon fisheries occur primarily in the Pacific Ocean, where most of the fishing effort focuses on chinook, coho, sockeye, pink, and chum. In 1985, for example, 94 percent of the world supply of salmon from capture fisheries was caught in Pacific Ocean areas. From 1979 to 1985, the world catch of the five major salmon species, in the aggregate, was relatively stable. Annual totals fluctuated moderately around a six year average of 765,000 metric tons for the five species.

The United States is the world's leading producer of wild (ocean/river caught) Pacific salmon. United States commercial salmon landings ranged from 91,400 metric tons in 1975 to 330,000 metric tons in 1985. In the 1980s, however, wild catches stabilized, hovering between 276,000 metric tons and 330,000 metric tons.

Much of the United States domestic production of salmon is aimed at export markets. In fact, the quantity of Pacific salmon sold domestically has declined as salmon exports have grown. Between 1970 and 1986, United States exports of salmon (fresh, frozen, and canned) increased more than tenfold, from 12,800 metric tons to 160,000 metric tons. Thus, despite a 60 percent increase in the United States salmon catch between 1970 and 1986, the amount of salmon available for the United States market, from the domestic catch, declined from 1.89 pounds (0.85 kg) to 1.23 pounds (0.57 kg) per capita.

Total world production of pen-raised salmon (Atlantic and Pacific) has expanded rapidly, rising from 6,880 metric tons in 1980 to an estimated 70,000 metric tons in 1986. In 1980, farmed salmon accounted for 1.2 percent of world production (wild and aquaculture). By 1985, this share rose to 5.3 percent, and appeared headed for 10 percent in 1986.

The National Marine Fisheries Service estimates that world production of farmed Atlantic and Pacific salmon could approach 226,000 metric tons by 1990, and equal 26 percent of total world salmon production (aquaculture and wild). Norway is the world's leading producer of farmed Atlantic salmon, and probably will continue in this role. Norwegian output is expected to grow from 46,000 metric tons to 100,000 metric tons between 1986 and 1990. Other likely top producers of farmed Atlantic salmon are the United Kingdom and Ireland, with combined production in 1990 totaling 35,000 metric tons.

Salmon aquaculture production estimates for the United States are uncertain. Private salmon aquaculture operations recently have started in Washington and Maine, and several permit applications are under review by state agencies. According to National Marine Fisheries Service, farmed output of Atlantic and Pacific salmon (in Idaho, Maine, Oregon, and Washington) will reach an estimated 7,600 metric tons. In Alaska, industry groups and the state legislature are debating the merits of allowing pen-culture operations.

Fresh pen-raised salmon first appeared on the United States market in significant quantities in 1970-80, and not long afterwards became one of the most widely sought after specialty seafood products by United States restaurants. Imports of fresh, farmed salmon rose from 726 metric tons in 1980 to more than 12,700 metric tons in 1986.

Norway literally dominates the United States fresh salmon import market. In 1986, 69 percent of United States imports of salmon were products of Norway. Canada was the second leading foreign supplier with 19 percent of the total, followed by Chile (5 percent), and the United Kingdom (3 percent).

Although the domestic market for farmed salmon is relatively new, imports appear to follow a fairly regular seasonal pattern. Fresh salmon imports peak in the December to March period. In comparison, landings of Pacific salmon in the capture fisheries peak in the summer months. This suggests that pen-raised salmon are filling a demand niche created because of the scarcity of wild salmon in the winter months.

Shrimp Production

World landings of shrimp (wild and aquaculture) have almost doubled over the past 15 years, from 1.08 million metric tons in 1970 to 1.90 million in 1985. However, the increase in production has not kept pace with world population growth. Thus, on a per capita basis, landings dropped from 0.413 kilograms to 0.388 kilograms.

Food and Agricultural Organization data suggest that the world catch of shrimp is not likely to increase significantly in the near future. In the late 1970s and into the 1980s, the catch stabilized in the 1.57 to 1.67 million metric tons range. In contrast, aquaculture production has soared, growing from 78,300 metric tons in 1982 to 216,500 metric tons in 1985. Farmed shrimp in 1985 accounted for almost 13 percent of total world shrimp production.

In 1986, United States shrimp landing totaled 182,000 metric tons. Between 1950 and 1977, United States shrimp landings had followed an upward trend, rising from 87,200 metric tons to 216,000 metric tons. Since then annual landings have fluctuated widely between 113,300 metric tons to 191,800 metric tons.

The demand for shrimp in the United States, at least for the past 20 years, has exceeded the harvest potential of wild shrimp in United States waters. As a consequence, the domestic market has become increasingly dependent on shrimp imports. For example, in the 1960s imports accounted for, on average, a little more than 50 percent of United States supplies. In the 1980s the import share was more than 60 percent, and peaked at 73 percent in 1983.

Countries in Latin America and Asia are the major suppliers of shrimp to the United States. In 1986, the United States imported 223,000 metric tons of shrimp. Imports from Mexico, Ecuador, Taiwan, and Panama have increased substantially since 1980. Most of this growth is attributable to sharp increases in the production of cultured shrimp.

A combination of stable landings and increasing demand has raised questions concerning the future adequacy of shrimp supplies to meet market demand. Current trends suggest that aquaculture is expected to provide much of the new supply source for shrimp in the United States and abroad.

By 1990, the National Marine Fisheries Service estimates that world production of cultured shrimp may reach 490,000 metric tons. If the world catch of wild shrimp stays at the 1980-1985 average level, by 1990 aquaculture could account for 28 percent of world shrimp production.

If the upward trend in seafood consumption continues, the United States is going to need new supply sources in the 1990s. The United States relies heavily on imports of both capture and aquaculture species, and faces an evergrowing trade deficit in fisheries products. With many of the world's principal capture fisheries at or approaching their maximum biological levels, the United States dependence on aquaculture imports will increase in the future. This also holds for other major seafood importers. In the case of salmon and shrimp, it appears that future increases in demand will be supplied primarily from aquaculture products, as indicated by the potential aquaculture production estimates.

As reflected in the sections on inland and Great Lakes fisheries, recreational demand for quality fishing also will grow. Given that wild stock production has leveled, state managers of such fisheries will undoubtedly turn to aquaculture production to augment wild fisheries. This may well open recreational fishing to more "put and take" particularly in small and large man-made impoundments. So too will the fisheries of the Great Lakes be supplemented by such techniques. The 21st century will see unprecedented growth in aquaculture for such purposes.

REFERENCES

Almeida, F.P. 1987. Status of the silver hake resources off the northeast coast of the United States-1987. Woods Hole Laboratory Reference Document 87-03. 60 pp.

Anthony, V.C. and S. Clark, 1979. A Description of the northern shrimp fishery and its decline in relation to water temperature, climate and fisheries. In **Proceedings: Workshop on the influence of environmental factors on fisheries production.** Center for Ocean Management Studies, University of Rhode Island, Kingston, R.I. 119 pp.

Anthony, V.C. and M.J. Fogarty. 1985. Environmental effects on recruitment, growth and vulnerability of Atlantic herring (*Clupea harengus*) in the Gulf of Maine region. In **The Biological Characteristics of Herring and Their Implication for Management.** Canadian Journal. Special Publication Fisheries and Aquatic Science, Vol. 42, Supplement No. 1, pp. 150-173.

Broutman, Marlene A. and Dorothy L. Leonard. 1988. Preliminary statistics on causes of shellfish bed closures. National Oceanic and Atmospheric Administration, National Ocean Service, Office of Oceanography and Marine Assessment, Ocean Assessment Division, Strategic Assessment Branch, Rockville, MD.

Dow, R.L. 1977. Effects of climatic cycles on the relative abundance and availability of commercial marine and estuarine species. Journal **du Conseil International pour l'Exploration de la Mer.**

Fisher, Diane, J. Ceraso, T. Mathew, and M. Oppenheimer. 1988. **Polluted coastal waters: the role of acid rain.** Environmental Defense Fund, New York, N.Y. 120 pp.

Flemer, D.S., G.B. Mackiernan, W. Nelson, and V.K. Tippie. 1983. **Chesapeake Bay: a profile of environmental change.** U.S. Environmental Protection Agency, Region 3, Philadelphia, PA.

Gosselink, J.G., E.P. Odum, and R.M. Pope. 1974. **The value of the tidal marsh.** Louisiana State University, Center for Wetlands Resources, Louisiana State University 74-03. 30 pp.

Houde, Edward D., ed. 1987. **Long range research need for Chesapeake Bay living resources: workshop** report. University of Maryland, Center for Environmental and Estuarine Studies, Report No. TS61-87. 150 pp.

Mager, Andreas, Jr., and Gordon W. Thayer. 1986. National Marine Fisheries Service habitat conservation efforts in the southeast region of the United States from 1981 through 1985. **Mar. Fish Rev.** 48 (3):1-8.

National Oceanic and Atmospheric Administration. Anonymous. 1988. In press. Status of the fishery resources off the Northeastern United States for 1988. NOAA Technical Memorandum National Marine Fisheries Service-FNEC. 135 pp.

National Oceanic and Atmospheric Adminstration/National Ocean Service. 1988. **How representative are the estuaries nominated for EPA's National Estuary Program.** Office of Oceanography and Marine Assessment, Ocean Assessment Division, Strategic Assessment Branch, Rockville, MD. 9 pp.

National Oceanic and Atmospheric Administration/Estuarine Programs Office. 1987. **Estuarine and coastal ocean science framework.** NOAA Estuarine Programs Office, Washington, D.C. 87 pp.

National Oceanic and Atmospheric Administration/National Ocean Service. 1987. **National Status and Trends Program: progress report.** Office of Oceanography and Marine Assessment, Rockville, MD. 82 pp.

National Wetlands Policy Forum. 1988. Draft Report of the National Wetlands Policy Forum. Washington, D.C. 75 pp.

Pope, J.G., T.K. Stokes, S.A. Murawski, and J.S. Idoine. 1988. A comparison of fish size composition in the North Sea and on Georges Bank. In **Proceedings of Ecodynamics: Workshop on theoretical ecology.** Kernforschungsanlage Julich (KFA), Conference Service, P.O. Box 1913, D-5170, Julich, FRG. October 1987.

Sherman, K., J.R. Green, and L. Ejsymont. 1983. Coherence in zooplankton of a large northwest Atlantic ecosystem. United States National Marine Fisheries Fishery Bulletin. 81:855-862.

Skud, B.E. 1982. Dominance in fishes: the relation between environment and abundance. Science. 216:144-149.

Sutcliffe, W.H.J., K. Drinkwater and B.S. Muir. 1977. Correlations of fish catch and environmental factors in the Gulf of Maine. Journal of the fisheries Research Board of Canada.

Tester, Patricia A., Richard P. Stumpf, and Patricia K. Fowler. 1988. Red tide, the first occurrence in North Carolina waters: an overview. In Oceans '88. Marine Technology Society. 4 pp.

Titus, James G., ed. 1988. Greenhouse effect, sea level rise, and coastal wetlands. EPA Office of Policy, Planning, and Evaluation, Washington, D.C. EPA-230-05-86-013. 152 pp.

Ulanowicz, Robert E. 1987. Depicting functional changes in the Chesapeake Bay ecosystem. Pages 117-124 in G.B. Mackiernan, ed., Dissolved oxygen in the Chesapeake Bay: processes and effects. Maryland Sea Grant College Program, College Park, MD. 176 pp.

U.S. Environmental Protection Agency. 1988a. Chesapeake Bay: basinwide nutrient reduction strategy. Chesapeake Bay Program Agreement Commitment Report. Chesapeake Bay Program, Annapolis, MD. 6 pp

U.S. Environmental Protection Agency. 1988b. Draft Chesapeake Bay wetlands policy. Chesapeake Bay Program Agreement Commitment Report. Chesapeake Bay Program, Annapolis, MD. 8 pp.

CHAPTER 10

Outdoor Recreation and Wilderness

H. Ken Cordell

According to the 1986 President's Commission on Americans Outdoors, outdoor recreation and wilderness are becoming increasingly important to American society. In recent years, however, the public sector has faced strong pressures to reduce recreation spending. Most severe at federal and state levels, cuts have been made in personnel, maintenance, and management. A positive result has been the stimulation of innovation, partnerships, and cooperation.

This chapter reviews recent past trends, the current situation and possible futures for outdoor recreation and wilderness. Based on this review, several observations are offered about the social significance of recent past trends. Opportunities for improving resource allocations and management are suggested.

President's Commission on Americans Outdoors and the Domestic Policy Council's Task Force

Recognition of the changing nature of recreation grew throughout the 1970s. Acknowledgment of the significance of this change led national recreation interests to gain the support of such figures as Laurance Rockefeller and Morris Udall for the concept of a new national recreation policy review. Rockefeller led the resulting Outdoor Recreation Policy Review Group in 1982, an effort that helped spark introduction of legislation to create a national commission in 1983. Successful efforts in the Senate, led by Malcolm Wallop of Wyoming, resulted in unanimous support for such legislation. House action, however, was stalled, causing President Reagan to create by executive order the President's Commission on Americans Outdoors in January 1985.

This commission began work in the fall of 1985 and completed its efforts in early 1987. It conducted a review of literature and research, solicited ideas and experiences from active interests, heard from more than 1,000 witnesses and received several thousand written submissions. The commission reports were released in early 1987 and provided a wide range of observations and recommendations.

In the summer of 1987, a Domestic Policy Council Task Force on Outdoor Recreation Resources and Opportunities was created to review outdoor recreation in light of the commission's report. Its report, *Outdoor Recreation in a Nation of Communities*, was completed and published in April 1988. This chapter reviews data in both the President's Commission on Americans Outdoors and Domestic Policy Council reports.

The Relationship of Outdoor Recreation and Wilderness to Conservation Interests

The outdoor recreation movement has important ties to conservation interests and their activities. For example, the impetus for the Outdoor Recreation Resources Review Commission, which was formed by President Eisenhower in the 1950s to study outdoor recreation needs, came from a small number of conservation leaders, principally Joseph Penfold of the Izaak Walton League, Dave Brower of the Sierra Club, and associated civic organizations. High on their agenda were concerns for parks; open space; opportunities for hunting, fishing and other outdoor recreation activities; and a concern for habitat, clean water, and wetlands.

The Outdoor Recreation Resources Review Commission's report in 1962 provided a unifying agenda for the conservation community. Congressional enactment of the commission's recommendations for protecting and expanding the public estate followed easily. The 1960s also produced broad concern for quality air and water. Lady Bird Johnson struck a responsive chord as she championed beautification plantings in cities and along highways, a fight against billboards, and an appreciation of aesthetics. Thus, public health, historic preservation interests, and women's and garden clubs allied with old line conservation groups. The result was clean air and water bills.

This activity contributed significantly to the environmental movement. A number of organizations came into being, carrying environment or ecology in their names. Some of the older organizations began to change focus, from natural resources and outdoor recreation to environmental quality for public health and safety, including nuclear and toxic wastes. While these evolving organizations retained their original interests, such as wildlife or wilderness, the overall shift was to more technical environmental problems. The broadest remaining point of consensus has been continued support for wilderness.

From the synthesis provided by the broad environmental interests of the 1960s, there has since developed divergence of interest between "modern" environmental organizations and those concerned about natural resources and recreation.

Using this brief review of history and issues as a springboard, the following section provides an overview of the resource base and its availability for outdoor recreation.

THE RESOURCE AND FACILITY BASE

The land base of the United States is about one-third each natural forest and range. With the associated water area, there are 1.6 billion acres of forest and range that include most of our public lands. Thirty-nine percent of forest lands and 42 percent of range lands are federal. Of these federal properties, over 690 million acres are available for public recreational use. Also, 53 million acres of state lands and over 2 million acres of local government lands are available for recreation (Figure 10.1), making a total of 746 million public acres. Private lands available for recreation include over 280 million acres. It is essential to note that the areas reported here are only those available for recreation and that *areas not available are not reported*.

Recreation Resources on the Federal Estate

Wilderness and Remote Backcountry Land. These lands are more than three miles from roads and are typified by little or no development beyond abandoned roads, foot trails, and occasional shelters. Many of the most remote and pristine of these lands are in the National Wilderness Preservation System. As of 1987, about 89 million acres of federal land had been included in the National Wilderness Preservation System; most, 56 million acres, were in Alaska. Of the 32 million acres in the lower 48 states, roughly 28 million are in the western regions, mostly in national forests. In the East there are only 3.9 million acres of the National Wilderness Preservation System, again, much of it in national forests. Estimates of remote backcountry not in the National Wilderness Preservation System include 102 million acres, mostly in the West, 70 million in Alaska. Outside of Alaska, there are only about 1.5 million nonwilderness remote acres.

Extensive Undeveloped Land. Bordering the most remote of federal lands are lands lying between a half and three miles from a road. More than 86 percent of these 87.3 million acres are in national forests. The East has comparatively little — about 2.2 million acres in the North, another 3.3 million in the South.

Roaded, Partially Developed Land. Within a half mile of a road there are an estimated 388.4 million acres — almost 80 percent managed by the Bureau of Land Management. The Forest Service manages 72 million acres. Only about five percent of federal roaded acreage is in the East. The most heavily used portions of the federal estate are these lands lying within a half mile of roads. They include the 760 trails, more than 8,400 miles, in the National Recreation Trail System. More than 500 of these trails are managed by federal agencies,

Figure 10.1. Resource and Facility Base in the United States, 1987

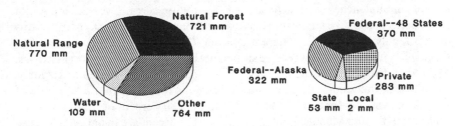

Source: Outdoor Recreation and Wilderness Assessment Group, USDA Forest Service, Athens, GA.

about 140 by local government, 80 by state agencies, and almost 30 by private concerns.

Developed Land Sites. There are a total of almost 5,000 federal campgrounds operated by eight different agencies. The majority of these campgrounds are in national forests (70 percent), followed by those in land managed by the Corps of Engineers (17 percent). The Rocky Mountain region has 35.2 percent, the Pacific region 34.9 percent. Only about 10 percent of the campgrounds are in the Northeast. Federal agencies also operate over 63,000 picnic areas, about 80 percent of which are located in the East, and have developed over 144,000 miles of roads.

Water Opportunities. Among the primary remote water resources is the National Wild and Scenic River System. As of 1986, 7,178 miles had been included, most in the Pacific Region, especially in Alaska. About 911 miles were in the East. Three agencies, the Forest Service, Park Service, and Bureau of Land Management, manage nearly 30 percent of the National Wild and Scenic River System. Almost 7,550 additional miles were under study in 1986.

Among water-oriented federal properties, those most suitable for outdoor recreation include most segments of national rivers, national seashores, lakeshores, and water-oriented national recreation areas. Among the acres in national rivers, lakeshores, and recreation areas, more than two-thirds are in the Rocky Mountain Region. The Northern Region has the least such area (413,000 acres), although much of it is near major metropolitan areas. Unlike these specially designated federal waters, more of the highly developed water areas are in the East. Most swimming areas are in the southern region. Over 60 percent are on Corps of Engineer's projects. A total of over 7,800 boat ramps are managed by five federal agencies, nearly half in the South.

Snow and Ice Opportunities. Combined, wilderness and other remote areas (more than three miles from roads) with sufficient snowfall for winter sports (16 or more annual inches) add up to about 171.5 million acres. Over 127 million of these acres are in Alaska; fewer than two million are in the East. Most of this area is highly inaccessible. There are about 71 million federal acres a half to three miles from a road that receive sufficient snowfall for winter sport activities. More than two-thirds are in national forests in the Rocky Mountain Region.

Most of the federal lands in snowfall regions that lie within a half mile of roads are available for winter sports. More than 80 percent of these acres are on Bureau of Land Management lands; about 17 percent are in national forests. More than half are in the Pacific Region, including Alaska. More than 2,000 miles of trails in the National Recreation Trail System have been designated for cross-country skiing, more than half in the Northeast. More than 1,500 miles of the National Recreation Trail System have been designated for snowmobiling use, again with the majority in the North, none in the South. During winter, more than 100,000 miles of roads on federal lands, when unplowed, may be used for winter recreation. About one-third of ski lifts are in national forests. Eighty-three percent of such sites in the Rockies and 78 percent in the Pacific Coast are in national forests.

Specially Designated Federal Lands

Special federal designations are mostly "overlays" of the federal land systems, such as the National Forest System. National designations, such as wilderness, are usually referred to as systems; for example, the National Wilderness Preservation System. They are not, however, managed as systems in the strictest sense. Congress usually designates special areas, particularly on multiple-purpose lands, to resolve disputes over competing land uses. Special designation represents a narrowing of management purpose. When accomplished at the congressional level, designation supplants administrative prerogatives.

Wilderness. Wilderness began with administrative designation of the Gila Wilderness Area in 1924. From these humble beginnings, the National Wilderness Preservation System has grown to nearly 89 million acres. Congressionally designated wilderness acreages occur in 44 states, two-thirds in Alaska. The National Park Service, Forest Service, Fish and Wildlife Service and the Bureau of Land Management manage wilderness to preserve and sometimes to restore natural conditions. While recreation is an important use, scientific research, species continuance and diversity, education, and gene pool preservation are equally important.

National Recreation Areas. Congress has individually designated 32 National Recreation Areas. The National Park Service administers 17 of these areas, the Forest Service 15. These areas generally exceed 20,000 acres, have high carrying capacity and have outstanding scenic qualities. While they vary from high mountains to seashores and inland waters, some are very close to major metropolitan areas. Each National Recreation Area carries its own particular requirements as prescribed by its act. The managing agency then prepares a management plan in accordance with these requirements, which reflect national purposes, but these requirements can be out of context with local conditions and desires.

National Wild and Scenic Rivers. The Act of 1968 authorized designation of national rivers. Subsequently, 75 river segments comprising 7,365 miles have come into the system. The federal agency having jurisdiction administers the designated river, sometimes in partnership with states. The states administer approximately 10 percent of the system miles. This national river system provides unique linear recreation opportunities for such activities as canoeing, rafting, hiking and trail riding. Its management gives primacy to protection and recreation.

National Scenic, Historical, and Recreation Trails. Congress has designated 14 National Scenic and Historical Trails, covering 23,500 miles. Again the agency with jurisdiction assumes management, typically emphasizing non-motorized uses and protection of natural and historic values. The Secretary of the Interior may designate National Recreation trails under the original act. A total of 760 trails or trail segments, including 8,400 miles, has been thus designated. Approximately 500 of these are on federal lands, 80 are on state, 140 on local, and about 30 on individually or organizationally owned lands. National Recreation trails are not limited to non-motorized uses.

Recreation Resources on State Properties

About 52.6 million acres (2.5 percent of the United States land base, excluding Alaska) of the land in state ownership are available for public recreation. The East contains 39.9 million state recreation acres. Combined, the North and South have 61.5 percent of the national total. Almost 50 percent is in state forests, the rest is in state parks (19 percent), or fish and game systems (31 percent).

Land Opportunities. An estimated 2.9 million acres of state lands are designated wilderness or are remote backcountry more than three miles from roads. State park agencies manage about 75 percent of these remote lands. The remainder of designated wilderness is on state forests, almost all of it in the

North. State-owned lands also include about three million acres of extensive backcountry between a half and three miles from roads, all of which are on state park properties. Nearly half of these acres are in the South. The greatest portion of state-owned recreation lands are within a half mile of roads, in all, more than 40 million acres. State forest agencies manage slightly more than half of these acres. State parks, forests, and fish and game agencies provide almost 2,100 campgrounds. Campgrounds on state park and forest lands are concentrated mostly in the eastern regions, especially in the North. More than 70 percent of state parks in the North have picnic facilities, compared with 67 percent in the Pacific Coast, 60 percent in the South, and 54 percent in the Rocky Mountain Region.

Water Opportunities. States have more than 60 thousand miles of rivers or sections of rivers under protected status. Most of these miles are in the North (35 percent) or South (37 percent). These rivers provide opportunities for remote as well as for the more accessible water-based recreation activities. The availability of state-provided, developed water facilities includes fishing and swimming opportunities at more than half of the state parks, including a few boating facilities.

Snow and Ice Opportunities. About 4.6 million acres of wilderness and other remote state lands provide winter recreation opportunities. More than half (53 percent) of these most remote acres are in the North, much of the remainder is in the Pacific Coast region. More than 35 percent of all state recreation lands with sufficient snowfall are less remote and lie a half to three miles from roads. About 45 percent of these 2.4 million acres are in the Pacific Coast Region; about one-third are in the North; one-fifth are in the Rocky Mountain Region. An estimated 29 million acres of state-owned recreation areas are within a half mile of roads and receive enough annual snowfall to provide winter opportunities. About three-fifths of these acres are in the North, another 7.4 million (25 percent) are in the Pacific Coast states. States also provide a modest amount of downhill skiing and winter resort opportunities.

Recreation Resources on Local Properties

Outdoor recreation resources provided by local governments span nearly a full spectrum, with the exception of remote, roadless opportunities. From outdoor festivals and sporting events, to nature preserves and overnight camping, local governments provide an important variety of close-to-home opportunities. The majority of local park and recreation agencies (77 percent) are under a municipal jurisdiction. Many of the remainder (15 percent) are county departments.

Local agencies are very active in providing sports fields and playgrounds; approximately 85 percent provide outdoor tennis and basketball; and about 50 percent provide fitness trails and outdoor courts. Data from the Renewable Resources Planning Act Assessment (U.S. Department of Agriculture Forest

Service 1988) indicate that tent and recreation vehicle campsites are as frequently provided as tennis courts, particularly in the Pacific Coast Region. Many local departments emphasize outdoor sites; the median number per local department in the United States was 12. Total land and water area per department was 160 acres in 1986. Mostly, local governments provide opportunities at the developed end of the spectrum. Sports fields are among the most abundantly provided opportunity; pools and playgrounds generally come next. Tennis courts and golf courses also are important.

Frequently, local departments provide relatively large areas of natural parks and lakes. Across the conservatively estimated 3,821 departments providing natural areas and 2,812 providing lakes throughout the United States, there are totals of more than 450,000 natural land acres and more than 60,000 acres of lakes. The total area local agencies provide for recreation is 2.3 million acres. Local departments also provide a wide variety of trails extending over 32,000 miles, most of which are for fitness, hiking, and biking.

Overall, local government departments seem most concerned with maintaining their existing outdoor sites and facilities, adding additional outdoor opportunities, adding indoor opportunities, increasing funding, and providing more information to users. These priorities put a strong emphasis on close-to-home outdoor recreation, most of which is complementary to that provided by federal and state governments.

Private Lands and Development

Rural private land makes up more than 60 percent of the contiguous United States land base, about 1.28 billion acres. All but five percent of this acreage are non-industrially owned. In 1987, more than 350 million acres of this non-industrial land were closed to all but its owners. Access to 576 million acres, or 48 percent of the private land base, was estimated to be restricted to those personally acquainted with the owner. Only about 23 percent, or 283 million acres, is open to the public (Figure 10.2). More than 80 percent of this open land is either free of charge or has a daily fee. The rest, mostly in the South and the Rockies, is under some form of exclusive lease agreement. In 1977, about 29 percent of private lands was open to the public, a decrease of almost 70 million acres in more than 10 years.

An estimated 31 million acres of open private rural lands are more than one-half mile from a road and are extensive enough to be categorized as backcountry. The vast majority of this private backcountry acreage is in the Rocky Mountain Region— almost 26 million acres. Three and one-half million of the private backcountry acres in the Pacific Coast region are leased for recreational use.

Approximately 2.3 million miles of the estimated 15.5 million miles of roads and trails on non-industrial private land are open to the public for recreation (15 percent). This represents about one mile of trail or unimproved road per 125 acres of open land. Lands in the East appear to be more heavily roaded than

Figure 10.2. Private Lands Open for Public Recreation in United States, 1987

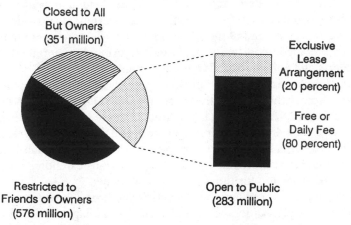

Source: Outdoor Recreation and Wilderness Assessment Group, USDA, Forest Service, Athens, GA.

those in the West. The North has more than one million miles of roads on private lands, compared to about 300,000 in the Rocky Mountain Region and about 120,000 in the Pacific Coast states. Many of these roads are little maintained and are rough.

Beyond non-industrial private lands, the private sector accounts for about 55 percent of all campgrounds in the United States and contains over 70 percent of campsite capacity. In general, private campgrounds cater to the camper who desires more facilities and services. Private campgrounds, more often than public, provide a store, hook-ups for trailers, and playground facilities. More than 50 percent of private campgrounds provide full hookups, compared to only four percent of public campgrounds. The North has more than 40 percent of private campgrounds; the South has another 30 percent.

Dude ranches and golf courses are among the myriad commercial enterprises operated by private entrepreneurs. Generally, private businesses provide resources and services not otherwise available. Often they facilitate access to public areas. The majority of land-based commercial enterprises are located near population centers. For example, almost three out of five resident camps and nearly half of the country's 11,000 commercial resorts are in the North. Another 18 percent of resorts are located in the South. Three-fourths of the over 6,000 golf courses open to the public are located in the eastern half of the country. The 2,400 members-only golf courses also are located primarily in regions with the greatest population. Golf courses also provide an important open space resource for walks and jogging in warm weather, or skiing and snowshoeing in winter.

Special Designations, Non-federal
State park, forest, and fish and game agencies manage sizable acreages of specially designated lands for recreation and wilderness. Local governments and some private organizations also manage specially designated natural, historic, and cultural sites, along with lake and river facilities.

Wilderness. Nine states have formally designated wilderness similar to, but smaller in size than, the federal system. These wildernesses are managed as a part of either state parks or forests. In total, almost five million acres, including two million managed by non-profit organizations, can be considered non-federal wilderness. Of these, about three-fourths are in tracts of 5,000 acres or more. Non-federal designations complement the federal system by filling gaps, particularly in the East.

Rivers. The states have placed approximately 6,000 miles of rivers under some form of protection for both recreation and to preserve natural values. Additionally, states administer more than 750 miles of federally designated wild and scenic rivers. Some states have river acts patterned after the federal act.

Trails. State and local jurisdictions manage about 35,000 miles of specially designated trails, including 776 National Recreation Trails approved through the Secretary of the Interior. These trails are significant because of their close proximity to populations, thus offering close-to-home opportunities.

EFFECTIVENESS OF RESOURCES FOR OUTDOOR RECREATION AND FOR PRESERVATION OF WILDERNESS

Recreation Opportunities
Marion Clawson is credited with conceptualizing a measure of the *effectiveness* of land and water resources for recreation opportunities (Clawson 1982). Reported here are regional comparisons and future projections of the effectiveness of recreational opportunities across federal, state, local and private providers, as conceptualized by Clawson. Effectiveness basically is an index of the availability of recreational opportunities across different types of recreational resources, facilities and services within the distances people are willing to travel and relative to the number of people living within these distance zones. Opportunities are downweighted because they are increasingly more distant from population centers. Effectiveness, as a supply measure, greatly improves the utility of raw data, such as acreages, miles or number of sites, as a statement of the appropriateness of the kind, mix, quantity, and location of available recreational opportunities, relative to the location and number of people living in the communities spread throughout our country.

On the average, effective opportunities per capita for each of the succeedingly less remote, more developed, land-based recreational environments are much greater in the West than in the East. Opportunities for all types of land-based recreation in both the Rocky Mountain and Pacific Coast regions are effectively five to 10 times greater than opportunities in the northern and southern regions. Within regions, average effectiveness indices of opportunities for land-based recreation vary only slightly.

The effectiveness indices for water-based recreation environments are nearly the same for the two eastern regions, but east-west differences for water opportunities are not as great as they are for land opportunities. Effectiveness indices reflect a three-fold greater abundance of water recreational opportunities in the West relative to the East. In the Eastern and Pacific Coast regions, intensively developed water recreation sites have provided the highest effective opportunities, nearly twice that of wild or remote water recreation. Wild water recreation has the highest average effectiveness value for the Rocky Mountain region. In this region, indices of effective opportunities are about the same across all four categories of water recreation environments.

Among the average snow-based effectiveness indices, the most notable are the expected near-zero values in the southern region. The average snow-based effectiveness values in the western regions are five to 10 times those of the northern region. The highest average effectiveness index values for snow-based recreational environments are in the Rocky Mountain region.

Observable recent trends, since about 1970, of the availability of public and private resources (land, water, snow-based), facilities, and services serve as a baseline for describing the result of implemented public policy and private sector reactions to markets. It is highly informative to examine the effect that continuation of these trends would have in the future if no conscious policy change or large-scale market shifts were to occur. General summarizations of recent past trends in resource availabilities are presented in the 1989 Renewable Resources Planning Act Assessment (U.S. Department of Agriculture Forest Service 1988) and are not repeated here for the sake of brevity.

Figures 10.3a, b, and c illustrate projections of future recreation opportunity effectiveness under a scenario where resource availability and facility development trends would continue in the future. These projections are based on computed models that account for policy, population and market dynamics. Using these models, it was possible to simulate a continuation of trends since 1970. With such continuation, some projections imply continued opportunity growth, sometimes rapid, in order to stay on trend lines established since 1970. These projection results are presented very briefly below.

Figure 10.3b indicates that continuing recent past trends in the provision of access, facilities, and services would result in future gains in opportunities for both road accessible, partially developed, and highly developed water opportunities. Continuing past trends would only slightly diminish remote and wild water opportunities, as well as those for all types of snow- and ice-based

Figure 10.3. Projections of Change In Recreation Opportunities

10.3a

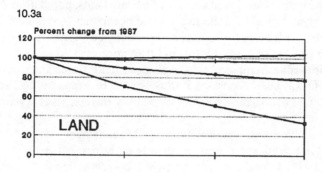

10.3b

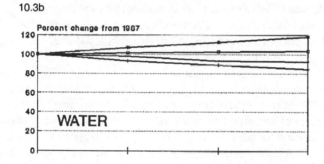

10.3c

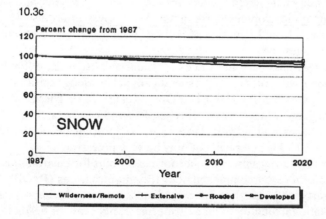

Source: Outdoor Recreation and Wilderness Assessment Group, USDA, Forest Service, Athens, GA.

activities. Effectiveness of land-based recreational opportunities would be quite a different matter. Continued closure of private lands, population growth, land conversions, and rural land subdivision and occupancy for residential purposes may well diminish those for roaded and partially developed land activities to as little as 50 percent of current levels in little more than 20 years. Wild, remote opportunities may diminish nearly 20 percent in this time. Developed opportunities would stay nearly constant, if they were to be expanded by about the rate of population growth, the prevalent trend over the last several years.

Future Wilderness Preservation and Management

The 1964 Wilderness Act specifically authorized that "wilderness areas shall be devoted to the public purposes of recreational, scenic, scientific, educational, conservation, and historical use." A number of these uses are further endorsed in subsequent acts, including the 1974 Forest and Range Land Renewable Resources Planning Act and the National Forest Management Act of 1976. The manuals of the Forest Service, National Park Service, Fish and Wildlife Service, and Bureau of Land Management accordingly acknowledge and support a variety of recreational and nonrecreational wilderness uses. In the past, wilderness has often been viewed and managed largely as a recreational resource. But recreation is only one of the values and uses of wilderness. The value to society of knowing that wilderness exists or vicariously experiencing it through television or stories, even though one does not personally visit a wilderness area, may equal or exceed the value of an on-site visit. There also are other critical values, such as maintenance of species diversity, protection of threatened and endangered species, protection of watersheds, and social uses, such as human development programs. Wilderness areas also are used for scientific research, and sometimes for such "nonconforming" commercial uses as mining and grazing.

Nonrecreational uses and values of wilderness are often difficult to document. National wilderness statutes specifically acknowledge spiritual values, but their meanings are highly variable (McDonald et al. 1989). The use of wilderness for spiritual growth may include the use of sacred places or things, organized group experiences, and individual experiences. Spiritual and aesthetic values of wilderness are highly personal, but may be very powerful.

Wilderness settings provide outdoor classrooms for environmental education and natural resource management training programs (Reed 1989; Spray and Weingart 1989). Lastly, wilderness landscapes may be important symbols providing national identity to many Americans, not only for aesthetic reasons, but for cultural, political, and religious reasons.

Because there has been little research on the extent of nonrecreational values and uses of wilderness, the public has not always been aware of these values. Benefits from wilderness are mostly intangible and not as easily measured as those of timber, water, forage, or mining. As a result, many uses of wilderness are not included in the forest planning process. Interest in the nonrecreational uses and values of wilderness is increasing and improved methods to measure and describe such uses will have to be developed.

Many feel that the National Wilderness Preservation System is not yet as complete as it should be. There are an estimated 189 million federal, 17 million state and more than 30 million private acres of remote, roadless lands not in the National Wilderness Preservation System; 112 million acres lie more than three miles and 124 million lie between a half and three miles of roads. Almost half of the federal, non-wilderness roadless area is in Alaska. As only one of many possible criteria, the current National Wilderness Preservation System contains representations of only 157 of the 261 different ecosystems of the United States. Threatened and endangered species occur in 57 percent of the wilderness areas. Both of these indicators point to a possible need to expand ecosystem representation and to assure continuation of habitat for threatened and endangered species. The rising interest in non-recreational uses and the existence of large areas of unroaded, remote lands could enhance future prospects for expansion.

ADMINISTRATIVE, LEGISLATIVE, AND PRIVATE INITIATIVES

Executive Branch

The report of the President's Commission on Americans Outdoors, one among several public and private national initiatives important to the future of outdoor recreation, has sparked a number of activities. In response to the commission, the Domestic Policy Council created a Task Force on Outdoor Recreation Resources and Opportunities. Its report emphasized needs for actions to create an appropriate recreation ethic, for steps to encourage recreational access to private lands, for a series of steps to expand recreational opportunities on federal lands, and for local initiatives. The focus on local initiatives mirrored the President's Commission on Americans Outdoors' emphasis on greenways, river protection, and other activities to be accomplished largely without federal dollars.

A variety of federal agency initiatives are underway, with the Forest Service clearly leading the way. Its National Recreation Strategy, which includes new programs such as the challenge cost-share and creation of a Scenic Byways System, is a bold departure for this agency. Included are broad new organizational goals and values, emphasis upon "customer satisfaction" and marketing, a new focus on cooperation with the private sector, and a clear invitation to field personnel to experiment. The Bureau of Land Management, the National Park Service, and other agencies have parallel efforts underway.

Other important initiatives underway within agencies include better coordination of policies. A National Recreational Fisheries Management Policy, cosigned by some 70 public and private organizations, has recently been developed. The Fish and Wildlife Service has been working with the Farmers

Home Loan Administration to exchange partial forgiveness of debt in exchange for restrictions on certain uses of lands that have high wildlife potential.

Legislative Branch

The volume and diversity of recreation-oriented legislation in the Congress have grown. Funding has been a major focus. The Wallop-Breaux Trust Fund, providing in excess of $200 million annually to enhance boating and fishing opportunities through matching grants to states, was recently re-authorized and strengthened. This legislation requires a national boating survey to more accurately estimate collections of federal motorboat fuel taxes, a key source for this fund.

Fee legislation has come before the Congress in several forms. Approval for higher park entrance fees and for special accounting of these revenues was achieved. The return of these revenues to the sites where the fees were collected, without a commensurate reduction of appropriations, remains to be resolved. The Congress has supported partnership funding, where federal dollars leverage private contributions for recreation and wildlife projects on federal lands. The re-authorized Sikes Act allows supplementary fees on state fishing and hunting licenses, with proceeds to be spent on federal lands. The 101st Congress will consider proposals for new, fee-financed trust funds to improve trails and protect wetlands.

Proposals to alter the Land and Water Conservation Fund were also considered, but not acted upon. One initiative would have replaced the Land and Water Conservation Fund with an American Heritage Trust sufficient to provide $1 billion annually for land acquisition and recreation facility development. The legislation did not prevail in the face of fiscal difficulties and concerns that the legislation may skirt normal appropriation processes. An alternative approach to strengthening the Land and Water Conservation Fund would have devoted a portion of federal oil and gas royalties from onland leasing activities, much as Outer Continental Shelf revenues are now used. It seems realistic that legislation amending the Land and Water Conservation Fund will be considered by the 101st Congress.

Other legislative efforts have focused on corridors for recreation. A number of river protection bills were considered and enacted. In nearly every case such legislation has called for special management of river corridors to accommodate local interests. Downstream river uses were added to the authorizing legislation for five major existing water projects. Legislation to encourage the conversion of abandoned rail lines into recreational trails was enacted in 1988, especially those lines abandoned on or near federal lands.

Finally, congressional sources and the highway lobby have begun discussions regarding the nation's long-term highway needs. A key component of those discussions is the recreational needs of American drivers, including the scenic byways movement. There is broad interest in this issue.

Private Sector Initiatives
New information and reservation systems have been developed to provide improved access to recreational opportunities. Leading systems are Mistix, a division of Home Shopping Network in California, Utah, and Colorado, and AIS, developers of the Official Recreation Guide, accessed through American Airline's Sabre computer system. In the Pacific Northwest, an information system about trail opportunities has been created.

Another important private sector initiative unites the nation's leading recreation interests with key private landowner organizations, ranging from the National Cattlemen's Association to the American Farm Bureau Federation. Together these groups seek to remove access disincentives facing private landowners and to establish new incentives for opening lands. A key part of this initiative is passage of "Good Neighbor" laws that strengthen limitations on liability. Still more private partners are involved in the Take Pride in America effort, designed to raise awareness about the outdoors and to encourage involvement in its protection.

SOCIAL TRENDS

Population
The population of the United States is growing at a slower rate than in the past. About 100 million people have been added over the past five decades, about two million people per year. Wharton Econometrics Forecasting Associates estimates that additional growth over the next five decades, to the year 2040, will total slightly over 90 million, an annual average increase of only 1.75 million. Immigrants will provide a substantial proportion of this expected increase. Geographic redistribution, apart from the well-publicized sunbelt/snowbelt shift, shows important changes in residence patterns, with some rapidly growing non-metropolitan areas. Continued extensive population growth is forecast in coastal states. In the 1970s, the growth rate of non-metropolitan counties exceeded that of central cities and the suburbs, reversing a long-standing trend. In the 1980s, however, the general trend has reversed again, with cities and suburbs growing more rapidly. But there are a number of non-urban counties that continue to grow at a rate more than twice the national average. Both retirees and the young are seeking these fast growing "exurban" counties because of quality of life factors, such as scenic and recreational amenities. Also, the estimated 40 percent of the population living within 50 miles of the ocean shore in 1984 is projected to double by the 21st century.

Socioeconomic Makeup
Aging of the population is a dominant characteristic. Although the segment of the population 65 years and older will continue to fall until about 1995, a result of the baby bust of the 1920s and the depression of the 1930s, more than half of

the population will be over 40 by 2000 (Snyder 1984).

The population is also becoming more diverse ethnically. Immigration and very high birth rates among minority populations are rapidly changing the make-up of American society. The American-Asian population increased 146 percent between 1970 and 1980, while the number of people of Spanish origin rose by 56 percent between 1970 and 1982. During this same period the black population grew by only 22 percent and the white population by only 11 percent.

Income distribution projections show polarization toward more high and low income families, but a decline in middle income families. Households with incomes of more than $50,000 (in 1980 dollars) are projected to triple by the mid-nineties. Older Americans have become more financially stable, and are an actively sought segment of the market in recreation, travel, and tourism.

Single-parent families doubled between 1970 and 1984, reaching 6.6 million. Although the divorce rate is expected to stabilize, estimates are that half of all children today will live in a home without a father.

Overall, changing social trends portend a much more varied and harried group of visitors and concentrations of these visitors at public facilities close to the centers of population where they live.

Employment and the Economy

Employment patterns are shifting to information and service sectors. Already, more than half of the working population is engaged in white collar or information work, while about 30 percent of the workforce is in the service sector. The share of industrial workers has dropped to less than 20 percent, and agriculture involves less than five percent of American workers. Recreation, travel, and tourism are important service and information components of many state and local economies, in some cases providing replacement jobs for those lost in agriculture, energy, mining, and timber.

Recreation is tied in several important ways to economies at all levels. It also has significant economic efficiency and welfare dimensions. Secondary economic benefits are realized through increased employment and personal incomes; investment in recreation facilities and services; tourist, visitor, and provider spending; regional and local economic growth and redistribution; and increased revenue and costs to local, state, and federal governments. Increasingly, states and localities are looking to outdoor recreation and tourism as a major source of economic growth. Some of the opportunities for expanding local economic activity will lie in activities involving extended stays, such as at ski resorts or campgrounds. Recent trends have shown greater development of private accommodations, food and other services and transportation associated with public land recreation than in the past. An expansion of recreation opportunities to meet projected demand would result in an increase of several hundred million recreation trips per year— most of them to rural areas. Local spending associated with these trips would likely exceed $15 billion per year, with an expected impact on total industrial production of between $20 billion and $25 billion per year.

Political Change
Authority in governance is being decentralized. Daniel Bell has said that "the nation-state is becoming too small for the big problems of life, and too big for the small problems of life" (Bell 1987). Domestically, the rise of activism and innovation among states has coincided with a decline of support for many federal programs. There appears to be an emerging need for regional groupings of states or counties to more effectively deliver services and satisfy needs for regional identity (Garreau 1981). The power of the electorate is shifting from political parties to special interest groups.

Population shifts to the South and West have shifted congressional seats from the Northeast, and should do so again after the 1990 Census. Population estimates show that California, Texas, and Florida will be the principal gainers, while New York and Pennsylvania will lose. As congressional district lines are redrawn, central cities are also likely to lose voting strength.

Many local jurisdictions are changing from a system of at-large seats to single-member districts. This will make those who are elected more accountable at the neighborhood level, a trend that could impact numerous recreation managers. The widespread desire of individuals to gain more control over their lives and of their environment is forcing such local changes, and is also surfacing in strong local opposition to uncontrolled development in all parts of the country. This desire for control of development will likely contribute significantly to the protection and dedication of lands for recreation, open space, and preservation purposes. This non-development posture will be most evident in suburban areas and in those non-metropolitan areas where population growth is being attracted by visual and recreational amenities.

Leisure
Available, unobligated time has declined. There is a continuing drop in the amount of leisure available to most citizens. Between 1973 and 1984 the average number of hours of leisure fell more than 31 percent (Harris 1984). The 1988 Harris survey revealed a further decline, an overall loss of about 37 percent in 15 years. Harris identified increased number of women in the workforce and longer hours on the job for factory workers as major reasons. The increase in time Americans devote to commuting has also depleted leisure. Retired individuals have the greatest amount of leisure, while households where both parents work have the least.

Leisure activities today tend to center more on the home. While outdoor recreation has embraced some new activities and developments that have made it easier to engage in traditional activities, there have been equally impressive changes in the home leisure technology. Contributing to the trend toward more "at-home" activity are the aging of the population, the rediscovery of the family as the baby boomer generation bears children, and electronic home-video entertainment.

The Influence of Technology
Technology directly creates new recreation equipment and uses, but a large part of technological advancement has come from the military and other nonrecreation sources. From military technology has come four-wheel-drive vehicles, rubber rafts, and the parachute. Much of the outdoor clothing and camping equipment have also come from military research. More recently, space technology has provided the lightweight "space blanket."

New technology creates new challenges to public land management. Some of these challenges relate to health or safety. Other problems rest upon questions of the appropriateness of new activities. Any number of problems may arise from this situation, including user conflicts, vandalism, adverse publicity, and inappropriate decision making. On the opposite side, new technology can also create opportunities for private providers. The private sector can usually respond quickly to new demands. Providing such opportunities as a commercial venture is one way rural areas can add to their economic vitality.

RECREATION DEMAND TRENDS

Much attention has been focused on whether recreation demand is growing, and if so, how fast. Some recent diagnoses speculate that the outdoor recreation market has matured, meaning that per capita growth rates are approaching zero. Below, we present an overview of the demand side of the recreation market.

Recreational Use of Public Lands
The number of visitor days at federal recreation areas (a measure of total time spent by visitors at these sites) grew about four percent between 1977 and 1987. However, this statistic is somewhat misleading because visits to federal areas (a measure of the number of times people come to sites for recreation) has continued to grow into the 1980s at about the same rate as in the 1970s. In national forests, growth in visits averaged almost four percent per year between 1977 and 1987 (Figure 10.4). The explanation for these seemingly incongruous trends is that visitors are spending less time per visit and are using off-site accommodations more frequently, rather than camping or otherwise overnighting at federal areas proper.

Another phenomenon is that people are not traveling as far for recreation. In 1972, many more trips were overnight trips of more than 100 miles, and most day outings were more than 50 miles from home. In the 1980s, the majority of overnight trips are within 100 miles and many more day trips are within 25 miles.

The ratio of overnight-to-day trips has also dropped dramatically from about seven of 10 and four of 10 for the Forest Service and Park Service, respectively, in 1977, to two of 10 and about one of 10 for these agencies in the mid-1980s. These are drastic changes reflecting much greater visitation at close-to-urban areas and some reductions of visitation to "far away" areas. The exceptions are those areas which effectively serve as major destinations and which have the necessary commercial accommodations to meet today's travel needs.

While federal visitation in the past has significantly involved overnight visits, state areas have mostly been used for day trips. The nine-of-10 day-to-overnight trip ratio for state parks has largely remained stable. Most visits to state lands for recreation have involved visits of three to four hours and visitors typically live within 35 miles.

As we move into the beginning of the 1990s, visitation patterns and the "draw" of federal areas seem to be approaching the close-to-home patterns that have long existed for state areas. Neither of these categories of public lands, however, provides the degree of near-home opportunities that local government does. Independent estimates place the number of different people who use local government outdoor recreation sites at about two-thirds of the United States population and three-fourths of the adult population. At all levels of government, visitation to public sites close to or within cities and other populated places is growing most rapidly.

Population Participation

Overall, 89 percent of the United States population reports participation in some form of outdoor recreation. In 1987, Americans spent some part or all of 28.2 billion personal days in outdoor recreational activities. The most popular activities, measured by the number of trips away from home, include:

(Millions of trips)

Swimming outdoors	461
Driving for pleasure	421
Sightseeing	293
Walking for pleasure	267
Picnicking	262
Attending outdoor sports events	261
Warm water fishing	239
Motor boating	220

Management of natural resources for outdoor recreation is most affected by consumption in the form of trips away from home. Of the approximate 4.6 billion outdoor recreation trips Americans took away from home in 1987, about 50 percent (some 2.25 billion) were taken to participate in activities that are

Figure 10.4. Millions of Visitor Days at Federal Areas

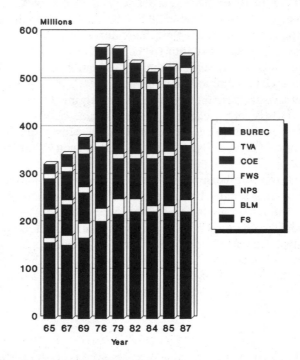

Source: USDI National Park Service Fee Reports.

highly dependent on natural environments (U.S. Department of Agriculture Forest Service 1988). Involved with these 2.25 billion trips were such traditional activities as camping, canoeing/kayaking, fishing, hunting, hiking, horseback riding, bicycling, wildlife observation, winter skiing and visiting prehistoric sites. In general, activities that are physically demanding, involve risk and adventure, are educational, or are equipment-oriented have been growing most quickly.

Forecasts developed for the 1989 Renewable Resources Planning Act Assessment provide an indication of what might happen in future years. Based on an assumed future that would continue the change of availability of public and private lands for recreation as they have occurred since 1970, estimates of expected future consumption of recreational trips away from home were developed (Table 10.1). Among land activities, the fastest growing are expected to be: 1) active pursuits — hiking, walking, running, bicycling; 2) educational pursuits — visiting museums, historic sites, and prehistoric sites; and 3) social-oriented activities — developed camping and family gatherings. All forms of snow activities and canoeing, rafting, and swimming are also projected to grow rapidly.

For comparison, forecasters estimated the numbers of trips Americans would prefer if opportunities were made available at a faster rate than has occurred in the past. In general, the greatest differences between futures if Americans could have all the opportunities they would prefer, and those we might expect if the rate at which opportunities are made available, are predicted for dispersed recreation. This "shortage" will mostly involve roaded, partially developed forest and range areas that currently provide the greatest share of dispersed, warm-season land and winter-snow opportunities. If the trend toward greater closure of private land continues and greater access to public land is not forthcoming, some shortages, as we have defined them, may be substantial. The most "critical" shortages are likely to be for warm-season, land recreation, both motorized and non-motorized. This category of setting alone accounts for almost three-fourths of the total predicted shortage of future recreational trip opportunities.

NEEDS FOR CHANGE AND ACTION

The nation's population is increasing, there is continuing growth of demand for outdoor recreation, and the public is becoming more diverse, as are their recreational pursuits. There are, however, many who do not participate in outdoor recreation or who do not participate as much as they would like, for a variety of reasons. One of the principal reasons is that many of the opportunities for outdoor recreation are located some distance from where the bulk of the population lives. There is growing interest in providing more outdoor recreation opportunities closer to the concentrations of populations, but this is also where recreation opportunities and open spaces are most threatened by development. Together with addressing this mismatch of location, there are a wide variety of options for change and action in order to improve the effectiveness by which land, water and facilities afford recreational opportunities.

Expand Opportunities on Public and Private Lands

Most existing public lands can accommodate substantially higher visitation. For the most part, most public lands see relatively little use. In some cases, new or improved access roads, facilities, trailhead parking, and trails would greatly improve effectiveness. Even in areas experiencing relatively high visitation, there are opportunities to accommodate greater use with little apparent adverse environmental effect. These opportunities include more intensive management to separate conflicting uses, encouraging use in the off-season, and better information on low-impact use of backcountry areas.

Private lands comprise nearly two-thirds of this nation's land base and can provide numerous outdoor recreation opportunities. According to recent research, however, an estimated 77 percent of the private land potentially available for outdoor recreation is closed to public access and this percentage is growing. This may in part be turned around if landowners can realize some economic or other gain from public use of their land.

Provide Opportunities Close to Home

More numerous, shorter-duration, close-to-home trips are quickly replacing the long vacation. Thus outdoor recreation opportunities close to where large numbers of people live are growing in importance. Such opportunities can be realized through acquisition of land in and near urban areas and through improved planning and provision of economic incentives to encourage recreation and open spaces as communities develop. Some public forest and range lands lie close to urban areas, particularly in the West. Examples are the national forests adjacent to Los Angeles-San Diego, Portland, Seattle, Salt Lake City, and Atlanta. These and other public lands can provide urban residents with expanded opportunities for outdoor recreation in natural settings.

Improve Quality

A quality environment is typically essential for quality outdoor recreational experiences. Through careful management of other uses, scenic qualities can be maintained and activities such as timber harvesting made more compatible. Necessary facilities, from roads to restrooms, can be designed and placed to maintain aesthetic quality while enhancing enjoyment of the outdoors. Trails can be located to improve the hiking experience.

Litter is a pervasive problem affecting aesthetic quality. Agencies must deal with the flooding tide of non-biodegradable containers and trash. There is an exceptional need for volunteers and civic organizations to assist in the collection of litter and the restoration of the aesthetic quality of federal, state, and local recreation areas. Moreover, public educational programs, such as Take Pride in America, and on-site interpretive programs can stress the prevention of littering and vandalism.

Because of inadequate funding, there has been a growing backlog of maintenance of public recreational areas. Poorly maintained or unsafe facilities reduce visitors' enjoyment and can actually deter use. The elimination of maintenance backlogs, a badly needed initiative, in part seems already to have begun.

Other aspects of quality include protecting historic and prehistoric sites from deterioration and erosion, vandalism, theft, overuse, and neglect. In addition to already identified significant prehistoric and historic sites, there are needs to identify, evaluate, and preserve areas now unprotected. Also, improve-

Table 10.1. Current Supply of Recreational Trips and Indices of Future Growth to 2040

Resource Category: LAND

Activity	Trips in 1987 (million)	Percentage of 1987 Supply				
		2000	2010	2020	2030	2040
Wildlife Observation	69.5	107	113	120	126	130
Primitive Camping	38.1	108	115	122	130	134
Backpacking	26.0	124	144	165	185	198
Nature Study	70.8	99	101	103	107	108
Horseback Riding	63.2	114	125	135	144	149
Day Hiking	91.2	123	144	168	198	229
Photography	42.0	115	128	141	154	163
Visit Prehistoric Sites	16.7	148	148	173	203	236
Collecting Berries	19.0	110	120	132	149	169
Cutting Firewood	30.3	109	118	130	144	161
Walking	266.5	116	132	148	168	183
Running/Jogging	83.7	131	160	192	229	260
Bicycle Riding	114.6	124	146	170	197	218
Off-Road Driving	80.2	104	108	112	118	121
Visiting Museums	9.7	118	134	152	172	187
Attending Special Events	73.7	115	129	144	161	175
Visiting Historic Sites	73.1	117	133	152	178	204
Pleasure Driving	421.6	110	120	129	139	145
Family Gatherings	74.4	121	139	160	182	202
Sightseeing	292.7	114	128	144	164	185
Picnicking	262.0	110	120	131	145	156
Developed Camping	60.6	120	138	158	178	195

Source: USDA, 1988

ments in the quality of the nation's waters, already improved over the 1960s and 1970s, is a significant need.

Improve Services

To take advantage of opportunities, the public must have information on both public and private facilities. Often, potential users simply are not aware of what is available nearby. The need is for imaginative efforts such as clear informational brochures, awareness of existing outdoor recreation sites and opportunities through marketing campaigns, "user-friendly" computer terminals in public places, and centralized information centers that provide one-step information offered by local, state, and federal agencies, local chambers of commerce, and private businesses. Expanded programs of visitor information, including on-site interpretive and educational services, are needed to help match users with recreational opportunities.

Increase Coordination, Cooperation, and Partnerships

Many organizations, agencies and private businesses provide or otherwise service outdoor recreation. In a continuing era of tight government budgets and growing potential for private investment, improved coordination among public and private entities can increase recreational opportunities cost-effectively. Research and technology transfer is a particularly fertile area for cooperation. The opportunities to bring public agencies and the private sector together in short-term, goal specific associations, or long-term, more comprehensive relationships, are nearly infinite. Cooperation and partnerships can also serve to build coalitions for support of federal, state, local, and private outdoor recreation programs and open space preservation.

Expand Non-recreational Benefits from Wilderness

There seems to be an increasing awareness of the non-recreational benefits of wilderness. Preservation of critical wildlife, fish, and plant habitats, watershed protection, gene pool preservation, scientific uses, human development and spiritual growth, education, and ecosystem representation and diversity are purposes of wilderness that need management emphasis, much as recreation already receives. Some actions which should be considered to enhance non-recreation uses of wilderness include:

1) Continuing inventory of roadless areas.

2) Establishing recreation opportunities on areas with wilderness character, but which are not in the National Wilderness Preservation System, in order to reduce pressure on sensitive wilderness.

3) Incorporating protection of non-recreational values into wilderness management plans.

4) Systematically assessing threats to wilderness.

Research opportunities transcend virtually all the needs for action and change discussed thus far. While there has been substantial research, there remain large gaps in knowledge. These gaps include:

1) Better information on participation trends, future demand, and effectiveness of supplies of outdoor recreation and wilderness.

2) Better understanding of how public opportunities and those provided by the private sector complement one another.

3) Better measures of recreation suitability and quality.

4) Improved knowledge of the motivations, barriers to, and norms of recreation participation.

5) Better understanding of the social and economic benefits of outdoor recreation and wilderness.

6) Improved valuation technology and models.

REFERENCES

Bell, Daniel. 1987. **The World and the United States in 2013.** Daedalus Vol. 116, No. 3. Summer 1987. 1-32 pages.

Clawson, Marion. 1982. Effective Acreage for Outdoor Recreation. **Resources,** Vol. 781, Fall.

Cordell, H. Ken and English, Donald B. K. 1988.

Garreau, Joel. 1981. **The Nine Nations of North America.** Houghton Mifflin, Boston, MA. 427 pp.

Harris, Louis. 1984. **Americans and the Arts** IV. Study Number 831011, October 1984. 21 pp. New York, NY.

McDonald, Barbara, Guldin, Richard, and Wetherill, G. Richard. 1989. The Spirit of Wilderness: The Use and Opportunity of Wilderness Experience for Spiritual Growth. In: **Proceedings Benchmark 1988: National Wilderness Colloquium.** Tampa, FL.

Reed, Patrick C. 1989. The National Wilderness Preservation System: The First 23 Years and Beyond. In: **Proceedings Benchmark 1988: National Wilderness Colloquium.** Tampa, FL.

Spray, Richard H. and Weingart, Paul D. 1989. The Wilderness Environment: Training Wilderness Managers. In: **Proceedings Benchmark 1988:** National Wilderness Colloquium. Tampa, FL.

Snyder, David Pierce and Gregory Edwards. 1984. **Future Forces.** American Society of Associate Executives, Washington, D.C. 109 pages.

United States Department of Agriculture Forest Service. 1988. **An Analysis of the Outdoor Recreation and Wilderness Situation in the United States: 1989-2040.** Draft Tech. Doc. Supporting the 1989 RPA Assessment. U.S. Govt. Printing Office, 1988, VIII. 24 pp.

CHAPTER 11

New Technologies

D. A. Holt
S. L. Rawlins

No single new technology has the potential to completely solve even one of the myriad of environmental problems faced by this nation. Computer and information management technologies, however, have the potential to link together the incremental improvements from a large number of new technologies, resulting in an overall improvement in natural resource management. Because of the explosive rate of advancement of computer and information management technologies, many natural resource managers are not fully aware of this tremendous potential.

Rather than cataloging all of the new technologies on the horizon that could contribute toward improved management of natural resources, this chapter highlights the one that we believe has the greatest potential to bring the fruits of technology advances to bear on natural resource problems. It then discusses the technological, psychological, and economic constraints that must be overcome to bring this potential to reality.

THE INDUSTRIAL MODEL

In modern manufacturing industries, computers, computer-aided design tools, sensors, programmable robots with machine vision, hearing, and touch, other electronically controlled machines and devices, expert systems, database management systems, and office automation software and hardware are networked to form computer-integrated manufacturing systems. These systems help managers integrate and coordinate strategic and tactical planning, research and development, finance, procurement, personnel management, production, quality control, distribution, marketing, and cost-accounting activities.

Such systems are designed to improve communication and coordination, improve intelligence gathering, reduce inventories of parts and products, shorten product development time, maximize product/service differentiation, increase market penetration, increase efficiency and productivity, respond rapidly to or anticipate market changes, enhance job quality, capitalize on employee creativity and ability, and, in general, make the firm more competitive and responsive to changes in the business environment. As the concept of computer-integrated manufacturing is developed and implemented, the robots and machines join printers and other equipment as peripheral devices of the computers.

Many of the principles of computer-integrated manufacturing are applicable to agriculture, which is the largest, most complex, most high-tech, and most important manufacturing industry. Because the components of United States agriculture are so diverse and so widely dispersed throughout the landscape, computer integration of agricultural activities promises to be even more beneficial than the integration of other manufacturing industries.

COMPUTER-INTEGRATED AGRICULTURE

The functions of farms, forests, and fisheries of the future will be monitored to an increasing extent by sensors connected to microprocessors and computers. This information plus detailed information on past and potential financial transactions and financial status will be stored in spreadsheets and other databases in the storage devices of computers. Other relevant information will be collected from outside individual operations, where it will reside in local, state, regional, national, and international databases, accessible through the Computer-Aided Agricultural Decision-Support Systems network.

Yet the human manager will remain at the heart of each farm, agricultural business, and organizational enterprise. The manager will use as principal tools powerful computer work stations with fully integrated packages of individual expert systems and other items of computer software, accessible locally and through telecommunications networks.

The work station will be the manager's port into the agricultural information universe. The manager will communicate with the computer system in symbols and natural language, at times merely by spoken word. Just as machines are extensions of limbs and muscles, this decision support system will be a powerful extension of the agricultural manager's mind.

Once decisions are made concerning the operation of the farm, agribusiness, or other agricultural organization of the future, the manager will implement them or they will be implemented automatically using machines and devices largely controlled by computers. Some of these will be conventional farm machines, such as tractors, chisel-plows, and combines, but equipped with elaborate electronic controls and microprocessors to guide, control, and adjust them. Others will be exotic machines and devices, such as robots, able to perform intricate tasks very precisely, with little or no help or direction from humans. Some robots will be able to traverse uneven terrain and grasp and manipulate objects and organisms moving in the wind or under their own power. They will operate 24 hours per day when needed, in cold and heat, dark and light, and under wet and dry conditions.

Transactions involved in purchasing and selling inputs and products of the farms and agribusinesses of the future will take place on the computer network, aided by expert systems. Network software will match quantity, quality, and price specifications of sellers and purchasers, debit and credit accounts, and compute the least-cost means of transfer. Using sophisticated agricultural software, producers will "lock in" profits at the beginning of production cycles by forward pricing of purchases and sales and will monitor the system continuously to identify ways to increase profit by changing production and marketing strategies.

The microprocessors of the future will have the enormous speed and memory of today's mainframe computers. They will be found in agricultural machines, robots, and devices. Powerful desktop and portable computers will be the work stations from which human managers control farms, agribusinesses, and agricultural research, development, and educational activities. Minicomputers will be communication nodes that broker information on huge, highly integrated communication networks.

At the top of this hierarchy of devices will be the supercomputers of the future, programmed to permit levels of analysis and prediction undreamed of today. The computer network and the information and accessible-information tools will be an essential part of each farm business, each agribusiness, every agricultural institution and agency, and every policy-making group, even more so than the telephone and mail networks of today.

Just as rivers, railroads, and highways provide conduits through which people and goods move throughout a nation, the telecommunications networks linking computers will be conduits for communication and transfer of agricultural information. The networks of the future will provide easy, almost instantaneous, often automatic connections among agricultural network participants. Information to be shared will be transferred so rapidly that a participant will be able to use shared databases and decision-aid software residing in the memory of someone else's computer as readily as that in his own computer.

BENEFITS OF COMPUTERIZATION

The integration provided by the computer network will enable the computer components of the agricultural decision-support system to function as a giant, shared computer. It will decentralize access to agricultural information and foster decentralized decision-making. At the same time, the system will integrate individual agricultural operations into efficient national enterprises, generating unprecedented levels of flexibility, responsiveness, efficiency, quality, and productivity.

As the computerized telecommunications networks develop, a vast parallel market for agricultural information will develop. Agriculturalists will be able to access an enormous number of information sources and information-processing tools and select alternatives that meet their specific needs and their quality and price specifications. Competition in this agricultural information market will lead to continuous improvement in the quantity, quality, and cost-effectiveness of information and information tools.

CONSTRAINTS TO ACHIEVING THE VISION

No matter how promising a technology may seem, there will be important technical, psychological, and economic constraints to its adoption. This certainly is true of computer technology. To the extent that the developers and promoters of new technology understand these constraints, they can take action to reduce or eliminate them. The following paragraphs provide a description of important technical, psychological, and economic constraints to the computer-integration of agriculture.

Technical Constraints
Computational speed. The quest for computational speed is ancient. The inventors of the abacus, the first digital computer, wanted to compute more quickly and more accurately. Mechanical calculators, invented in the 1800s and perfected in the 1900s, greatly increased computational speed, accuracy, and capacity. The electronic computer enabled tremendous increases in speed. High-end personal work stations execute MIPs (millions of instructions per second) and supercomputers can work in the mega-MIPs (billions of instructions per second) range.

It is hard for most people, even those familiar with computers, to understand why there would ever be a need to have faster computers than are presently available, but many applications require greater speeds than are possessed by the fastest computers. For example, certain structural analysis problems utilizing finite difference equations take several hours or even days on a supercomputer, and thus are very costly to conduct. Real-time simulations of such phenomena as air flow and turbulence around aircraft wings require enormous computational speed. The cost of running these computer programs is reduced considerably as computational speed increases.

In agriculture, stochastic-dynamic simulations of complex biological and economic systems were impossible until the advent of supercomputers. Yet when variables are added to these models to make them realistically complex, they suffer the so-called "curse of dimensionality." This means that addition of each new variable and its interactions with variables already depicted in a model adds greatly to the computation required to operate the model and obtain realistic predictions of system behavior.

Image-processing, which makes possible machine vision, hearing, and touch, requires extremely fast data processing. The "reaction time" of the machine may need to be even faster than that of a human. Thus images must be analyzed very rapidly; correct, detailed conclusions must be drawn; and actions must be implemented extremely rapidly and accurately. For example, a robotic fruit picker must identify ripe fruit, determine the precise position of the fruit, which may be moving; extend the picking mechanism and pick the fruit; and deposit the fruit in a container.

The advent of parallel processing, in which several processors are used simultaneously on the same problem, has the potential to shorten drastically the time required to perform the calculations and other manipulations required to solve certain kinds of problems. In this approach, the problem is subdivided into portions that can be processed separately. Each sub-task is assigned to a different processor. The processors, working in parallel instead of sequentially, make the necessary computations and the final result is assembled. Of course, to benefit from parallel processing, the problem must be broken down to separate sub-tasks that need not be accomplished in sequence.

Memory. The capacity to store and retrieve very large quantities of data and information is essential in modern computers. The solution of some problems requires that very large amounts of input data are stored and then processed. Also, when millions of instructions per second are being executed, it does not take long to accumulate tremendous quantities of output which, in many cases, must be stored for further analysis.

Large electronic databases are very useful. They can be marketed for profit. Thus, the demand for large electronic information-storage devices continues to increase. Great amounts of space are saved by storing information in electronic format rather than hard copy. The capacity to search for and retrieve specific information very rapidly and efficiently from such repositories is extremely important.

Personal computer users will continue to demand greater memory in their computers, so as to enable multi-tasking. They need to be able to load several applications (programs) in the RAM (random-access memory) of their computers and then be enabled to switch back and forth among the applications very rapidly. They may wish to interrupt their work on one application, perhaps a spreadsheet, switch to another, such as word-processing, and work on that application while the first application either remains static or continues to run in the background. To work efficiently, the user must be able to return to any application and resume work immediately where he left off.

Speed of transmission. Not only will the computer-aided decision-support system for natural resource management require fast computers with great information storage capacity, it will require high-speed communication of information between computers. Current computer networks include AR-PANET (INTERNET), HEPNET, MFENET, NSFNET, NASNET, and MILNET, which are government-supported, as well as commercial facilities such as TYMNET, TELENET, and BITNET. The data transfer rate of the most widely used networks varies from 1.2 to 56 kilobits (thousands of bits) per second. Because it takes about eight bits to encode a number or a letter, most existing transmission rates limit communication to relatively short messages and documents.

Since much of the information most useful to managers will be generated by computers in graphic form, transmission of pictures will be essential. In many cases communicating the results of computer simulations will require transmitting moving pictures. To transmit moving black and white pictures digitally will require transmission rates of 10 to 60 Mbits (millions of bits) per second. For color pictures, the required rate is 320 to 1,920 Mbits per second.

NSFNET backbone circuits linking the five National Centers for Supercomputing Applications permit transmission at about four Mbits per second. Researchers have achieved experimental microwave transmission rates of gigabits (billions of bits) per second. An extensive fiber-optic and satellite communication network, plus ongoing improvement in communications hardware and software, will permit the high rates of transmission required to serve users of the decision-support system for natural resource management.

Compatibility. To achieve the necessary level of integration, many different types and brands of computer hardware, software, and computer-controlled machines and devices will have to function and communicate compatibly. Recognizing this, several private sector and government groups are working to develop standards and protocols that will enable universal computer and machine connectivity and compatibility.

Telecommunications networks are moving toward the universal acceptance of such standards as TCP/IP (Transmission Control Protocol/Internet Protocol) and OSI (Open Systems Interconnection Protocol). Firms installing CIM (Computer-Integrated Manufacturing) systems are converging on MAP (General Motors' Manufacturing Automation Protocol), and office systems are accepting TOP (Technical and Office Protocol).

Integrated software. If the potential of knowledge-based systems, commonly known as expert systems, is to be fully exploited to meet the needs of natural resource managers, software must be developed and assembled in integrated packages. Only then will the specific decisions supported by one expert system be related to and consistent with other decisions the manager must make. These integrated expert systems will be central components of the computer-aided decision-support system. Scientists at Texas A&M University have pioneered the concept of integrated expert systems (Naegele et al. 1986).

Natural resource managers and their advisors will need access to software packages similar to the Computer Aided Design/Computer Aided Management (CAD/CAM) packages used by design engineers and architects. For agricultural managers, the equivalent of CAD/CAM might be called Computer-Assisted Agricultural Planning/Computer-Assisted Agricultural Management (CAAP/CAAM).

These packages of integrated expert systems will help natural resource managers choose among alternative input products and practices, assemble them into effective operational systems, and manage the systems. This will include diagnoses of problems, prescription of site-specific management practices and spatially distributed inputs, and delivery of inputs through electronically controlled machinery to optimize system performance. Computer-Assisted Agricultural Planning/Computer-Assisted Agricultural Management packages will allow managers to explore alternative scenarios based on various assumptions about supplies, costs, returns, weather, government policies, and other uncertainties, and to evaluate and manage risks.

In use, the knowledge base of integrated expert systems for natural resource managers will need to be periodically revised. Users of the packages will have to draw on external databases that are maintained with up-to-date information by a wide range of public and private organizations. Geo-referenced databases with site-specific information will be updated by remote sensing from aerial platforms as well as from sensors mounted on tractors or from data entered manually. Some of the most powerful expert systems will require supercomputers to operate large, complex simulation models, optimization routines, and statistical packages.

Updating and refining the knowledge base of expert systems, accessing external databases, and using mainframe computers will be much easier and more efficient if expert systems are available via large-scale telecommunications networks involving wires, satellites, microwave transmitters and receivers, and packet radio. Managers need to be able to access expert systems and databases wherever they may exist, download the information they need to their work stations, and upload data or knowledge they have acquired to databases and expert systems on host computers. The integrated computer-aided decision-support system will provide these capabilities.

Using the computer-aided decision-support system should be as simple as dialing the telephone, perhaps even simpler. In many cases the computers should establish the connections automatically. Sophisticated electronic interfaces, involving natural-language communication, will provide each network participant easy access to information other participants wish to share. In this way, expert systems will become the user-friendly interfaces to the natural resource information sources of the world.

Psychological Constraints

A student in computer system management at Creighton University in Omaha, Nebraska recently told one of the authors that one of the first things he learned was to expect resistance to computerization from people working in public institutions and private firms being computerized.

An important responsibility of persons implementing and managing computer systems is to convince others that they will be able to learn to use computers, and that learning these new skills will make them even more valuable to their firm, organization, or institution.

Those who wish to foster the use of computers must be aware that some managers, advisors, and clients are concerned about the complexity of computers. When people understand that a well-designed system will actually make it easier for them to perform complex tasks and analyses, they will be motivated to learn the basic skills associated with the technology.

One of the best ways to overcome the fear of computerization is to involve potential users of computer systems early in the design and development of systems. A good way to do this is to develop prototype software, such as expert systems, and ask users to participate in further development by testing the prototypes and proposing ways to improve them.

Other advantages of involving users early in the development of knowledge-based systems are that users' knowledge and experience can be incorporated into the systems and the effectiveness of user interfaces can be evaluated. An extremely important indirect effect of user involvement is that users help evaluate the overall knowledge base for use in decision-making.

Economic Constraints

Natural resource managers, whether they be farmers, people engaged in agribusiness, or public agency managers of forests and wildlife, have certain problems and opportunities in common. They must serve the real and perceived needs of the customers, clients, and other constituencies that ultimately provide their financial support. They must deliver value in return for money. Natural resource managers, including farmers, must manage resources over which they do not have complete control. The public is increasingly asserting control over natural resources. Public concerns about resource conservation, environmental quality and safety emerge as restrictions and regulations that limit the options open to natural resource managers.

Natural resource managers must compete with other interests for financial support, whether it comes in the form of revenues from sales or fees; gifts, grants, or contracts; or from appropriations of public funds. As is the case with any business manager, natural resource managers must be concerned about the balance between costs and returns, the "bottom line." As competition becomes more intense and profit margins dwindle, the issue of the "bottom line" assumes overriding importance to the individual manager. It is the primary factor determining whether each enterprise will survive.

During the late 1950s, the National Farmers Organization organized farmer members in county chapters in order to increase farm prices. Their strategy, similar to that of a labor union, was to sponsor holding actions, during which participating farmers would withhold their grain and livestock from the market. Some farmers disagreed with this approach, for various reasons. One of the authors (D.A. Holt), who was farming in Illinois at the time, argued with a young neighbor farmer who was struggling to get established. He predicted that if the young man joined the organization, in five years the National Farmer's Organization would "own his soul." The response was, "If I don't survive this year, it won't matter what happens in five years." When the chips are down, the desire to survive as a manager takes precedence over almost any other goal.

Legislators and others forming public policy on natural resource issues need to be sensitive to the "bottom line" financial concerns of those who must implement the policies and regulations. This is especially true in agriculture, where conservation and environmental quality regulations must ultimately be implemented by farmers.

To illustrate this point, for decades beginning in the 1930s, soil conservationists encouraged farmers to adopt conservation plans for their farms. These plans, prepared by Soil Conservation Service staff members using sound land-use principles, were designed to prevent soil erosion and sustain soil productivity. County soil conservation district personnel worked closely with participating farmers to develop and implement plans for tillage and cropping systems that were agronomically appropriate for the soil types and topography of each individual farm.

While some conservation farm plans were implemented with great success, they were not widely adopted in the Midwest. Many of those that were adopted were abandoned. A major reason for the lack of success of farm plans in the Midwest was that they did not adequately address the "bottom line" constraints faced by managers.

Conservation farm plans often called for increased acreages of cover crops, usually forage crops, with corresponding decreases in grain crop acreages. To use the forage crops, the participating farmers often had to establish or expand their livestock enterprises. This created new management challenges, including the provision of adequate housing and other facilities for livestock production.

Learning to finance, manage, and market livestock successfully is not a trivial undertaking. The livestock enterprises increased the risk associated with farm operations, further increasing the need for capital and credit reserves.

Apparently, many of those developing conservation plans and many of the farmers trying to implement them could not assemble enough information and management expertise to design and manage farming systems that were both profitable and conserving of soil and water. Such farming systems are very complex. The systems-design and systems-analysis skills necessary to establish and manage effective and profitable systems exceeded that of the designers and participants. In short, the decision-support system serving conservation-minded farmers was inadequate.

Will Benefits Outweigh Costs?

Experience in the private sector suggests that traditional cost-benefit analyses are not always appropriate for evaluating computerization opportunities. Such analyses are usually based on estimates of potential cost reductions alone. For example, computer systems are often sold on the basis of how many employees they will replace.

Computerization of a firm or institution usually does not reduce total costs. In fact, the cost of providing effective computer capabilities, relative to other costs, will usually increase with time. This definitely will be the case as we develop and implement powerful knowledge-based applications in natural resource management.

On the other hand, well-designed, effectively implemented, and well-managed computer systems usually do improve overall productivity, sustainability, and competitiveness. This improvement comes from more rapid response to change, better product/service differentiation, better communication within organizations, more thorough analyses, better intelligence gathering, better overall management, and other benefits. Often these benefits are manifested as several small, incremental improvements in productivity and efficiency that can only be evaluated in the aggregate, as they affect overall performance.

There are situations in which computerization of a private firm is not beneficial. Often such situations arise when only one or a few aspects of the business are computerized. For example, if a private firm's purchasing operation is computerized without corresponding changes in related operations, such as accounting, the net result may be an overall decrease in productivity and efficiency. In those situations, labor savings in one area may be offset by increased labor requirements in another, uncomputerized area.

Private sector experience also suggests that computerizing or automating a basically inefficient operation may result in an inefficient computerized operation. Thus, it is important to make sure the basic operation is well-planned and efficient. Then computerization has the potential to improve efficiency and productivity even more. These experiences suggest that the overall system of computer-aided decision support for natural resource management should be carefully designed, using systems-design principles and drawing on systems-engineering science, technology, and experience.

Implementing a computer-aided decision-support system for natural resource management will probably not reduce total costs, but it has the potential of providing the tools necessary to gain control over processes that are now dangerously out of control. Left out of control, some of these processes could result in damages many times greater than the cost of developing and implementing the computerized decision-support system. To be effective, however, such a system should be carefully designed, using systems-design principles (Wymore 1987) and drawing on the expertise and experience of systems engineers and scientists who have developed similar systems for industry.

Adequacy of Investment

The fully integrated, computer-aided, decision-support system for natural resource management will be very expensive to develop and even more expensive to maintain. It must pervade virtually everything we do in natural resource management and it must go on forever. The old saying "If you want to float big ships, you've got to go where the water is deep" applies here. The natural resource system required to meet the increasing demands of a rapidly growing and increasingly complex society represents a very "big ship." Failure to keep it afloat will endanger those whom it supports.

Those responsible for providing resources to maintain an effective natural resource system should recognize that development of the required computer-aided decision-support system is open-ended. As it grows, it will take more resources to maintain it. It must be built, maintained, expanded, continuously refined, and parts of it must be replaced when they become obsolete. It must be extended throughout the nation and the world, linking the suppliers and users of natural resource information wherever they may be.

As with many other potentially useful technologies, the potential capabilities of computer-aided decision-support and knowledge-based systems technologies have been both understated and overstated. As a consequence, some of our colleagues, clients, and administrators have developed unrealistic expectations. Pessimists say, "You have been working on these models and expert systems for years and you haven't finished any of them. It's something you do because you like to play games on computers."

Perhaps worse, some optimists are convinced that expert systems are not only very powerful management tools, but also that they will be cheap ("Just finish them and put them on the computer") and easy to develop ("Develop them in a few weeks, using powerful development tools"). Giving decision-makers a realistic appraisal of the capabilities and costs for developing these systems is an essential element for long-term progress.

Eventually, the cost of the computer-aided decision-support system can be born by its users. Economies of scale will reduce the cost to individual participants. A substantial investment of both public and private venture capital will be needed initially, however, to provide the telecommunication, computer, and prototype software components of the system.

Fortunately, some components of the system, such as the telecommunications networks, will serve many other purposes besides supporting natural resource management. In fact, integrating the system with systems serving other functions and needs will be the principal method by which the necessary economies of scale can be achieved.

Whether the necessary funding from public and private groups will be provided for this initial investment depends on whether or not they become convinced that the potential return on investment is substantial. Favorable initial experiences with the system will be important. The strategy of producing prototype components and involving prospective users early in the process of evaluation and further development will help users to understand and appreciate the potential contributions of the system.

Federal Investment in the System

Budget deficits have recently created a siege mentality among federal legislators and administrators who undoubtedly will be asked to provide resources to create this system. Recently David Gibbons, who is responsible for evaluating natural resource proposals in the Office of Management and Budget, told an agricultural lobbying group, the Council of Agricultural Research, Extension, and Teaching, that under no circumstances will resources be shifted from such nationally important programs as defense and entitlements to other activities, such as agricultural research and extension. Much of the research essential to natural resource management research is conducted under the umbrella of agricultural research.

Dr. Gibbons said, in effect, count on having fewer resources. He may be right, from the standpoint of political reality, but if he is, the nation is in danger of losing its ability to compete effectively in the global economy, manage its natural resources effectively, maintain a high standard of living, and address all the other items on the ambitious national agenda.

We need to foster a systems perspective among ourselves, our leaders, and the general public. If and when we all think about the nation as a social, economic, and bio-physical system and understand the flow of resources through that system, we will recognize that agricultural and natural resources research and development are inputs to the system, and that defense and entitlements are outputs. If you want to increase outputs, you ordinarily don't do so by decreasing inputs, particularly inputs of research and development. A policy of investment in natural resource management research and development will pay high dividends to the nation.

Individuals and groups with a stake in good management of natural resources, and that includes almost everyone, must learn how to form the political coalitions necessary to bring about meaningful change. Agriculture, which is basically a natural resource management enterprise, has not been effective in forming coalitions for support of natural resource research and development. It is simply too fragmented and speaks with too many voices on too many diverse issues.

As soon as the advocates of increasing productivity, efficiency, and competitiveness in agriculture and the advocates of conserving natural resources and protecting the environment realize that they can better achieve their individual goals by working together, the door to progress will be open. The secret to such cooperation is the ability of individuals and groups to emphasize areas of agreement and de-emphasize appropriate areas of disagreement. An objective analysis usually reveals that the areas of disagreement are relatively few and of minor practical importance.

EXTENDING THE CONCEPT OF CONSTRAINTS TO TECHNOLOGY ADOPTION

In a series of lectures several years ago, Dr. Louis B. Leakey, famed anthropologist, described an ancient species of pre-man that became extinct because its members were overspecialized for vegetarianism. When they were faced with changing climatic conditions and competition from a more omnivorous species, they were unable to survive. Dr. Leakey extrapolated this observation to modern times, suggesting that modern man might be overspecialized in capacity to develop technology, particularly military technology. Lacking adequate social concerns and skills, a species armed with atomic weapons, he suggested, might destroy itself.

Another parallel may exist in the modern world. Man has employed technology to create production systems that, in some situations, are not sustainable. These systems often consume or destroy the nonrenewable natural resources that are used to produce them. The problem usually arises when a specific, specialized technology is used without knowledge of or regard for the possible effects of the technology on other parts of a system or other related systems. The systems analysis and design approach to developing, implementing, and managing new technology promises to help deal with these natural resource management problems.

There are several technologies, including biotechnology, that show great promise of helping improve natural resource management. Opportunities exist to improve the resistance of agricultural plants and animals to stress and pests, without endangering the environment. Similar efforts might help natural resource managers adapt production and utilization systems to expected global climatic changes.

Researchers using biotechnology techniques are developing highly specific, biodegradable, and otherwise safe pesticides that can be applied in extremely small quantities. Natural biocontrol mechanisms are being transferred among organisms, using biotechnology approaches, thus increasing the utility of these mechanisms.

An improved systems design and development approach to natural resource management promises to permit deceases in the levels of input required to obtain necessary levels of output. Increased productivity engendered by biotechnology should make it unnecessary to destroy natural areas for crop and animal production. Intensive crop and animal production can be confined to areas that can sustain it without environmental degradation.

In each situation, there will be constraints to adopting new technology. These constraints will parallel those identified in this paper as inhibiting the computerization of agriculture. Research, development and education can address the technical and economic constraints. Psychological constraints are more difficult to deal with but should be considered an integral part of the total development and implementation effort.

CONCLUSIONS

Opportunities abound to improve agricultural management, which is a very important component of natural resource management, by computer integration of the diverse components of agriculture. To computerize agriculture in this manner is an important strategic planning and systems-design challenge.

In a highly competitive, global, agricultural economy, those who evaluate the potential costs and benefits of any new technology should also estimate the risk of not adopting technology that may make them more competitive. Typical cost/benefit analyses may not be adequate to evaluate the potential of computer-integrated agriculture.

The pace of technological, economic, political, and social change continues to quicken. If new technologies are designed, implemented, and managed so as to empower rather than to replace the potential users, to make them more adaptable to change, and to make their activities more productive, efficient, and sustainable, the problems of technology adoption will be minimized and the benefits maximized. Involving the users and potential beneficiaries of new technology closely in its development is a step toward achieving these goals.

REFERENCES

Holt, D. A. 1985. **Computers in production agriculture.** Science, 28:422-427.

Naegele, N. A., Coulson, R. N., Stone, N. D., and R. E. Frisbie. 1986. The use of expert systems to integrate and deliver IPM technology. In: R. E. Frisbie and P. L. Adkisson, eds., Integrated pest management in major agricultural systems. Texas A&M University, College Station, Texas. 743 pp.

Porter, Michael E., and Victor E. Millar. 1985. How information gives you competitive advantage. Harvard Business Review. July-August, 1985.

Wymore, A. Wayne. 1987 (unpublished draft). A mathematical theory of system design. System Engineering and Design Systems, Tucson, Arizona. 560 pp.

Zuboff, Shoshanna. 1988. **In the age of the smart machine: The future of work and power.** Basic Books, Inc., New York, New York. 457 pp.

CHAPTER 12

Recycling

Florentine Liegerot

Recycling in America has existed for almost as long as the country itself. It has appeared in distinctly different forms, and has seen both success and failure. An understanding of the factors that influenced the ultimate outcome of earlier recycling programs gives us a distinct advantage when looking at the role of recycling in the future.

Long before the word recycling was added to the dictionary, Americans were consciously extending the life of everything they owned. It was a common practice for women of a community to gather together for a visit, especially on winter days after the harvesting was finished and the food preserving was completed. This was a social time, but it also served a serious purpose. Dresses, shirts, and trousers that had been worn threadbare and mended as many times as possible were cut into small squares and other shapes. Then, every usable scrap from these garments was stitched together to become a form of bed-clothing known as "patchwork" quilt. In the truest sense of the word, these women were recycling. The quilts they made kept the family warm, and added beauty to the home.

America's founding fathers were also recyclers. Because they were far away from the mining and manufacturing centers of Europe, obtaining valuable raw materials needed in the manufacture of new products often required many months of waiting. Consequently, these early Americans were forced to repair and remanufacture their broken tools, firearms, and other metal goods. And so, the village blacksmith shop became America's first recycling center.

As the nation grew, and long before urban discards appeared to threaten the environment, entrepreneurs began collecting metals, rags, and even paper fibers for resale and remanufacture. These "ragpickers," as they were called, were responsible for the formation of the secondary materials industry early in this country's history.

One industry that developed strictly through recycling was paper making.

The first United States paper-making plant was founded in 1690 near Philadelphia, Pennsylvania. The paper was made exclusively from recycled fiber derived from cotton and linen rags and waste paper made from these textile fibers. It was not until the 1860s, when the demand for paper increased, that producers developed techniques to utilize wood fiber in paper making. The use of fibers and waste paper declined significantly until shortage of raw materials brought it back in the 1940s.

America's industrialization, coupled with improved modes of transportation, began to make delivery of materials less expensive and much faster. Consumer goods were more easily acquired and our natural resources seemed infinite. This new feeling of prosperity and plenty caused consumers to be complacent and interest in recycling dwindled.

The outbreak of World War II began to change things. Precious imports such as rubber, tin, and aluminum, vital to both domestic and military needs, were no longer available. Americans returned to recycling on an unprecedented scale. Schoolchildren were planting Victory Gardens and collecting string and the foil from chewing gum wrappers. A demand for paperboard packaging made recycling waste paper important once more. Families washed and flattened cans to salvage tin. Broken metal toys and cooking utensils were also turned in for remanufacture. Used tires were no longer discarded, but were consolidated to provide new tires for the war effort and industry. Americans, united in purpose, recycled like never before.

Soon after the war ended, industry returned to normal. Great advances and improvements were made in United States manufacturing. Goods became plentiful and cheaper, and the former impetus that encouraged the recovery of materials faded away. Americans became preoccupied with consumption; therefore, recycling was literally ignored.

As the country's affluence continued to grow, so did the demand for more conveniences and time-saving devices. Americans, understandably, wanted more leisure time to enjoy this affluence, and so the "throw away" society was born. Nearly everything became disposable; diapers, paper plates and cups, plastic flatware and table covers. Even appliances were no longer manufactured to last. It became less expensive to purchase a new radio than to repair the old one. Thus, the old one was thrown away.

Although Americans have every imaginable convenience, there is a serious drawback to this lifestyle. Instead of the 2.9 pounds of household trash per day Americans disposed of in 1960, by 1986, the average American was discarding 3.5 pounds per day, a dramatic increase considering the significant growth in our population. Citizens once again became complacent toward the country's resources, both natural and man-made, and the environment suffered. As waste loads have grown and environmentally acceptable disposal options have dwindled, disposal of solid waste has become a national issue requiring the attention of government, industry, and the general public.

WASTE DISPOSAL OPTIONS

Can we reduce the amount of waste we discard? Can waste be given a second life? Can individuals make a difference in waste disposal? These are some questions that must be answered to preserve the quality of life for future generations.

Three different kinds of wastes exist today: hazardous waste, commercial/ industrial waste and municipal solid waste (MSW). The following discussion focuses exclusively on MSW.

Americans currently generate approximately 160 million tons of MSW annually. Paper is the single largest component of MSW, comprising 40 percent of all solid waste — approximately 64 million tons annually. Yard wastes account for 48 million tons, and glass and various metals make up 32 million tons each year. An additional 16 million tons are attributed to plastics and miscellaneous wastes. Experts estimate that 50 percent of all these materials could be diverted from the waste stream for recycling each year. Currently, however, only about 10 percent is recycled.

A national public policy supporting the use of a "waste management hierarchy" has been in effect since 1976. Under the hierarchy, source reduction and recycling are the preferred options — incineration and landfilling are to be used only as last resorts.

In reality, the waste management hierarchy has been largely ignored. The majority (80 percent) of wastes is currently landfilled. Another 10 percent is incinerated, and as noted above, a mere 10 percent is recycled. The U.S. Environmental Protection Agency has responded to the situation by setting ambitious recycling goals of 25 percent by 1992 and 50 percent by 1998. Some cities, including Portland, Oregon, Islip, New York, and Montclair, New Jersey have already reached the 25 percent rate, but they are the exception rather than the rule.

Why isn't recycling more commonplace? One reason is a general lack of knowledge on the part of the public concerning the garbage crisis. Many citizens have an "out of sight, out of mind" attitude, never thinking about where the trash goes once it leaves the curb.

However, recycling will inevitably play a larger part in the solid waste arena, if only because other alternatives are becoming less feasible.

Landfills will not be able to bear the brunt of our wastes much longer. Nearly half of the 5,500 landfills in the United States will reach capacity within the next five years, and siting new landfills is extremely difficult because of the

"Not In My Backyard," or NIMBY, attitude prevalent in many communities. Americans want wastes disposed of safely, but not in their neighborhoods.

State and local politicians are bowing to the pressure from their constituencies; many states and cities have or are considering moratoriums on new landfills and/or expansions. As a result, 25 states will be out of landfill space within the next 10 years. Tipping fees are already escalating at both landfills and transfer stations, which means higher refuse bills for citizens. Also, many states, particularly in the Northeast, have to haul their wastes out-of-state for disposal, causing resentment among citizens in states on the receiving end.

Incineration is gaining popularity among public officials, but again, the NIMBY attitude is preventing companies from building and operating them. Environmental groups express concerns about ash disposal and air pollution, further complicating and slowing new construction. Other commonly voiced concerns about both landfills and incinerators include increased noise level, odor, truck traffic and anxiety over property values.

Many state legislatures are dealing with the solid waste problem by mandating that some type of recycling program be incorporated in large communities within the next few years. Rhode Island was the first state to implement such a law, and several states and large cities are following the lead. Some smaller communities exempt from these state laws are taking the initiative on their own. Citizens are realizing the benefits of recycling, including saving landfill space and preserving natural resources.

Communities have three basic types of recycling programs from which to choose: curbside collection, drop-off centers, and buy-back centers.

Curbside Collection

Curbside collection is the most visible type of recycling program and therefore easiest to publicize. It is popular among residents because of its convenience— residents merely separate their recyclables from regular trash, store them in separate bins and leave the bins on the curb for pickup, usually on the same days as regular garbage pickup. The recyclables are taken to a recycling plant for processing and sale.

Involving multi-family dwellings in community recycling programs can help their visibility because of the large number of citizens living in such housing — more residents mean higher tonnages are available per pickup point.

Recycling can be made easier for apartment residents by installing separate waste chutes near regular garbage chutes to collect recyclables. The maintenance staff simply collects the recyclables and places them in containers for pickup.

Recycle America, a program sponsored by Waste Management, Inc., the nation's largest curbside recycler, offers cities the option of providing recycling services to multi-family dwellings in a majority of its contracts. Recycle America establishes drop-off centers near regular garbage bins for apartment dwellers to drop off their recyclables.

In Seattle, officials are considering revising the building codes to require that all new multi-unit buildings incorporate a recycling plan before they are built. New Jersey has a similar statewide law. All told, more than 500 cities nationwide have curbside programs in place, and ten states have mandatory recycling laws. It should be noted, however, that none of these recovery efforts are fully supported by revenue and disposal savings. They require additional support either through increased fees or surcharges.

Public/private partnerships are another option, whereby cities and waste services firms work jointly to implement recycling programs. In San Jose, Recycle America has been operating a curbside program for nearly three years, boasting an average 60 percent participation rate. The contract with the city stipulates the program's profits are split 50/50. When markets are down, the loss is absorbed evenly; conversely, when markets are up, the revenues are split equally.

Drop-Off and Buy-Back Programs

Drop-off and buy-back centers can either stand alone or complement curbside programs. They work well in rural areas where curbside programs are impractical.

Drop-off centers typically collect several materials and are usually operated by scrap dealers or not-for-profit organizations. Paper drives are probably the most well-known type of drop-off program. A waste hauler or paper dealer furnishes containers at a school, church, shopping center or other location for people to drop off their newspapers. Proceeds are donated to a not-for-profit organization.

Buy-back centers give people money for turning in their recyclables. They tend to be successful in depressed areas because they provide an additional source of income.

CORPORATE RECYCLING

Many corporations have taken the lead in recycling by implementing office recycling programs. Waste Management, Inc., began such a recycling program in 1988, in which more than 1,100 employees participate. Approximately 36,000 pounds of recyclable paper is being collected per month and the total amount of office waste requiring disposal has been reduced by 50 percent. The company also collects aluminum cans.

McDATA Corp., a computer networking systems firm in Broomfield, Colorado, instituted an office recycling program at the suggestion of employees.

In just a few months, employees collected 1,100 cans of aluminum, 7,000 pounds of glass, and 42,000 pounds of paper. The company will add plastics to its program in 1989.

PLASTICS RECYCLING

Plastics pose a unique problem because although they comprise only 7 percent of MSW by weight, they account for 30 percent of MSW in volume. They also take hundreds of years to decompose. Some local governments are addressing the plastics problem by enacting laws banning plastics. In March 1989, Minneapolis and St. Paul, Minnesota, approved ordinances banning most nonreturnable and nonbiodegradable plastic food packaging, to take effect the summer of 1990. Suffolk County, New York, passed a law banning the manufacture of plastic grocery bags and other types of plastic.

The plastics industry has responded by positioning itself as a proponent of plastics recycling, and many manufacturers are entering joint ventures to develop plastics recycling plants. For example, the DuPont Company joined forces with Waste Management, Inc. to build several plastics recycling plants across the country, with the first one opening in early 1990.

MARKET SUPPORT

The success of any recycling program is heavily dependent on the economic market for recyclables. Materials are marketed through local scrap dealers and brokers or directly to the end user. Because these secondary markets are cyclical, revenues from the sale of recyclables are highly variable. These fluctuations in the market are one reason why local officials may not consider recycling to be a reliable way to handle MSW. Recycling programs tend not be self-supportive, either, requiring some type of subsidy to operate.

To ease the dependence on open market conditions, recycling operators can enter into contract sales, which protect against the normal fluctuations in recycled materials markets and insure materials will be sold for a fair price.

The open market usually allows the supplier of recovered materials to get the highest price when prices are good, while the sale by contract usually levels out the price. When markets are down, dealers and end users may not be buying on the open market at all, but recyclers selling by contract still have buyers. Contracts are most often used in the waste paper industry.

In many areas, used newspapers have glutted the available market. In the Chicago area, the market for old newspapers is so satiated that recycling operations cannot find buyers for the material. Many city and suburban buy-back centers have stopped paying for old newspapers people drop off, and some newspaper drop-off sites are closing. As a result, prices have fallen to only half of previous levels. Other markets have such a surplus that cities are paying recycling operations to haul the newspapers away. Even foreign markets, such as Taiwan, Japan, and Mexico, are so overstocked they no longer purchase recycled newspaper. If the current newspaper glut is not absorbed, it could force the government to raise taxes or disposal fees to cover the costs of recycling.

The basic problem is that there has been no increase in the capacity of paper mills to recycle all the collected paper. The latest surge of citizen participation in recycling caught the industry by surprise. This may result in government intervention. In Connecticut, for example, the legislature has approved a bill requiring newspapers to substantially increase the amount of recycled paper they use. Though the bill has run into a few snags, proponents are optimistic about its eventual passage.

Other states are encouraging market support by instituting procurement provisions favoring recycled goods. Twenty-four states mandate that a certain percentage of finished products be made from recyclables, and they allow purchasing agents to pay 5 to 10 percent more for recycled goods.

Some states offer businesses investing in recycling equipment substantial tax credits for the cost of the equipment.

PUBLIC EDUCATION

To preserve the environment for future generations, the public needs to be educated to a new version of "three R's" — reduce, reuse, and recycle.

The foundation for a new wave of public attention was laid in 1987 when the infamous "garbage barge" from Islip, New York spent months looking for a place to unload its cargo — several tons of MSW. The crisis resurfaced again in the media in 1988 when medical waste washed up on Eastern shores during the height of the tourist season. But the garbage crisis does not rise and fall in proportion to media exposure. It is a growing problem affecting everyone living in this country. And as the old adage goes, "If you're not part of the solution, you're part of the problem."

And the problem is growing at a rapid pace. Recycling is part of the solution, but where recycling is mandatory, it is hard to enforce. Where it is voluntary, there is little incentive to change habits. Finding the right mixture of regulations and incentives is, therefore, one of the major challenges facing communities as they contemplate recycling as one part of their solid waste strategy.

Some local governments are providing the incentive by instituting a "buy the bag" program, in which municipalities sell various size garbage bags to residents. Residents pay for disposal according to the amount of waste they generate. This type of program motivates citizens to reduce the amount of waste they generate and start recycling, for a lower garbage bill. "Buy the bag" programs are catching on, but they are still in the early stages. In the meantime, other types of efforts should be increased to involve the general public with recycling.

The first step is to educate the public about the merits of recycling: save money, extend the useful lives of landfills, and reduce litter. The education process can be as elementary as informing people that buying in bulk means less packaging to throw away (with the additional benefit of usually being cheaper in the long run), telling them to request paper instead of plastic bags from grocery stores, and informing them how long certain products take to decompose, e.g. a tin can, 100 years; an aluminum can, 200-500 years; and a glass bottle, up to 1,000,000 years!

Another selling point of recycling is the amount of natural resources it conserves. For example, each ton of recycled newsprint replaces the pulp from approximately 17 trees; recycling cans conserves 65 to 95 percent of the energy needed to produce new cans; and nine gallons of fuel are conserved through recycling one ton of glass.

The public should also be made aware of the value of reuse, e.g., using sponges and cloth towels instead of paper towels; reusing plastic containers for leftover food storage and so on.

The public must also be educated to the fact that developing markets for recyclables is just as crucial to recycling as collection. They should be encouraged to purchase products made from recyclables whenever possible.

The bottom line is the majority of Americans are unaware of the impending landfill crisis. They are oblivious to the need to reduce sources of waste because neither public education nor market incentives have successfully driven their point home.

WASTE MANAGEMENT IN THE 21ST CENTURY

Dealing with America's trash will require a combination of solutions. No single method of handling solid waste— landfilling, incineration, waste reduction or recycling— will work on its own. All components need to be integrated for a responsible and safe solid waste management plan.

The 21st century is just over the horizon. To preserve the environment, Americans must protect it. Recycling is not the total solution, but it is a very significant way to set an example for future generations. Converting a waste problem to a resource supply will need to be one part of a new approach to natural resource management in the decades ahead.

PART II
Perspectives
and Analyses

Introduction

R. Neil Sampson

The preceding overview of the status of our natural resources provides the reader with detailed information about population, climate, soils and croplands, forests, rangelands, water resources, wetlands, fisheries, wildlife, and recreational resources. Insights about the economic trends and technological developments permeate the chapters. But what do these data and trends mean as a whole?

The following six chapters each provide some assessment. Harvard social scientist Daniel Bell comments on the overall historic and global context for interpreting these trends. Department of Agriculture analyst John Fedkiw points to the new horizon opened when understanding of interacting trends leads to more holistic resource management. Adela Backiel, a natural resource specialist at the Congressional Research Service, names the challenge for natural resource professionals who recognize the trends and the call to action implied by them.

The last three chapters join reporting on a panel of experts with the authors' own insight in reflection on the trends cited in this book. Charles E. Little focuses on the new concept of sustainability; Richard Collins provides one explanation for why experts seem to differ in whether the trends imply danger or simply challenge to change; and Sara Ebenreck sums up conference reflections on the import of all the data for quality life in the future.

These chapters, as the foregoing ones, are designed as the beginning of a dialogue, not its conclusion. As each author makes clear, if we are to have resilient natural resources for the 21st century, a response will be demanded from us all.

We are deeply indebted to the 18 moderators and panelists who provided so much food for thought. Their ideas, as well as comments from the floor, are woven throughout this document. Each of them, whether or not they are quoted directly, made significant contributions. They are: Mollie H. Beattie, Commissioner, Vermont Department of Forests and Parks; John R. Block, President, National Wholesale Grocers Association; M. Rupert Cutler, President, Defenders of Wildlife; Dr. John Gordon, Dean, Yale School of Forestry; Ralph E. Grossi, President, American Farmland Trust; James Hildreth, Farm Foundation; Laurence R. Jahn, President, Wildlife Management Institute; Laird Noh, Senator, Idaho State Senate; Jerry J. Presley, Director, Missouri Department of Conservation; Dale Robertson, Chief, United States Forest Service; Robert Rodale, Rodale Press; Milo Shult, Associate Director, Cooperative Extension Service; Stewart Udall, Former Secretary, Department of the Interior; Scott Wallinger, Senior Vice President, Westvaco Corporation; Robert Wetherbee, President-Elect, National Association of Conservation Districts; Douglas Wheeler, Vice President, Conservation Foundation; Gerald Winegrad, Senator, Maryland State Senate; and Robert E. Wolf, Congressional Research Service (Retired).

CHAPTER 13

Overview of Resource Discussions

John Fedkiw

The preceding chapters on resource trends in use, management and conditions each provides an in-depth perspective on the status of the resource and its performance in the past. Each is comprehensive, systematic, and quantitative in content. None claims to be more important than any other. Each is the mark of a resource expert's work supported by several other cooperating experts in the field.

The presentation on the status of wildlife described the need for a holistic management approach that attempts to recognize the ecologic and economic trade-offs among resources and guide decisions toward a societal optimum. These chapters reveal many interrelationships and linkages among the resources, a factor which calls for a step beyond traditional functional management in which foresters manage trees, hydrologists manage water, and wildlife specialists manage wildlife. Holistic management seeks to apply the knowledge of all species and their environments in an integrated manner. It is still a largely unrealized ideal, however, and although the learning experience made possible by this information leads to the need to move toward a new idea, the information itself does not tell us how to do so.

As the conference session in which information in these chapters was presented closed, there was a sense among the participants that the resources and their management, except for marine fisheries and wetlands, had generally fared well. Global warming was a source of uncertainty for most resources and raised questions about their future performance. Asked about the resilience of resources and their responsiveness to management, the experts were positive but qualified. For example, rangeland trends are demonstrating resilience and management response, but major improvements take a long time. The much debated issue of appropriate fees for animal grazing on federal lands takes range management into the political arena and limits the capability for range science to improve range conditions without external pressures.

Wildlife trends demonstrate similar resilience and responsiveness to management but, again, there are limiting factors such as public tolerance for big game and habitat adequacy for some species. There is also uncertainty about the retention of habitat for some 2,000 to 2,500 plants and animals that have the potential to be listed as threatened or endangered species. Forest conditions are pretty good for producing more timber, but the threat of global warming raises a long-term uncertainty about their health. Fisheries are resilient, but management will be needed to reduce predators in the North Atlantic marine fisheries to restore a balanced species mix. Although the resilience is there, recovery can be slow. Visual quality resilience is more limited for recreation. There is a need to compensate landowners for access to wildlife opportunities to prevent the loss of land available for wildlife recreation. Where fees or leases have been introduced, some of the revenues are being invested in wildlife management to better those opportunities.

Soil scientists noted that the health of the cropland soil base is holding steady. While there may be a slight decline in the soil quality itself, yields are rising. It is possible to build and improve soil economically but this process is variable with the type of soil. The practice of no tillage, for example, can add to Virginia topsoil. Chemicals can increase yields but some topographies limit fertilizer use.

While we cannot increase the absolute quantity of water, water experts emphasized opportunities to conserve and extend supplies. More effective management and a market approach to allocation of available waters would improve conservation and the effectiveness of supplies for alternative uses. The decline in irrigation contributes to water supply flexibility. The declining trend in the use of pesticides and the United States Department of Agriculture's new emphasis on water quality as a national priority should also benefit water quality, but the program needs to be targeted to be most effective.

The outlook for declining acres of cropland cultivation with rising yields suggests a reduced pressure for conversion of wetlands. Experts, however, are not yet willing to accept cropland use trends as reliable indicators. There still are incentives to convert wetland potholes in the prairie area. An approach that rewards farmers for saving wetlands may be necessary. The forthcoming update of the wetlands inventory will be the best measure as to whether their conversion is slowing or stopping.

Overall, in sum, resource experts seemed reassuring about the resilience of the natural resources and their responsiveness to management. Their cautions addressed: a) the rate at which resources could improve, b) just how much policy and management would do at both public and private levels, and c) the impacts of uncertainties such as greenhouse warming or a long-term rise in oil and transportation costs. But resource capacity to produce more or to provide better quality services or greater benefits is real. It is not questioned.

Chronic problems do remain. Agriculture must become more sustainable in the use of soil and water resources. There are areas of inland waters and estuaries where health advisories have been issued on the hazards of eating fish. There are places where groundwater is not drinkable. Conference experts, resource managers and educators acknowledged that teamwork is the route to a solution: we must work together to establish standards that can integrate the management of the various resources.

CHAPTER 14

Making Intelligent Decisions in a Democratic Society

Daniel Bell

The 1988 presidential campaign made everyone an environmentalist. Both Mr. Bush and Mr. Dukakis vied for the title of "Mr. Clean," and the public responded vocally to the 1988 summer spectacle of garbage barges floating back and forth on the horizon, hypodermic needles washed upon the shore, toxic wastes in landfills, the possibility of a "greenhouse effect" in the sky, and the threat of a widening window in the protective ozone layer overhead.

The question now is (to paraphrase Thomas Paine) whether Mr. Bush, the winner, and John and Jean Q. Public will be only summer soldiers and sunshine patriots, when the cold winds begin to blow and everybody but the homeless retreats to their heated (and overheated) houses.

What we have seen in the past 20 years has been what Neil Sampson, in a recent editorial in *American Forests*, has called an issue-attention cycle. People get excited, stampede, want answers and then get bored and walk away or simply get onto a new issue. It is very difficult to provide a continuing and more comprehensibly sustained effort to identify issues.

One of the problems, of course, when you have an issue-attention cycle is that it leads to a search for a quick technological fix. A few years ago, as many of you know, the concern with garbage and waste and exhaustion of landfills led to the panacea of incineration of municipal waste with the presumed further gain of generating electricity in the process. The difficulty was that mass-burn incinerators proved to be more expensive than other solutions, there was air pollution from the burning, and since 35 percent of the initial waste contained dangerous toxic material that could not be burned, one had to find specialized landfills. So it turns out that quick fixes are no answer.

What I want to do here is to lay out certain contexts for the 21st century and, in those contexts, identify the major issues that may require attention and possibly some positive solutions.

To begin, I wish to lay out the basic historical context out of which our present-day dilemmas arise. Only since World War II has economic growth become the social objective of almost every nation of the world. We take it so much for granted now that we don't realize how recently this occurred. Before World War II, as some of the older people remember, we had the idea of mature capitalism, of cartelization, of simply maintaining control, through devices such as administered prices, to maintain a uniform price throughout the country. World War II basically broke that lock and brought out the fact that one could produce tanks and airplanes in large numbers. This led to the belief that economic growth could continue steadily. Something else has happened, too. Again, the context is important. Before World War II, 80 percent of the land mass of the world and 80 percent of the world's population were under domination of the western powers. Then, within 30 years, 120 new nations were created. Many are still floundering but, by and large, they are all eager to maintain a degree of economic growth.

In the West we have had the creation of a large middle class of about a half billion people, according to the estimates of one of my colleagues. Now that kind of growth and that aspiration transfers itself to Bengali farmers, Chinese peasants, and Papuan Stone Age men seeking bicycles, radios, domestic appliances, housing, electricity, and more education. And this becomes a driving force of the world economy. In other words, there is a sustained hunger for material goods that becomes a growing pressure on resources.

Yet a contrary recognition has also arisen and this is what creates a continuing dilemma. It is the realization that natural resources are not inexhaustible, so we face the difficult question of the appropriate rate of use, given exhaustible resources. That becomes the crucial element of political, and even moral, decisions.

In addition, another limit on growth is the recognition of externalities: the side effects and social costs of actions initiated by one set of individuals, yet borne by others. It is also the recognition that growth alone is not a measure of welfare or quality of life. Growth alone is simply the addition of goods and services that we register by calculating the gross national product. The British economist A.C. Pigou, who first defined the concept, said wittily that if a widowed Vicar maintained a housekeeper and paid her a wage, that is an addition to national product; but if he marries her, and stops the wage, that's a subtraction. And that's the way economists figure it.

What we don't have is a definition of net national welfare. Yet without it, we will not have adequate indicators of the quality of life. We have also learned that there are no free goods. Economics textbooks a long time ago essentially said that air and water are free goods because they are so plentiful. This was the basis of the famous diamond-water paradox put forward by Adam Smith. Water has a higher utility, but it is cheap because it is plentiful. Diamonds are scarce, and thus cost more. In recent years we have had so much pollution because we did not put a price on use of air and water, and without a price on something we misuse it.

Finally in this inventory of awareness there is also the idea of an eco-system as a natural equilibrium of the intertwined elements. Yet, ironically, so many people who praise the idea of eco-systems often fail to recognize that the eco-systems are a form of social Darwinism in which the stronger survive at the expense of the weak. (Marx in one of his earlier essays talked about the German forests as strong oaks that beat back the smaller bushes.) So an eco-system, by and large, is a form of social Darwinism, too.

These elements come together to form a basic dilemma: the universal desire for economic growth and the recognition, from exhaustible resources and externalities, of a set of limits. The basic need is to define socially optimal use of resources. Economic growth has become a social goal, but it cannot have free rein.

DEMOGRAPHY

There are other challenges we have to confront as we move into the 21st century. The first and most obvious challenge is the pressures on economic growth from population. The fact is that of the 10 largest countries in the world today (of a population of 5 billion), only two, the United States and Japan, are fully developed societies. The two largest, China and India, with 1.75 billion people— 35 percent of the world's population— are just on the rising slope of economic development and economic growth, making claims for more and more resources for society. The third largest country, the Soviet Union, is a dual economy with a highly developed military sector and a weak consumer sector, so that the Soviet Union is 60th among countries of the world on the standard-of-living list. It wants to move up. The remaining five largest countries— Indonesia, Brazil, Bangladesh, Pakistan and Nigeria— make up another 750 million people, though the growth rates of population is such that Nigeria in the next 35 years will have almost 340 million inhabitants because of a 3.4 percent growth rate in its population.

It is not simply the enormous overall pressure that forces us to look ahead to the 21st century, but something more immediate: the demographic imbalances in the world. Simply stated, it is this. In all of Africa, 46 percent of the population is under age 17. In all of Latin America, between 35 and 45 percent of the population is under age 17. In countries like Bangladesh and Afghanistan, 45 percent of the population is under age 17. In Europe, the United States and Japan, we have, of course, a graying population.

Because of these large imbalances, we will see a tidal wave of population coming into the labor force of these countries. This combines with growing urbanization— almost all of Latin America today is largely urbanized. As more and more people leave their farms— about 65 percent of the people live in urban areas— you have unemployment rates of 20 to 30 percent. Today, for example, Mexico has 80 million people, more than any country in Europe, and its population is growing at the rate of 2.5 percent. Forty-six percent of the Mexican population is under 15 years of age. In North Africa, in the Maghreb— Algeria, Morocco and Tunis— more than 75 percent of the population is under 25 years of age. In the next 10 years we will see a doubling of the entry rates of the labor force.

What can we do? There are only three logical alternatives. Take their people; buy their goods; or give them money. Most societies don't want immigrants. Europe, which after World War II had the *Gastarbeiter* to do the dirty work in the society, now tries to expel them. We admit some Mexicans, particularly for migrant agricultural labor, but by and large there is great uneasiness about the scope of immigration. In Europe today we have hostility to immigrants, as in France, where the Algerians try to come. What are we to do? Immigration creates tensions. Give them capital? They are already overburdened with debt. Buy their goods? That undercuts our industries, so we have three swords of Damocles hanging over us.

Nobody is doing anything about it. I don't know of any international meetings, United Nations or otherwise, which confront these issues. There is some emphasis on birth control and population development. But that doesn't take care of the immediate issues of the next 10 or 15 years; we may be swamped by the tidal wave.

TECHNOLOGY

The second context is technology. We have seen in recent years a demonization of technology, as if it were the sorcerer's apprentice who has spun out of control. Yet technology is not an autonomous force, but an instrument used in different ways and different patterns through political or market decisions. The most extraordinary accomplishments of this century are the great advances in technology; the great advances in medicine— where most children's diseases have been eliminated— and in food. By and large, in most places famine is no longer a real issue in the world today.

But I want to call attention to what I think is the most important aspect of technology in relation to natural resources. This is the revolution taking place in science that leads to substantial reductions in natural resource requirements per unit of real output. Today, for example, material scientists do not think in terms of a particular product such as copper, tin or zinc, but what properties we need. We can specify ductility, tensility, conductivity, in what combination and at what cost. Thus, we have increasing independence from natural resources because of the ability to create new materials in different combinations. (Parenthetically, I may point out, this has led to great economic blows for primary-products producing countries who have not re-deployed their economies. A United Nations report a few months ago pointed out that a basket of exports by African countries today is worth half of what it was 10 years ago. And if we subtract oil, it is a third. This has been due to the depressed prices of metals in this decade, until recently.)

The challenge set by this trend of reducing raw material requirements? Develop a government tax policy that encourages these kinds of materials and energy-saving developments.

POLITICS

The third context is political. Other things being equal, the resource and environmental problems of the world are not naturally created or technologically induced, but the results of political and social factors.

Consider food, for example. Today almost all countries of the world, with the possible exception of Bangladesh and parts of sub-Sahara Africa, are producing their own food. The Soviet Union's wheat growing areas are very similar to North Dakota and Saskatchewan, but the U.S.S.R. uses 30 percent of its labor force for agriculture. In Canada and the United States, less than five percent of citizens work in agriculture. Social organizations and politics make the difference, not soil.

It used to be said that "capitalism" in its ruthless surge for profit is destructive of the environment. Yet one sees the bureaucratic mangling of areas in the non-capitalist Soviet Union. Lake Aral, the fourth largest lake in the world, is shrinking (will vanish by 2010, says *Izvestia),* because two major rivers were diverted for irrigation to grow cotton. Lake Baikal, the world's largest fresh-water lake, is despoiled by dumping from nearby pulp mills which only wish to fulfill individual quotas— the environment can go hang. Self-interest is self-interest, whether "public bureaucracy" or "private enterprise."

Let me turn to this hemisphere. One of the looming ecological disasters is the destruction of tropical rain forests in Brazil. The Brazilian government says they need to do this to deal with growth of population. They defend it as land reform. It is not land reform, but the inversion of land reform, for what we have in most of Brazil are large land holdings run by absentee landlords. Cutting down the tropical rain forests is the easier way out, the path of least resistance.

If one turns to the United States, one of the major problems is the administrative anachronisms of 50 states and 3,000 counties that do not follow any natural lines or boundaries. In the Midwest, counties were laid out on a 25 mile square grid. There are 1,400 local governments in the New York metropolitan area. States that bisect natural regions, estuaries or bays are not effective units of environmental management. This is not decentralization, but disarray. The challenge is to find effective government compacts appropriate to the scale and size of the actions needed.

SOCIO-ECONOMIC METHODOLOGIES

How do we manage a stock of nonrenewable but essential resources? What is the optimal rate of use?

The "traditional" way of approaching these questions— one used by Gifford Pinchot 80 years ago— was the utilitarian criterion of "the greatest good for the greater number." It is still pretty much the fall back theme when individuals are pressed to provide a criterion. It is the basis of gross national product as a quantitative measure of the health of the economy. Yet it is misleading.

There is a distinction, implicit even in utilitarian thought, between the sum total of individual decisions and the social decision. In most instances, the utilitarians thought that men, acting either rationally or for civic virtue, would not press these apart. Yet as we know, this separation of individual and common goods constantly happens. If a government asks, during wartime, should we reduce cloth available for private sale so that we can make uniforms; every patriot says, yes. But each man or woman fingers his or her threadbare jacket and thinks, I need a suit. Ask if we should have speed restrictions on the highways in order to reduce energy consumption (or reduce highway deaths), and most individuals might say, yes. But each person may also seek exemption, for "I have to get there in a hurry"; or if a trucker, "I have to save time." This is the basis, of course, of Garret Hardin's famous parable of the Tragedy of the Commons. Unless there is a social mechanism such as price to allocate usage, the common becomes ravaged by the sum total of individual behavior.

The same problem— and distinction— holds in the question of the rate of use of exhaustible resources. Let us follow the logic of the economists— here I take the reasoning of Robert M. Solow.

A pool of oil or a vein of iron is a capital asset— and even with recycling (because of the laws of thermodynamics), there is a diminution. An owner, private or government, has to make a judgment as to how to use that resource. When left in the ground, it produces a return for the owner only by appreciating in value. Since it yields no dividend so long as it is in the ground, the condition of a stock equilibrium in the asset market, the value grows at a rate equal to the rate of interest. In respect to the flow equilibrium— the rate of production is a function of the demand curve. In the perfect situation, where flows and stocks are coordinated through a futures market, the last ton produced will also be the last ton in the ground. This is a simple market-clearing approach to rate of use.

But is it an optimal social policy? It is a "rational" policy from the viewpoint of the private owner. But does society wish to discount the rate of wasting deposits at the same rate that resource owners choose to discount their future profits? What if we say that the resource may be exploited too fast and exhausted too soon? From whose point of view? For one, there is the inter-generational question. Do we have the right to deprive future generations of resources to satisfy primarily ourselves?

The choice of a social discount rate is, in effect, a policy decision about inter-generational distribution; it cannot be made by the sum total of individual decisions. One may wonder: if people, by their preferences vote for a rapid rate of depletion, is that not their free choice? But who, then, speaks for the unborn, particularly if, as Edmund Burke once said, "Society is a partnership of the living, the dead and the still unborn."

We also have to be mindful of the deceits of the word "social." For many old liberals, social meant governmental or political intervention. Yet government, as we know, is also a cluster of competing bureaucracies; so it is not easily clear that the political process is automatically more future-oriented than the average corporation. The long view and the right path are not that easily defined. How is this behavior to be induced, and by whom?

Is this approach I have suggested substantially an attack on the free market philosophy which has kept this economy growing and relatively free? Here I have to make another crucial and relevant distinction between the free market, or laissez faire, and market mechanisms.

A free market is fair and equitable if there is a rough equality in the distribution of income or power, so that preferences are actual registers of an individual's willingness to forgo something and pay for something else in accordance with his choices. But when there is a preponderance of market power in various areas, by the ability to fix or administer prices in oligopolistic situations, or because of skewed income distribution, the market is a response to demand, but it not necessarily fair or equitable.

A social decision is an effort to define social goals and establish social frameworks, for a need such as the control of pollution. But within that framework there is a choice of bureaucratic regulatory mechanisms, or market mechanisms. Compared to the clumsy and heavy-handed administrative mode, with its multiplication of regulations and bureaucracy that monitor situations by seeking to measure precisely the amount of pollutants discharged in the air or water, the pricing system *is* a far more flexible mechanism. Here individuals have to decide to bear the cost to reach the social objectives either by reducing the externalities or paying the amounts required for others to do it for them. Market mechanisms provide for flexibility and choice within varying time frames as judged by the producer. But they have meaning largely within the framework of social goals. So I make a necessary distinction between a free market and market mechanisms. I seek a social consensus on policy, and the use of market mechanisms to achieve this.

None of this is a recipe for utopia. We are, after all, human and sometimes all too inhuman. It is an effort to more completely understand our problems and dilemmas so as to make clear the actual costs and painful choices.

CHAPTER 15

Choices for Natural Resource Professionals

Adela Backiel

The last great debates about overpopulation affecting our natural resource base occurred in the late 1960s and early 1970s. Basically, as the theory went, resources were being used at a nonsustainable rate that compounded the already existing problem of resource scarcity. The popular notion of the time was that resources were not inexhaustible and needed to be used conservatively, while searching for alternatives. The issues of resources scarcity, optimal use of resources, and population growth were all part of the prelude to the environmental movement which began with the publication of *Silent Spring* by Rachel Carson and went public with the celebration of Earth Day.

In response, our political leaders enacted numerous laws relating to the environment. Some of these laws were specific to individual natural resources. Many were broader and encompassed general guidelines and rules that set the environmental tenor of the country for the next two decades. With passage of these laws, natural resources management was now equated with environmental management. Forest policy, for example, is not only defined in terms of specific forestry laws, but also by these broader, more encompassing acts of Congress. Most notable is the National Environmental Policy Act of 1969.

After a respite in which, in a political sense, the environment seemingly was only a budget line item to be cut, natural resources and the environment are again an important variable in policy and political equations. This political re-awakening is not just a repeat of the environmental movement of the 1970s. The public has continued to show its support and concern for the environment and that growing concern is beginning to be heard.

We are still discussing many of the same issues, but the era we are entering is one of globalism. Our current problems no longer belong only to developed nations. We are no longer in a position just to warn against what Harvard sociologist Daniel Bell describes as a "demographic tidal wave" of population; we are living with it. No longer are resources regarded only as ripe for development, or needing protection in their own right; they have become a primary focus in many policy debates over broader issues. How much should pollution emissions be reduced in the industrial Midwest to improve human health and forest health without putting West Virginia coal workers in the unemployment lines? Can enough forests be planted or halted from destruction to absorb some of the increased output of carbon dioxide from our industries? What effect will that have on development in less developed nations? How many forests should be transformed into farms to feed starving nations or into housing developments along the coasts of the United States? How can we manage the demographic tidal wave?

These issues have put natural resource professionals at a crossroads where our traditions and beliefs meet the future policy choices governing our earth's natural resources.

THE ROLE OF SCIENTISTS IN PUBLIC POLICY-MAKING

Politics and natural resources management have something in common: both make public choices about public values. The result is policy. Policies identify and define our society's desires. Policy and politics encircle the arena of the most important challenges facing natural resource professionals.

As natural resource scientists and managers, we have the responsibility to speak out, tell what is known, and admit what is not, while continuing to do research. But it is also our responsibility not to hide behind the data, the uncertainty, the demand for more research. In spite of the risks we need to project what will happen if action is not taken, or money not funded, or cooperation not achieved.

Laird Noh, state senator from Idaho, has urged that "we manage with fact, not folklore." But we need to guard against equating knowledge with wisdom — our scientific input does not make the decision, but is combined with other facets of the issue involving the welfare of our society. Data may provide information, but it does not give us the next step. Decisions are not based on scientific input alone. Nor should they be. Decisions require that value judgments be made, by us, or by politicians.

As Bob Wolf (Congressional Research Service, retired) has pointed out, natural resource issues are a small percentage of the federal budget and consequently occupy a small percentage of politicians' attention span. In many countries resources are not even a budget item. Higher priority issues that confront and monopolize our politicians' time and attention include defense, social programs, and the federal deficit.

To make natural resources and the environment a bigger agenda item in both the national and global agenda, scientists must become interested and involved in the policy process. We need to translate scientific knowledge and information to our public constituents and those in political power. We must decide if we want to let issues evolve or if we need to start a revolution. To fit science into the political agenda we must learn to speak the language of politicians, or else be ignored. We must get excited about politics, if we expect politicians to get excited about science.

If the ultimate political power lies with the people, as many conference speakers emphasized, then political resource management involves educating and listening to the public. People can make a difference. As the public's definitions of good public policy and natural resources management evolve, so, too, will political decisions.

Public policymaking is slow; consequently, most situations and issues suggest our working with the system, not against it. There are certain issues and circumstances, however, that require a new approach. The area that seems most ripe for change is the development and active involvement of global institutions as an international response to the ever-broadening environmental issues of today.

We must try to thrive on change within ourselves and our profession, if we expect change in our institutions. To speak out to the public and to politicians, as clearly as possible, about the current state and management of natural resources will require that natural resource professionals change our habits. People and organizations often resist change because it is a venture into the unknown. A common response is to turn inward and become creative about ways to stay the same.

But we must reach out and create ways to talk to each other. Changing our habits means striving to find common themes and understandings. Disagreement among educated professionals is part of a dynamic, changing profession, but there are times when those disagreements must be overcome for the good of society.

A CALL FOR LEADERSHIP

Former Colorado Governor Dick Lamm says we have been electing weather vanes instead of compasses. If, as he also believes, our politicians mirror those who elect them, then we have a responsibility to educate and incite our political leaders to action.

We are in charge of our own destiny. We need to help find the solutions, but not just by doing more research. Professionals must communicate, educate, and make value judgments when asked; they must sound the alarm of revolution when necessary, and become the beacons for our political leaders regarding solutions to natural resources issues.

In a recent speech, William Schneider, a political analyst for the *Los Angeles Times* and the *National Journal*, described Americans as a nation of problem-solvers. He said that Americans scheme to solve problems, but need a vision to create commitment. Natural resource professionals can be described in the same way. We have the techniques, we have the knowledge. We need to help create the vision so that our professions, the public, and our political leaders will show commitment to solving our national and global environmental problems.

CHAPTER 16

Resource Sustainability

Charles E. Little

Sustainability: surely this is the watchword for the management of natural resources as one century gives way to the next. At such times, it seems to me, people are inclined to think in longer cycles than ordinarily on all matters, especially on resource issues. The questions here are: Will the soil last *another* century, after all the hard farming with tractors and chemicals? Will the forests yield up their planks and beams and chips in the century to come as they did the century before when the vast, primeval American forest was still partially intact? Will the wildlife stay in balance, and will the creatures of the sea survive the present rate of harvest and pollution? Such are the issues of sustainability.

Yet at the conference on which this book is based, one expert after another with very few exceptions, reported that the American resource base was, by and large, in good shape. For me, and some others, this is an astonishing assessment. What of acid rain and water pollution, the disappearing vestiges of the old growth forest, the ravages of droughts to come given the inevitability of global warming? The answer seemed to be: market forces and technological advance and resource substitution have worked so far; there's every statistical indication that they will work in the future; so who's to argue?

In effect, and with a good deal of indirection and politeness, the panel on sustainability did mount an argument of sorts. For implicit in the "I'm all right, Jack" view of resource management is the notion that a conscious effort to establish sustainability in the United States is unnecessary, that the mechanisms of a free economy and human invention are automatically sufficient to this purpose. The panel, evidently, disagreed, for what they discussed were not the *techniques* of resource sustainability— conservation tillage or catfish aquaculture or new ways of tree-farming— but the communications dynamics required to move the nation toward sustainability and away from resource degradation and depletion. In this way the panelists did address sustainability as, essentially,

309

a political challenge; as we shall see, there was nothing shallow or merely technical about their thinking.

REACHING FOR SUSTAINABILITY

The motif of dealing broadly with sustainability, as opposed to treating with how-to, was established at the outset by panel moderator John Gordon, dean of the Yale School of Forestry and Environmental Studies, who in his introductory remarks said that technical specialists— the definition fitting most of the participants at the conference— should not merely talk to one another, but should have "a larger message." The principal message had been established in the keynote speech by Harvard sociologist Daniel Bell, said Gordon. It was "intergenerational equity," a jargon term that I'd guess is greatly appreciated by hard-nosed scientists and resource managers who do not wish to appear soft-hearted. It means something other than the allocation of resources among ourselves; it has to do with what we manage to pass along to our children and to the generations that follow. Will they have as good a resource base as we?

"By and large," said Gordon, a plant physiologist, "resources are being sustained. But we still must address the issue of intergenerational equity." Thus, the implicit question Gordon raised was "sustainability for whom?" And the implicit answer: "For posterity."

James Hildreth, an agricultural economist and president of the Farm Foundation, responded that he believed that posterity's equity really had to be a matter of policy not left to chance. Regulation, he noted, establishing legal limits to resource use, was not the only way to express such a policy, although that is the approach most often called for. A far better course, he intimated, would be to "change the rules of the game," which would necessarily influence market outcomes. "Suppose," he said, "we could think of a rule that would include the cost of disposal in the cost of the good. If that were the case, we'd have a quite different mix of products produced." Anyone maddened by the mindless excess of modern packaging, which not only depletes resources but causes air and water pollution, visual blight, and noxious odors, not to mention enormous public expense and inconvenience, would cheer the day.

"Many of our disputes over resources," Hildreth went on, "rest with value questions— good versus bad, which is subjective. But they also rest on non-value questions— what is, and what isn't, scientifically." Hildreth reminded the conference that much could be done for sustainability by dealing effectively with the nonvalue questions. "I would rather light a candle," he said, "than curse the darkness."

Laurence Jahn, president of the Wildlife Management Institute and a wildlife biologist, agreed with the idea that "we should fight for a factual base," but he was not quite so loath to do a little darkness cursing. Soil erosion, he said by way of example, simply should not be tolerated, nor should the draining of wetlands, which are not as well protected by law as they appear to be under the Clean Water Act and the Food Security Act. Nor did he feel that there was anything wrong with regulatory policies. Such policies, he said, could be utterly decisive in protecting sustainable resources for future generations if grounded in "the public trust doctrine of law," which he characterized as, simply, "doing what is right." Such a doctrine can justify public regulation, on a pre-emptive basis, of all manner of resources, although constitutional strictures concerning the taking of property without just compensation may be invoked later. In protecting wetlands, for example, he said, "You can establish a legal presumption that wetlands are unique to society and that they should be maintained. Such a presumption may work against the individual, but there is an appeal process through the courts." Jahn said the public trust doctrine to protect resources has been used successfully in Massachusetts, Florida, and elsewhere. "There is plenty of precedent for doing what's right," he said. "All voting citizens of this country should be familiar with the public trust doctrine. There is no other choice, and it does provide hope for the future."

If Hildreth argued for changing the rules of the game, and Jahn for regulation based on the public trust doctrine, Henry Webster offered yet another approach. What's needed for a high level of resource output on a sustainable basis, Webster said, is "to put your money where your mouth is." Arguing for a "considerable level of investment" in resource management, the Michigan state forester cited the Canadian experience. The Canadians, he said, are able to spend much more on forest management than we because they have successfully linked resource management solutions to well-perceived public needs— greater employment opportunities and higher export earnings. "That's a simple enough concept," he said, "to be grasped by newspaper reporters or mayors or others affecting public opinion."

Webster did acknowledge that money was tight, difficult to come by for resource management, which was a lower priority than it ought to be. "Not having to buy all the new firecrackers in various forms would help," he said, in a reference to wasteful defense expenditures, adding, "We've got to get hold of our tendency toward what historian Paul Kennedy calls 'imperial overstretch.' Both the U.S. and the U.S.S.R. have a tendency to bite off more than they can chew, and get screwed up in the process." In order not to screw up the resource base any further, Webster would have us develop adequately financed programs on a state or regional basis, where the linking of resource sustainability with other public values is more easily conveyed. "That way," he said, "resource management can be seen as part of the socio-economic solution rather than part of the problem."

I have left the remarks of the remaining panelist, Robert Rodale, for last because Rodale, a magazine editor and publisher of Rodale Press, introduced a stunning pronouncement that called the panel's most basic assumption, conservation — into question. In so doing he greatly influenced the general discussion which followed the panelists' remarks.

"One of the most fascinating things about this conference," Rodale began, "has been the silence on the word 'conservation.' I haven't heard that word once, either yesterday or this morning." But he went on to say that this was no bad thing. "Conservation as a concept is essentially dead. Its life span is over, although that is not to say it wasn't a good idea in its time." He explained the origins of conservation, via first forester Gifford Pinchot nearly a century ago, and pointed out that while the concept had been effectively applied to forestry, it was for agriculture simply a bandage over a faulty system that had led to more erosion and damage to the soil than ever before.

In fact, the death of conservation, Rodale said, "can be a very constructive thought — we *need* to move from a conservation mentality to a mentality that can actually produce sustainability." In his view, the route to sustainability is not through resource-industry conservation measures, which merely postpone resource depletion, but through "regeneration," which is to say those small human actions that taken in the aggregate can restore depleted soils, forests, and fisheries, leaving them more productive than they were found. Rodale said that this was, in effect, an affirmative, solution-oriented approach to resource management rather than rear-guard, negative, and problem-oriented. "You need to get people's attention with the negative sometimes," he said, "but if you keep talking about the problem, they become immune to your blandishments. People do *not* become immune to solutions, however."

In the general discussion following the panelists' prepared remarks, there was considerable challenge to Rodale's "conservation is dead" assertion. To a questioner who asked whether we really ought to change the concept, as opposed to restructuring the conservation "model," Rodale replied, "We are now in a different time (from the days of Pinchot), and we need an idea that's fully integrated with the public's capacity to carry it out." He meant, I believe, that the new idea would have to be actionable, and energizing, on an individual as opposed to an industrial basis. "The idea of conservation can only be sustained by government money," he said, as opposed to regenerative actions undertaken on an individual or community basis for their own sakes. In a society, he said, as in a burned-over forest, "you need pioneer species to bring it back, small steps that will eventually solve the problem, but that by themselves do not seem to have much effect." Was this not simply a restatement of Aldo Leopold's "land ethic"?, another questioner wanted to know. "An ethic," Rodale replied, "is a legalistic concept; more lawyerly than I really like." Under a concept of regeneration, he said, "the land ethic is replaced by the idea of a 'land spirit.' People are looking to the land for the regeneration of their spirit. When they do this, they regenerate the land. "I think we need a *new* Aldo Leopold," Rodale concluded, "to write about the land spirit."

BLOWING THE WHISTLE, POPULATION . . . AND MORE

A tactical issue much on the minds of all the panelists was whether resource managers, as representatives of government or industry, should or should not "blow the whistle" on the degradation of resources in their care. The topic came up in an earlier session when Lawrence Libby, chair of the Department of Food and Resource Economics at the University of Florida, said that a certain amount of yelling and screaming was necessary to help shape the resource management agenda. Many took exception that this view was unprofessional and unscientific, though panel moderator John Gordon charged, "If professionals will not stand up and be counted in defense of resources, who will?" A serious question, and taken as such.

Another motif was the impact, and importance of, population dynamics. I've yet to attend a conference on resources when someone does not rise to state that all discussion of improved management is useless unless and until population growth here as well as in the third world is not brought under control. This is one of the great conversation stoppers of all time, like the Marxian view that no social reforms are valid unless or until the means of production are taken out of the hands of the bourgeousie. There were some effective responses to the population-is-the-only-problem view, however, offered by panel members as well as members of the audience. Hildreth, for example, pointed out tellingly that it was the combination of population and the growth of technology that was the problem, not population alone. With modern technology, he said, "a very small population can do untold damage."

And then there were some fascinating digressions, such as Robert Wolf's discussion of the possibility of re-instituting homesteading on unused land. Wolf, a member of the audience (Congressional Research Service, retired), provided a lengthy and riveting historical analysis of homesteading— from Jefferson, to Hamilton, to Lincoln, to the Taylor Grazing Act of the 1930s, and finally to the present status of the public lands.

But none of these seemed to me to be the thread, the connective tissue, that led, sometimes quite tortuously, through the deliberations of this panel on sustainability. The object of the discussion was to deal with the question: "How do we achieve a sustainable resource base, especially in view of the need to provide intergenerational equity with respect to allocation of resources?" This was the question effectively framed by moderator Gordon. There were, in sum, four answers to the question:

James Hildreth said: We need policies that change the "rules of the game," so that economic self-interest operates in behalf of resource sustainability rather than in contravention of it.

Laurence Jahn said: There is an emerging opportunity to regulate the use of resources through the "public trust doctrine of law" which all Americans should become familiar with, and which they should demand be applied.

Henry Webster said: We need to invest more money in resource management; and to get it appropriated, we must be able to show how the public can benefit directly from the investment at the state and regional level.

Robert Rodale said: We need to redefine the public role in resource management, through the concept of regeneration, to empower the individual and the community to protect and enhance the resource base on their own initiative.

Which of these would be the most effective course to follow? The answer, obviously, is "all of the above." These are sophisticated, thoughtful responses, every one of them. Readers of the technical papers in this volume may wish to keep them in mind— as benchmarks, you might say, to interpret and evaluate the presentations of those who represent professional resource managers and research scientists in the United States. Will they, as a group, have the wit to propose new "rules of the game," to find new means to regulate resource use, to demand — and get — increased revenues for their work, to seek ways to empower individuals and communities for the regeneration of the resource base?

Or will they simply put their faith in the technological fix? Or that all-purpose cop-out, "market forces"? We should fervently hope not. As Laurence Jahn put it at the very end of this session, "There's no market mechanism that can adequately recognize the value of the micro-organisms in a column of soil." This is the nub of it: whether or not we can create, to pass along to our children and to theirs, a sustainable natural resource base whose yields in economic prosperity, social improvement, environmental quality, and natural beauty will go on and on, tomorrow and forever— because of political choices we are willing to make today.

CHAPTER 17

Challenges, Opportunities, and Choices

Richard Collins

During the Resources for the 21st Century conference which led to the production of this book, the news from the "outside world" that caused the most topical discussion and speculation was the election victory of George Bush. What would the Bush victory mean for conservation? What would it mean in terms of the types of appointments to critical positions within the government? Would there be substantial change from the Reagan years? Was George Bush really an "environmentalist" as he had asserted during the campaign?

But a persistent and deeper-running theme was also evident in many of the panelist presentations, in the discussions over coffee, and in the corridors. Environmentalists, scientists, and politicians alike expressed that theme in troubling tones and in questions that went beyond the data or even specific resource topics: How do you assess the state of the world? How do you interpret the accumulated views of the panel members? Apart from discrete problems, is there a reason to believe that our central institutions and underlying drives are sound and capable of producing a better, safer, more prosperous, and environmentally benign world? Or is the situation one so complex and tenuous that a gloomy future is in store for us?

No one would have guessed that President Mikhail Gorbachev would come to the United Nations in New York within a month and deliver a speech of encompassing importance that would address those same questions.

President Gorbachev's speech drew headlines for his proposal to reduce the number of Soviet troops in Central Europe. But within the speech he noted: "... the growth of the world economy reveals the contradictions and limits inherent in traditional-type industrialization. Its further extension and intensification spell environmental catastrophe." Gorbachev also asserted that a "radical review of approaches to the totality of the problems" was necessary if the world was to create a more secure future.

Gorbachev's words suggested that he was subscribing to the central tenets of those who believe that "growth" itself is the vital issue of our time and for the century ahead. Whatever Gorbachev meant, it was my impression that the panelists throughout the conference had to declare their positions on the growth issue. Although I never heard the title of the book *Limits to Growth* mentioned, the thesis of that book provided an implicit, yet pervasive and brooding presence. In specific terms of identifiable renewable resources, the various panelists appeared to have little fear that there would be a timber famine, food shortages, or that water would be unavailable. However, there was an interesting paradox: those who declared themselves generally optimistic were quick to note that there were definite, even forbidding challenges. Those who declared themselves pessimistic were not so much forecasting inevitable catastrophe as they were expressing an urgency about the depth and interconnectedness of the problems that the future presented.

It reminded me of the situation that followed the *Global 2000 Report to the President* subtitled "Entering the Twenty-First Century" prepared by the Council on Environmental Quality and the Department of State for President Jimmy Carter in 1970.

The major findings and conclusion of that report began with the words:

> If the present trends continue, the world in 2000 will be more crowded, more polluted, less stable ecologically, and more vulnerable to disruption than the world we live in now. Serious stresses involving population, resources, and the environment are clearly visible ahead. Despite greater material output, the world's people will be poorer in many ways than they are today.

Soon after the release of that report, the Heritage Foundation released another entitled *Global 2000 Revised,* and described the *Global 2000 Report* as "dead wrong." This report went on to say that their study "presents the relevant reliable trend evidence, which mainly reassures rather than frightens" and concluded.

> If present trends continue, the world in 2000 will be less crowded, less polluted, more stable ecologically, and less vulnerable to resource-supply disruption than the world we live in now. Stresses involving population, resources, and environment will be less in the future than now ... the world's people will be richer in most ways than they are today ... The outlook for food and other necessities of life will be better. ... Life for most people on earth will be less precarious economically than it is now.

It would seem that two views could hardly be more opposed. While the *Global 2000 Report* is often described as a "doomsday," the "sky is falling" or the "Cassandra" approach, the *Global 2000 Revised* is "encouragingly optimistic" and/or "reassuring."

What often goes unnoted after one gets beyond the initial pyrotechnics is that the differences between the two are not nearly as pronounced as one might initially conclude. The differences are less with data than with how it is compiled and presented; and the view of the future is less one of optimism or pessimism than it is how the partisans choose to present the common challenge which both sides clearly recognize. And, finally, it is how the parties deal with the relationships between physical resources and the institutional context that is decisive for understanding the differences in their attitudes.

In the *Global 2000 Report*, for example, the authors go to some lengths to indicate that their major concerns flow from institutional problems and the inequalities and unpredictability of these institutional relationships rather than limits of specific resources. In fact, they maintain that "there is reason for hope" and specifically note that the projections are based on the assumption that current policies will remain essentially unchanged through the end of the century. But as they also note, "policies are beginning to change" and these changes are "encouraging."

On the other hand, in *Global 2000 Revised*, the authors maintain, "Our conclusions are reassuring, though not grounds for complacency." And that "global problems due to physical conditions (as distinguished from those caused by institutional and political conditions) are always possible, but are likely to be less pressing in the future than in the past."

So, they stress the physical facts and trend data on specific resources rather than the institutional features and policies which must be assessed in order to provide a production of the future. As the *Global 2000 Report* concluded, an "era of unprecedented cooperation and commitment is essential" both to clearly establish the leadership of the United States in dealing with resource issues, and to be a responsible partner in working the "global commons." The *Global 2000 Revised* authors indicate that "enthusiastic and vigorous efforts to do even better, even faster will benefit the public in their response to the challenges of the future."

So, in the "Cassandra" orientation of the authors of *Global 2000*, there is an approach that emphasized the inertia of existing policies and the difficulty of change, and hence of the likelihood that their voices will go unheard or unheeded. The "optimistic" approach is one which, to be sure, is based on a different factual base, but which more importantly expresses a confidence that markets and governments will respond to overcome an admittedly difficult situation.

THE OWNER/MANAGER PANEL RESPONDS

All the panelists, who were asked to respond to summaries of the data presented in the book, expressed an implicit or explicit stance on the potential for positive reponse to resource issues as we move toward the 21st century. The audience, in turn, made implicit evaluations about whether each panelist's presentation justified optimism or pessimism. After all, when assessing the future and forecasting trends and developments, we all want to know if it looks rosy or somber.

Robert Wetherby, then the president-elect of the National Association of Conservation Districts and the first of the owner/manager panelists to speak, took on a somewhat combative tone in his initial statements. He felt that the previous day's panels had given too little emphasis to the very considerable accomplishments of the conservation movement in recent decades. By implication, he took a position counter to that of Robert Rodale, chairman of Rodale Press, who the day before suggested that "sustainability" or "renewal" were the words that captured the sense of the historic conservation movement.

Wetherby pointed out that the drought of 1988 had been as severe as the drought of 1936, but there was no evidence of a dust bowl to equal that of the 1930s. Something has changed for the better, he maintained. Wetherby asked for a show of hands from the audience to see how many were actually engaged in farming. He was presented with a sizable if scattered response, but it was apparent that he felt that there had been some straying from the farm, and perhaps from down-to-earth practicalities in some of the presentations of the day before.

It was Wetherby's comments about the 1988 National Wetlands Policy Forum that seemed to resonate with the other panelists and set the tone for their presentations. Wetherby had been one of a panel of 20 members that included three governors, other elected and appointed public officials, academic experts, and members of the business and environmental communities. Chaired by New Jersey Governor Thomas M. Kean, and conducted under the auspices of the Conservation Foundation, the forum's report had been released in early November 1988 and had gained special attention because President-Elect Bush had said during his campaign that if he were elected, he would adopt a policy of "no net loss of wetlands."

Perhaps no state had a more emotional or acrimonious struggle with the wetlands issue than Wetherby's home state of North Dakota. The proposed Garrison Diversion, North Dakota's premier water project, had been delayed for years by opposition from the United States Fish and Wildlife Service as well as state and wildlife groups who mustered both public criticism and litigation. The antagonistic and adversarial approaches had produced a stalemate that all sides wished to overcome.

The forum approach and its subsequent report had impressed Wetherby with the potential of such policy dialogue for other resource issues. He expressed his own frustration at the history of wetlands controversy in his own state, and he indicated that without something like the forum approach, the public could expect further confrontation, extensive legal and political conflict, expensive, and ultimately frustrating, litigation. It was clear that he was talking not only about wetlands, but forest planning, water resource issues, erosion and sedimentation plans, and other initiatives that involved public and private interaction.

Wetherby emphasized that the use of economic incentives would be important in the development of regulations or laws that affect landowners, but he also said that the use of dialogue, mutual understanding, persuasion and good will were likely as important. Agreements reached by consensus had the advantage of developing commitment to the programs by those participating in the process. He suggested that it was only the recalcitrant few who really needed to be constrained by penalties. He was confident that fuller understanding of the issues, goals, and interests among the various parties involved would go far in generating the "motivation" to carry out desired public purposes of resource management.

R. Scott Wallinger, executive vice-president of Westvaco and president of the American Forestry Association, followed Wetherby; starting from a different point, he arrived at a similar destination.

Wallinger noted that Westvaco was celebrating their own centennial, and that the theme of looking ahead to the next century was something he had experienced in his firm. Operating in 150 different countries gave him a strong sense of the contextual issues that he felt were more important for the future than projections of the availability of any particular resource.

Although Westvaco is a multi-national company, Wallinger stressed that even local potholes are not immune from the influences of international currencies and commodity prices. The complexities and uncertainties associated with international competition, currency and resource demands are realities. A global economy is a fact of life.

Resource projections are always valuable and useful, he noted, but they must always be given a skeptical eye because of the interactions in the social, economic, and political realm that were often the decisive factors in the resource outcome. Managers would be wise to look at the general institutional capabilities of government and of business rather than to focus too narrowly on specific forecasting tools, he asserted.

He referred to a comment made in an earlier panel by M. Rupert Cutler, executive director of The Defenders of Wildlife, who had responded to a question from the floor: Is there any common forum among the major environmental organizations? Cutler noted that there was no formal federation among environmental organizations. He also noted that in some cases the various environmental organizations had different priorities, and were sometimes competitive with each other for funds. He did mention that a "Group of

10" (the 10 largest membership organizations in the environmental community) occasionally met and worked on common agendas, issues, and strategies.

Wallinger recommended that it become the "Group of 50" and include not only environmental organizations but also industry councils and government agencies. Like Wetherby, he felt that there was a strong need to avoid "destructive conflict" and to replace it with "healthy competition." There should be forums and opportunities for people to find areas where "mutual goodwill" might be demonstrated.

Wallinger then made an interesting turnabout in characterizing the relations between resource professionals and the general public. An earlier panel had placed a very strong emphasis on the inability of the general public to make the connections between their everyday behavior and actions as consumers and citizens and the implications their actions had for resources and the environment. Gerald W. Winegrad, a Maryland legislator, had related an anecdote that served as a kind of symbol of this problem. He recalled addressing a session of intelligent young people who were involved in a Chesapeake Bay environmental education program. When he began to question them about where the energy came from that cooled their refrigerators and freezers and other amenities of modern life, they did not connect these appliances with the demand for nuclear reactors, fossil fuel power plants, or dams on free-flowing rivers.

Many conference professionals made the call for education of the broader, presumably less informed, less caring, and less committed public. Wallinger, without directly challenging that need, suggested that the reverse might also be true.

He told of a Swedish forester who had developed a management practice that had impressed Westvaco's corporate leaders. They invited him to meet with them to consider the feasibility of introducing the processes he had developed into the company. Wouldn't the workers resist such innovation? Wouldn't there be a kind of unthinking opposition because of the force of habit among their workers? The Swede replied, "I won't have any problem introducing this concept or getting acceptance of it from your workers. It is your supervisors and senior people who will resist it. They are committed to ideas and theories about how it should be done. They will be the source of difficulty."

Wallinger then went on to indicate how little understood or appreciated were the grass roots efforts of volunteers, voluntary organizations, and others who provided "sweat equity" and enthusiasm to attack resource and environmental problems. He suggested, through examples, that these volunteer efforts often provided the ideas and the energy, while more institutionalized leadership lagged behind. National environmental organizations, large government bureaucracies, and industry are often barriers to change and innovation rather than sources of leadership with vision and energy, he said.

Wallinger asserted that incentives and financial subsidies to encourage responsible actions by private landowners are perhaps less necessary as compensation than as a catalyst for individuals and organizations to develop new relationships. How the five percent who owned the forest and farmland or the 95 percent dependent upon its uses are going to jointly frame the issues and the responses is one critical question, for example. He concluded, as had Wetherby, that there was a vital need for creating a climate of mutual cooperation and for avoiding "unproductive warfare." Less formal ways for leaders to meet and discuss common concerns hold real promise for improving resource management, he suggested.

Jerry Presley, of the Missouri Department of Conservation, talked enthusiastically about the improvements made in Missouri as a result of public support for conservation initiatives and programs. He described himself as a "cockeyed optimist" because he believed the evidence showed that the public would support well conceived and targeted programs. He talked of his personal experiences as a young man; he had seldom seen turkey or deer, yet now they are much more evident and plentiful.

Presley indicated that there was a need for continued efforts to get "politics out of conservation" and to create a strong direct tie between professionals and the public. He outlined a number of initiatives in Missouri that demonstrated public support for well conceived programs, support that might not have developed except for direct efforts by conservationists with the voting public. Through a popular referendum the people of Missouri had earmarked one-eighth of one percent of the sales tax and dedicated it to the Department of Conservation, for example. Presley described the "charter" for this referendum, "Design for Conservation," a paper prepared by conservationists, which was widely distributed, reviewed, and obviously influential in the voting.

The ideas that had been set out in "Design for Conservation" were the continuing guidelines for his department, Presley said. Pressures to stray from those commitments arose, he suggested, but those pressures were resisted and public support had continued and strengthened because of this unwavering commitment.

The same concept had worked when the citizens of Missouri approved one-tenth of one percent of the sales tax to be dedicated to controlling soil erosion. The original tax had been scheduled to "sunset," but a coalition of environmental groups, professional conservationists, and university researchers and educators mobilized support that was successful in renewing the measure. Both urban centers as well as the rural areas of the state had supplied support. Like Wallinger and Wetherby, Presley cited strong evidence of citizen support and encouragement for many conservation initiatives. He pointed to the North American Waterfowl Plan as a notable example of private initiative and voluntary action. Public managers ought to heed the public's desires, organize clear goals, and vigorously advocate them, but the "public is more wise and discriminating" than the politicians or some professionals think, he concluded.

Dale Robertson, chief of the United States Forest Service, gave a kind of "mixed bull and bear" perspective. He noted that the United States is much better off than the rest of the world, but if the world is in considerable pain and difficulty this will necessarily affect us. World debt, poverty, and the pressures to overuse natural resources in other parts of the world will necessarily impact this country as well as the global environment.

He expressed special concern about the potential effects of global warming and what this could mean for the people of the world. Indicating that he shared many of the concerns and worries expressed about the future, he emphasized this was not because of specific resource shortages, but because of the complexity of the interacting forces such as population increase, poverty, political instability, and world monetary problems.

Robertson asserted that basic management skills needed to be cultivated and encouraged. The ability to adapt and respond to change is essential. Since the forces of change were probably not directly controllable, and yet change was going to be a compelling force, the ability to adapt to, or even thrive on, change was going to be imperative for effective management.

He then shifted his focus to some of the immediate concerns he felt that conservationists needed to address. To a considerable extent, he pointed out, resource agencies and organizations were rivals or competitors for increasingly limited resource dollars. He urged that this competition be one in which organizations build more on each other's strengths and capabilities than the old win-lose rivalries for common turf.

The pertinence of that point seemed to reside in the fear that rivalry among the larger organizations— public and private— concerned with the allocation and use of resources might stultify or repress grassroots initiatives or citizen organizations. It was clear that groups using public lands, so marked by controversy and competition, must cooperate or mutually suffer from the conflict. One such competition or conflict exists between groups who emphasize the use of resources for economic development, such as grazing, mining, timber production, and those who are more concerned with wilderness, wildlife values, wetland, water quality, and biodiversity.

The forest planning process, Robertson suggested, was evolving in such a way that through intensified interaction among the concerned parties and the Forest Service, many of these competitive pressures were being shaped into mutually acceptable plans. He stressed the need for institutional and managerial capabilities to deal with competition and conflict, and referred to the Forest Service's efforts to take a leadership role in accommodating the necessary changes.

He extolled the potential of "conservation partnerships" between the public and private sector. The United States Forest Service, for example, had shared with organizations like the Rocky Mountain Elk Foundation. This organization, a virtual newcomer to the conservation field, had raised over $1.5 million for habitat protection. He also praised Trout Unlimited and the Wild Turkey Federation as organizations which had taken leadership roles in conservation partnerships on national forest land.

Robertson spoke for the entire panel and its strong theme of developing creative ways to develop partnerships, consensus, and conservation when he reminded the audience of Benjamin Franklin's words to the assembled revolutionaries in Philadelphia: "If we don't hang together, we'll hang separately."

CHAPTER 18

Quality of Life for the 21st Century

Sara Ebenreck

At the heart of all living things, whether green shoots or human beings, is the urge to grow. But obvious as that impulse is the fact that not all growth yields equally appealing results. In the images of the conference which led to this book, the return of the pronghorn antelope in the Southwest signals our growing human ability to understand the importance of other species and to wisely manage land for wildlife habitat. But unlimited growth in the numbers of humans driving internal combustion engines over the same road equals both gridlock and air pollution, and 20 years of escalating growth in the use of farm chemicals and the production of toxic wastes is connected to degradation of water quality throughout the nation.

The impact of choices about preferable paths for human growth, in our society and worldwide, is so powerful that discussion about quality of life at this conference circled insistently around those options. Put simply, what paths should we choose if we are to ensure, not destroy, the quality of life we want for the 21st century?

The data experts tell us something about the path we're on now. That just opens up questions about which forks to take for the future. In the great eastern estuary of the Chesapeake, where once the English explorer John Smith saw crystal waters filled with fish, the oyster fisheries may well be on their way to extinction— despite major efforts at cleanup— for example. If the real estate economy of the region is booming, and oystermen are few indeed, is it important to our quality of life to undertake the long-range effort required to make the bay a safe home for oysters once again? In 1986, seven percent of the nation's rivers, lakes, and estuaries surveyed by one research group were too contaminated to support any of their "designated uses." Is that, and other resource degradation, simply the tough price to be paid for the more important human goals of economic progress and meeting growing consumer demands in a nation that likes to think of itself as leading the world?

National trends fit within overarching global ones. It is those global trends — greenhouse warming, worldwide population growth, species extinctions, and the likely environmental side-effects of conventional economic growth on a world-wide scale— that combine to trouble many experts as they project to the future. How will exploding numbers of people, many of whom think of success in images derived from the lifestyle of western developed nations, affect the carrying capacity of the earth and quality of life for us all? "Remember, only since World War II has economic growth been seen as an objective of every nation," prodded Harvard social scientist Daniel Bell.

If making long-range choices about levels of resource protection depends on decisions about what counts as important for our quality of life, the national guidelines are unclear, Bell implied. "We don't have a notion of 'net national welfare,'" he noted. "We need indicators for quality of life."

How will we formulate those indicators? How deeply are protection and restoration of natural resources related to our quality of life? Is it truly a foundation, without which such quality is not possible? And is there any hope of a national consensus about such matters as we move forward into the next century?

If we want insight about such matters, it must come from people who have pondered both facts and questions in the light of their best vision. To evoke some of that insight, this conference gathered a panel of four who were charged with the task of defining challenges, opportunities, and choices related to our quality of life for the next century.

The panelists were: Mollie Beattie, commissioner of the Vermont Department of Forests, Parks, and Recreation; Ralph Grossi, president of the American Farmland Trust in Washington, D.C.; Rupert Cutler, president of Defenders of Wildlife in Washington, D.C.; and Gerald Winegrad, member of the Maryland state Senate from Annapolis. The panel was moderated by John Gordon, dean of the Yale University School of Forestry and Environmental Studies.

MOLLIE BEATTIE: TREND IS NOT DESTINY

Opening the panel, Mollie Beattie pointed to the importance of publicly naming the elements which we see as important for quality of life. "I have a strong sense," she said, "that we tend to look at trends and say 'Here's what will happen.' We behave like passengers firmly strapped into our seats on an economic and demographic airplane, gripping our armrests, and saying 'I hope we land in the right place.'

"But trend is not destiny," Beattie continued. "And economics are not autonomous. They are an expression of people's values and they are controllable through public policy. We can certainly propose concepts of quality of life into the public debate. For example, I believe that quality of life should be include two critical factors that are usually left out: the integrity of natural systems and public access to the natural world."

In fact, Beattie challenged, many of the trends reported in the conference "point to a quality of life which I don't especially like. And you may not either." She followed with several questions.

> Do you want to live in a society that no longer values solitude and the opportunity to experience nature in quiet? In your heart of hearts, is it really okay to substitute aquaculture for a healthy marine system in the Chesapeake Bay and other estuaries? Do you really believe that people will be educated to value natural resources through publications instead of through experiencing the natural world? Are you happy with a world in which shopping is identified as a bona fide recreational leisure activity? Is it all right that our recreational access to the natural world is dependent solely on land prices? Is global warming okay with you as long as we can adapt our cropping systems sufficiently to survive?

The core of the problem, Beattie insisted, is our displaced sense of quality. "Most of the standards against which I've heard us measuring the quality of our resources tend to relate to capacity to meet demands. But real needs are not the same as the 'demands' measured by statistics." In short, we ought to be careful about measuring our capacity to achieve quality of life by our capacity to meet marketplace pressures. "Perhaps the basic question we face is this: why we are willing as a nation to risk our natural resources for a 'quality of life' increasingly marked by pollution?"

If natural resources are central to the quality of human life, ought not natural resource professionals provide the leadership for achieving 21st century goals? Beattie was not so sure. In listening to presentations at this conference, she noted, "I'm not sure we haven't screened out what we can't deal with. I didn't hear too many admissions here that we are dealing with absolutely unprecedented problems for which our old institutions and old analysis lack adequate responses."

Beattie also raised questions about the narrow range of voices heard in evoking a vision for the 21st century at this conference. "Look around you," she suggested. "Does the group here (predominantly white and male)— or, importantly, the range of speakers— represent the diversity of the American public?"

Engaging the American public in a dialogue about values and quality of life will take more than quoting numbers, Beattie emphasized. It will take people with the courage to name for public debate their own concept of what qualities are important.

An instance? "Consider the matter of access to public lands for recreation," Beattie said. "As a commissioner in Vermont, I am not just going to broker a compromise that gives every special interest some portion of the public land. I want to stand for the importance of people experiencing the natural world. So if the motorcyclists or bulldozer racers come to me and say, 'We need a piece of public land to do our racing,' I'm going to say 'no.' That will catalyze a debate and bring out public views on the matter."

RALPH GROSSI: NAMING GOALS FOR AGRICULTURE — WITH INCENTIVES

"I'm intrigued by references to the need for land ethics at earlier sessions of this conference," led in Grossi. But "the real problem is that as a California dairy farmer I have yet to be able to cash a philosophical check at my bank." Shift perspectives, for a moment, to the viewpoint of a national leader who is also an experienced farm operator in rural America. What's it like from that angle?

"We have serious issues in rural America today. We don't have to go to Third World countries to find families who lack basic medical care, whose educational opportunities are limited, and who are drinking polluted ground water. With a shrinking rural population, the disparity between urban and rural America is likely to grow, not shrink."

And focus on the relationship between agriculture and the environment. "The public is growing much more sophisticated about how agriculture relates to quality of life issues," said Grossi. "Consider the fact that a Washington coalition organized to work on farm policy had seven or eight members when it started on the 1985 farm bill — and now it has over 40, including multiple environmental groups — getting ready to work on 1990 farm policy."

Why? For one thing, because developments over the last 50 years in agriculture tended to ignore environmental constraints. "When American farmers ran out of new frontiers to plow, they turned to new technology. We measured the quality of our natural resources in terms of farm productivity. But in doing that, we inadvertently masked the issues that lay underneath."

Soil erosion and water quality are two issues now surfacing for questions by environmentalists. Also on the broad agenda are wildlife habitat destruction and water use rights for other purposes than farming, Grossi said. "So is the effect of chemical residues — which we haven't heard much about here. The drive in agriculture toward low-input farming is fueled heavily by public concern about chemicals in food and water.

"So the public is confronting agriculture with quality of life issues," he continued. "That's what happened in 1985 when the public said to farmers, 'If you want our tax dollars in farm programs, we want you to be good stewards of the land in return.' That's what happened in California with Proposition 65, which told both agriculture and business that they are accountable for what they do to the environment. It's what's beginning to happen about animal welfare."

The public is voting in favor of farmland protection, Grossi said, for reasons that relate to food, but also to the aesthetic and cultural values of farmland. Citizens in Lancaster County, Pennsylvania were deeply opposed to plans for a super highway through the historic Amish countryside— and they stopped it. "Here in Maryland, 100,000 acres of farmland are now preserved; in Massachusetts, it's 35,000 acres. Pennsylvania has a $100 million bond issue for farmland protection; California just passed a bond issue which gave $70 million for farmland protection. And everyone of those initiatives passed by a two-to-one vote."

What does it all signify? "We have to develop conservation programs that build on broad societal goals while recognizing equity issues important to individual landowners— all in a national political climate which functions in two to four year cycles. We need to figure out how to name quality-of-life factors and then quantify them so that landowners gain some economic value for protecting them."

RUPERT CUTLER: IS SPECIES EXTINCTION A TRIVIAL MATTER?

A half century back, conservationist Aldo Leopold talked about how tough it was to get economic-minded people to think of themselves as fellow-citizens in a natural community with other species and elements. To hear Rupert Cutler open his remarks by describing a recent meeting he had with seminarians and other church folk was to remember that it is not only profit-blinded people who fail to see the importance of other strands in the web of life. "I was told," Cutler related, "that while work to halt the global warming trend might be important, the work of saving the gray wolf habitat was pretty trivial. 'We haven't missed the dodo bird,' they told me, 'and we won't miss the wolf either.'

"Is species extinction a trivial matter? Do we have any real idea of the importance of any single species in the web of life which includes humanity? How many species must we lose before we call a halt to the vast oversimplification of our wild plant and animal endowment?"

Defenders of Wildlife is organizing a state-by-state program to protect native wildlife habitat, Cutler said. "We must determine which habitats are essential for all fish and wildlife and then see to it that the habitat in public or private hands is protected for that purpose." Cutler named some outstanding causes of habitat destruction: urban sprawl, fragmentation of our national forests into tiny islands of habitat as a result of logging, tropical deforestation.

The distance between Cutler's proposal and the present comes to mind: imagine housing developers needing to square their plans with adequate provision of native wildlife habitat before counties approved construction, for example.

"Millions of Americans do value nongame wildlife and contribute to protect it," Cutler said. "The state of California now charges hikers as well as fishers and hunters to use its wildlife areas. If we let hunters bid on the chance to hunt big game in national forests in the same way that we auction off forest timber, the government would make far more money in a more benign way. We simply haven't been creative enough with respect to management of wildlife. Protection of habitat and quotas is one path."

But population growth and quality of life are on collision paths, Cutler warned. "One species I'd like to see extinct is the sacred cow notion that population growth is inevitable. We have a clear choice. We can continue to stick our collective heads in the sand, refuse to bring down population rates through education and jobs for women as well as birth control assistance— or we can give the population issue the political attention and support it deserves."

GERALD WINEGRAD: WHO'S IN THE END ZONE VS. STATE OF THE OZONE

"We are a democracy," Winegrad began. "How do we build public support and political will for these quality of life issues when people are more concerned about who's in the end zone than about problems with ozone? When they're more focused on work to build Star War systems than work to build a sustainable society? When the focus of the presidential campaign is more on who is saying the pledge of allegiance than on who has allegiance to protecting the biological diversity of the nation and life on this planet?

"I'm concerned about the lack of leadership and the lack of understanding among our populace." This is not a far-off issue, Winegrad emphasized. "To think about quality of life issues, you just need to go outside the doors of this conference motel and look at the traffic, the sprawl, the population, and the choices about land use.

"Public policy reflects what American people tend to shy away from. So I find I always need to ask planners: What are you planning for? What are the priorities? When I look outside this door, I wonder: Just what is it we are planning for? Environmental and resource catastrophe? People piled up on top of each other? If we don't speak up about the need for limits to growth, who is going to speak up?"

Some of our growth is guided purely by myth, Winegrad said. One myth is the idea that rural areas need to grow, to embrace development to improve their tax base. "That is nonsense," he asserted. "A study by the American Farmland

Trust of Loudoun County, Virginia [a county within commuting distance of Washington, D.C.], found that for every dollar of new tax revenues there was a consequent cost of $1.28 in out-of-pocket county services. So every resident in that county was contributing 28 cents on the dollar for the developer's profits.

"What other benefits come along with development? Traffic congestion, overcrowded schools, and loss of forest cover. In my district of Annapolis, in 30 years, we have dropped from having 170,000 acres of trees to under 100,000. We have saltwater intrusion from overdrafts of water. We have more crime so we need more courthouse and jail space. We have sewage problems. We don't meet air quality standards."

Like others in the panel, Winegrad continued on a grave note. "What's more basic to life than being able to leave your home and go out and breathe the air? But what about the days in this Washington metropolitan area when the government is forced to tell the elderly and anyone with respiratory problems not to go out— to stay inside and turn on the air conditioner to filter that air?

"What does it mean when we solve our problems with lack of school space by building more schools; our problems with contamination of groundwater by drilling deeper; our need for homes by bulldozing more trees? It's a never-ending cycle in which building one highway generates another cycle of growth.

"Shortsightedness is our problem," he warned, "and not discussing or even asking the right questions. Yes, we need education— of congressmen, state legislators, local councils. We need people writing letters to editors, joining advocacy groups, and running for office. If we who understand something of these issues are not going to raise them, who is? As we move toward the 21st century, we can continue forward as usual— or we can seize the opportunity to control and limit growth."

SPEAK THE TRUTH TO ONE ANOTHER

What path through the thicket of questions about quality of life emerges from this discussion? Or, in Daniel Bell's phrase, what "indicators" of quality of life appear?

First is a clear consensus that quality of life does indeed include protection of environmental quality. On reflection, even the supposed "value-free" trend estimates which occupied so much of the conference can be seen as a manifestation of public valuing of certain kinds of environmental quality. Would national agencies and conservation organizations be devoting massive amounts of time and budget to compiling numbers about water quality related to agricultural chemicals if headlines from Iowa and the Dakotas to Connecticut and Long Island, New York had not screamed concern about farm chemicals found in groundwater? Would soil conservation programs be succeeding if the public did not value clean surface waters and a sense of farm productivity ensured for the future?

As our panelists reminded us and polls often tell us, Americans are willing, within limits, to pay for wildlife and farmland protection, for clean water and air, for restoration of soils. They have chosen to do this in Vermont and California, in Pennsylvania and Missouri, and countless other places. But this affirmation of environmental protection as a quality of life value already existing in America does not explain the sense of all the panelists that some form of education or further clarifying of values is critical for our future. What peculiar mixture of knowing and not-knowing is involved here?

"Consistency," the American writer Ralph Waldo Emerson once said, "is the hobgoblin of small minds." Perhaps, by that criterion, the issue is a curious sort of "large-mindedness."

We want environmental quality— yes. Who, when asked, is outspokenly opposed to clean air and water, soil conservation, and continued life for endangered species? But do we as a nation want it clearly and strongly enough to educate ourselves about our interdependence with ecological systems and then act in ways that respect the integrity of those systems? Are we willing to accept restraints such as strong limits on automobile fumes or clear boundaries to the sprawl of human habitats? Are we ready to begin new rounds of action about alternatives to production and disposal of toxic wastes— now standing at the rate of one ton per person per year in the United States? Are we ready to develop the cooperative industry/government/citizen forums that will be needed to address these issues in truth and with new creativity, with all interests involved in seeking solutions?

Or are we instead avoiding some tough choices? Are we asking that Utah wildlands be both recreation places and dumps for our growing nuclear and toxic wastes, without quite considering if it is possible to have both for the long range? Do we believe that we can limitlessly use our estuaries and their shores for recreation and housing while still protecting wildlife habitat and water quality in those places? That we can continue a throw-away culture and yet avoid finding dead sea turtles and waterfowl whose stomachs are full of plastic offal?

Given the genius of American technology, do we believe that no choices are really necessary? That, given time, new gene-manipulated bacteria will "fix" the water quality problems of the Chesapeake Bay or those of our underground aquifers? That new biodegradable "plastics" will create a market for farm products while relieving our need for controls on waste? That perhaps, as cartoons have it, we'll be able to shoot up a rocket full of "ozone-layer-fixing" stuff in time to save fatal deterioration of our atmosphere?

If so, in the words of United States Department of Agriculture Deputy Secretary Peter Myers, who welcomed the conference, it is time "to speak the truth to one another." It is time, the panelists agreed, to put facts about resource and population-pressure trends clearly in the public view. But it is also time, as Mollie Beattie and Gerald Winegrad emphasized, to put our visions of a desirable future before people, to openly clarify some of the choices we face, and to empower each other to speak and act.

How important is engaging that public dialogue about choices as we move toward the 21st century?

Imagine, if you will, a 21st century in which natural resources are protected by a cadre of experts who endlessly measure their chemical state and the species inhabiting them, while the vast majority of humans are locked into bubble-covered urban areas where they rotate endlessly between hours at their workplaces, their home television sets, and vast enclosed shopping and sports malls.

Quality of life? Not by anyone's vote. What about the joy of people splashing in the ocean surf? The inner hush of respect as children stand close to an old-growth redwood? The pleasure of seeing and smelling ripening corn fields? The rich rewards of give and take in all sorts of work and play with the natural world?

Quality of life, in short, can't be achieved simply by restoration of natural resources. Integral to it is the process of nurturing in people life-giving ways of being and working with the earth. Quality of life is a matter of human character as well as of the land's character. Experts can't give us quality of life; we must all together achieve it.

That, it seems, is why conference participants kept returning to the importance of fostering a "land ethic" or "land spirit" among people as a second indicator of quality of life. It is not only that this land ethic will lead people to restore the earth; it is that this spirit restores people themselves. In a society which is not only naming resource degradation as an issue, but which also lists drug and alcohol abuse, loneliness, lack of community, and teenage suicide as major problems, the promise of a renewal of spirit coming from a different relationship to our earth would be welcome news indeed.

A DECLARATION OF INTERDEPENDENCE

Some 500 participants in the conference that led to this book, lured by a sense that addressing these 21st century issues was an important enterprise, slogged through two and a half days of detailed presentations and debate in a drab and often darkened conference room. It was, at many moments, neither glamorous nor exciting to work at connecting the numbers, the projections, the questions. But then, one might imagine, neither were the endless and surely trying meetings that preceded July 4, 1776, in the seaboard colonies of America. Somehow, in the very process of joining in concern, we slowly articulate our vision and our intentions about matters essential to the future of the nation.

In 1989, as in 1776, it is perhaps time to face a new revolutionary choice. This time, the challenge is not to declare independence, but to acknowledge our interdependence and to undertake the protective actions that flow from that new sense of identity. In the words that American Indian Chief Seattle addressed to President Franklin Pierce in 1855, we must openly recognize, "Whatever we do to the web [of life], we do to ourselves." As our panelists emphasized, our human quality of life is not separable from the quality of our land, water, air and wildlife. And as the air that freely flows over national borders and the migrating wildlife that span several continents in their yearly journeys tell us, our national resource quality is not separable from global resource qualities.

What path to the 21st century? What kinds of growth do we need? The outline of a goal is clear from participants in this conference: a path which promises our children more than mere survival on an overcrowded and degraded planet. We seek life in spirited communities on an earth which is responding with renewed resilience, productivity, and beauty to deepened levels of human awareness and restorative action.

This conference, in its facts and discussion, was one step toward making *that* 21st century a reality.

Contributors

Adela Backiel is a natural resources management specialist at the the Congressional Research Service of the Library of Congress in Washington, D.C.

Sandra S. Batie is a professor at Virginia Polytechnic Institute and State University.

Daniel Bell is a Henry Ford II professor of social science at Harvard University.

Thadis W. Box is a professor at Utah State University.

Rodney L. Clouser is an associate professor of the Department of Food and Resource Economics at the University of Florida, Gainesville.

Richard Collins is director of the Institute for Environmental Negotiations at the University of Virginia.

H. Ken Cordell is project leader of the Outdoor Recreation and Wilderness Assessment Group for the United States Department of Agriculture Forest Service.

Fred Deneke was the national program leader of the forest land management extension service for the United States Department of Agriculture.

William E. Easterling is a Fellow in the Climate Resources Program at Resources for the Future in Washington, D.C.

Sara Ebenreck is a writer and teacher in environmental ethics in Prince Frederick, Maryland.

John Fedkiw is associate director for Renewable Resources and Special Studies at the United States Department of Agriculture in Washington, D.C.

Kenneth D. Frederick is a senior Fellow at Resources for the Future in Washington, D.C.

William G. Gordon is executive vice president at the New Jersey Marine Sciences Consortium in Sandy Hook, New Jersey.

Perry Hagenstein is director of Resource Issues, Inc. in Wayland, Massachusetts.

Dwight Hair is research coordinator at the American Forestry Association.

D.A. Holt is director of the Illinois Agricultural Experiment Station in Urbana, Illinois.

Lawrence W. Libby is a professor and the department chair at the Department of Food and Resource Economics at the University of Florida in Gainesville, Florida.

Florentine Liegerot is a recycling specialist for Waste Management of North America, Inc.

Charles E. Little is writer, editor, and conservationist in Kensington, Maryland.

Peter C. Myers is deputy secretary of the United States Department of Agriculture.

S.L. Rawlins is on the National Program Staff and Agricultural Research Service of the United States Department of Agriculture in Beltsville, Maryland.

R. Neil Sampson is executive vice president of the American Forestry Association and the author of numerous conservation books and articles.

Daniel B. Taylor is an associate professor at the Virginia Polytechnic Institute and State University.

Billy Teels is the national biologist at the United States Department of Agriculture Soil Conservation Service in Washington, D.C.

Jack Ward Thomas is chief research wildlife biologist at the United States Department of Agriculture Forest Service in La Grande, Oregon.

Index

Page numbers in *italics* refer to illustrations

ALSO AVAILABLE FROM ISLAND PRESS

Americans Outdoors: The Report of the President's Commission
The Legacy, The Challenge
Foreword by William K. Reilly
1987, 426 pp., appendixes, case studies, charts
Paper: $24.95 ISBN 0-933280-36-X

The Challenge of Global Warming
Edited by Dean Edwin Abrahamson
Foreword by Senator Timothy E. Wirth
In cooperation with the Natural Resources Defense Council
1989, 350 pp., tables, graphs, index, bibliography
Cloth: $34.95 ISBN: 0-933280-87-4
Paper: $19.95 ISBN: 0-933280-86-6

The Complete Guide to Environmental Careers
by The CEIP Fund
1989, 300 pp., photographs, case studies, bibliography, index
Cloth: $24.95 ISBN: 0-933280-85-8
Paper: $14.95 ISBN: 0-933280-84-X

Creating Successful Communities: A Guidebook to Growth
Management Strategies
By Michael A. Mantell, Stephen F. Harper, Luther Propst
In cooperation with The Conservation Foundation
1989, 350 pp., appendixes, index
Cloth: $39.95 ISBN: 1-55963-030-2
Paper: $24.95 ISBN: 1-55963-014-0

Resource Guide for Creating Successful Communities
By Michael A. Mantell, Stephen F. Harper, Luther Propst
In cooperation with The Conservation Foundation
1989, 300 pp., charts, graphs, illustrations
Cloth: $39.95 ISBN: 1-55963-031-0
Paper: $19.95 ISBN: 1-55963-015-9

Crossroads: Environmental Priorities for the Future
Edited by Peter Borrelli
1988, 352 pp., index
Cloth: $29.95 ISBN: 0-933280-68-8
Paper: $17.95 ISBN: 0-933280-67-X

The Poisoned Well: New Strategies for Groundwater Protection
By the Sierra Club Legal Defense Fund
1989, 400 pp., glossary, charts, appendixes, bibliography, index
Cloth: $31.95 ISBN: 0-933280-56-4
Paper: $19.95 ISBN: 0-933280-55-6

Reopening the Western Frontier
From *High Country News*
1989, 350 pp., illustrations, photographs, maps, index
Cloth: $24.95 ISBN: 1-55963-011-6
Paper: $15.95 ISBN: 1-55963-010-8

**Shading Our Cities: Resource Guide for Urban
and Community Forests**
Edited by Gary Moll and Sara Ebenreck
In cooperation with the American Forestry Association
1989, 350 pp., illustrations, photographs, appendixes, index
Cloth: $34.95 ISBN: 0-933280-96-3
Paper: $19.95 ISBN: 0-933280-95-5

War on Waste: Can America Win Its Battle with Garbage?
by Louis Blumberg and Robert Gottlieb
1989, 325 pp., charts, graphs, notes, index
Cloth: $34.95 ISBN: 0-933280-92-0
Paper: $19.95 ISBN: 0-933280-91-2

Wildlife of the Florida Keys: A Natural History
By James D. Lazell, Jr.
1989, 254 pp., illustrations, photographs, maps, index
Cloth: $31.95 ISBN: 0-933280-98-X
Paper: $19.95 ISBN: 0-933280-97-1

These titles are available from Island Press, Box 7, Covelo, CA 95428. Please enclose $2.00 shipping and handling for the first book and $1.00 for each additional book. California and Washington, D.C. residents add 6% sales tax. A catalog of current and forthcoming titles is available free of charge.